CAT vs HUMAN

TO VICTOR, MY FAMILY,
MONEY, SHELLEY, OSCAR,
PUPPY, AND TO ALL
CAT LADIES AND GENTS

CAT vs HUMAN

ANOTHER DOSE OF CATNIP

YASMINE SUROVEC

Andrews McMeel
Publishing®

Kansas City • Sydney • London

Andrews McMeel Publishing, LLC
an Andrews McMeel Universal company
1130 Walnut Street, Kansas City, Missouri 64106

www.andrewsmcmeel.com

14 15 16 17 TEN 10 9 8 7 6 5 4 3

ISBN: 978-1-4494-3331-4

Library of Congress Control Number: 2013901160

ATTENTION: SCHOOLS AND BUSINESSES
Andrews McMeel books are available at quantity discounts with bulk purchase
for educational, business, or sales promotional use. For information, please
e-mail the Andrews McMeel Publishing Special Sales Department:
specialsales@amuniversal.com

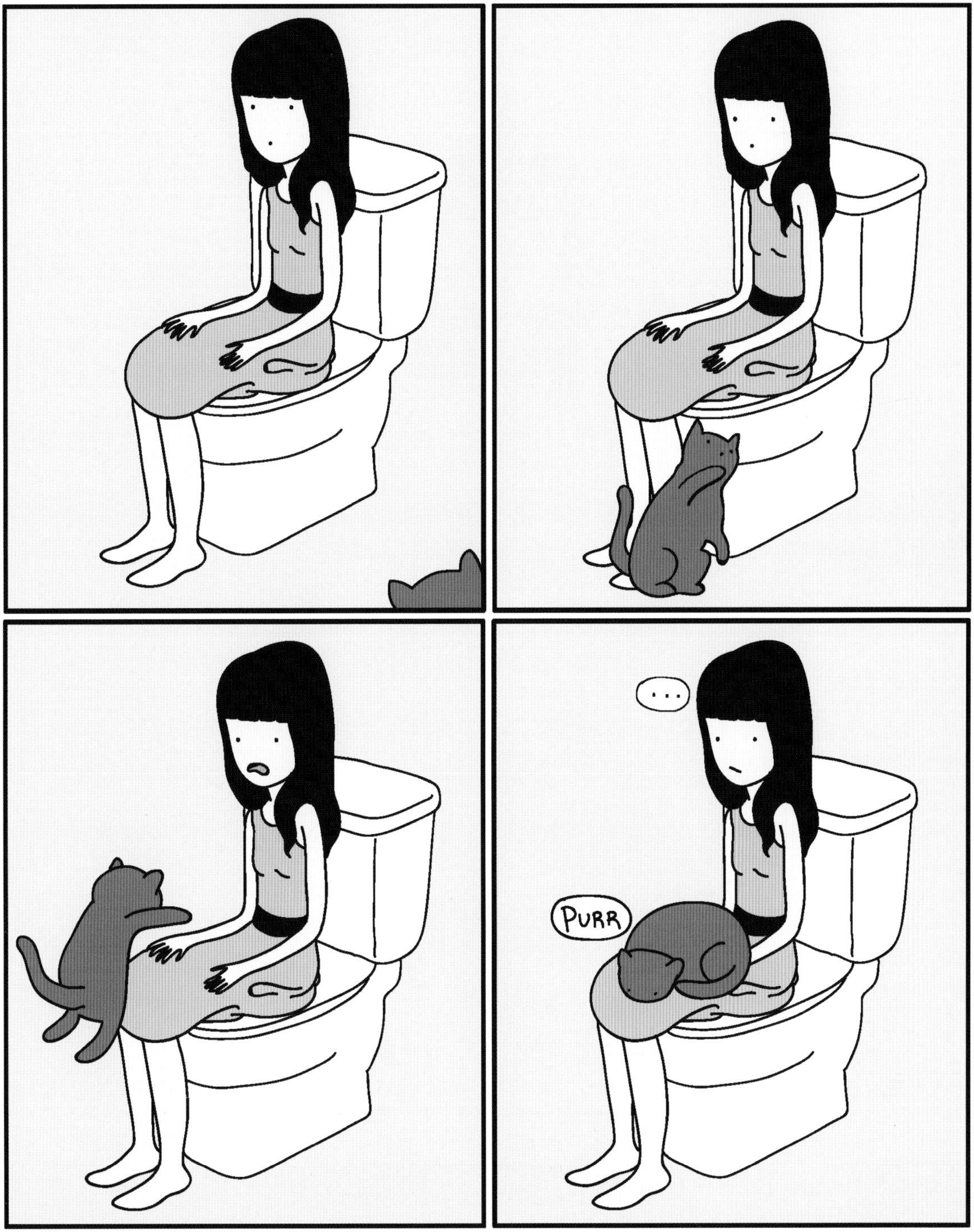
...
PURR

HOW MY CATS SEE ME

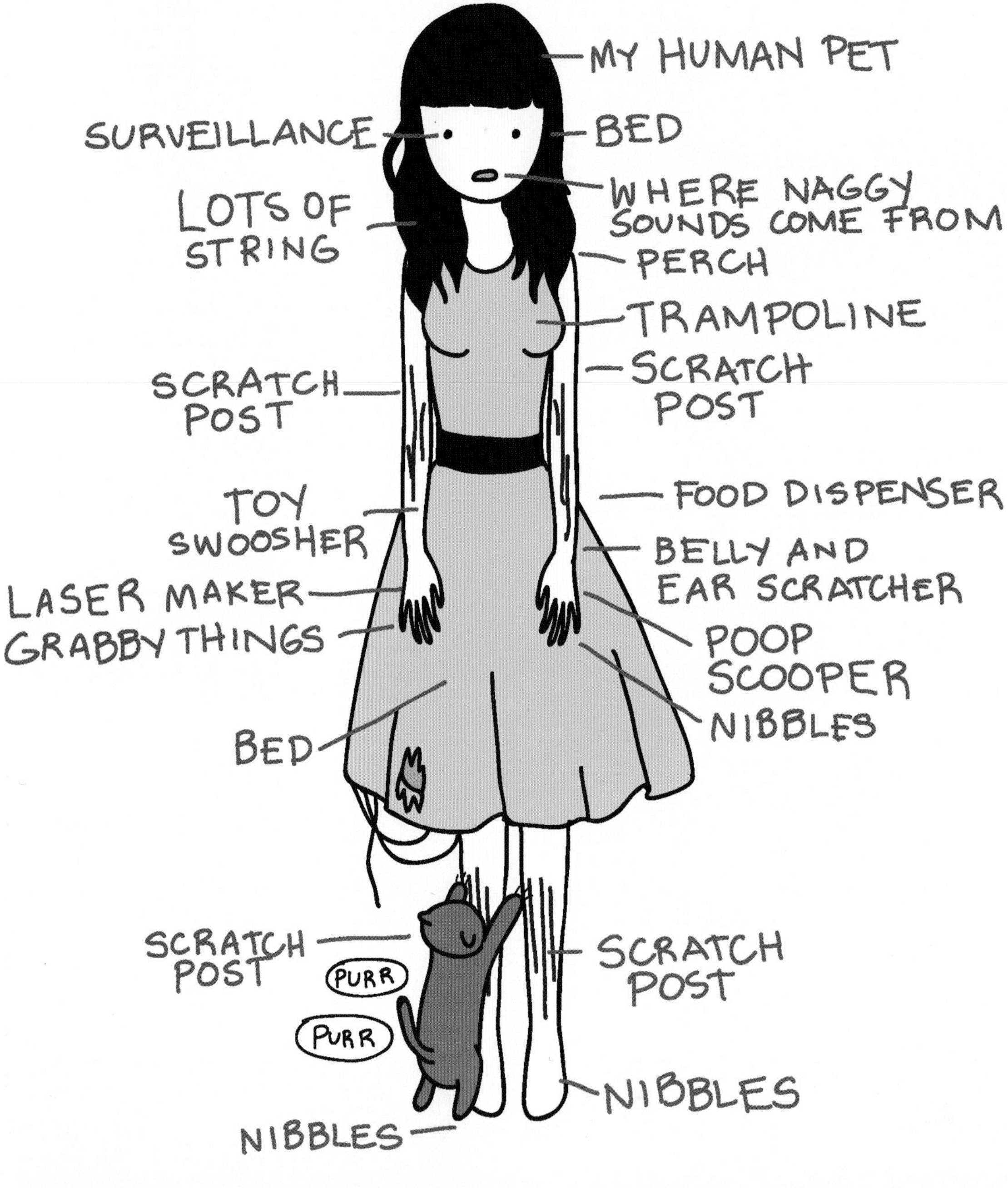
MY HUMAN PET
SURVEILLANCE
BED
WHERE NAGGY SOUNDS COME FROM
LOTS OF STRING
PERCH
TRAMPOLINE
SCRATCH POST
SCRATCH POST
FOOD DISPENSER
TOY SWOOSHER
BELLY AND EAR SCRATCHER
LASER MAKER
GRABBY THINGS
POOP SCOOPER
NIBBLES
BED
SCRATCH POST
PURR
PURR
SCRATCH POST
NIBBLES
NIBBLES

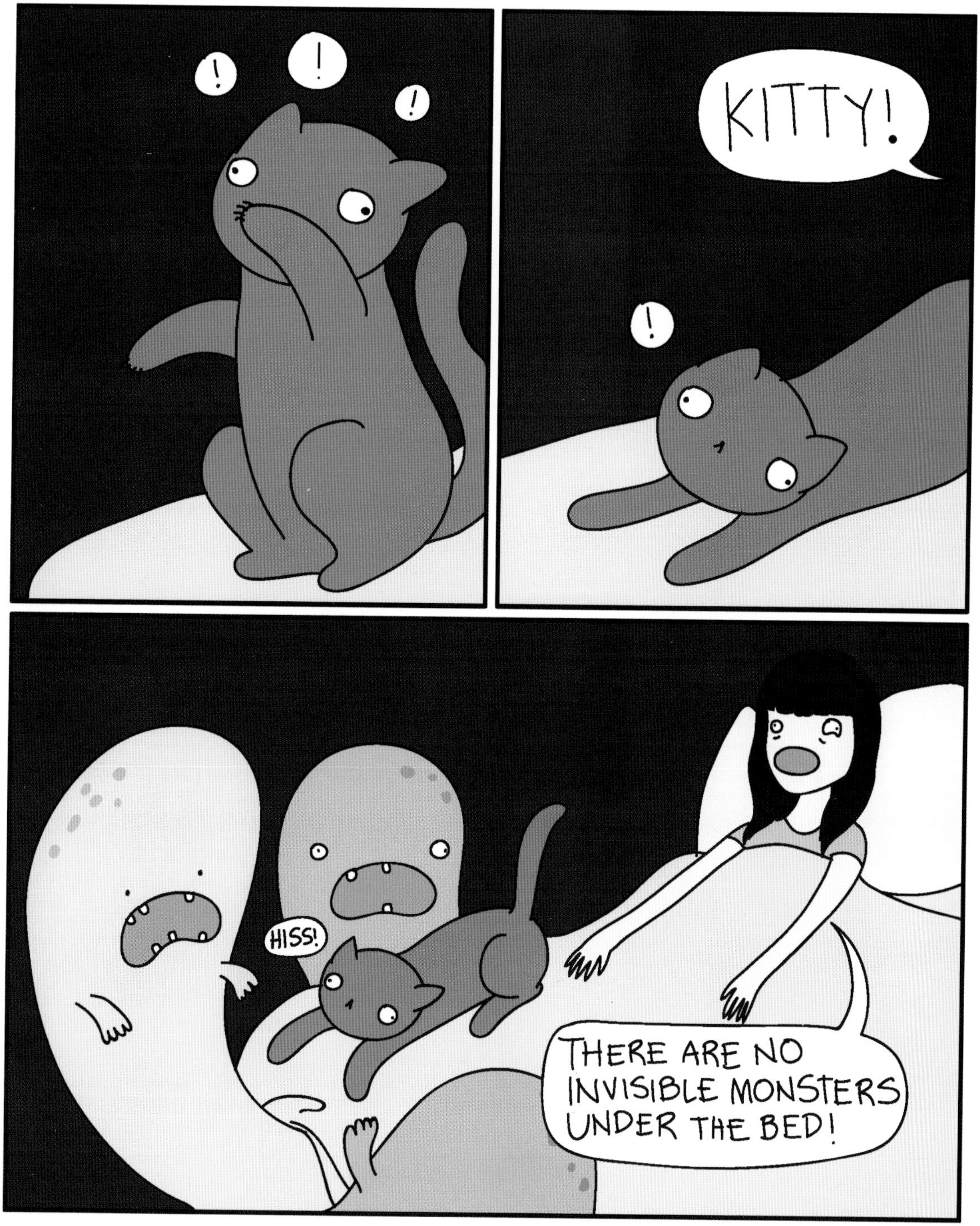
!
!
!
KITTY!
!
HISS!
THERE ARE NO INVISIBLE MONSTERS UNDER THE BED!

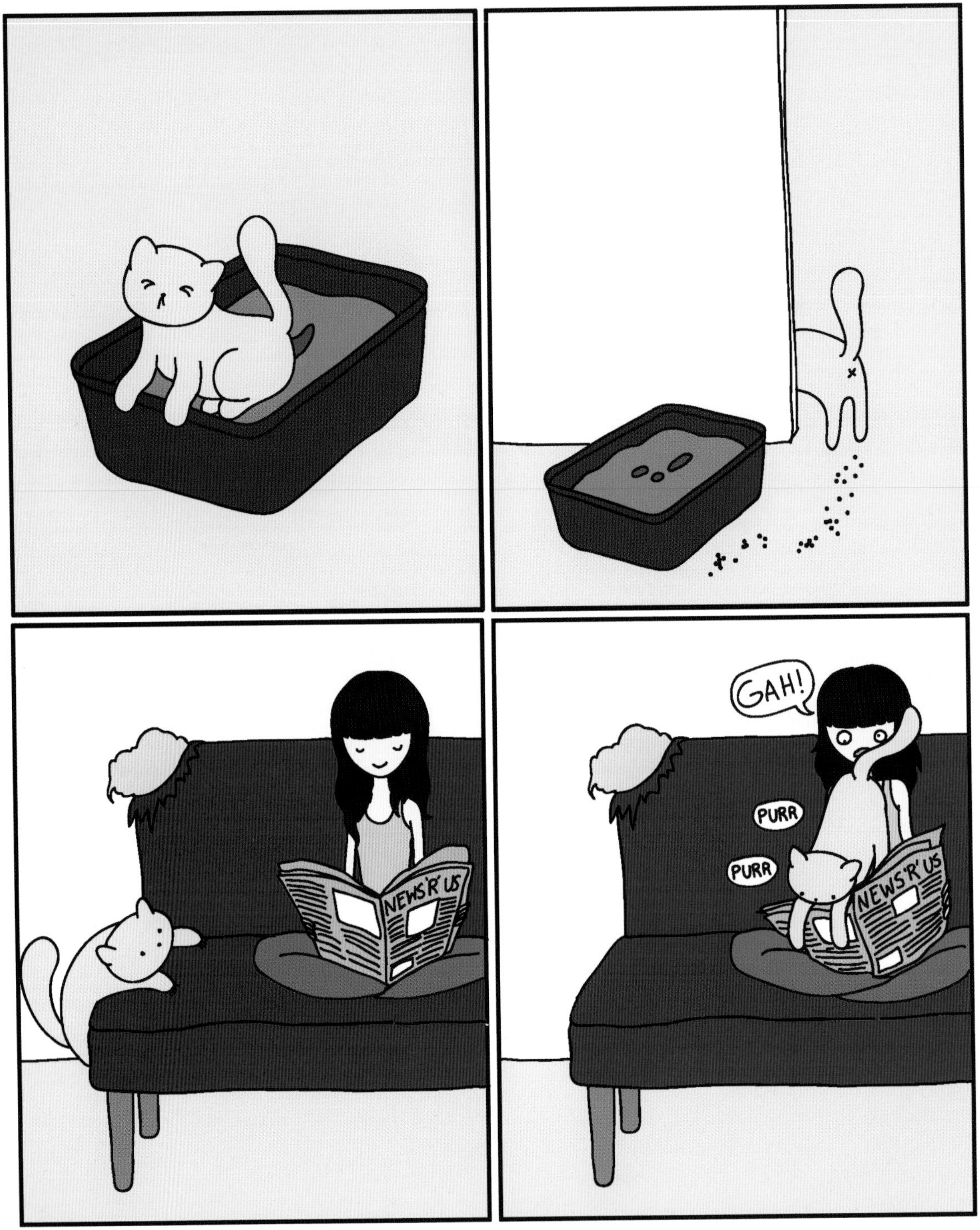
NEWS 'R' US
GAH!
PURR
PURR
NEWS 'R' US

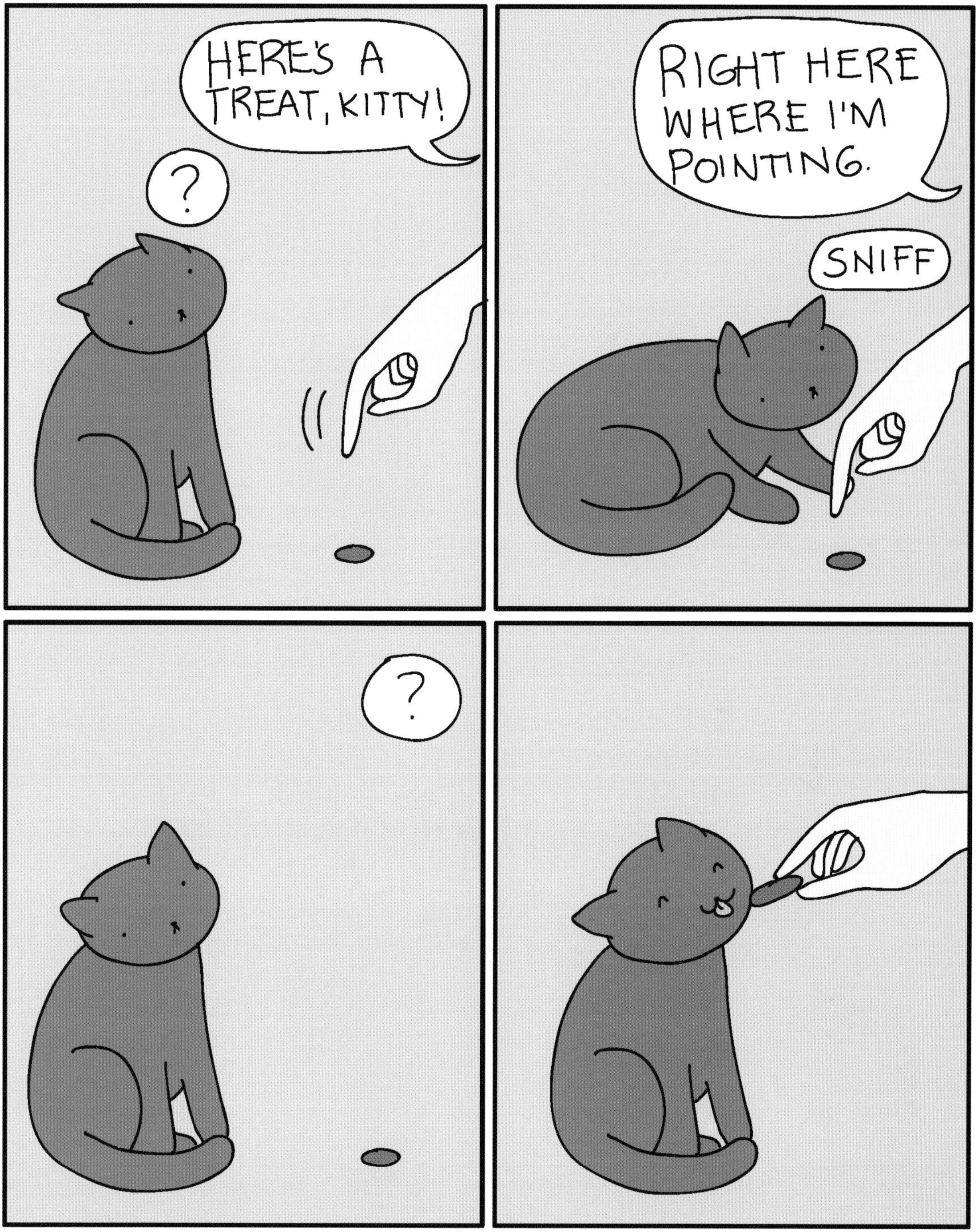
HERE'S A TREAT, KITTY!
?
RIGHT HERE WHERE I'M POINTING.
SNIFF
?

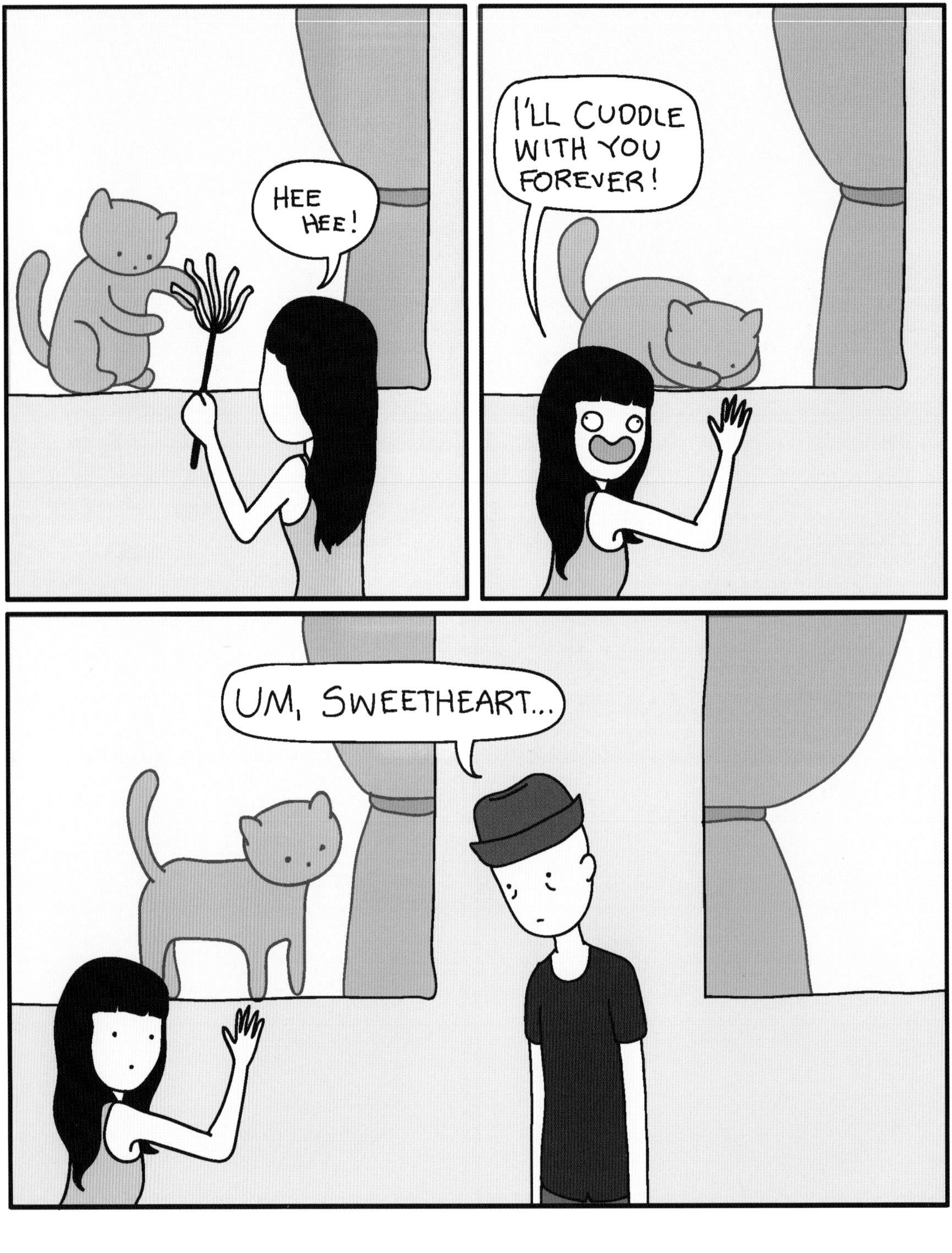
HEE HEE!
I'LL CUDDLE WITH YOU FOREVER!
UM, SWEETHEART...

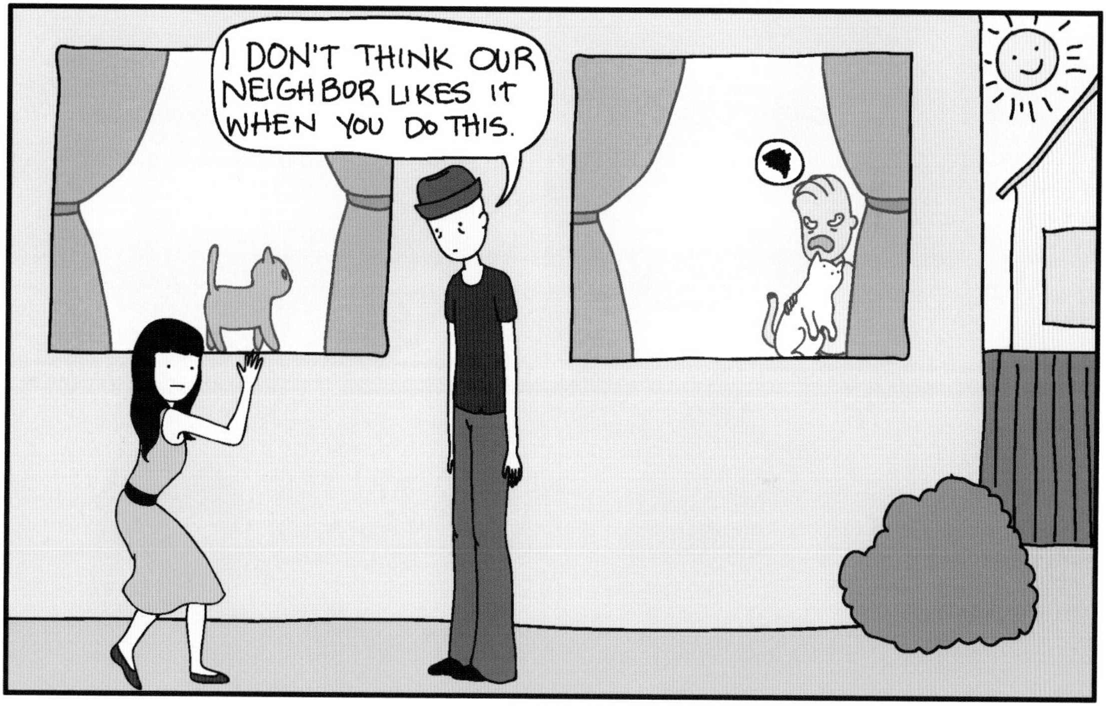
I DON'T THINK OUR NEIGHBOR LIKES IT WHEN YOU DO THIS.

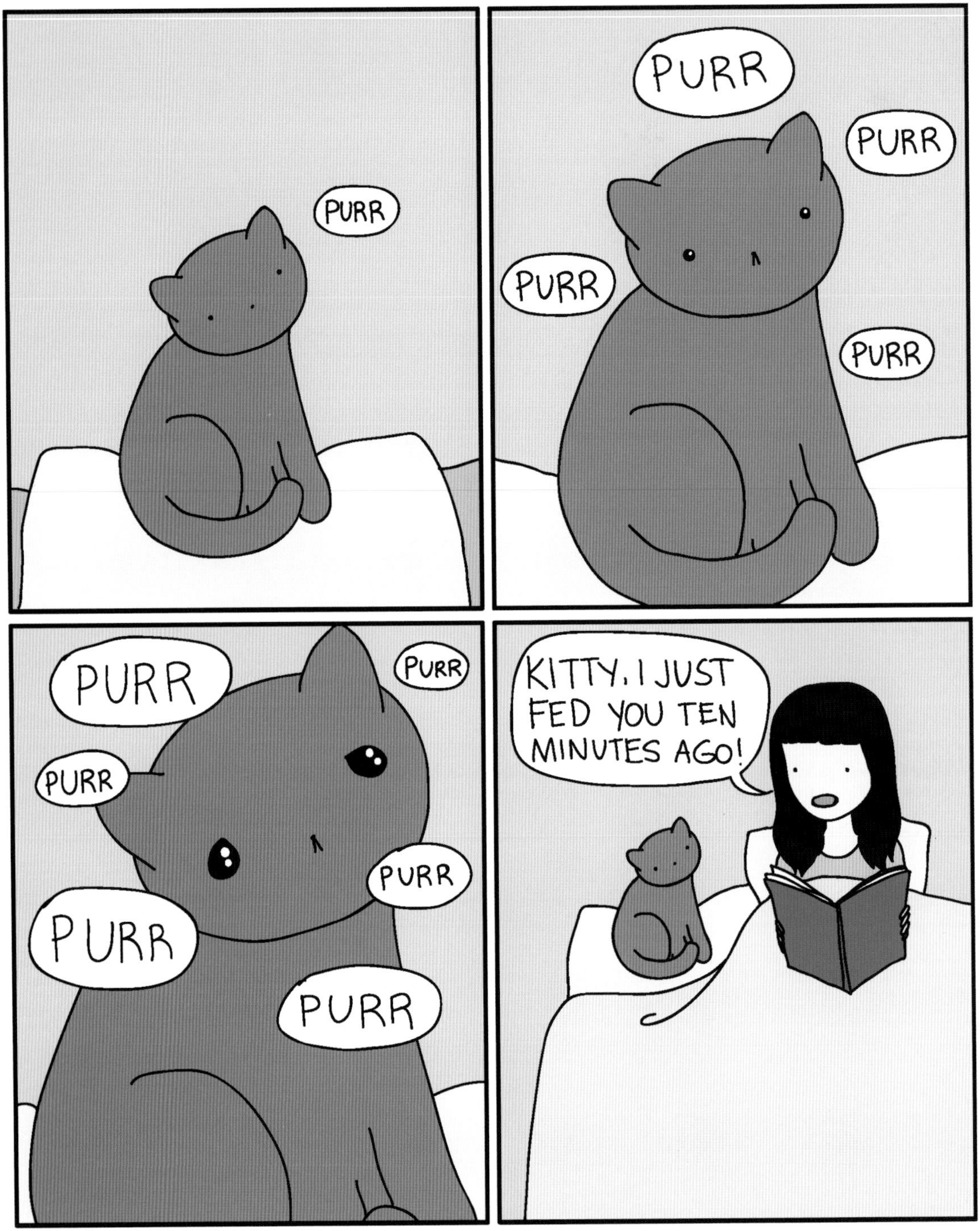
PURR
PURR
PURR
PURR
PURR
PURR
PURR
PURR
PURR
PURR
PURR
KITTY, I JUST FED YOU TEN MINUTES AGO!

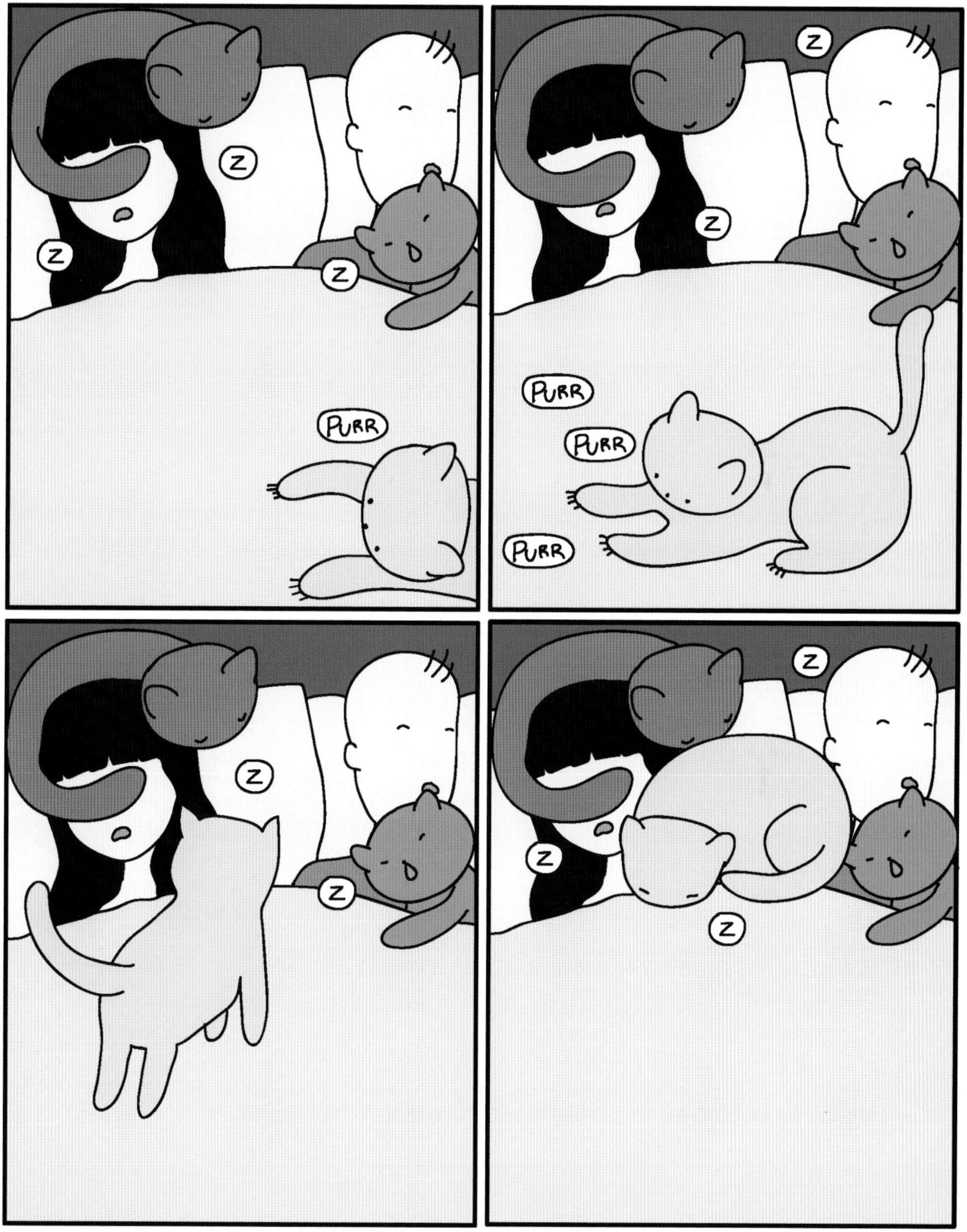
Z
Z
Z
PURR
Z
Z
PURR
PURR
PURR
Z
Z
Z
Z
Z

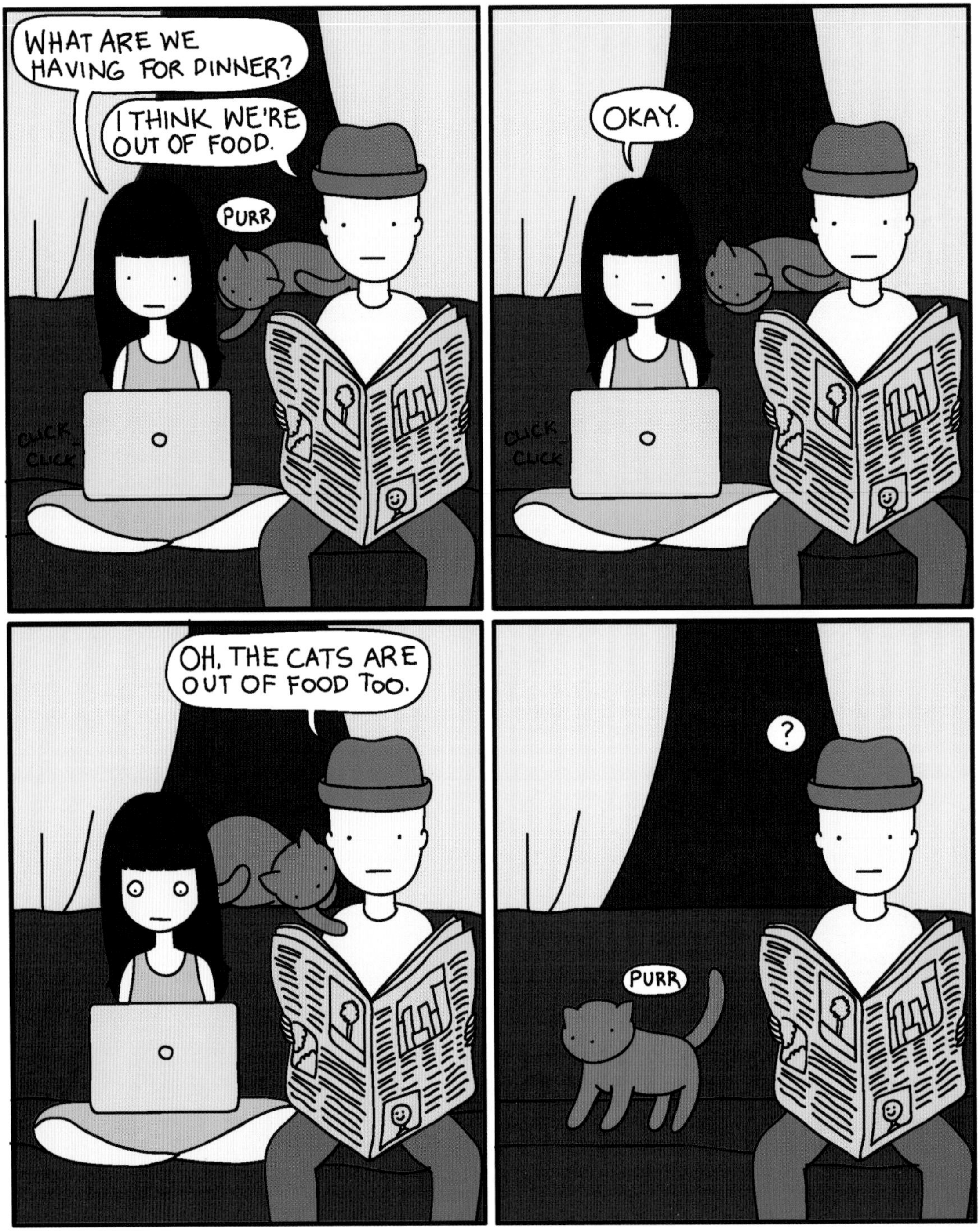
WHAT ARE WE HAVING FOR DINNER?
I THINK WE'RE OUT OF FOOD.
PURR
CLICK CLICK
OKAY.
CLICK CLICK
OH, THE CATS ARE OUT OF FOOD TOO.
?
PURR

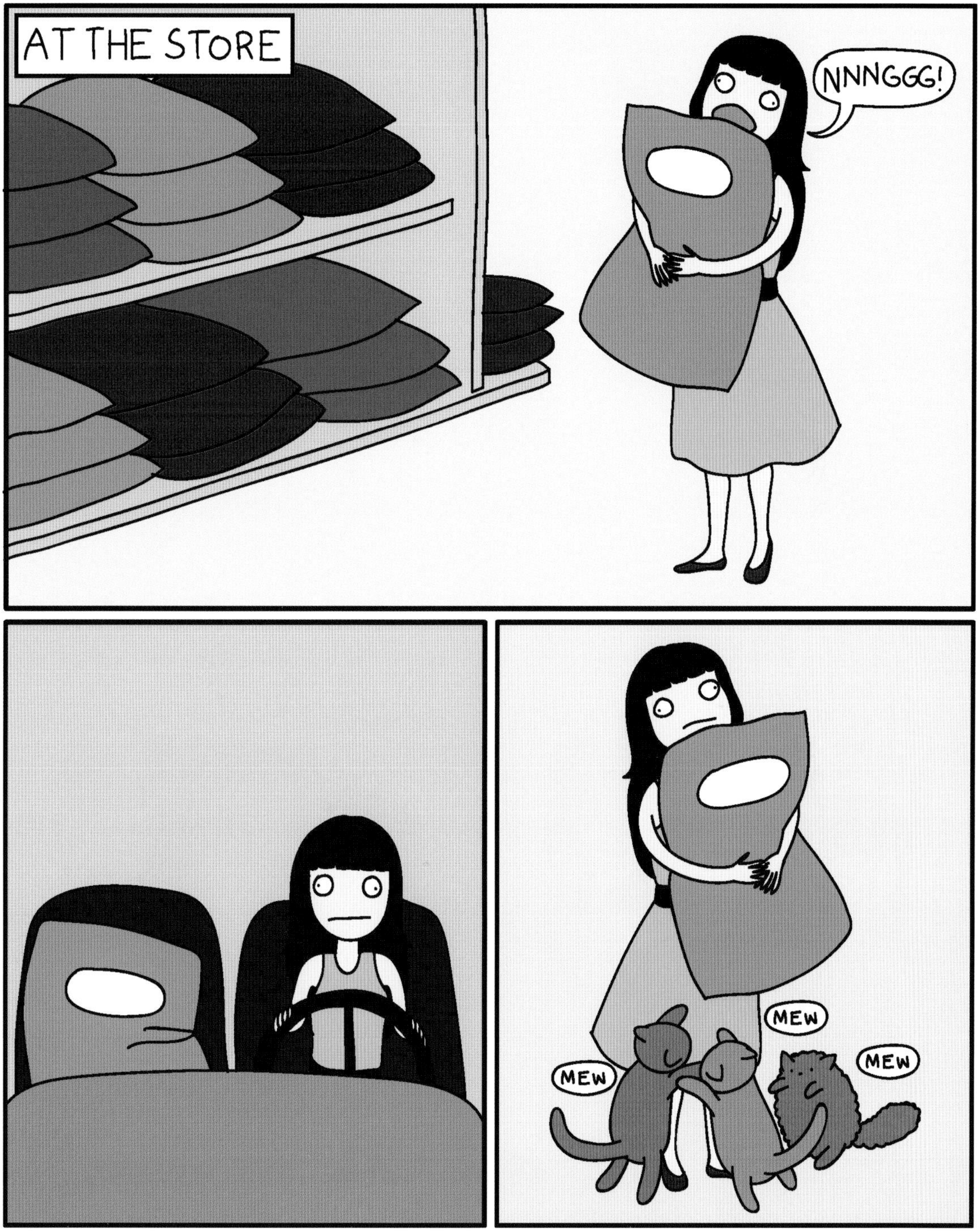
AT THE STORE
NNNGGG!
MEW
MEW
MEW

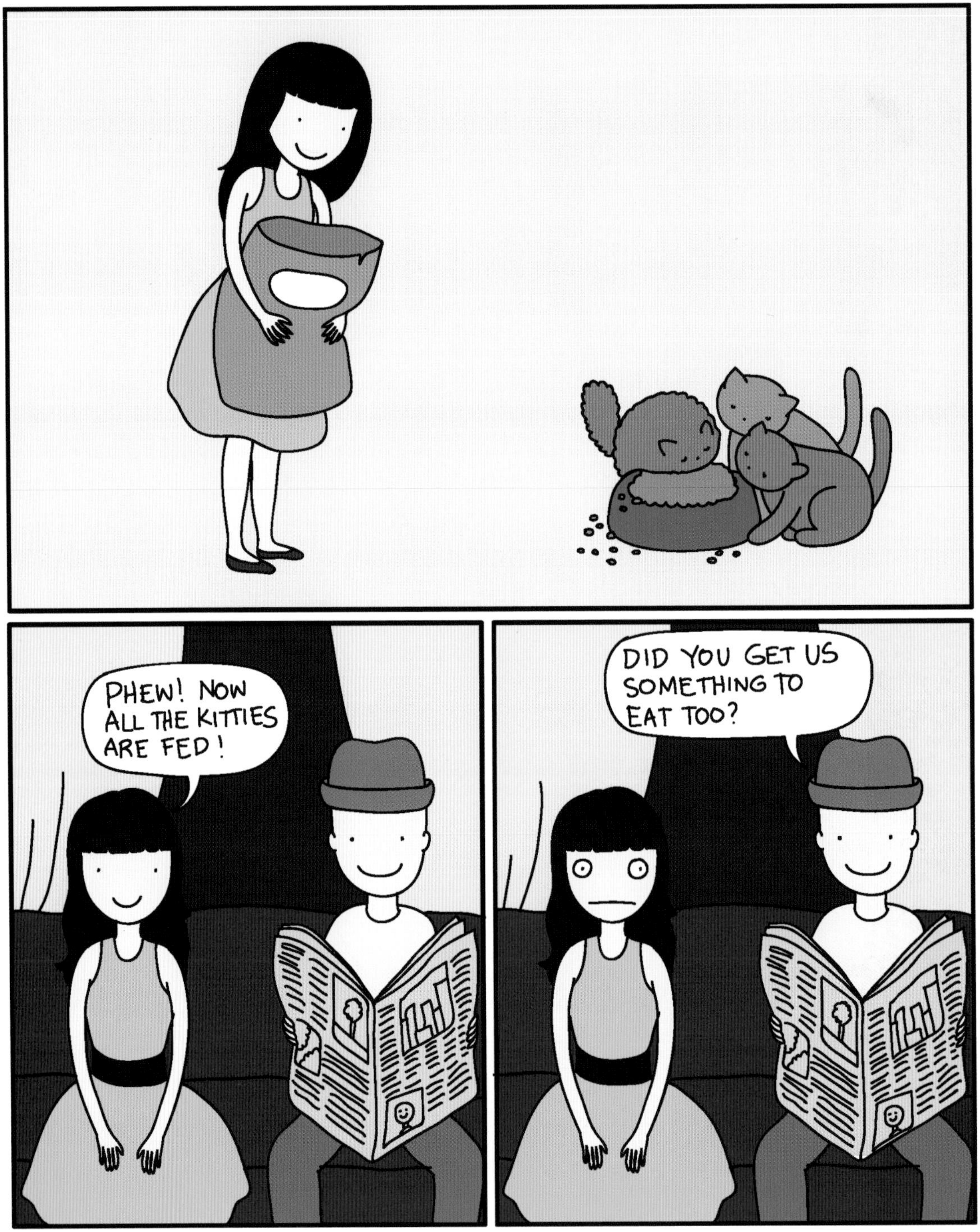
PHEW! NOW ALL THE KITTIES ARE FED!
DID YOU GET US SOMETHING TO EAT TOO?

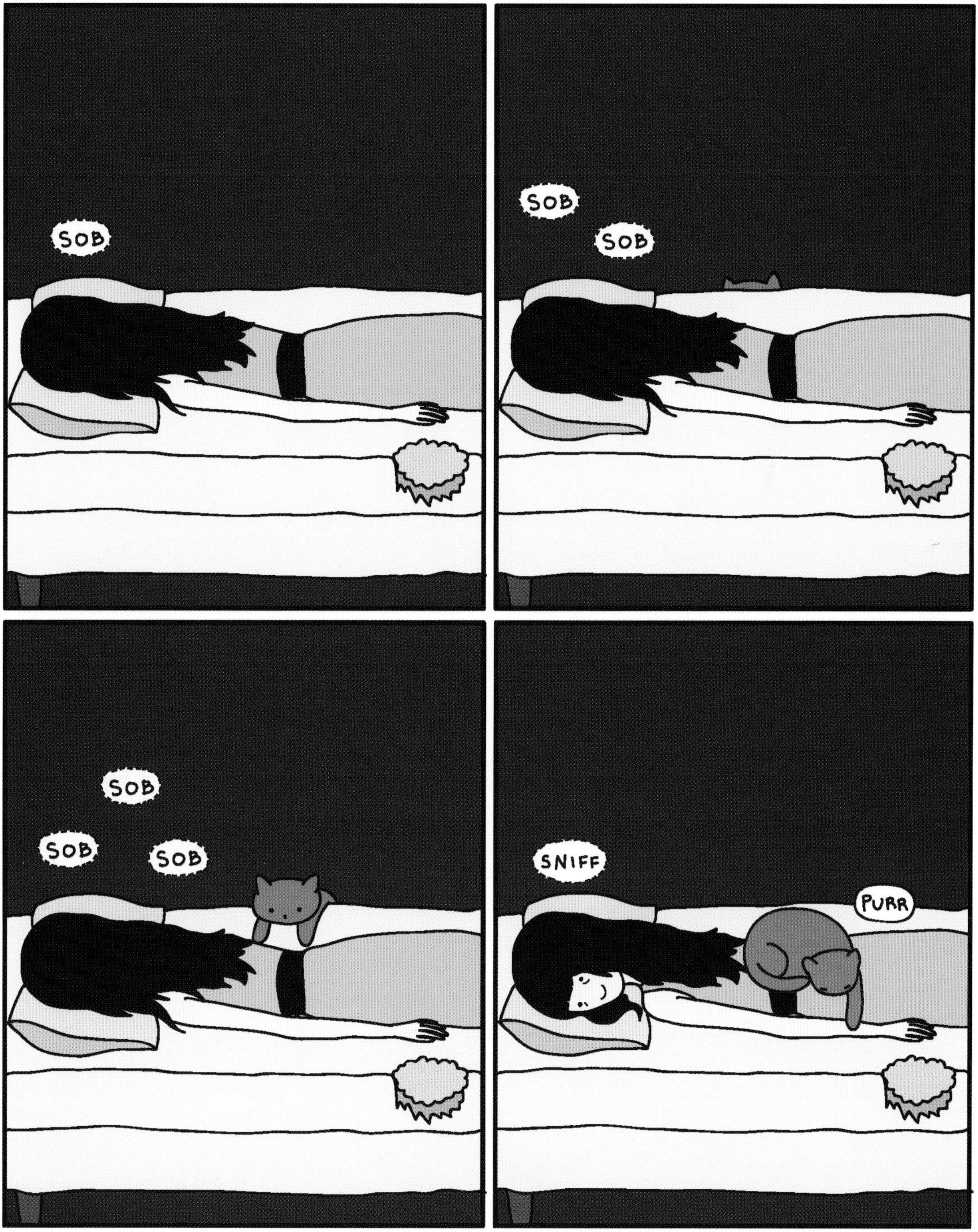
SOB
SOB
SOB
SOB
SOB
SOB
SNIFF
PURR

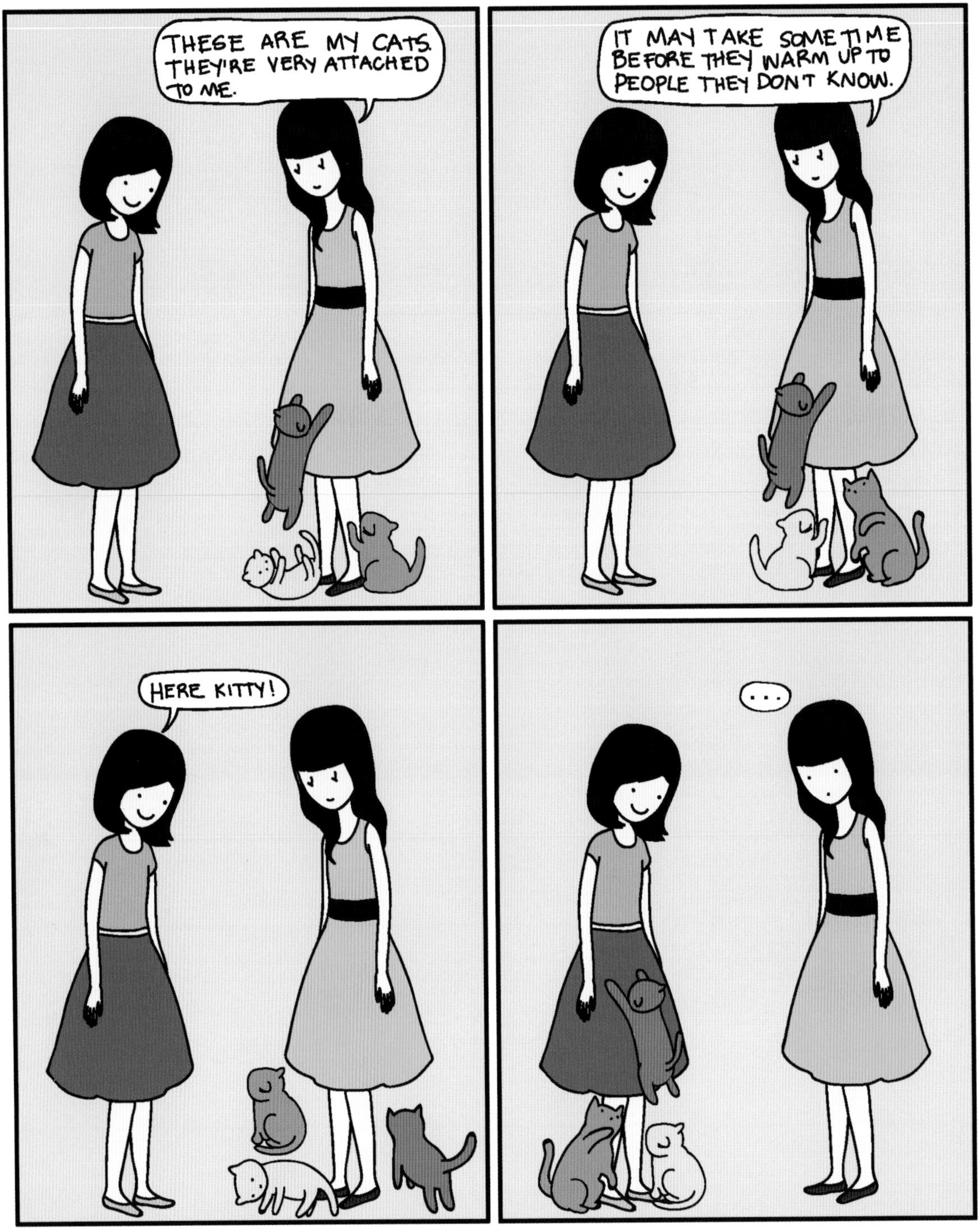
THESE ARE MY CATS. THEY'RE VERY ATTACHED TO ME.
IT MAY TAKE SOME TIME BEFORE THEY WARM UP TO PEOPLE THEY DON'T KNOW.
HERE KITTY!
...

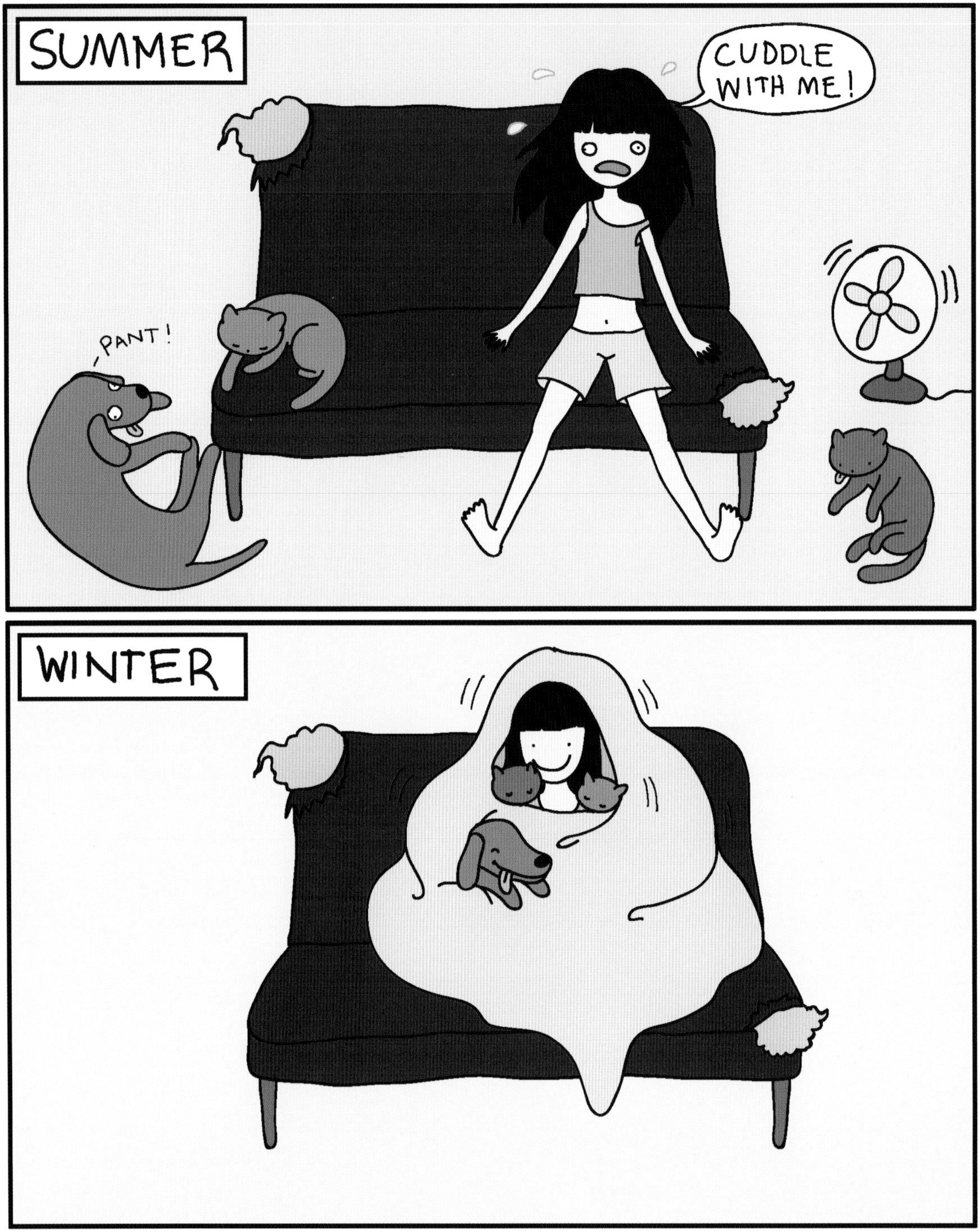
SUMMER
CUDDLE WITH ME!
PANT!
WINTER

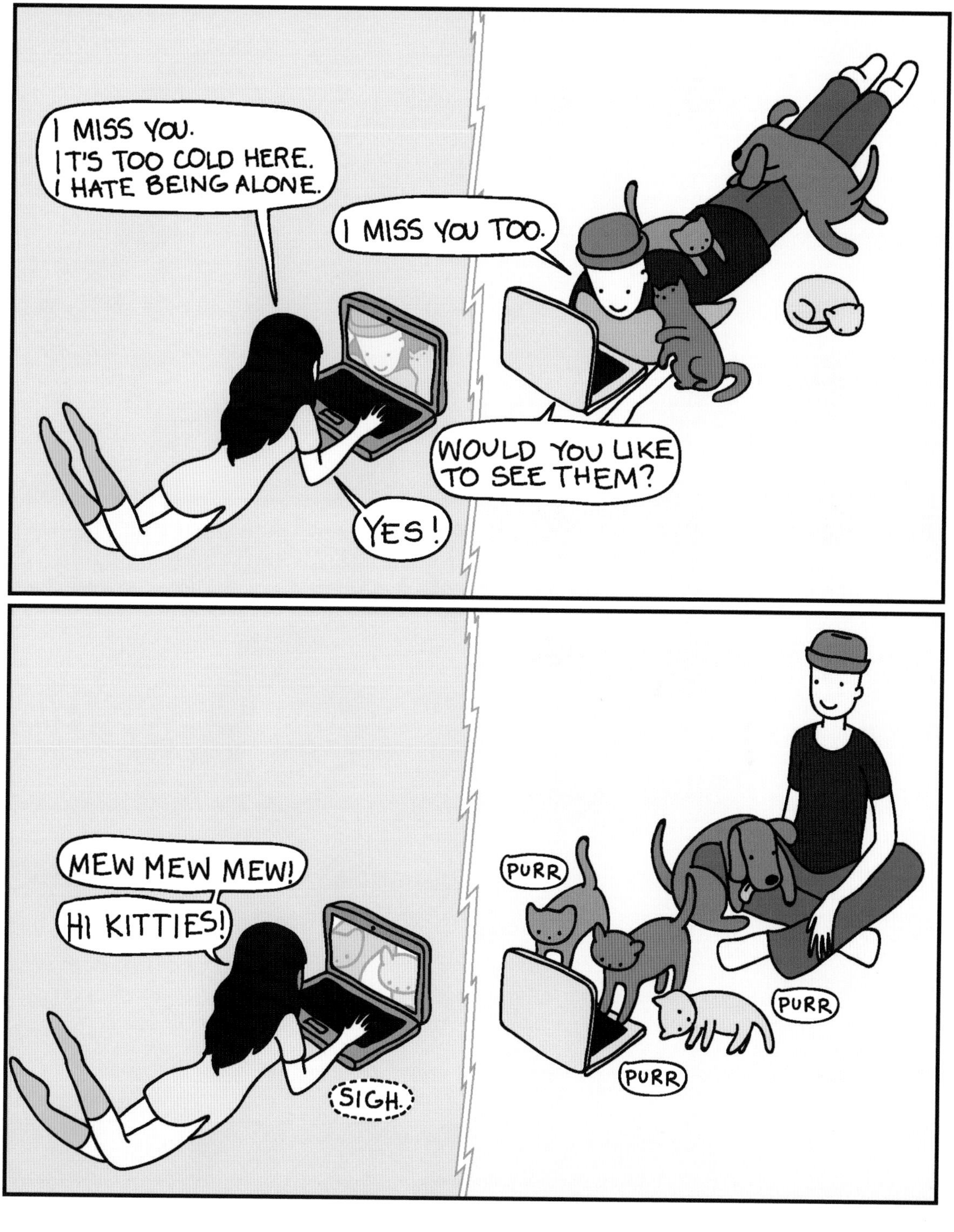
I MISS YOU.
IT'S TOO COLD HERE.
I HATE BEING ALONE.
I MISS YOU TOO.
WOULD YOU LIKE TO SEE THEM?
YES!
MEW MEW MEW!
HI KITTIES!
PURR
PURR
PURR
SIGH.

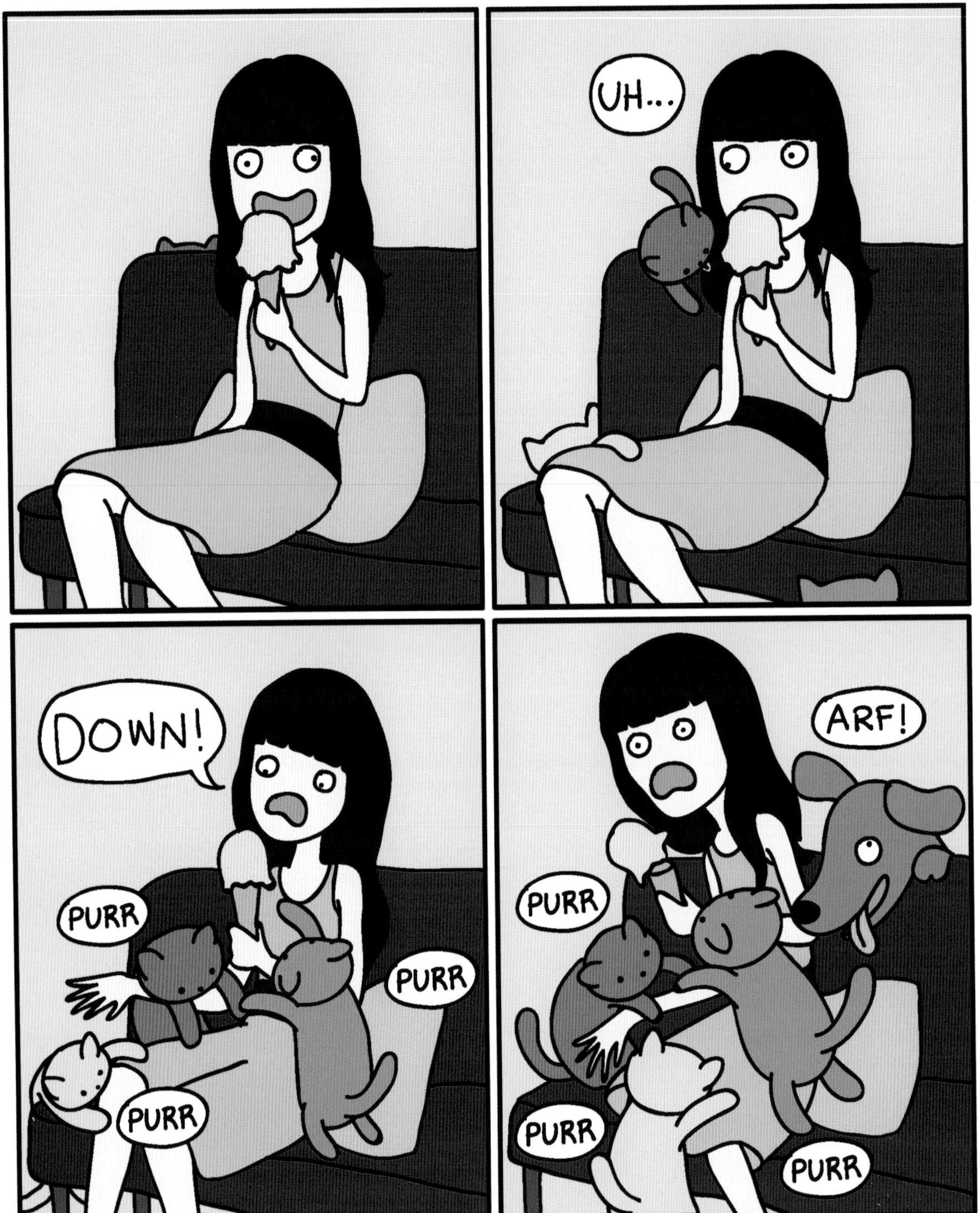
UH...
DOWN!
PURR
PURR
PURR
ARF!
PURR
PURR
PURR

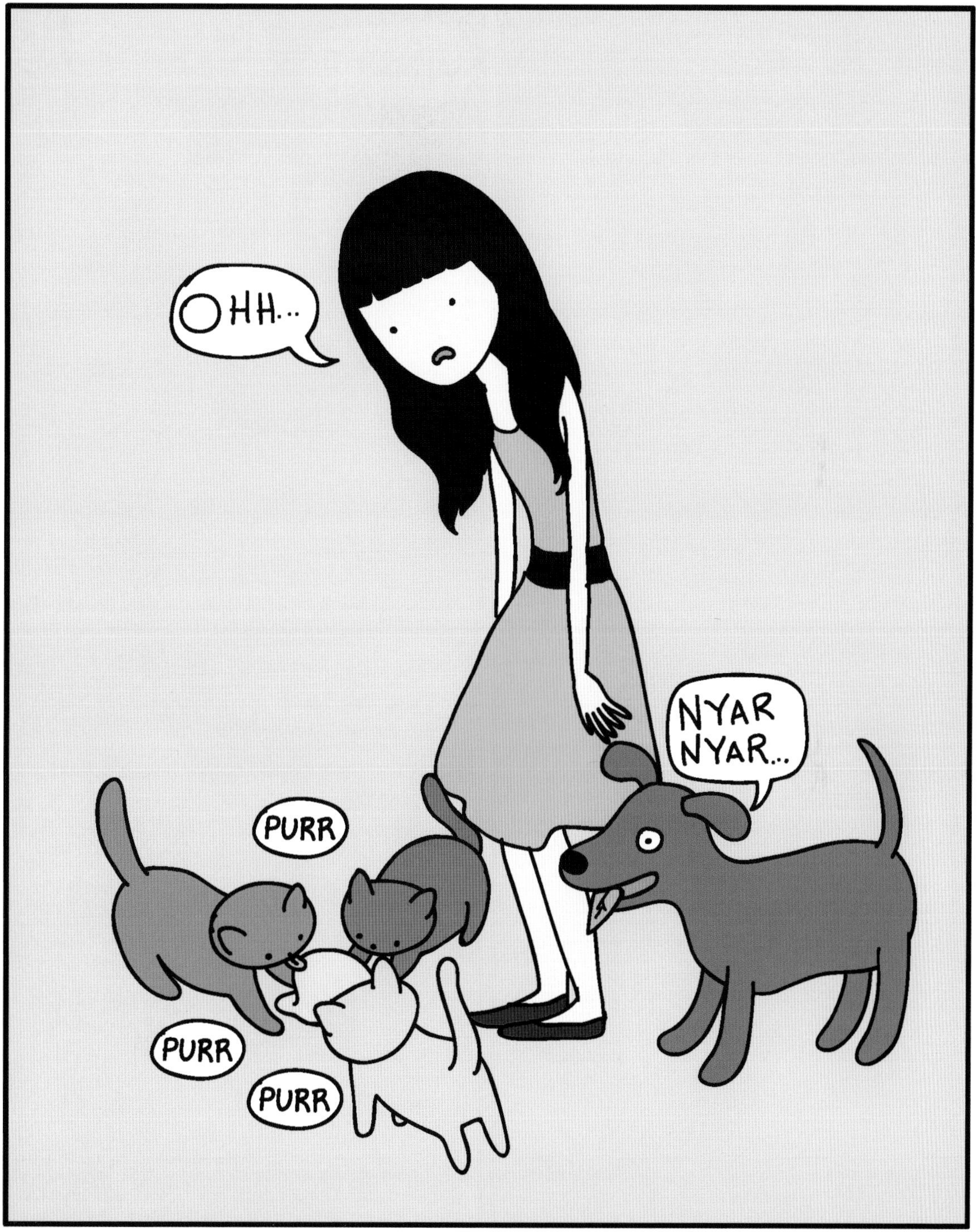
OHH...
NYAR NYAR...
PURR
PURR
PURR

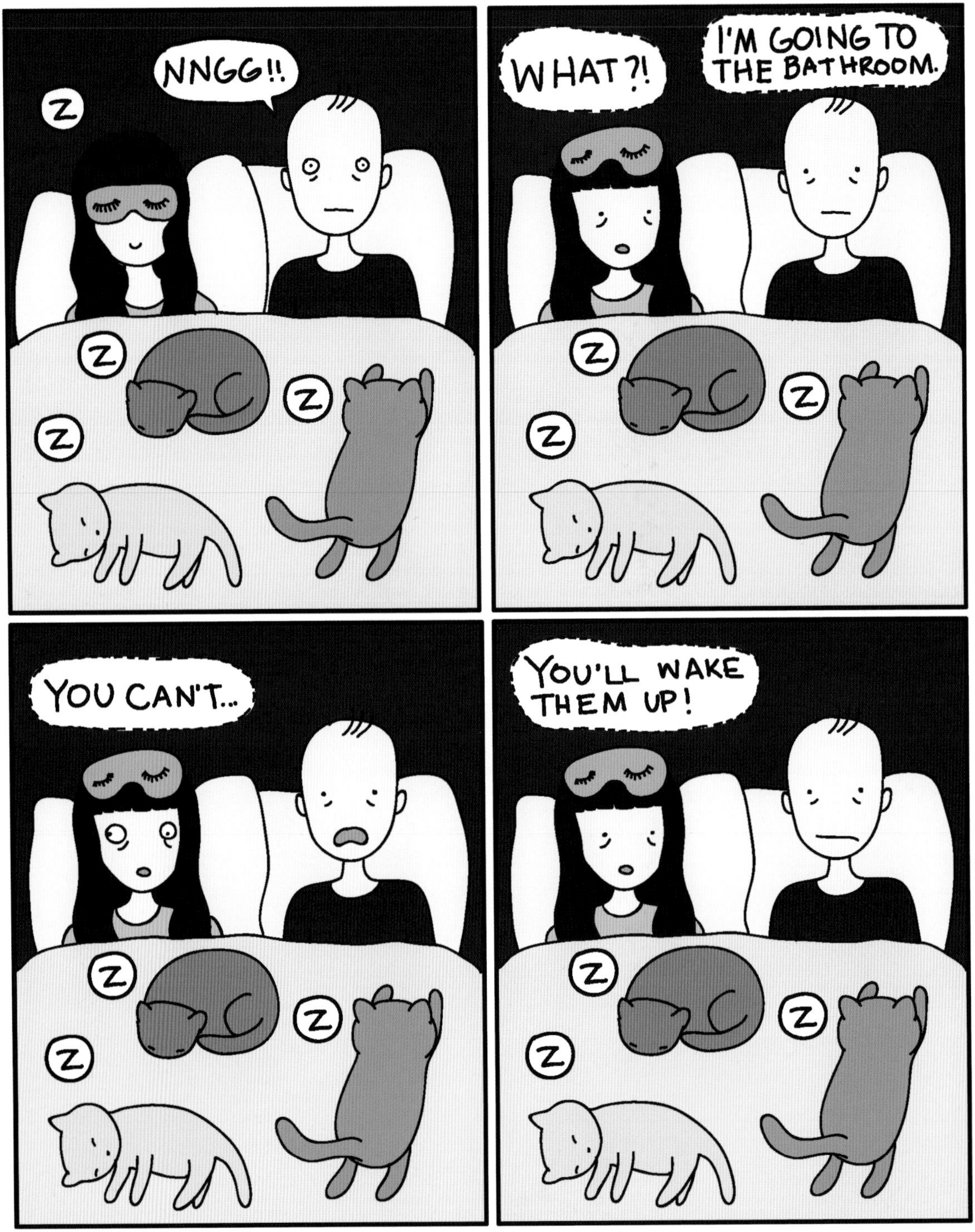
Z
NNGG!!
Z
Z
Z
WHAT?!
I'M GOING TO THE BATHROOM.
Z
Z
Z
YOU CAN'T...
Z
Z
Z
YOU'LL WAKE THEM UP!
Z
Z
Z

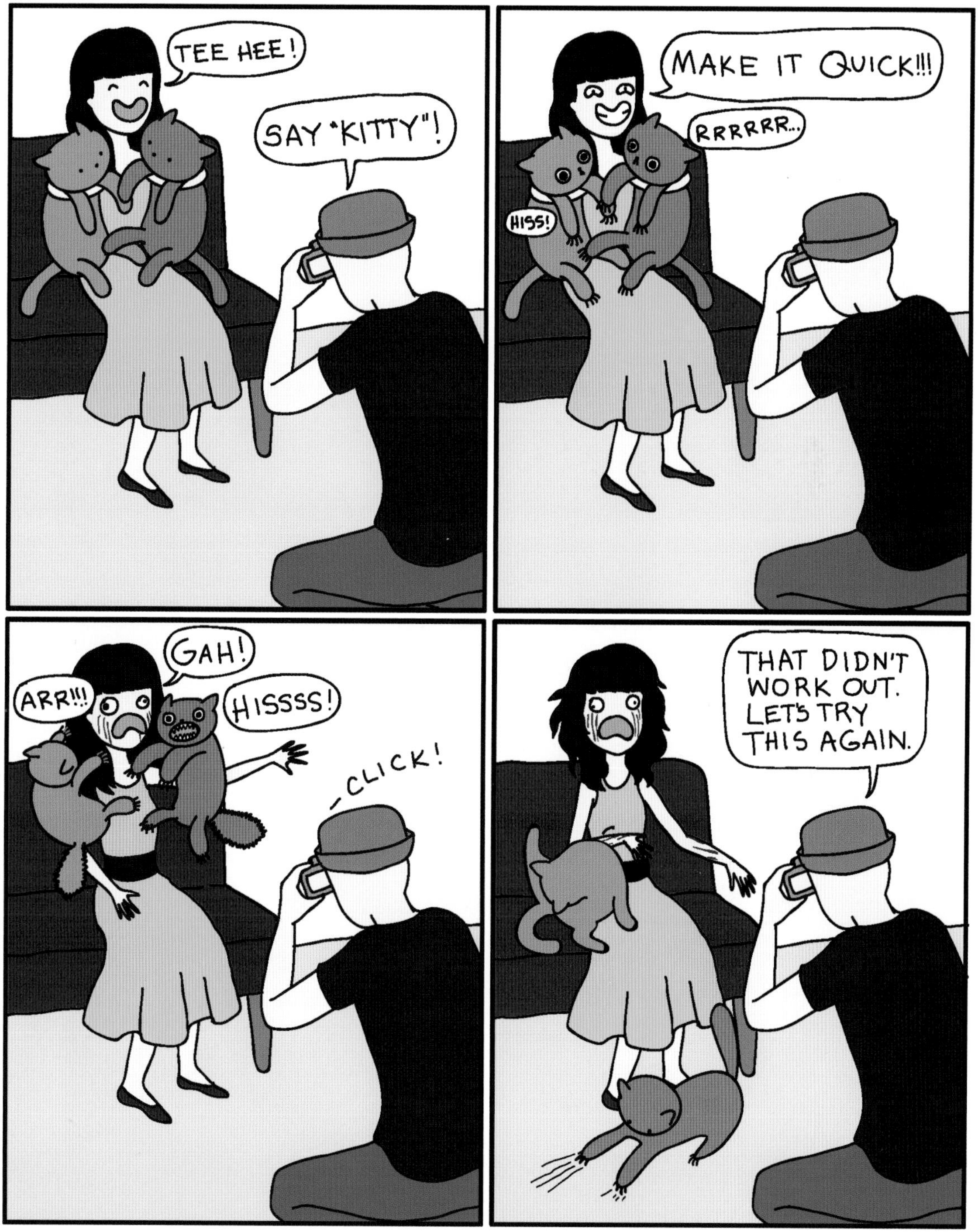
TEE HEE!
SAY "KITTY"!
MAKE IT QUICK!!!
RRRRRR...
HISS!
GAH!
ARR!!!
HISSSS!
CLICK!
THAT DIDN'T WORK OUT. LET'S TRY THIS AGAIN.

LESSONS FROM MY CAT

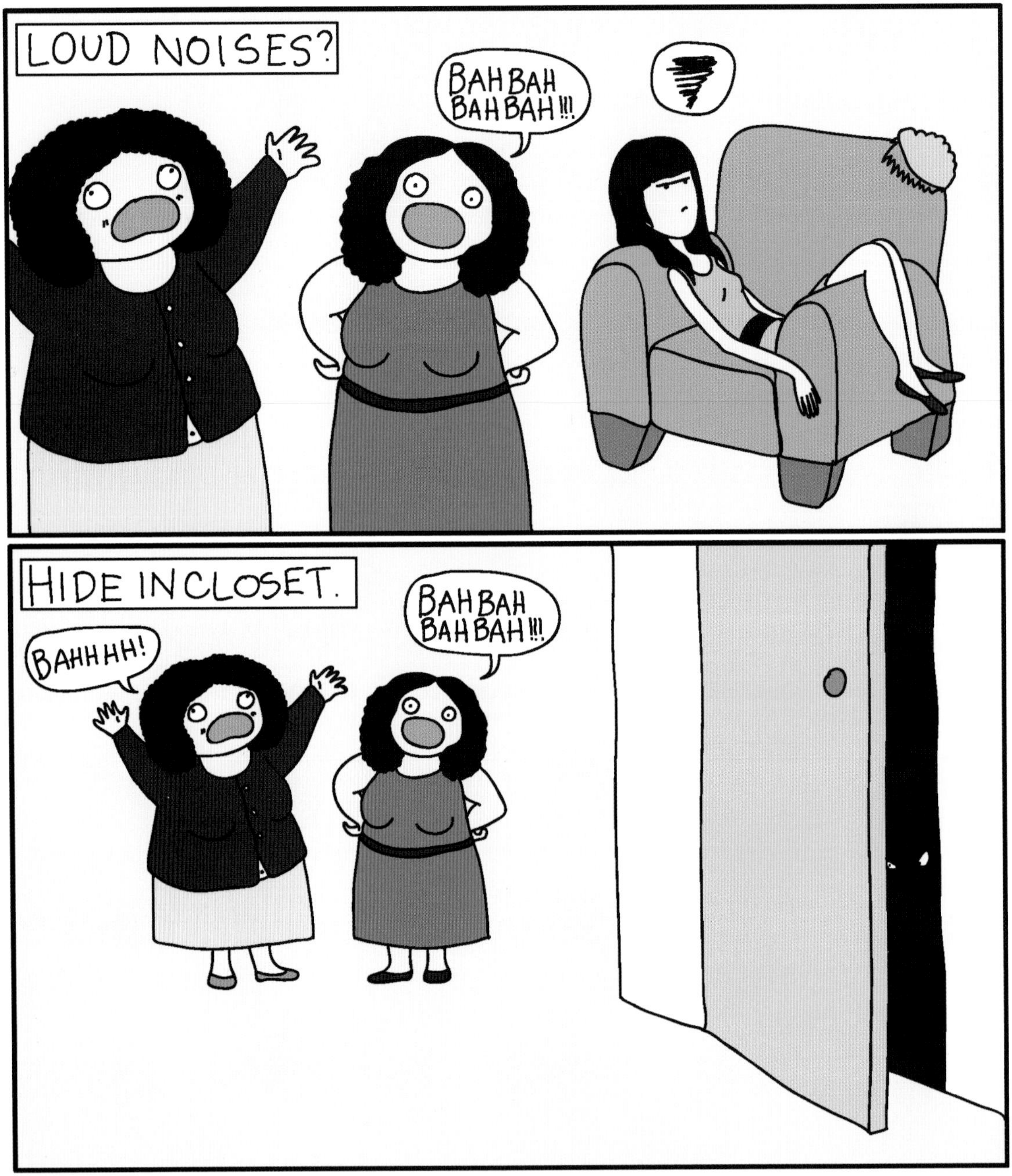
LOUD NOISES?
BAHBAH BAHBAH!!!
HIDE IN CLOSET.
BAHHHH!
BAHBAH BAHBAH!!!

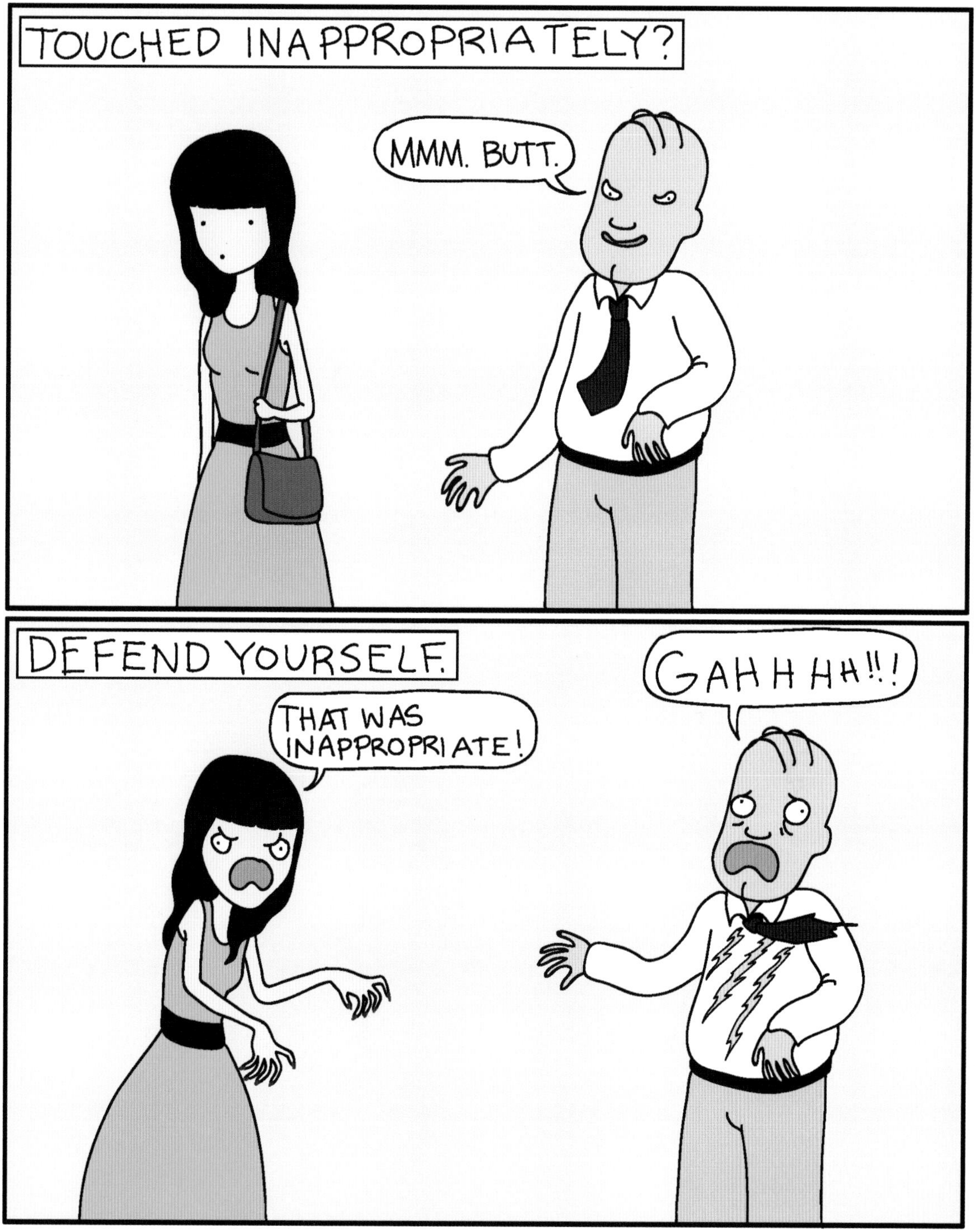
TOUCHED INAPPROPRIATELY?
MMM. BUTT.
DEFEND YOURSELF.
THAT WAS INAPPROPRIATE!
GAHHHH!!!

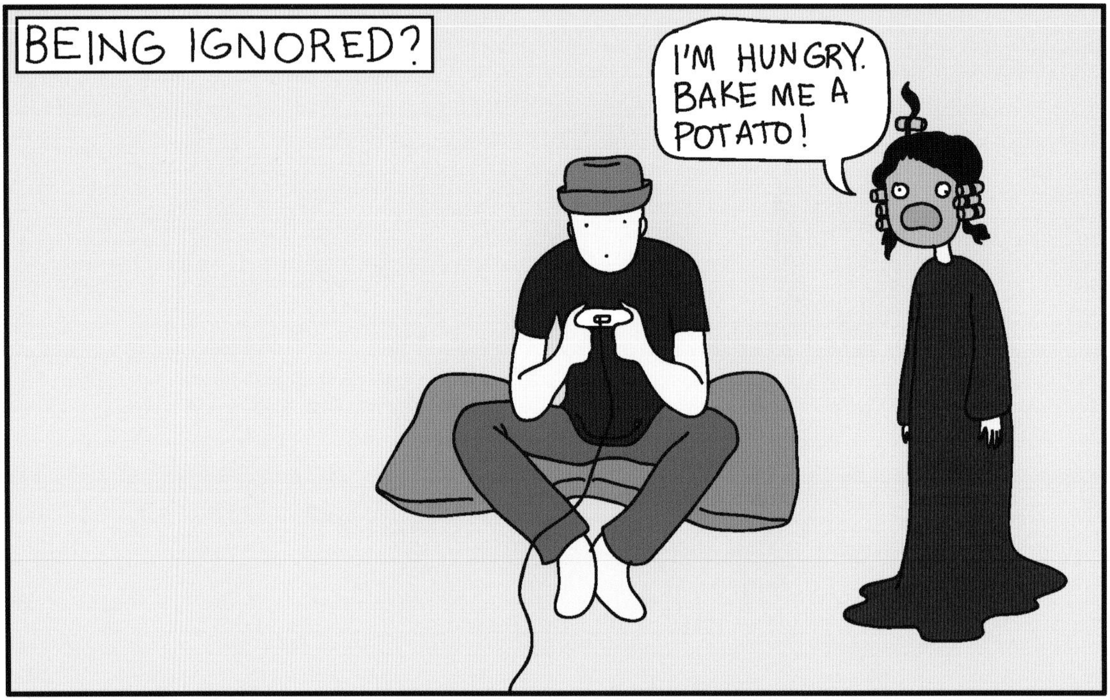
BEING IGNORED?
I'M HUNGRY. BAKE ME A POTATO!

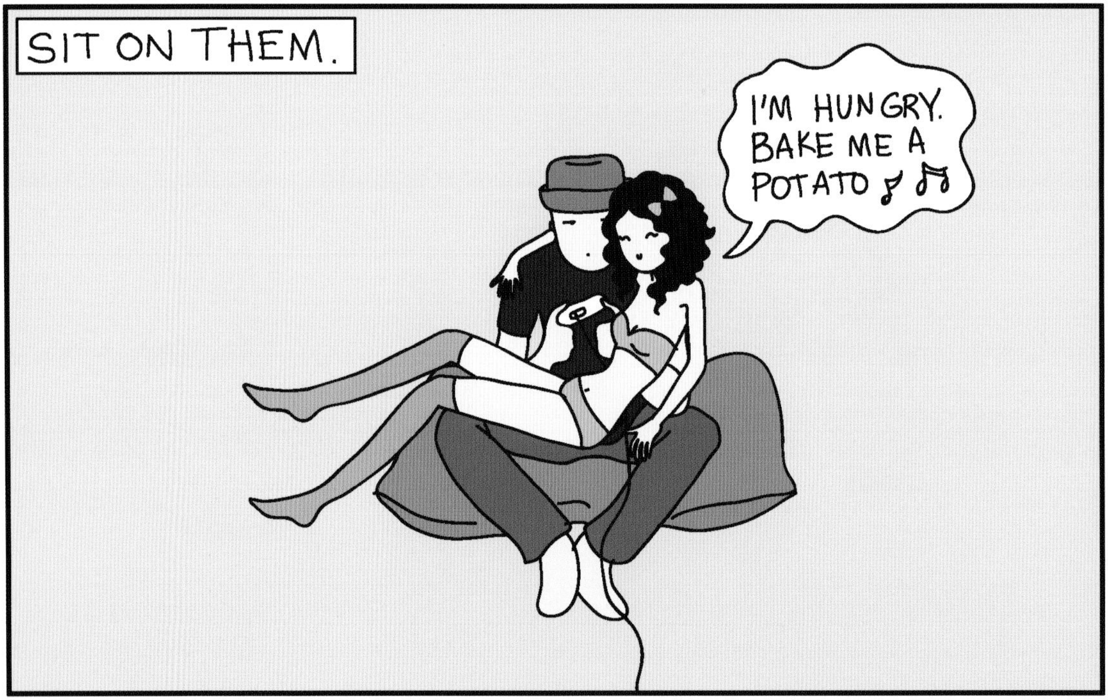
SIT ON THEM.
I'M HUNGRY. BAKE ME A POTATO

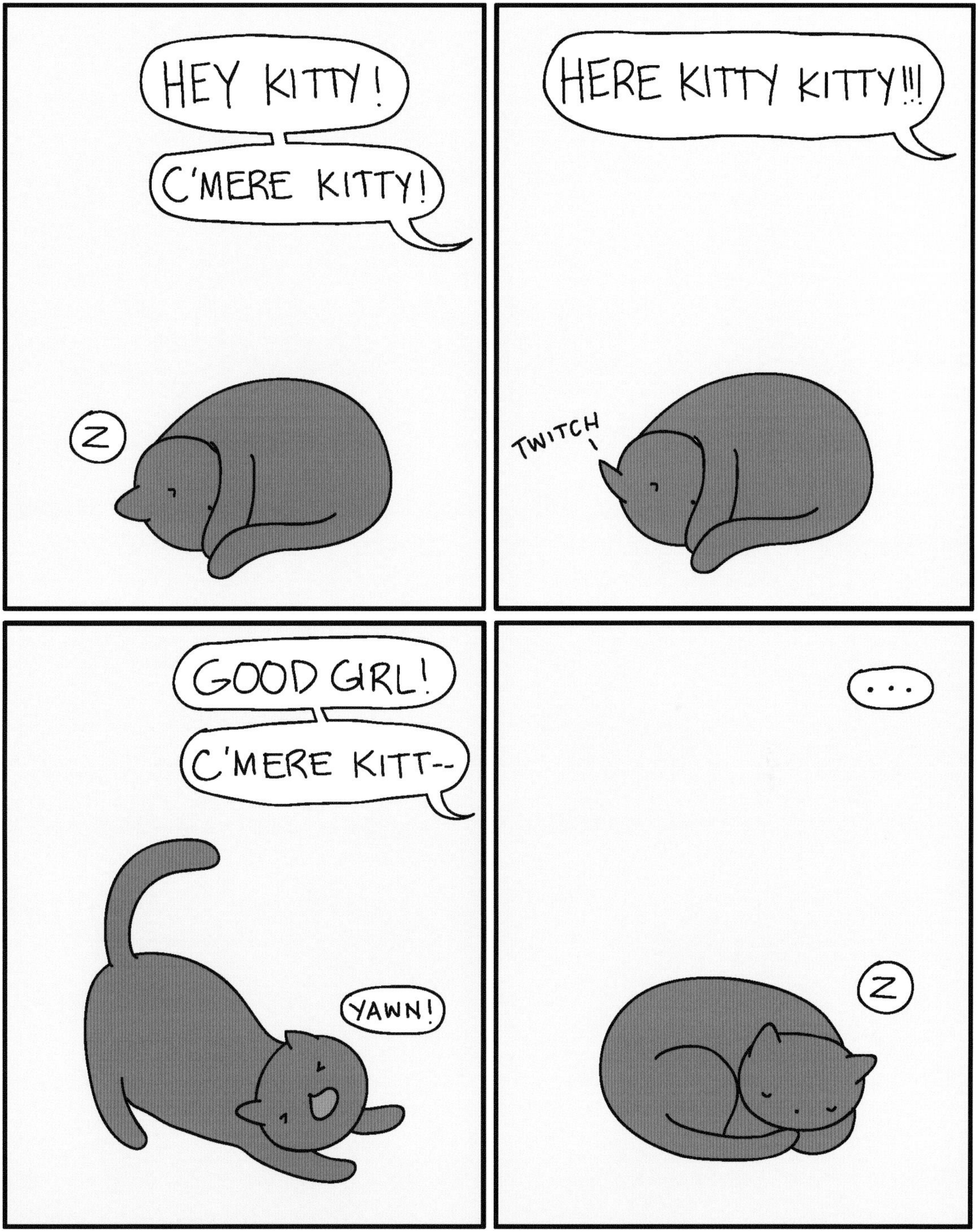
HEY KITTY!
C'MERE KITTY!
Z
HERE KITTY KITTY!!!
TWITCH
GOOD GIRL!
C'MERE KITT--
YAWN!
...
Z

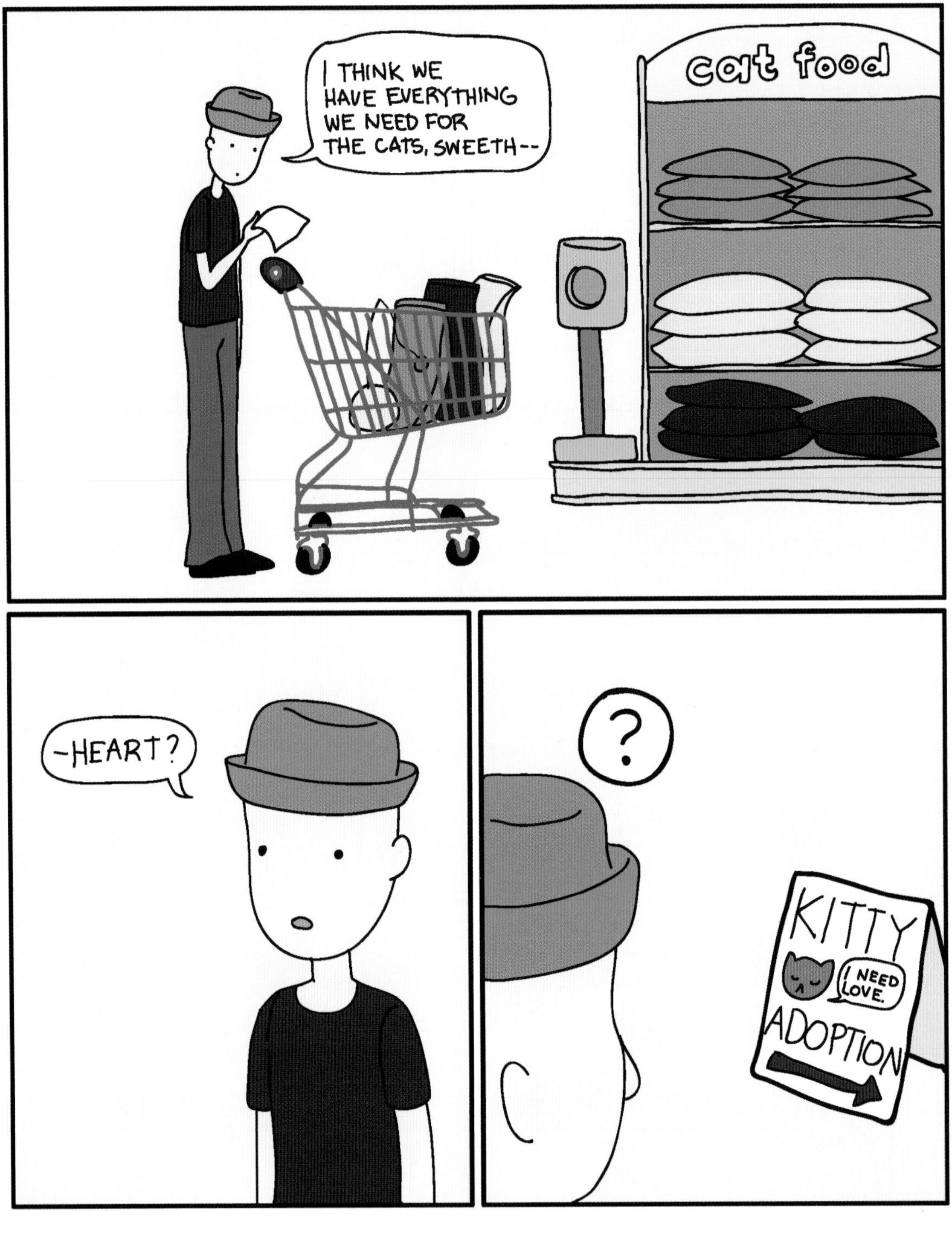
cat food
I THINK WE HAVE EVERYTHING WE NEED FOR THE CATS, SWEETH--
-HEART?
?
KITTY
I NEED LOVE.
ADOPTION

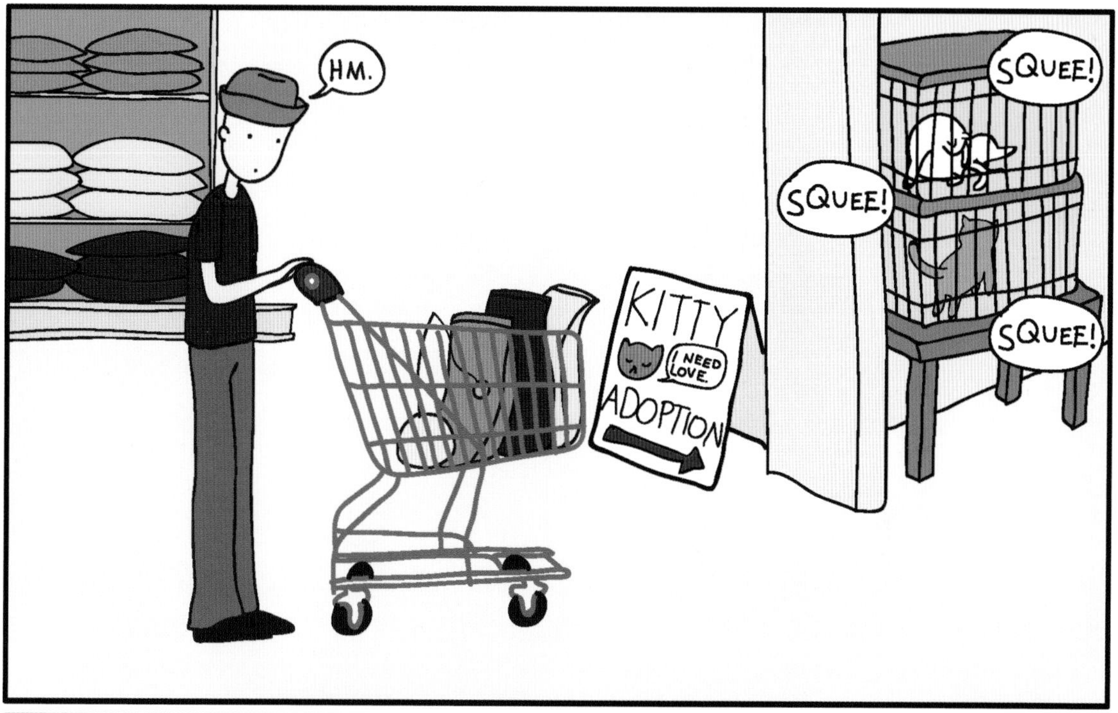
HM.
SQUEE!
SQUEE!
SQUEE!
KITTY
I NEED LOVE.
ADOPTION

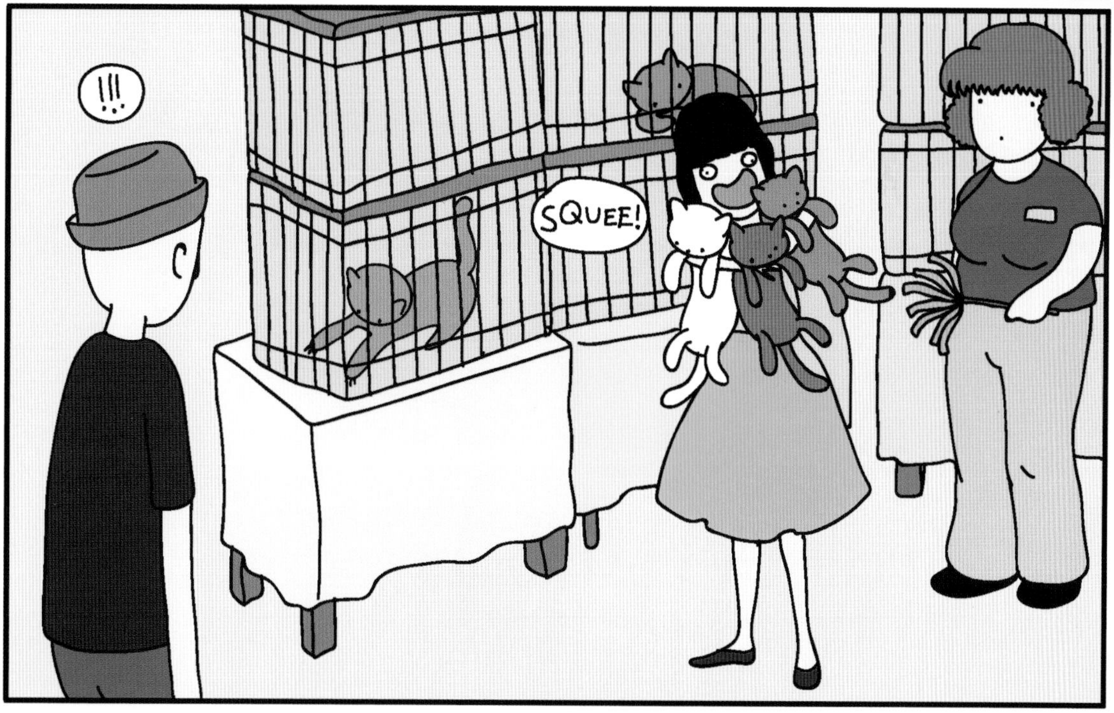
!!!
SQUEE!

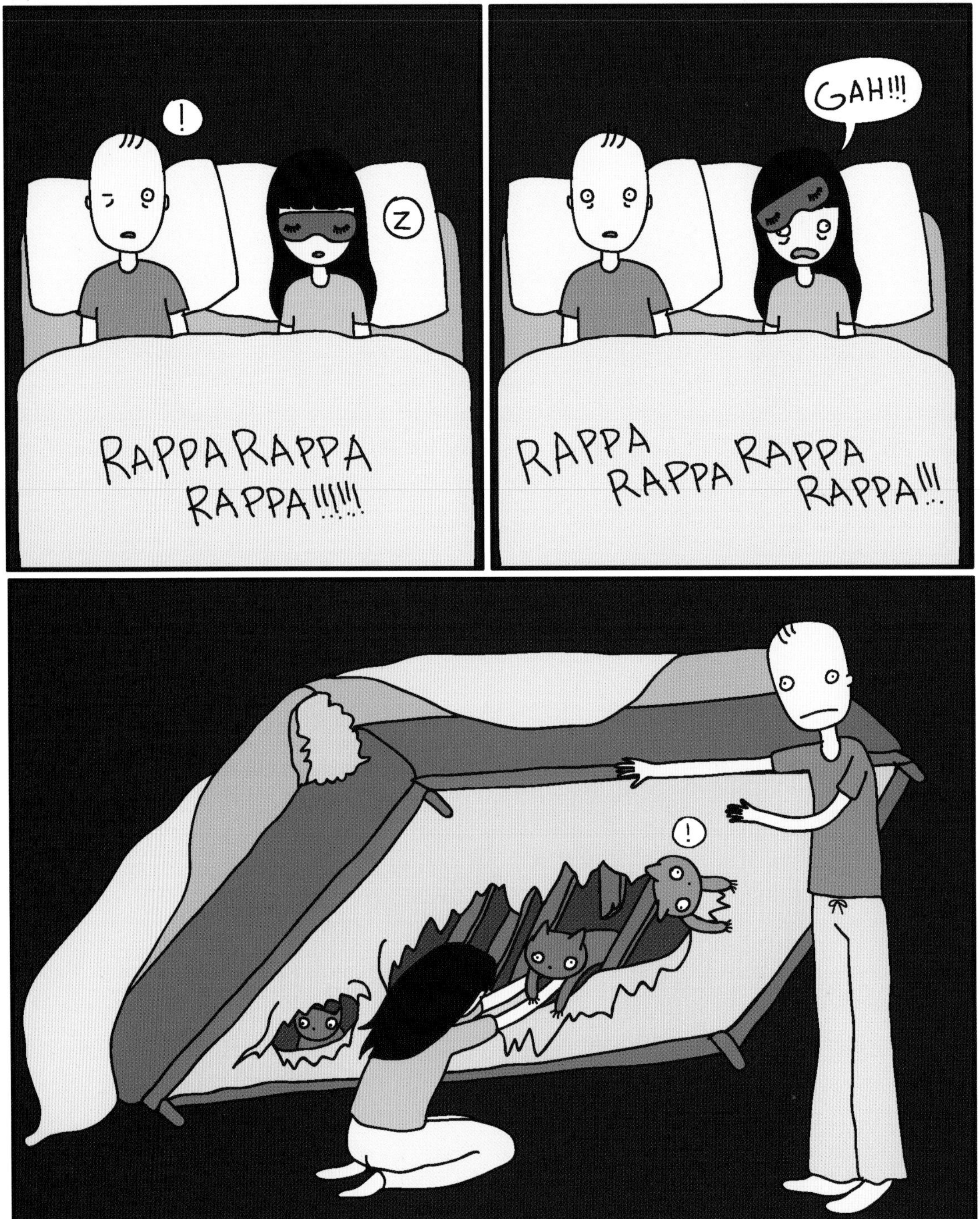
!
Z
RAPPA RAPPA RAPPA!!!!!!
GAH!!!
RAPPA RAPPA RAPPA RAPPA!!!
!

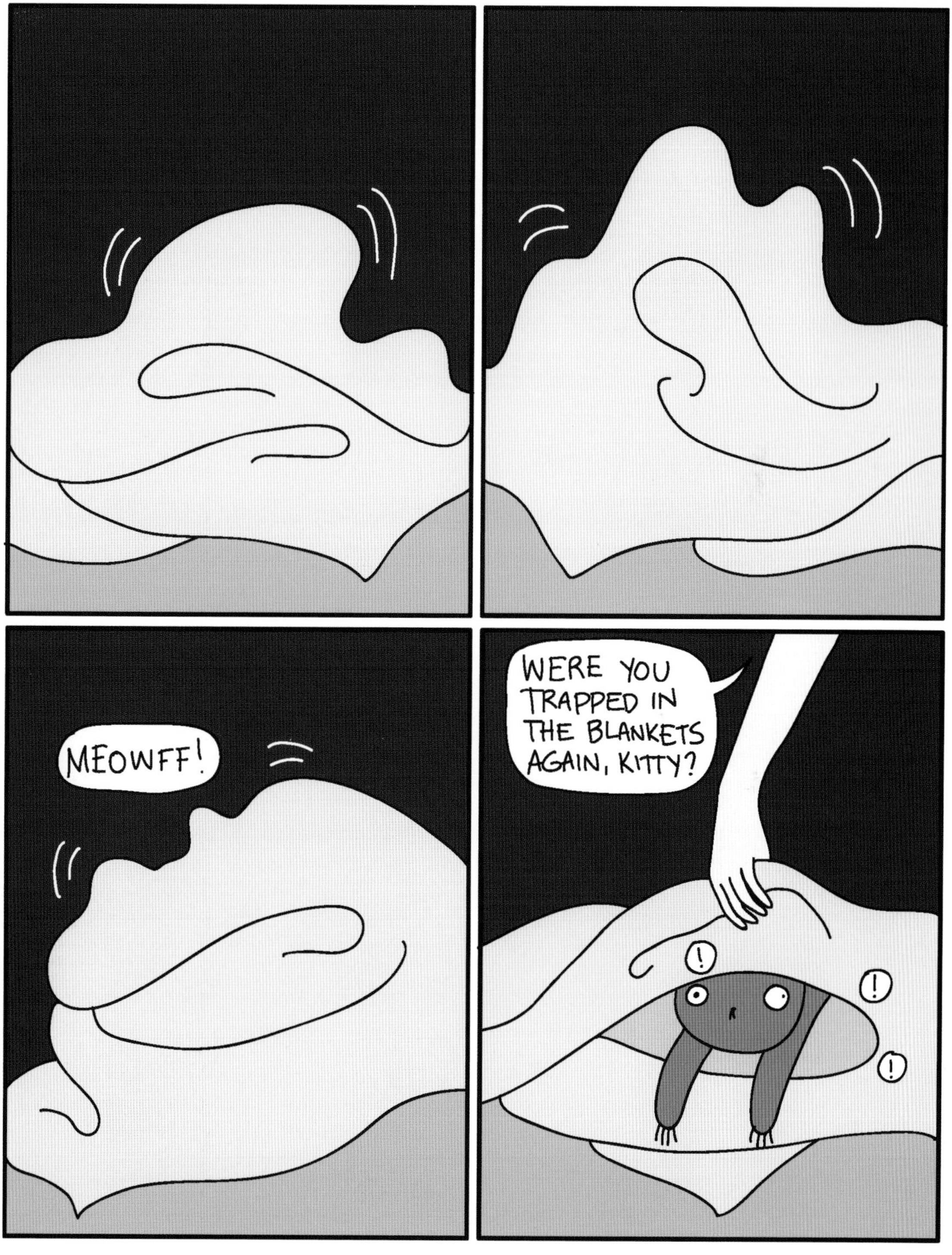
MEOWFF!
WERE YOU TRAPPED IN THE BLANKETS AGAIN, KITTY?

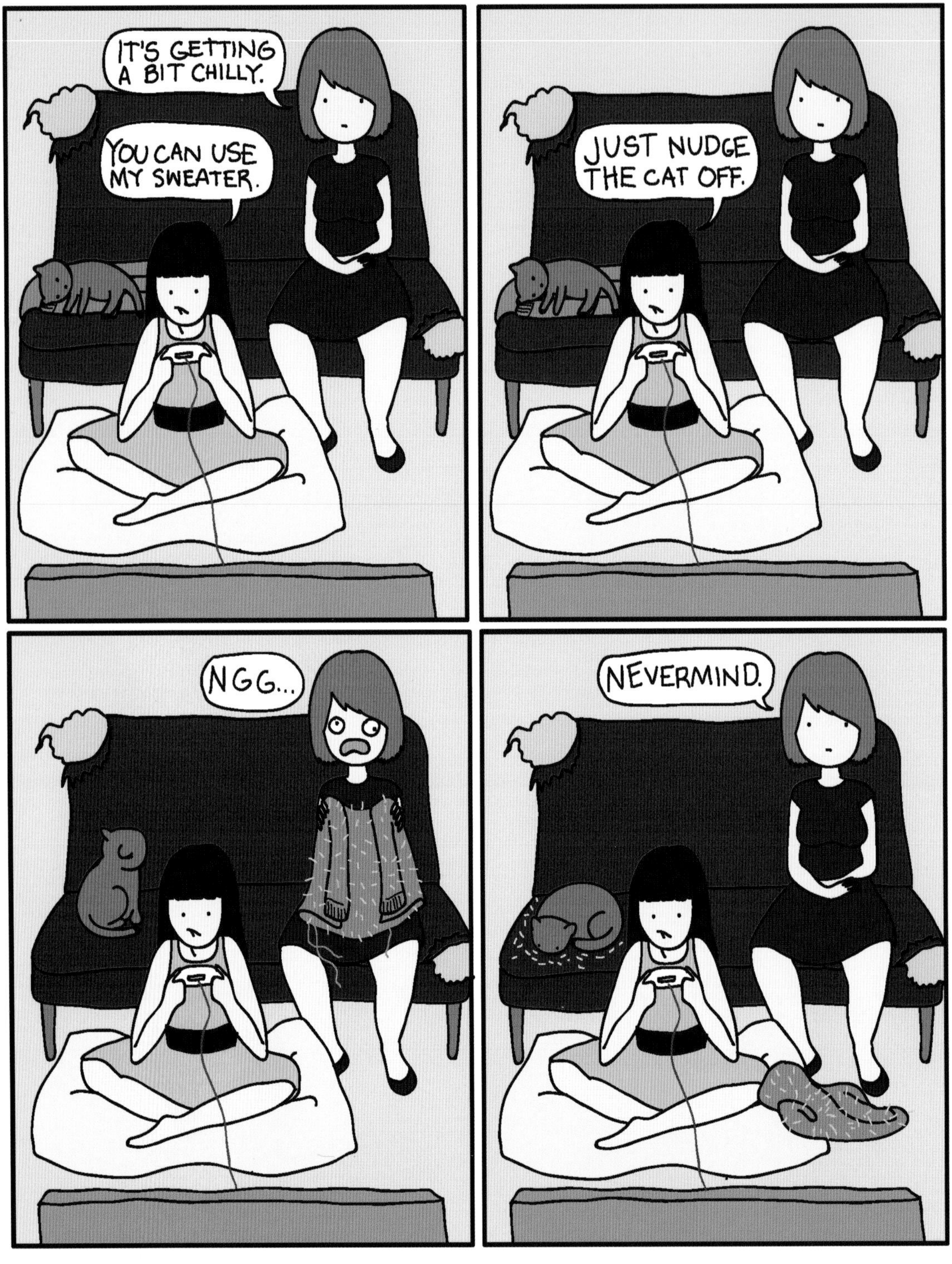
IT'S GETTING A BIT CHILLY.
YOU CAN USE MY SWEATER.
JUST NUDGE THE CAT OFF.
NGG...
NEVERMIND.

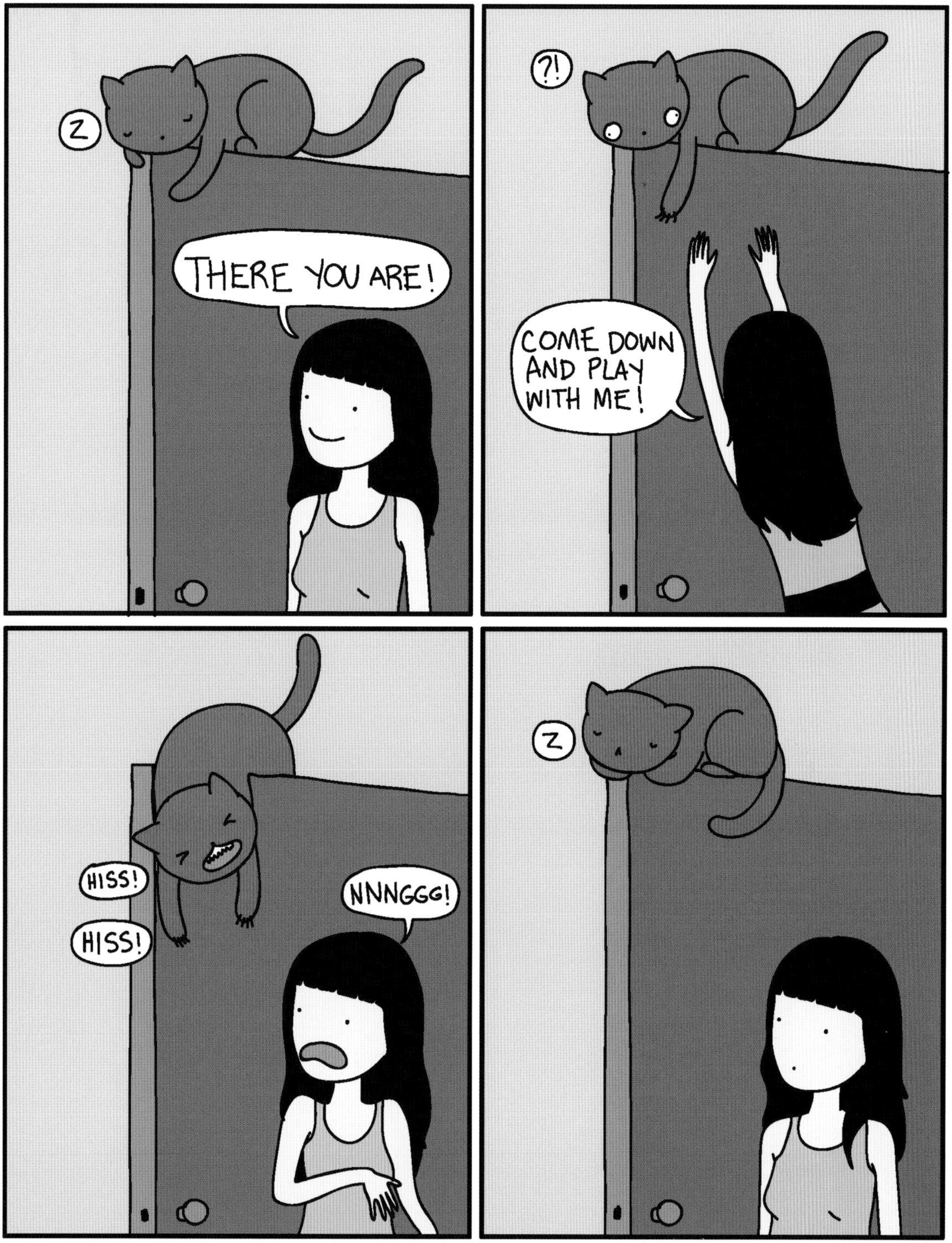
Z
THERE YOU ARE!
?!
COME DOWN AND PLAY WITH ME!
HISS!
HISS!
NNNGGG!
Z

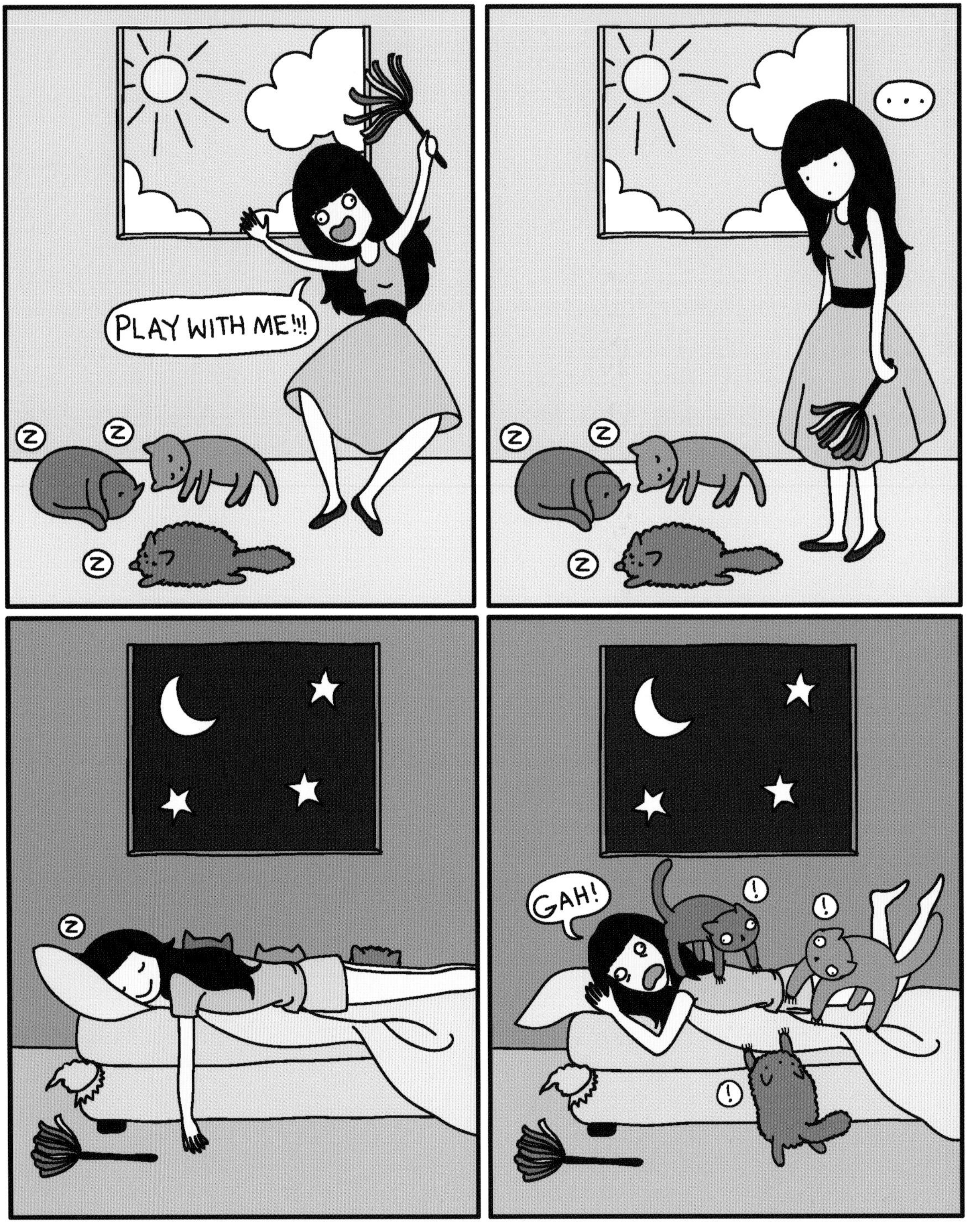
PLAY WITH ME!!!
z
z
z
. . .
z
z
z
z
GAH!
!
!
!

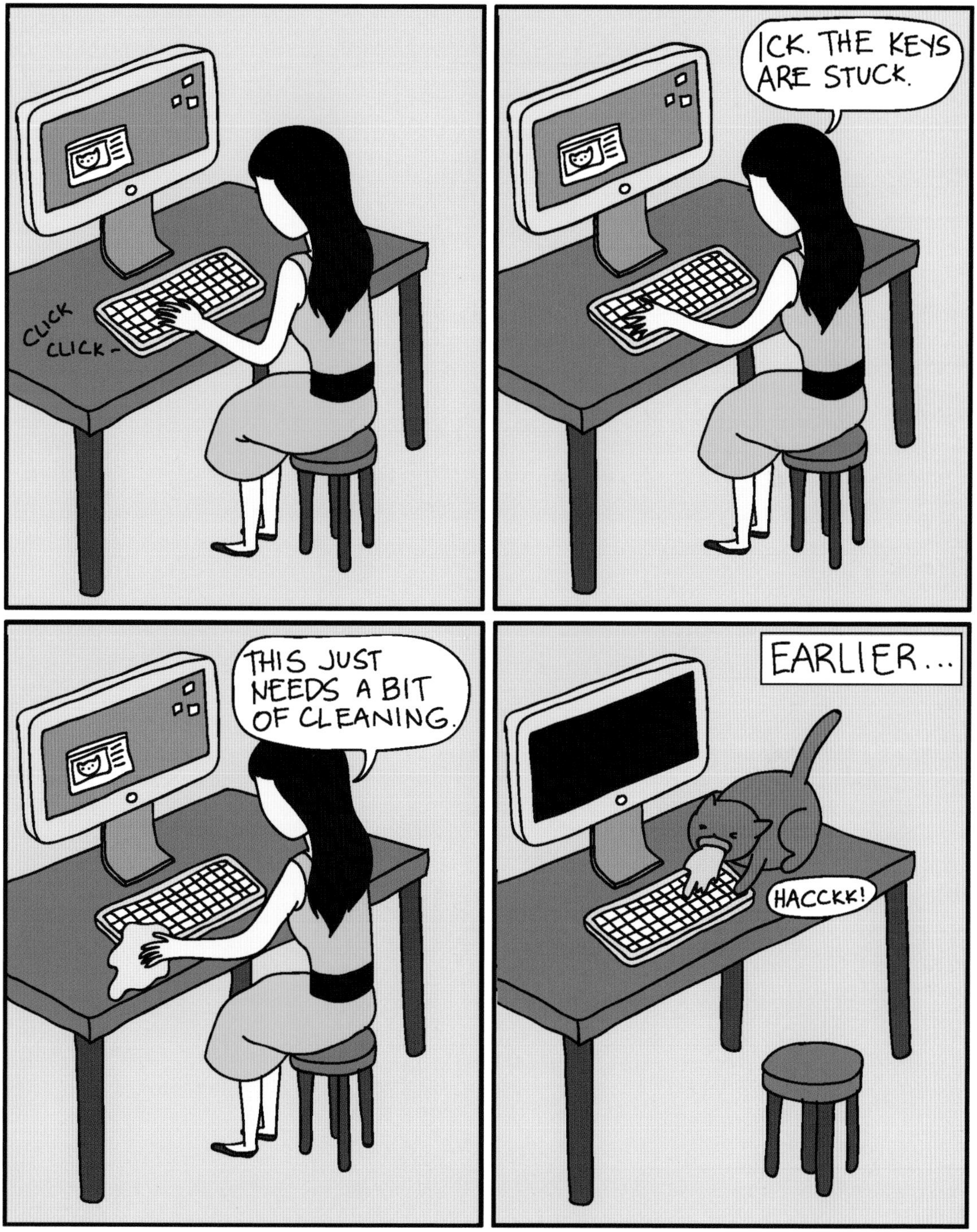
CLICK
CLICK -
ICK. THE KEYS ARE STUCK.
THIS JUST NEEDS A BIT OF CLEANING.
EARLIER...
HACCKK!

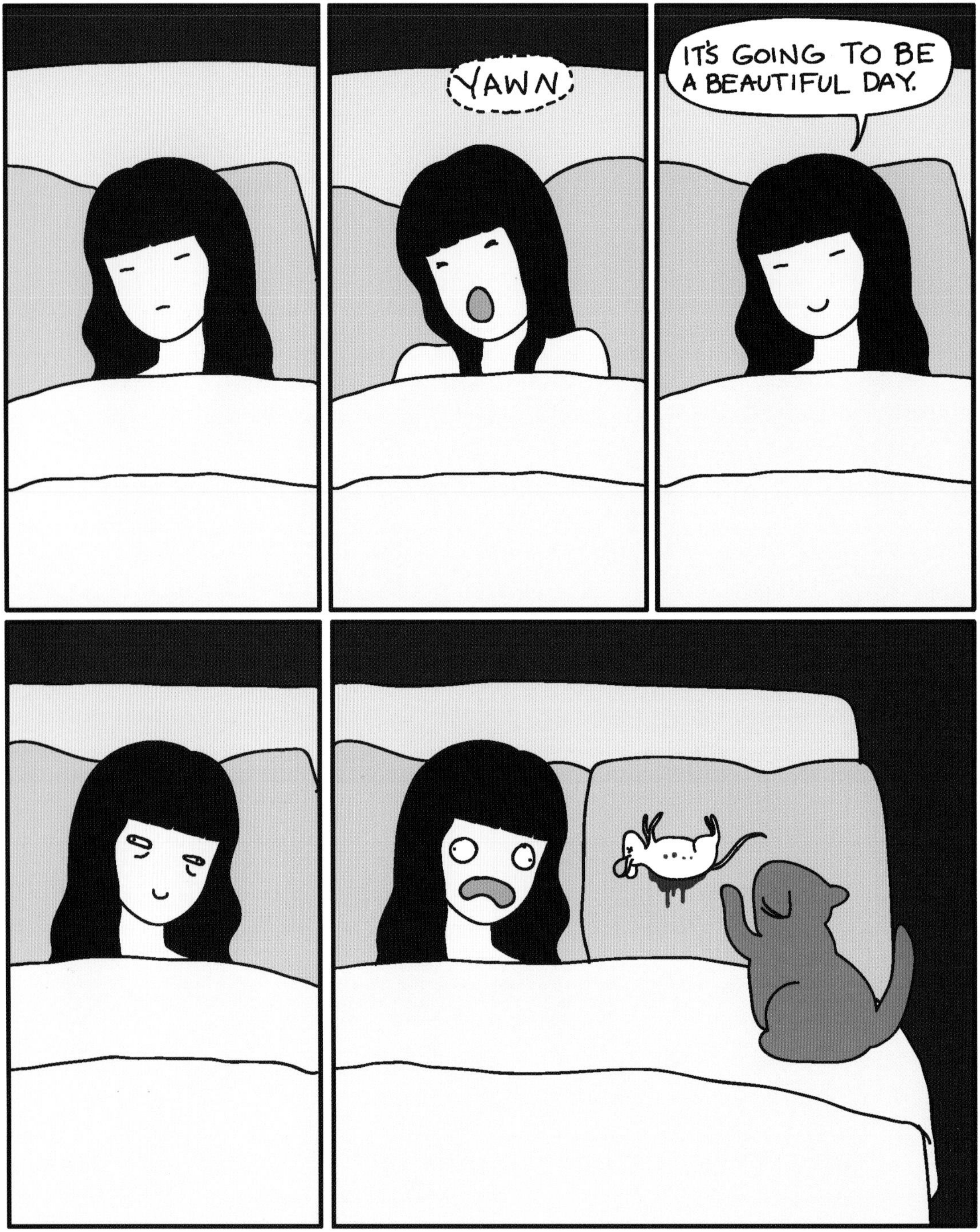
YAWN
IT'S GOING TO BE A BEAUTIFUL DAY.

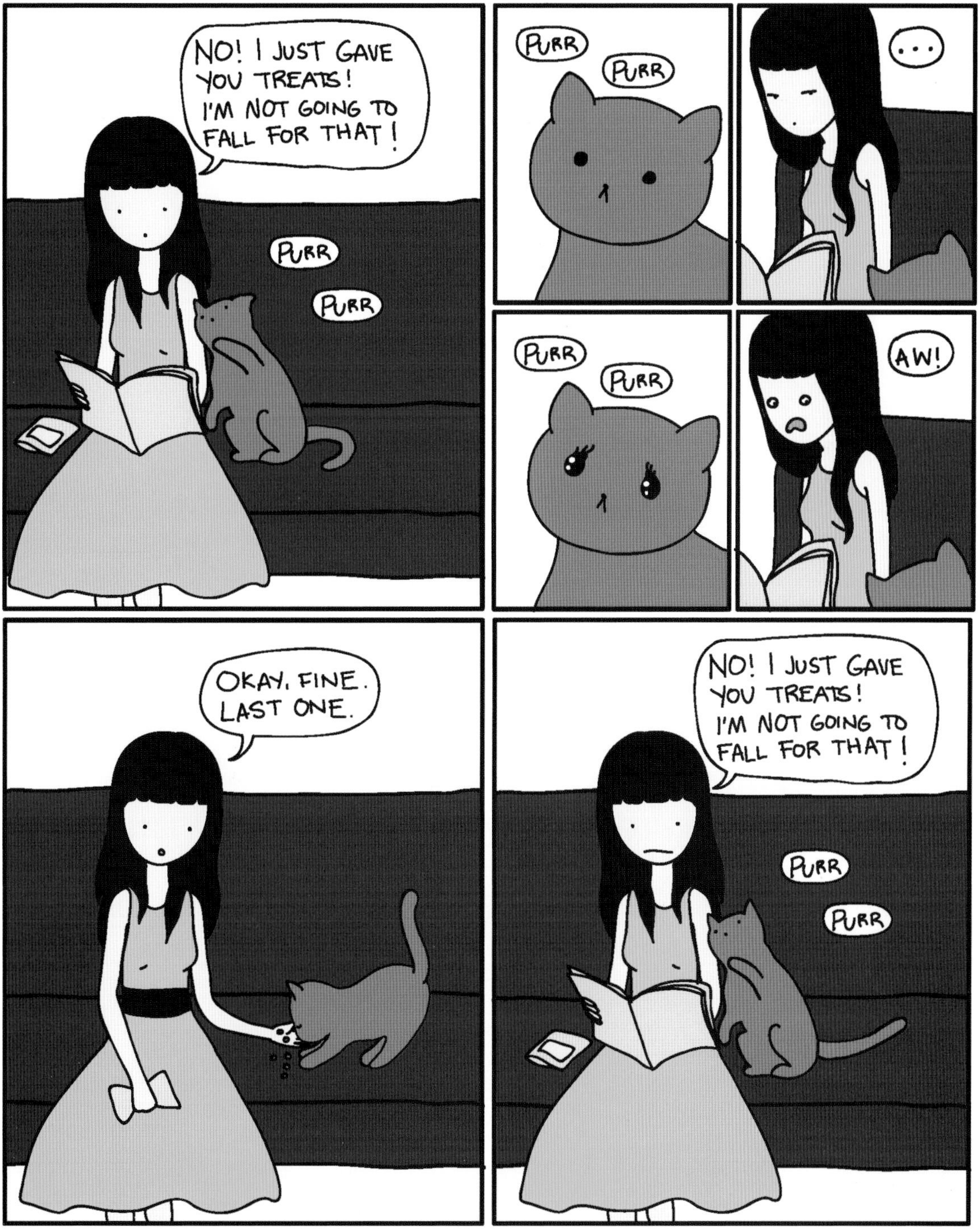
NO! I JUST GAVE YOU TREATS! I'M NOT GOING TO FALL FOR THAT!
PURR
PURR
PURR
PURR
...
PURR
PURR
AW!
OKAY, FINE. LAST ONE.
NO! I JUST GAVE YOU TREATS! I'M NOT GOING TO FALL FOR THAT!
PURR
PURR

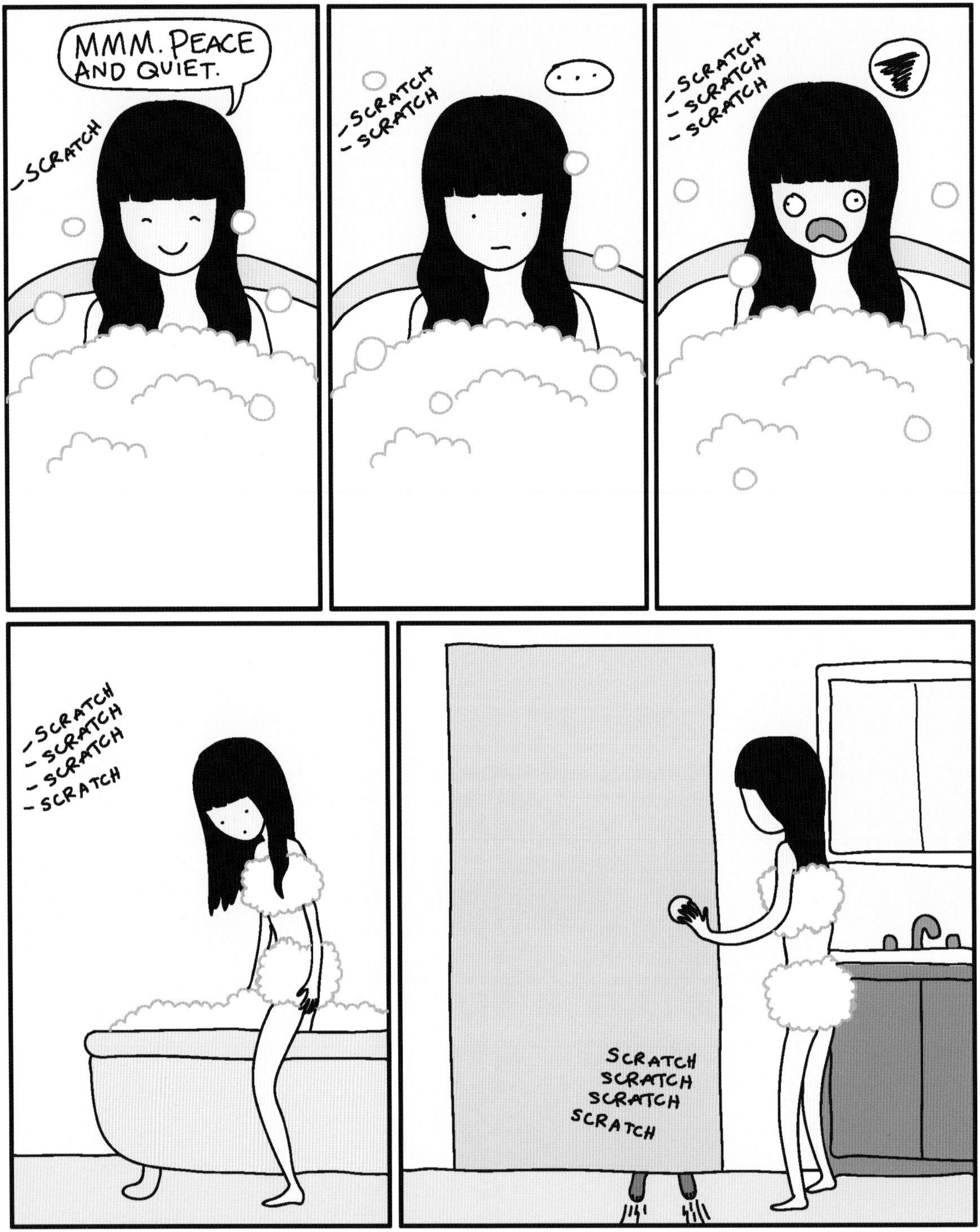
MMM. PEACE AND QUIET.
-SCRATCH
-SCRATCH
-SCRATCH
. . .
-SCRATCH
-SCRATCH
-SCRATCH
-SCRATCH
-SCRATCH
-SCRATCH
-SCRATCH
SCRATCH
SCRATCH
SCRATCH
SCRATCH

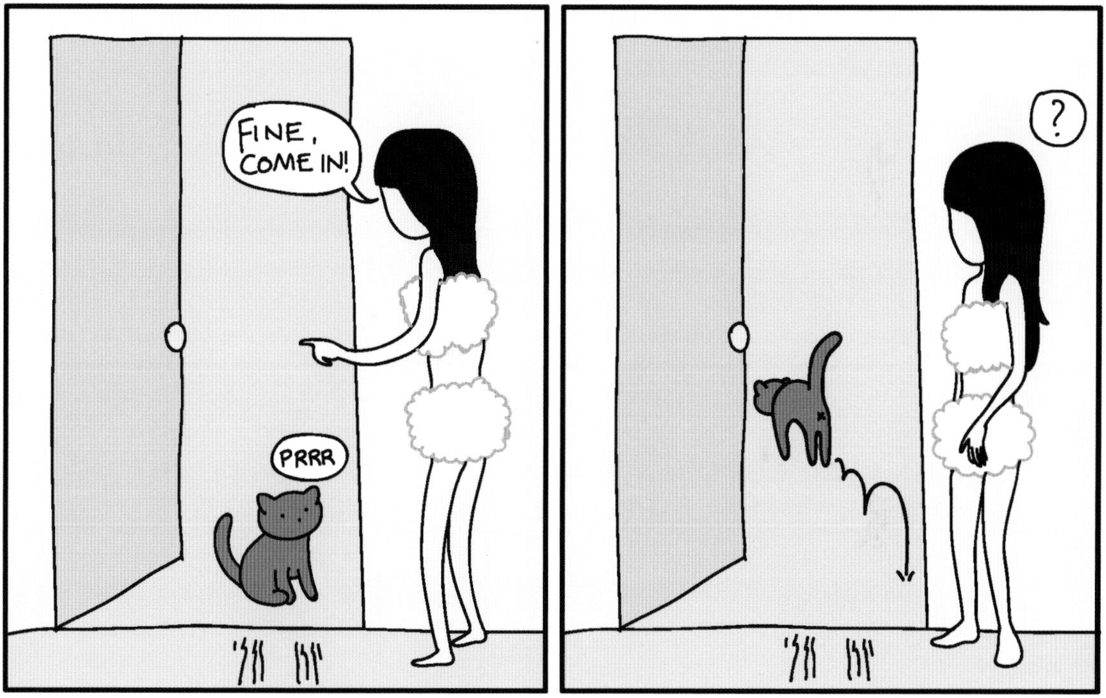
FINE, COME IN!
PRRR
?

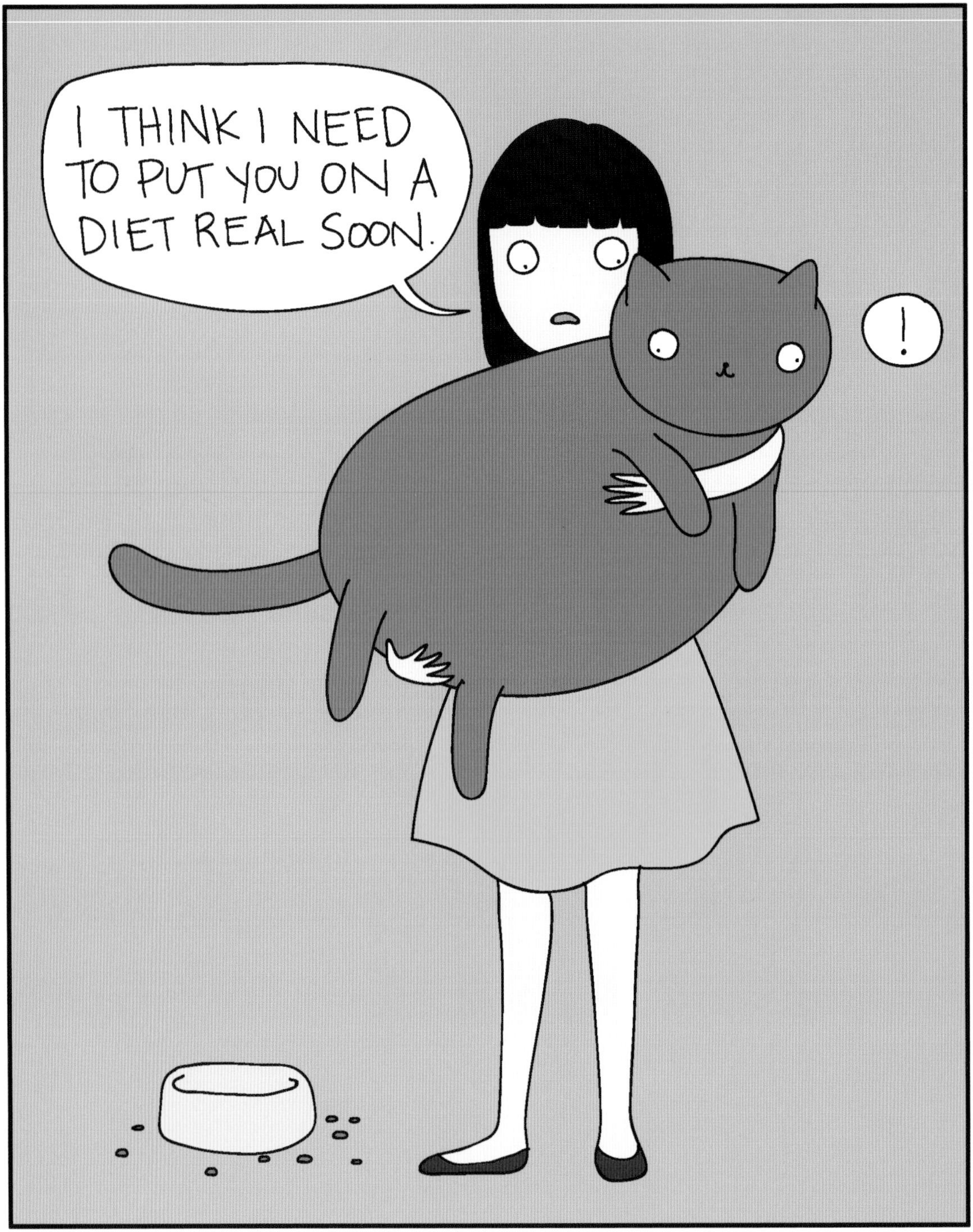
I THINK I NEED TO PUT YOU ON A DIET REAL SOON.
!

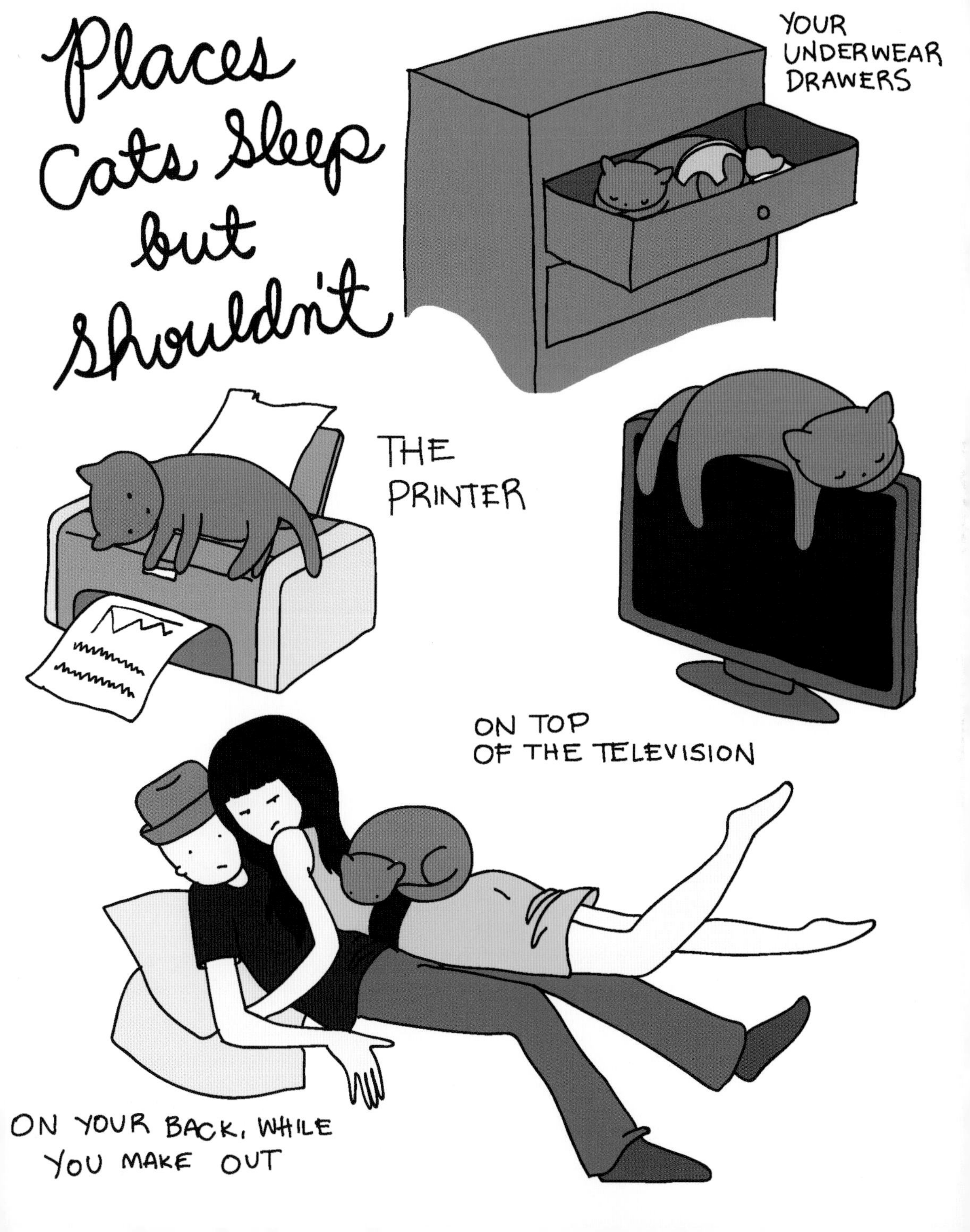
Places Cats Sleep but Shouldn't
YOUR UNDERWEAR DRAWERS
THE PRINTER
ON TOP OF THE TELEVISION
ON YOUR BACK, WHILE YOU MAKE OUT

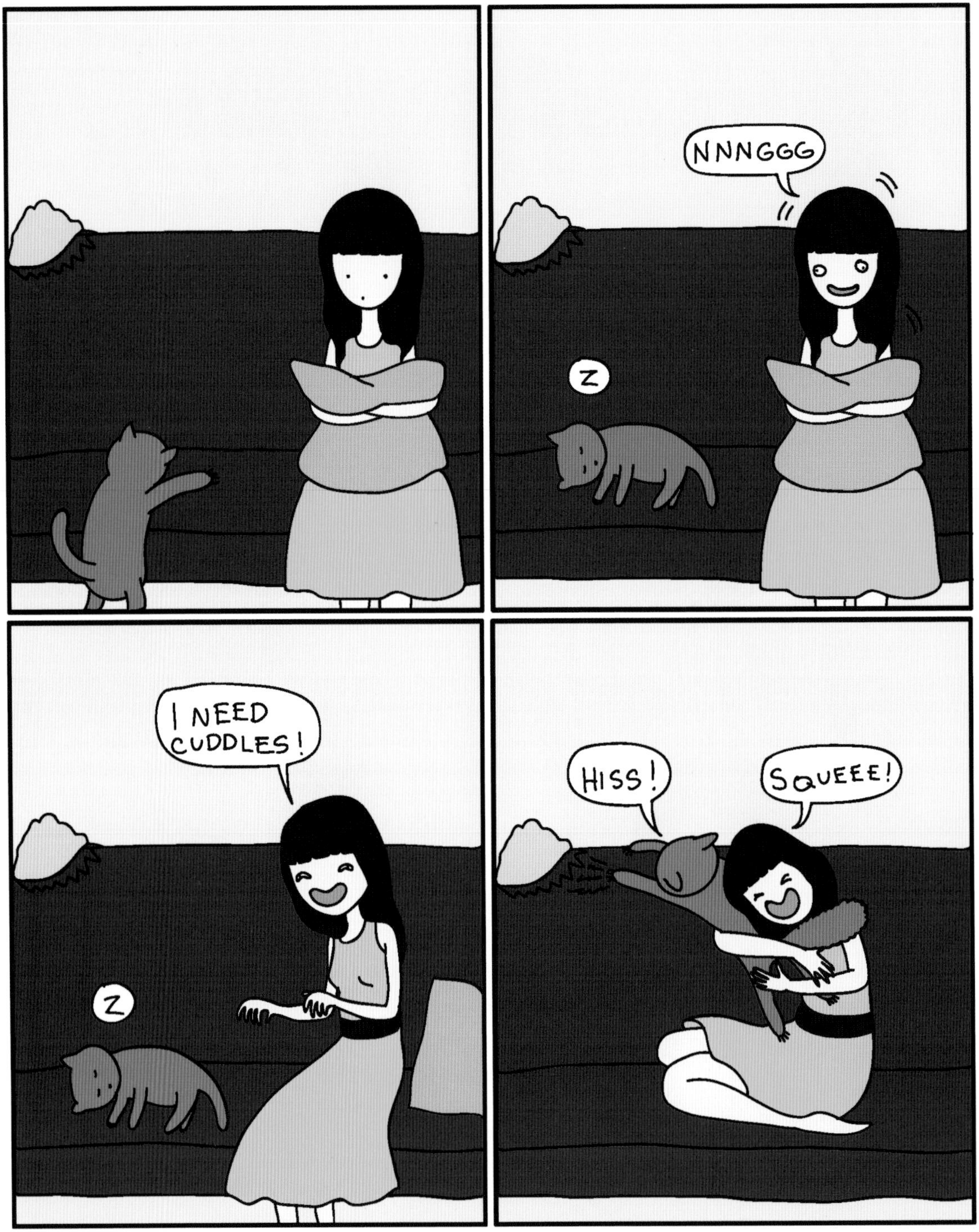
NNNGGG
Z
I NEED CUDDLES!
Z
HISS!
SQUEEE!

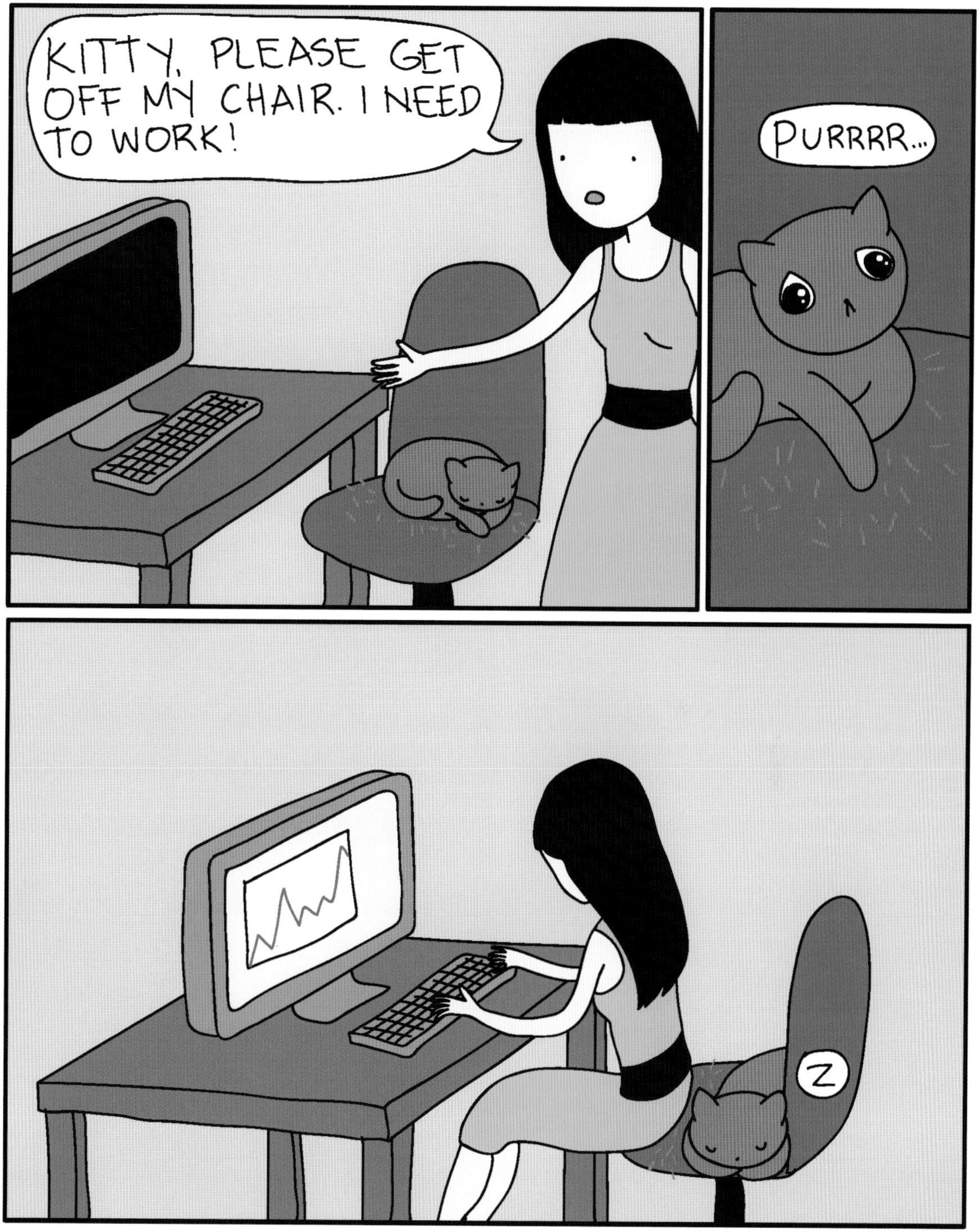
KITTY, PLEASE GET OFF MY CHAIR. I NEED TO WORK!
PURRRR...
Z

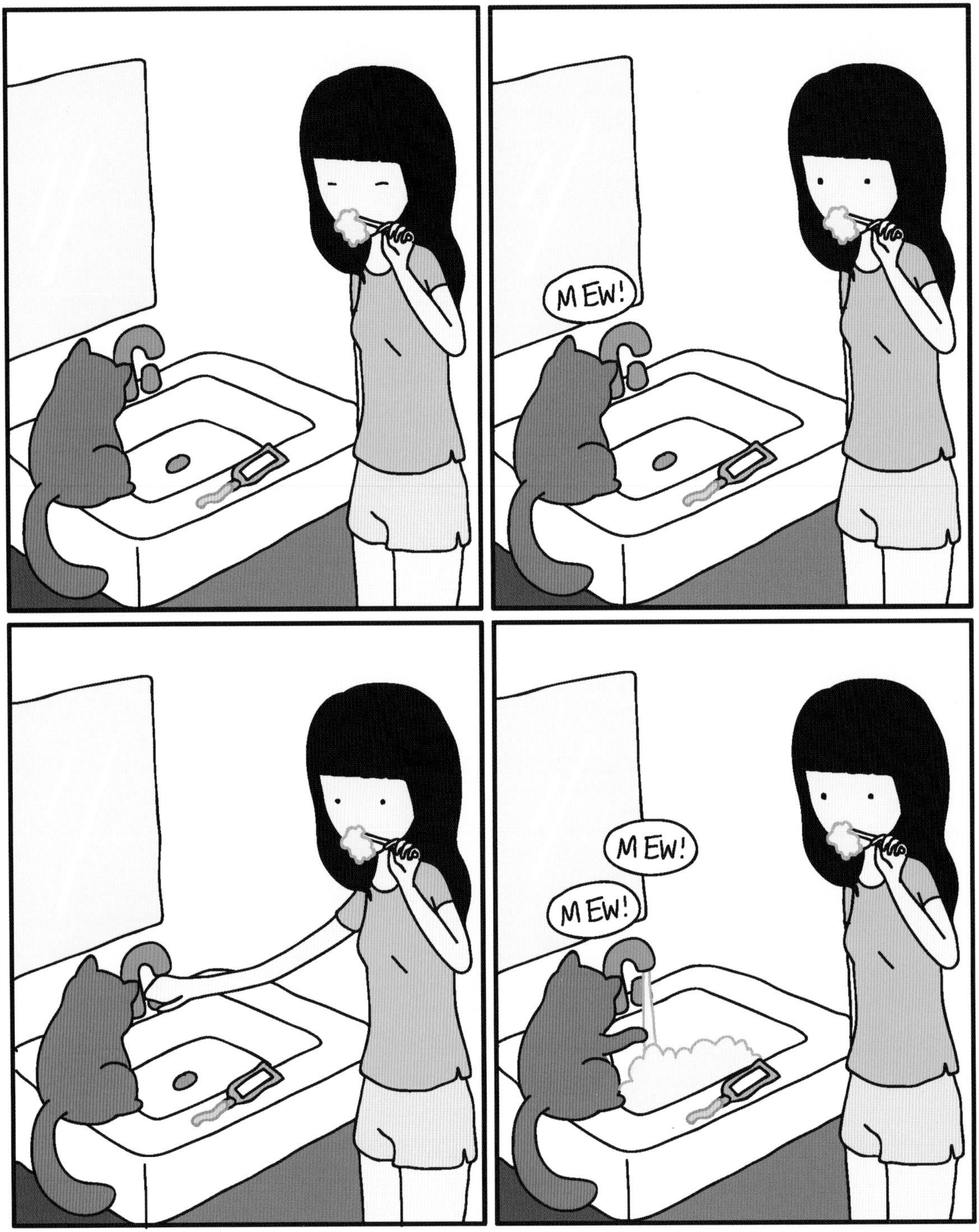
MEW!
MEW!
MEW!

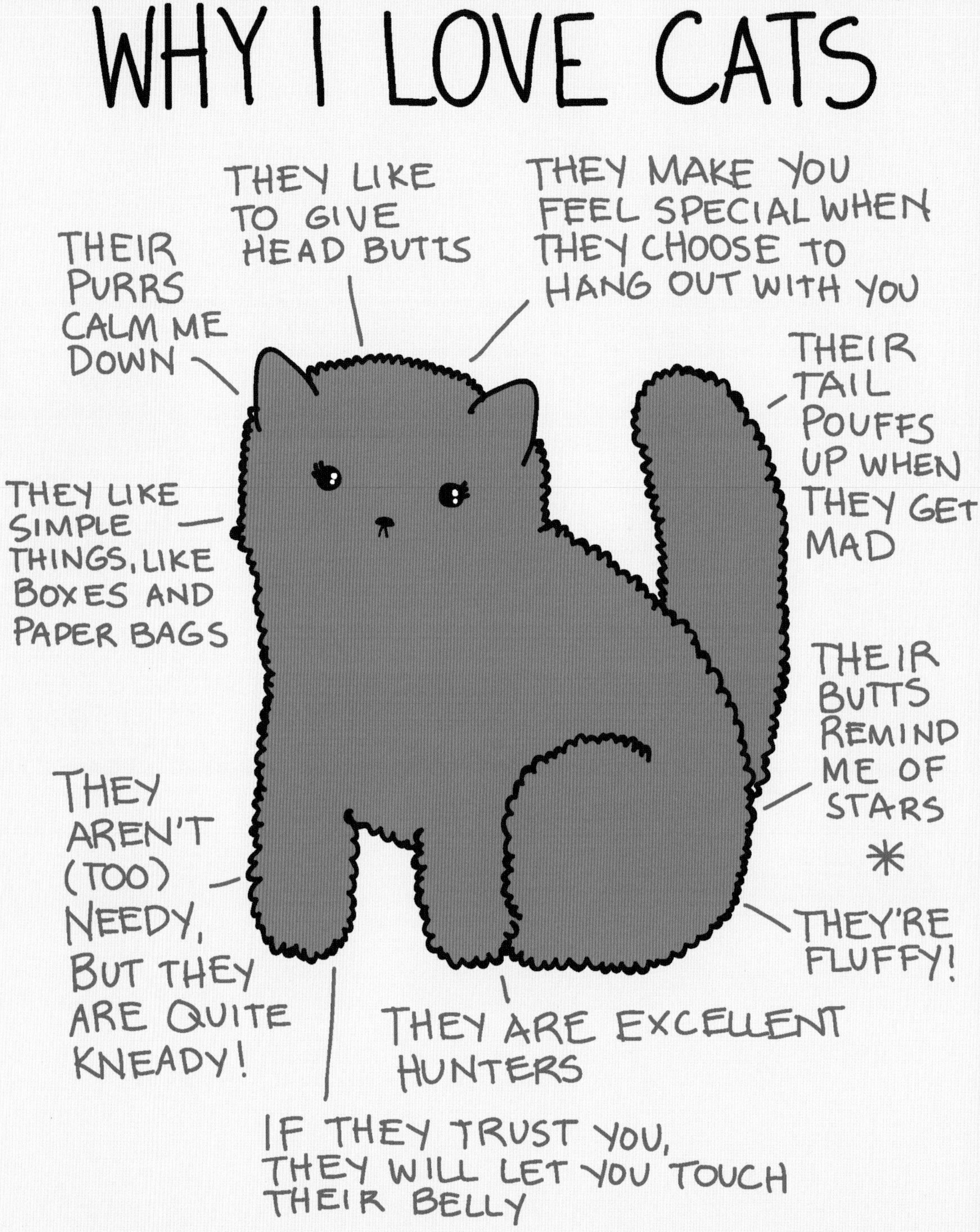
WHY I LOVE CATS
THEIR PURRS CALM ME DOWN
THEY LIKE TO GIVE HEAD BUTTS
THEY MAKE YOU FEEL SPECIAL WHEN THEY CHOOSE TO HANG OUT WITH YOU
THEIR TAIL POUFFS UP WHEN THEY GET MAD
THEY LIKE SIMPLE THINGS, LIKE BOXES AND PAPER BAGS
THEIR BUTTS REMIND ME OF STARS
*
THEY AREN'T (TOO) NEEDY, BUT THEY ARE QUITE KNEADY!
THEY'RE FLUFFY!
THEY ARE EXCELLENT HUNTERS
IF THEY TRUST YOU, THEY WILL LET YOU TOUCH THEIR BELLY

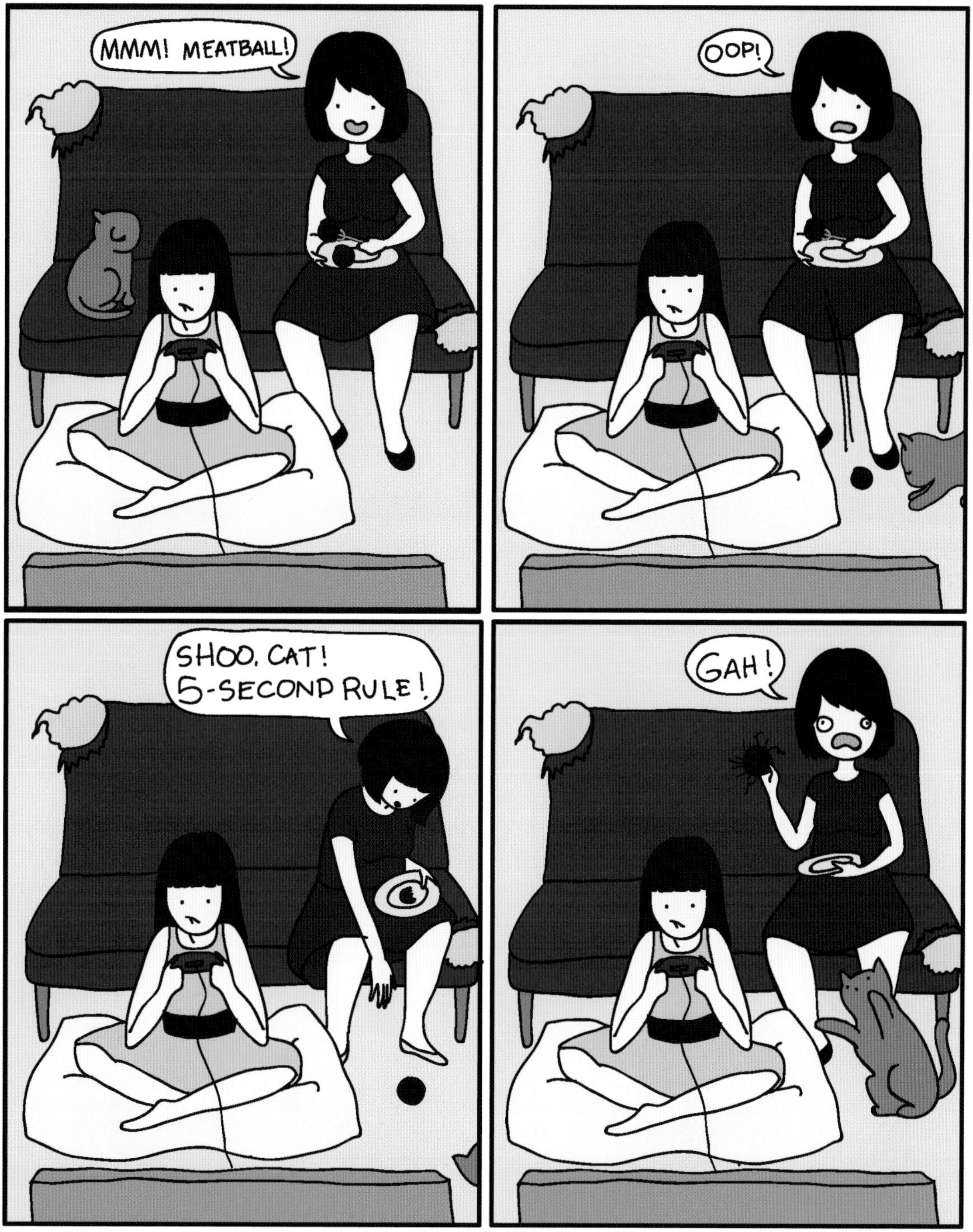
MMM! MEATBALL!
OOP!
SHOO, CAT! 5-SECOND RULE!
GAH!

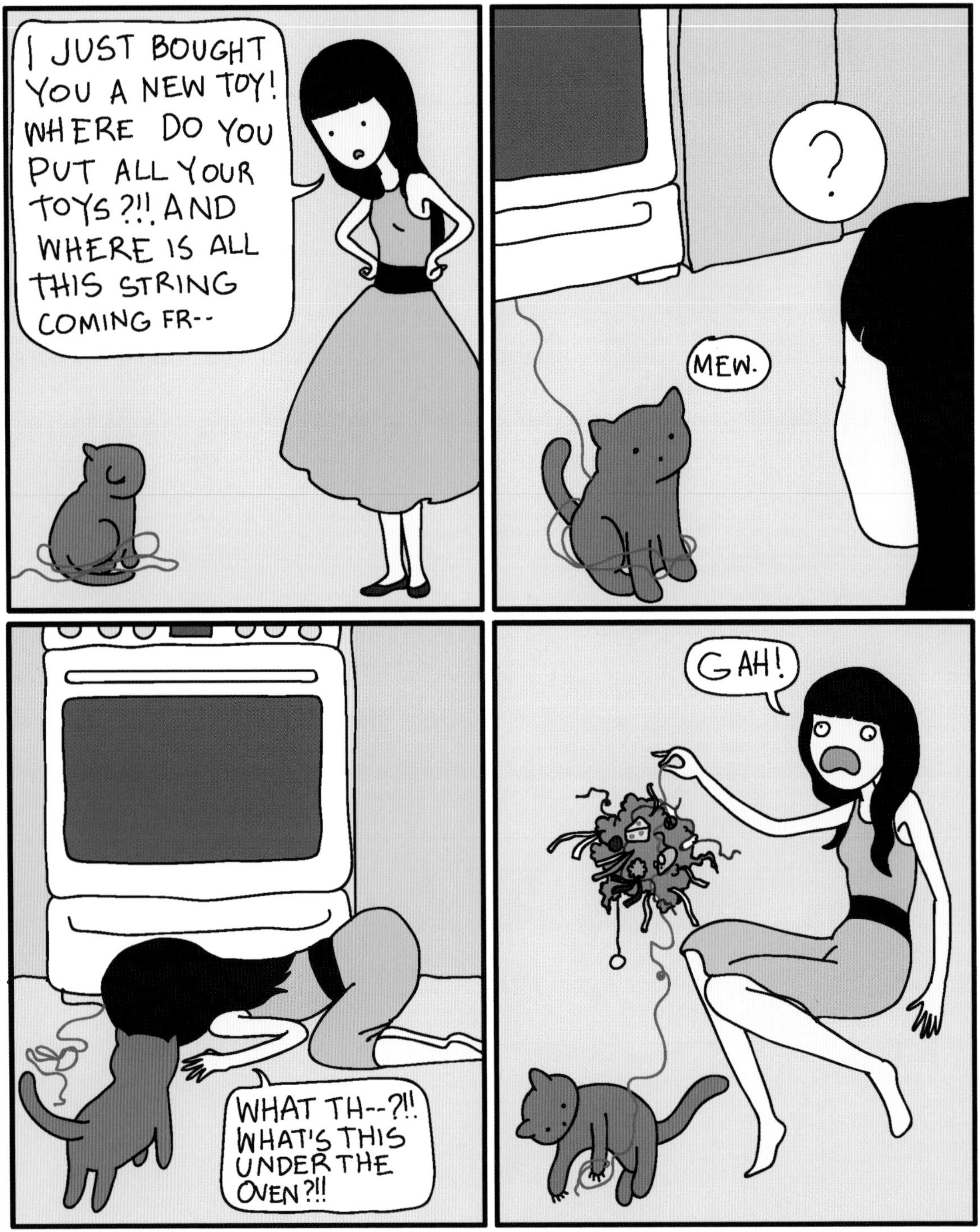
I JUST BOUGHT YOU A NEW TOY! WHERE DO YOU PUT ALL YOUR TOYS?!! AND WHERE IS ALL THIS STRING COMING FR--
?
MEW.
WHAT TH--?!! WHAT'S THIS UNDER THE OVEN?!!
GAH!

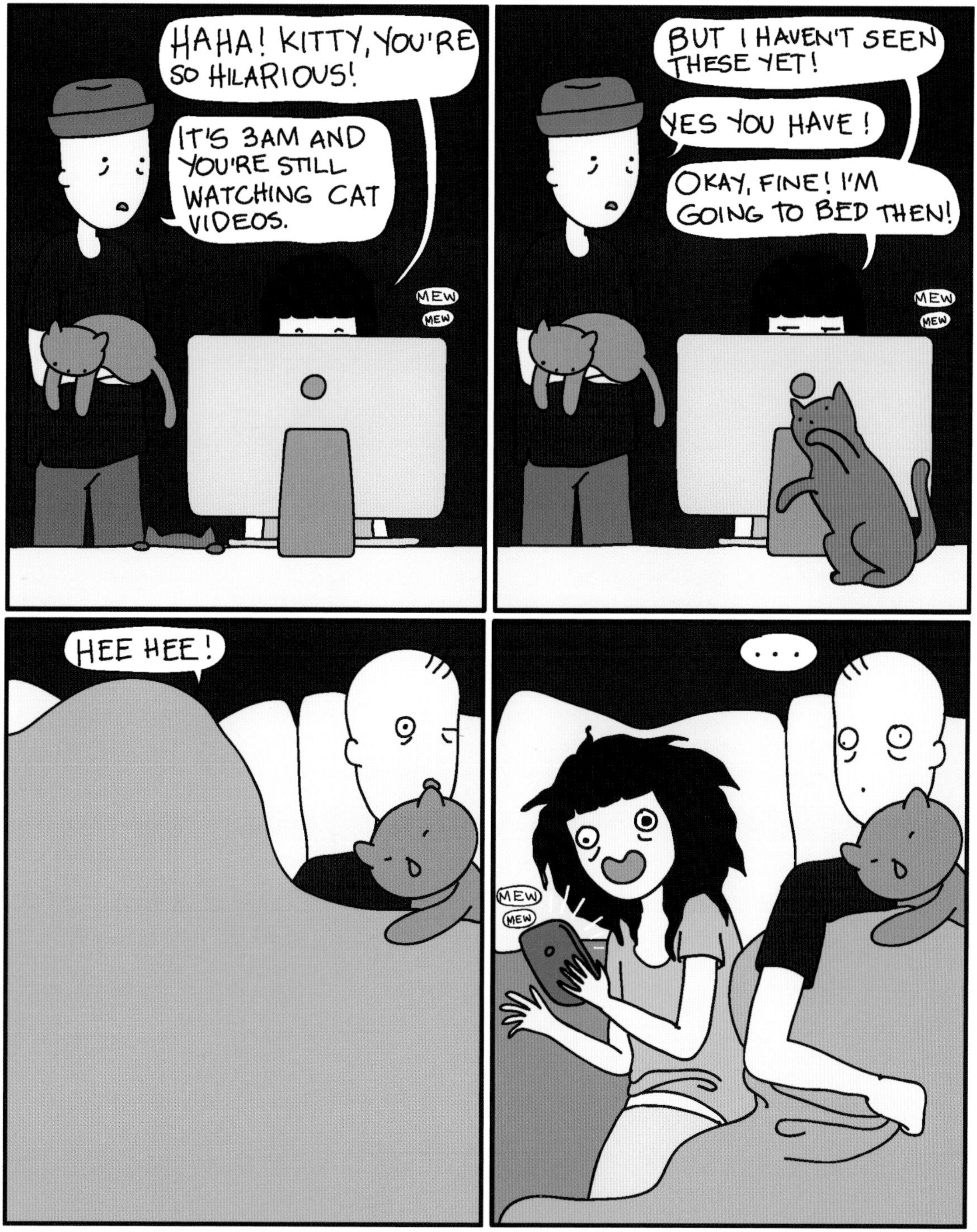
HAHA! KITTY, YOU'RE SO HILARIOUS!
IT'S 3AM AND YOU'RE STILL WATCHING CAT VIDEOS.
MEW
MEW
BUT I HAVEN'T SEEN THESE YET!
YES YOU HAVE!
OKAY, FINE! I'M GOING TO BED THEN!
MEW
MEW
HEE HEE!
...
MEW
MEW

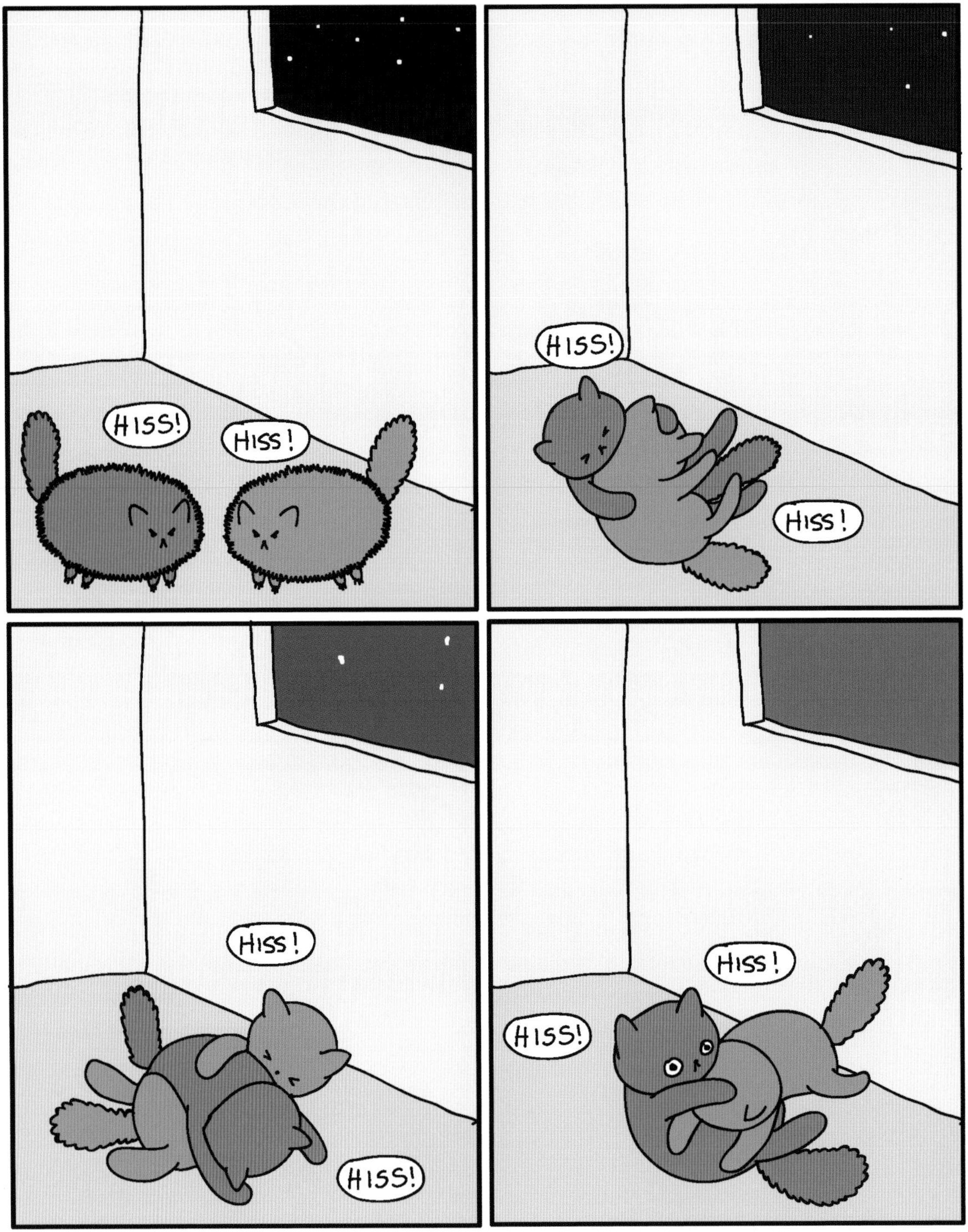
HISS!
HISS!
HISS!
HISS!
HISS!
HISS!
HISS!
HISS!

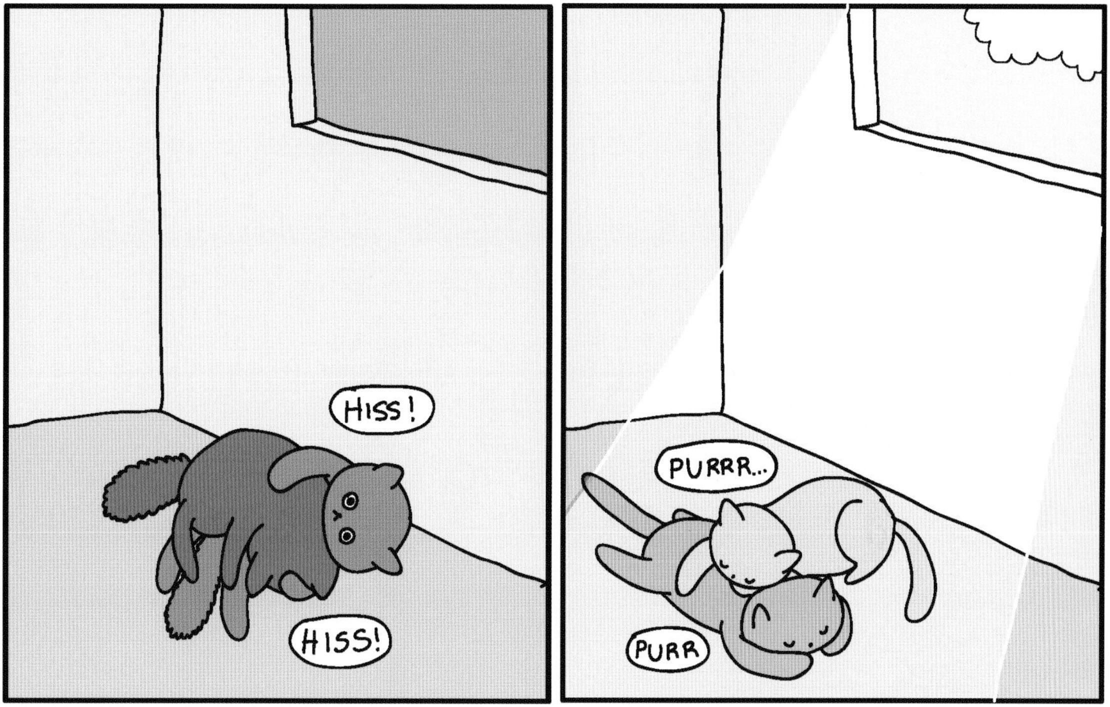
HISS!
HISS!
PURRR...
PURR

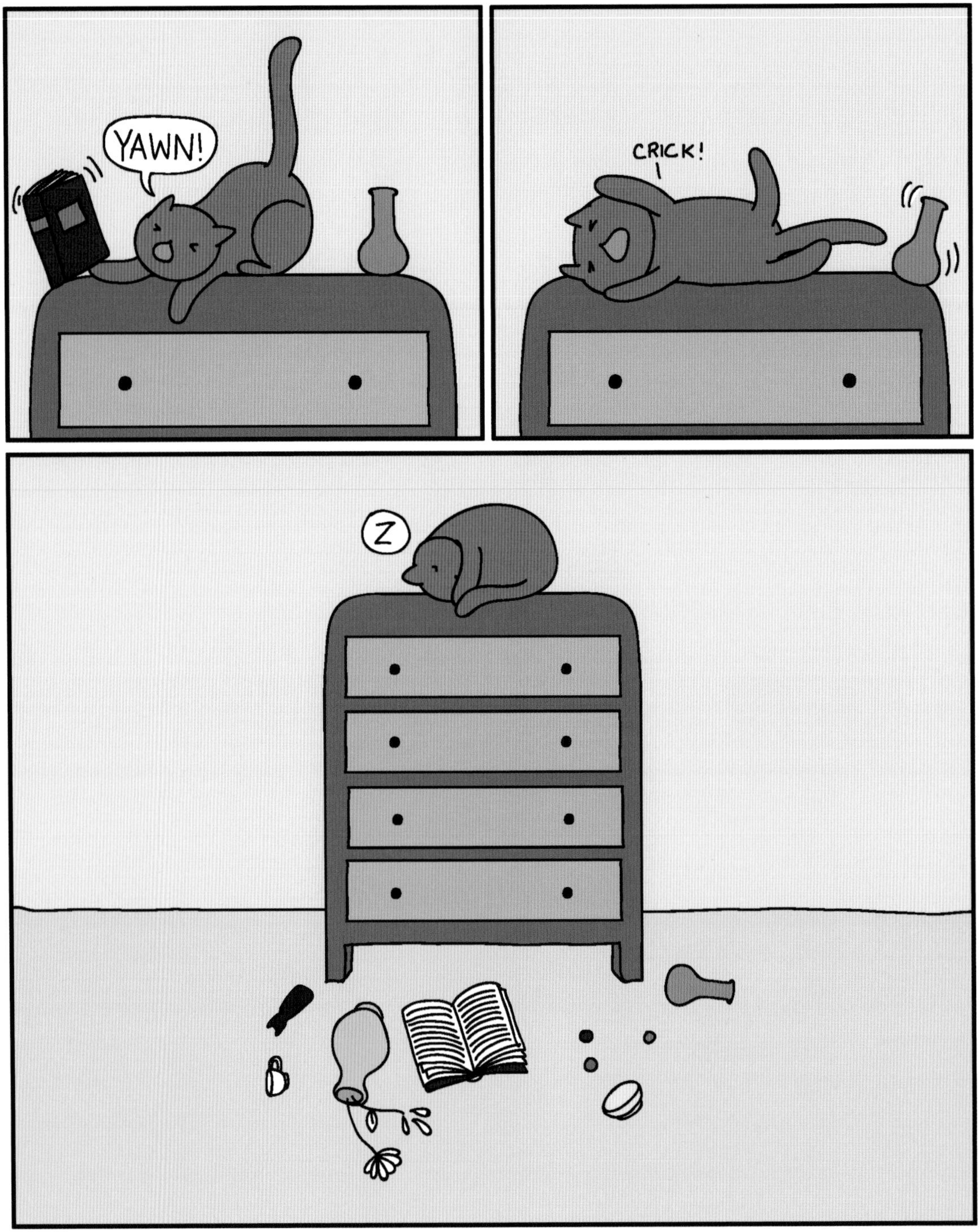
YAWN!
CRICK!
Z

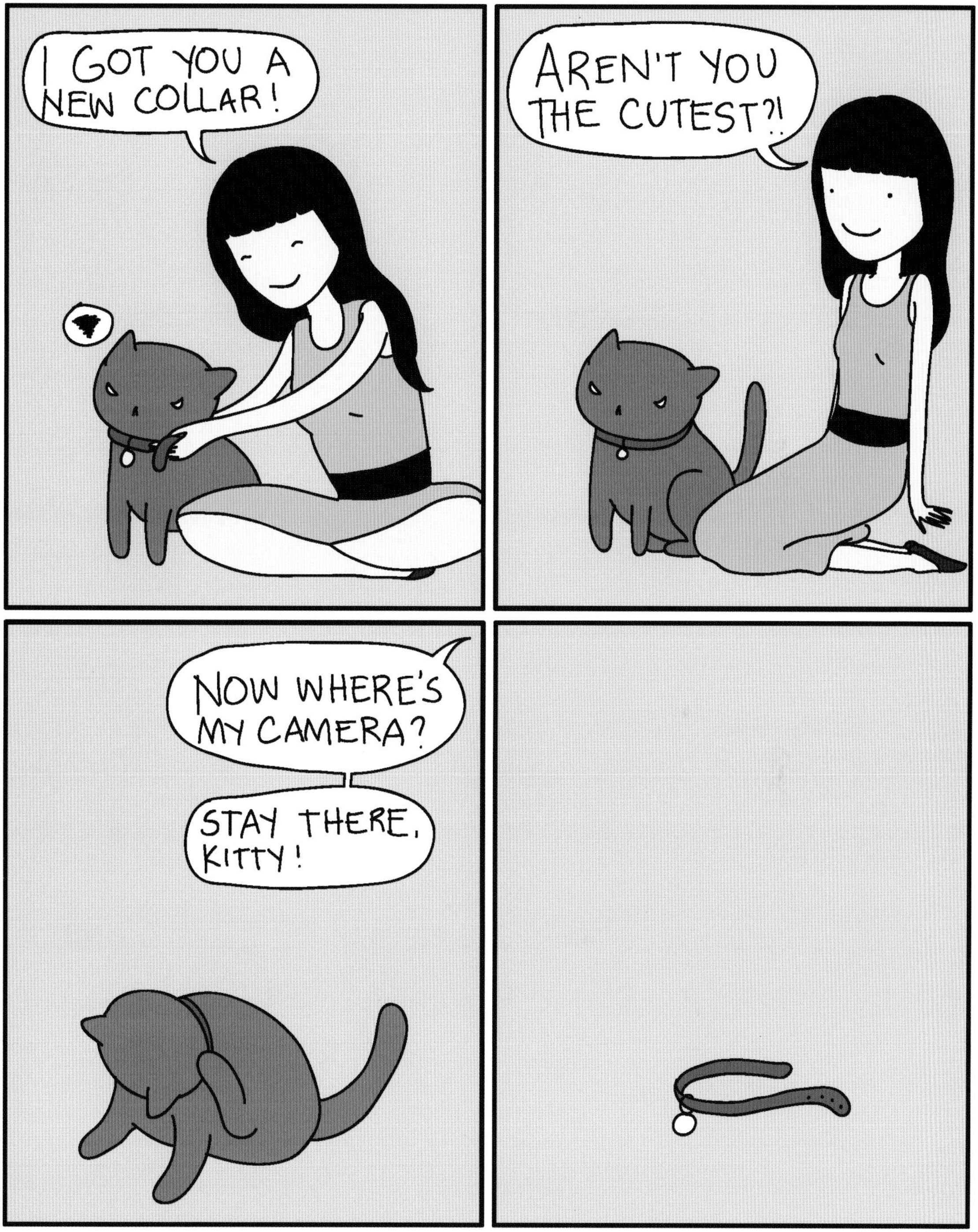
I GOT YOU A NEW COLLAR!
AREN'T YOU THE CUTEST?!
NOW WHERE'S MY CAMERA?
STAY THERE, KITTY!

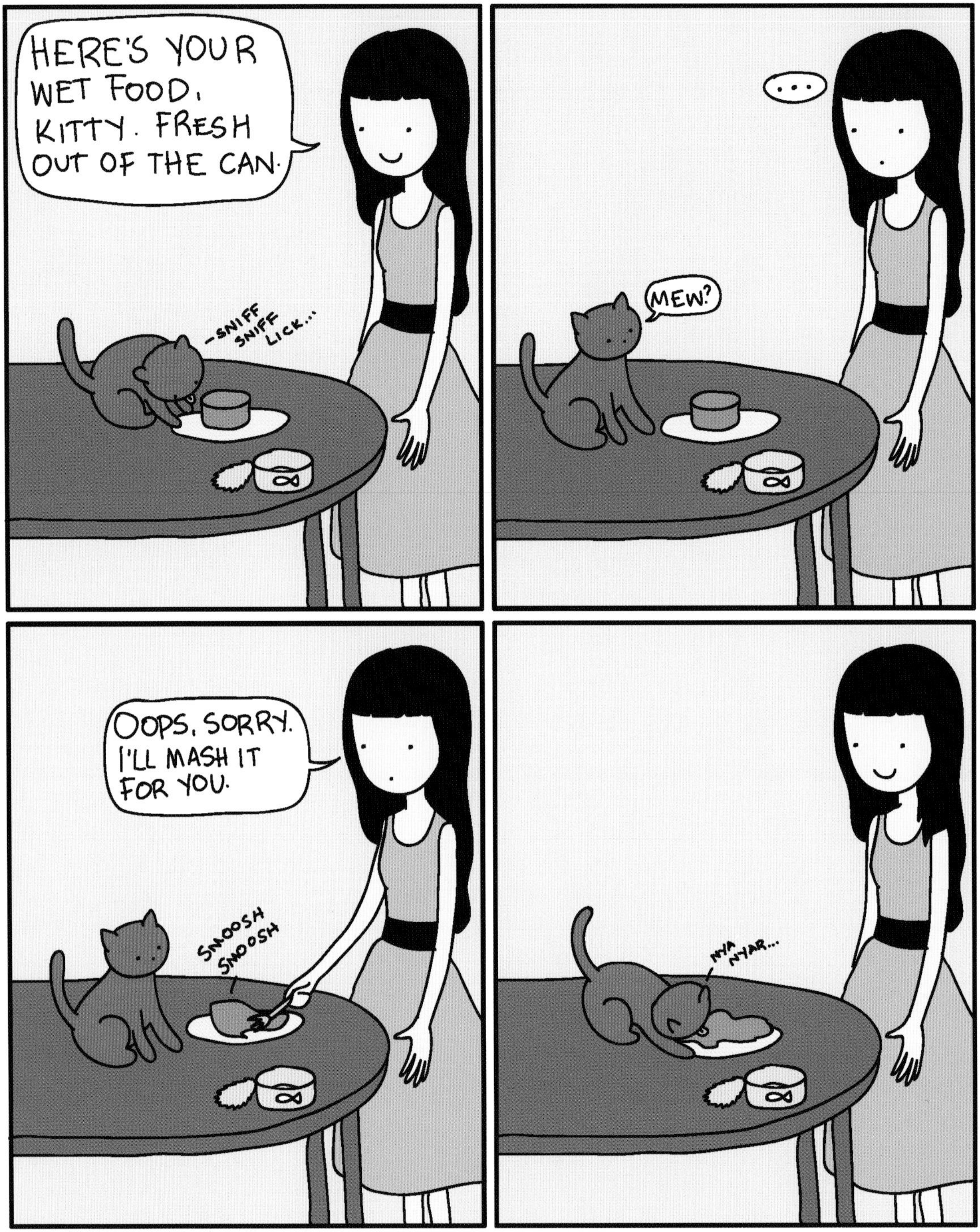
HERE'S YOUR WET FOOD, KITTY. FRESH OUT OF THE CAN.
-SNIFF SNIFF LICK...
...
MEW?
OOPS, SORRY. I'LL MASH IT FOR YOU.
SMOOSH SMOOSH
NYA NYAR...

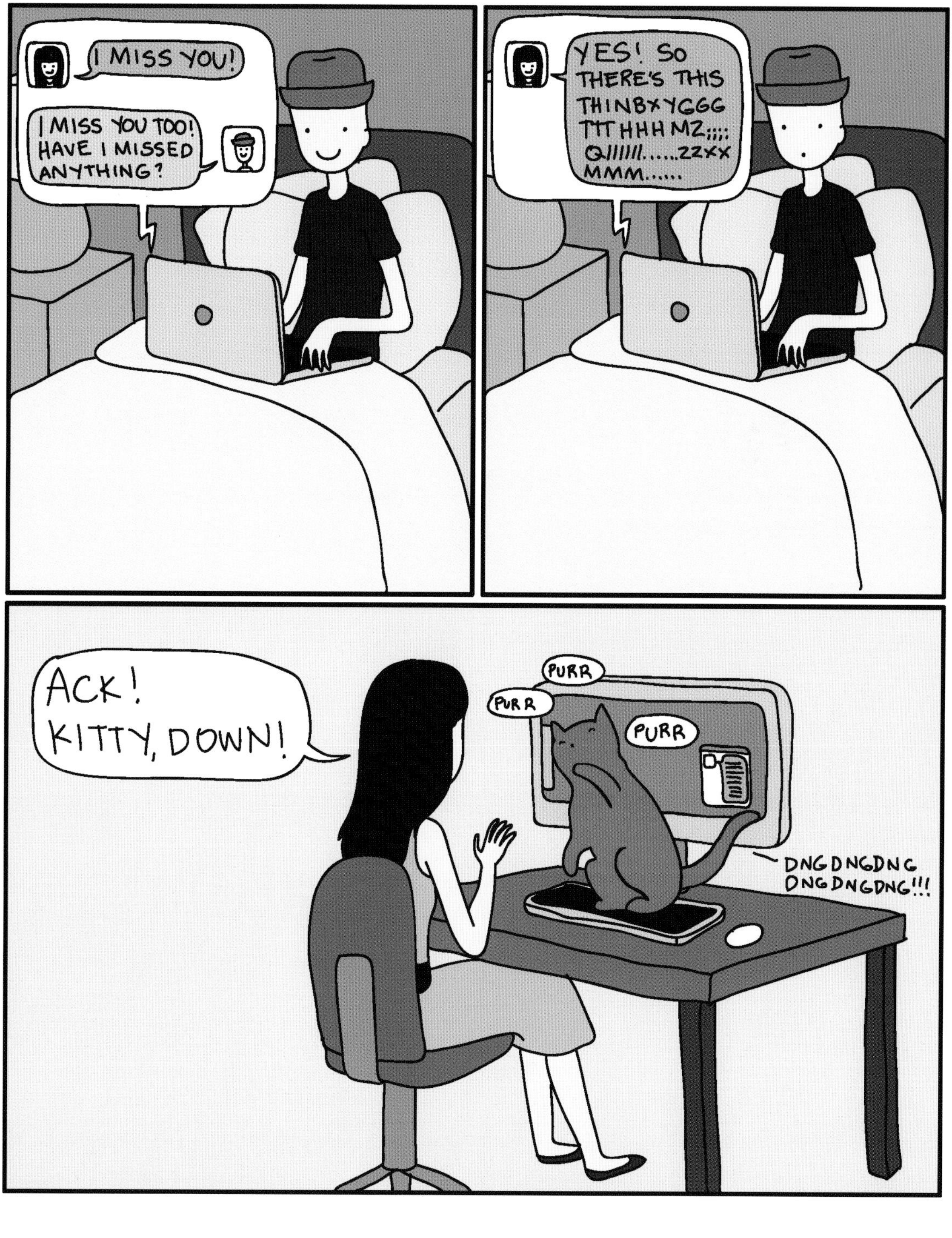
I MISS YOU!
I MISS YOU TOO! HAVE I MISSED ANYTHING?
YES! SO THERE'S THIS THINBXYGGG TTTHHHMZ;;;; Q//////......ZZXX MMM......
ACK! KITTY, DOWN!
PURR
PURR
PURR
DNGDNGDNG DNGDNGDNG!!!

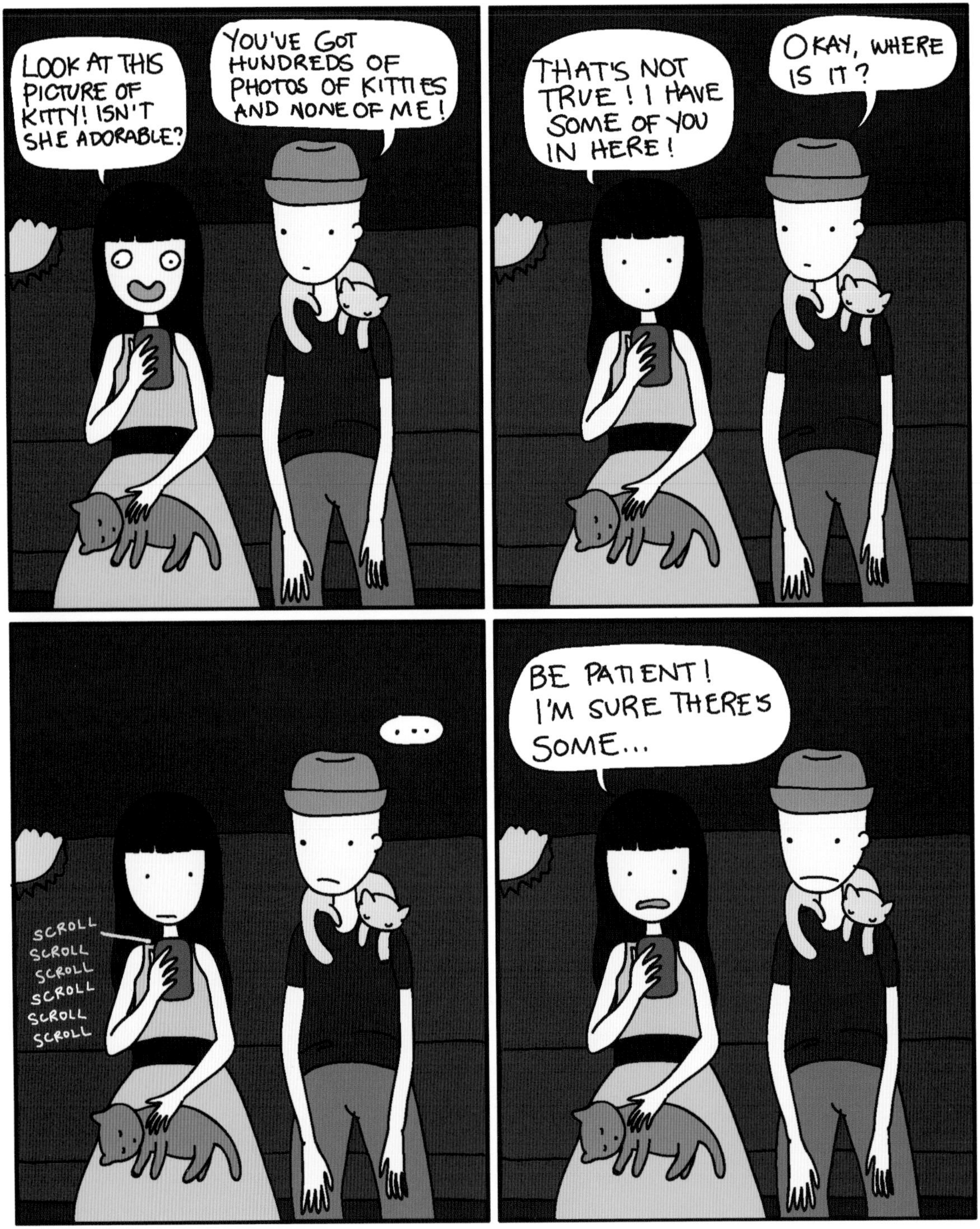
LOOK AT THIS PICTURE OF KITTY! ISN'T SHE ADORABLE?
YOU'VE GOT HUNDREDS OF PHOTOS OF KITTIES AND NONE OF ME!
THAT'S NOT TRUE! I HAVE SOME OF YOU IN HERE!
OKAY, WHERE IS IT?
SCROLL SCROLL SCROLL SCROLL SCROLL SCROLL
...
BE PATIENT! I'M SURE THERE'S SOME...

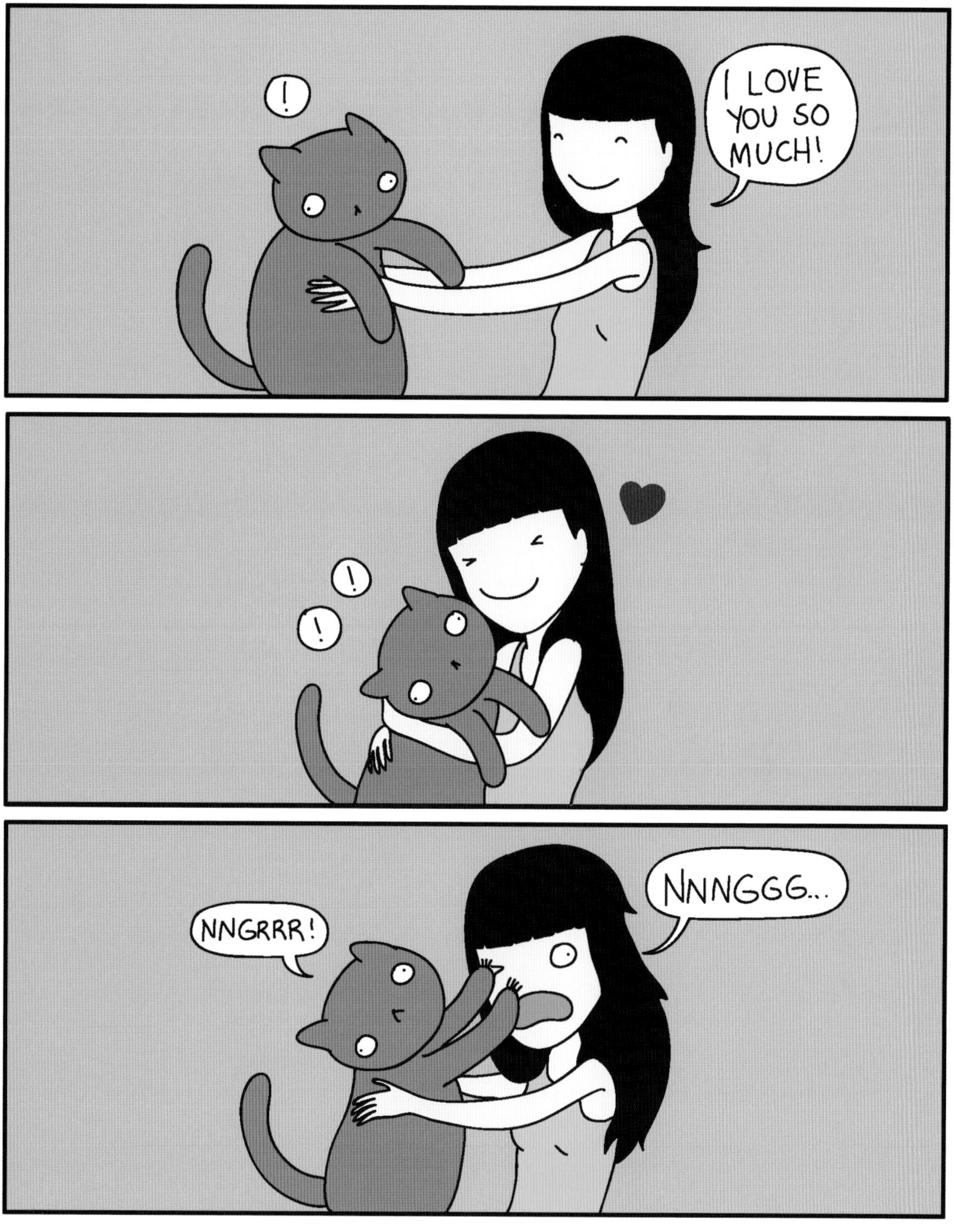
!
I LOVE YOU SO MUCH!
!
!
NNGRRR!
NNNGGG...

THINGS MY CATS DO WHEN I AM AWAY

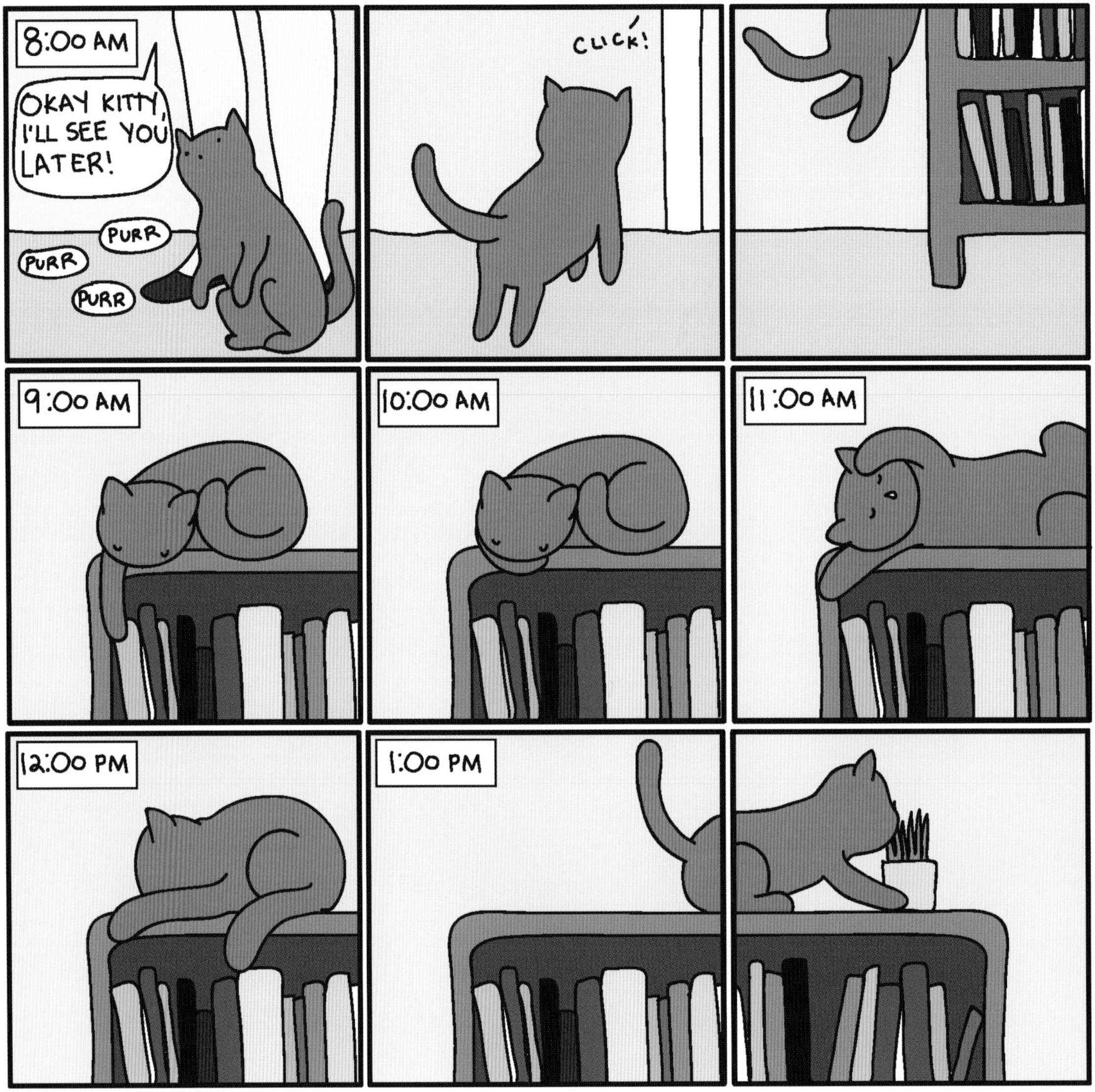

8:00 AM
OKAY KITTY, I'LL SEE YOU LATER!
PURR
PURR
PURR
CLICK!
9:00 AM
10:00 AM
11:00 AM
12:00 PM
1:00 PM

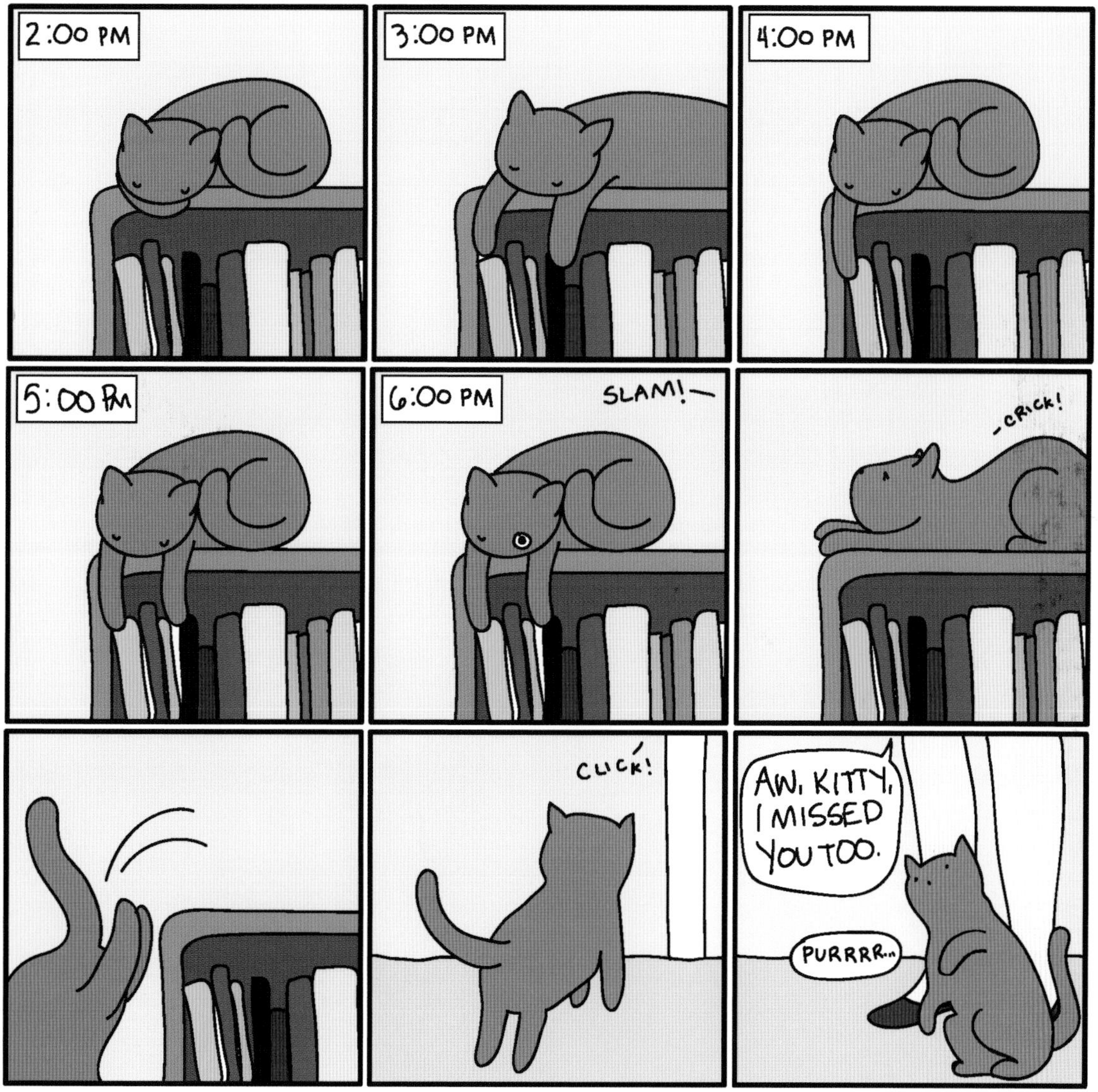
2:00 PM
3:00 PM
4:00 PM
5:00 PM
6:00 PM
SLAM!
CRICK!
CLICK!
AW, KITTY, I MISSED YOU TOO.
PURRRR...

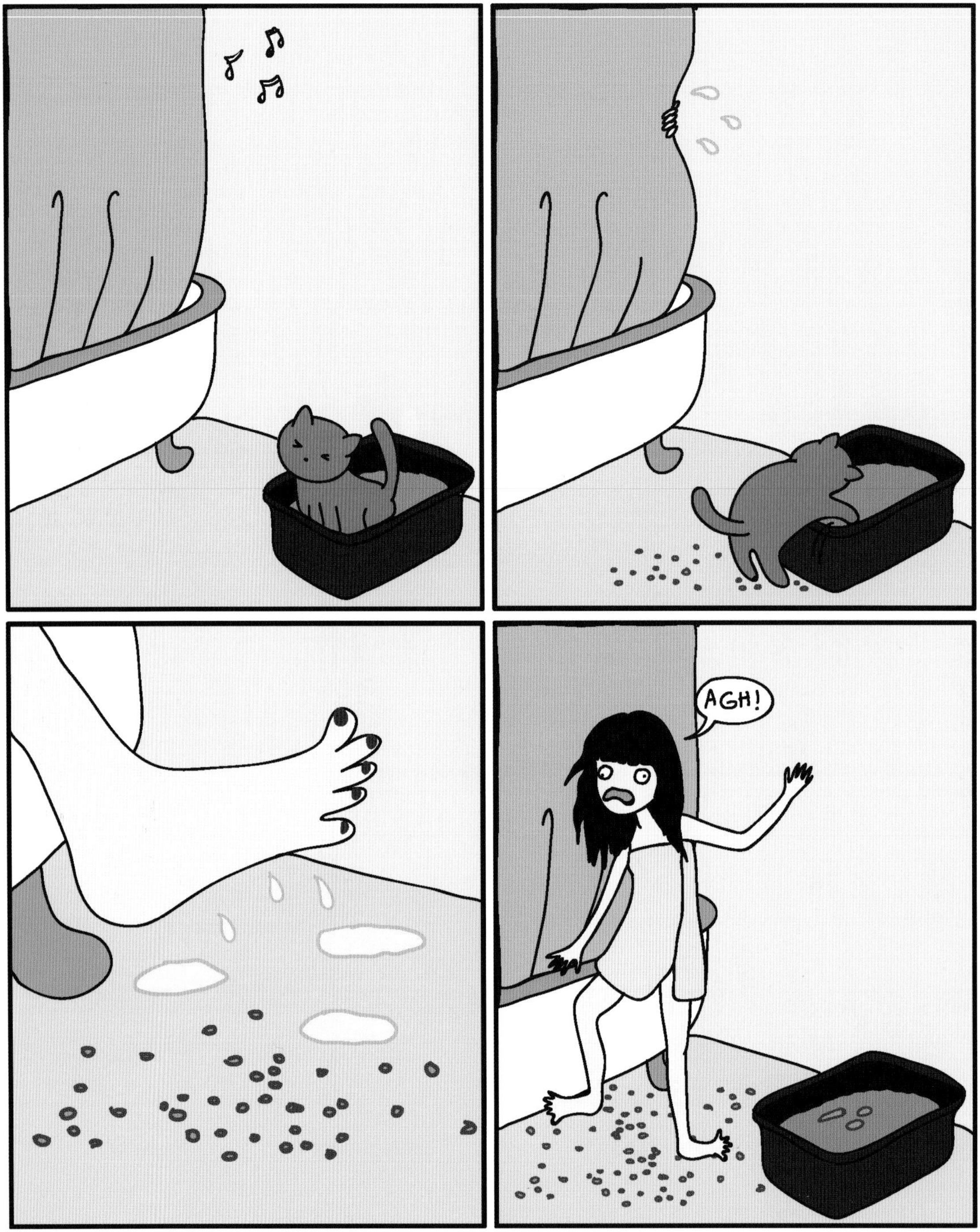
AGH!

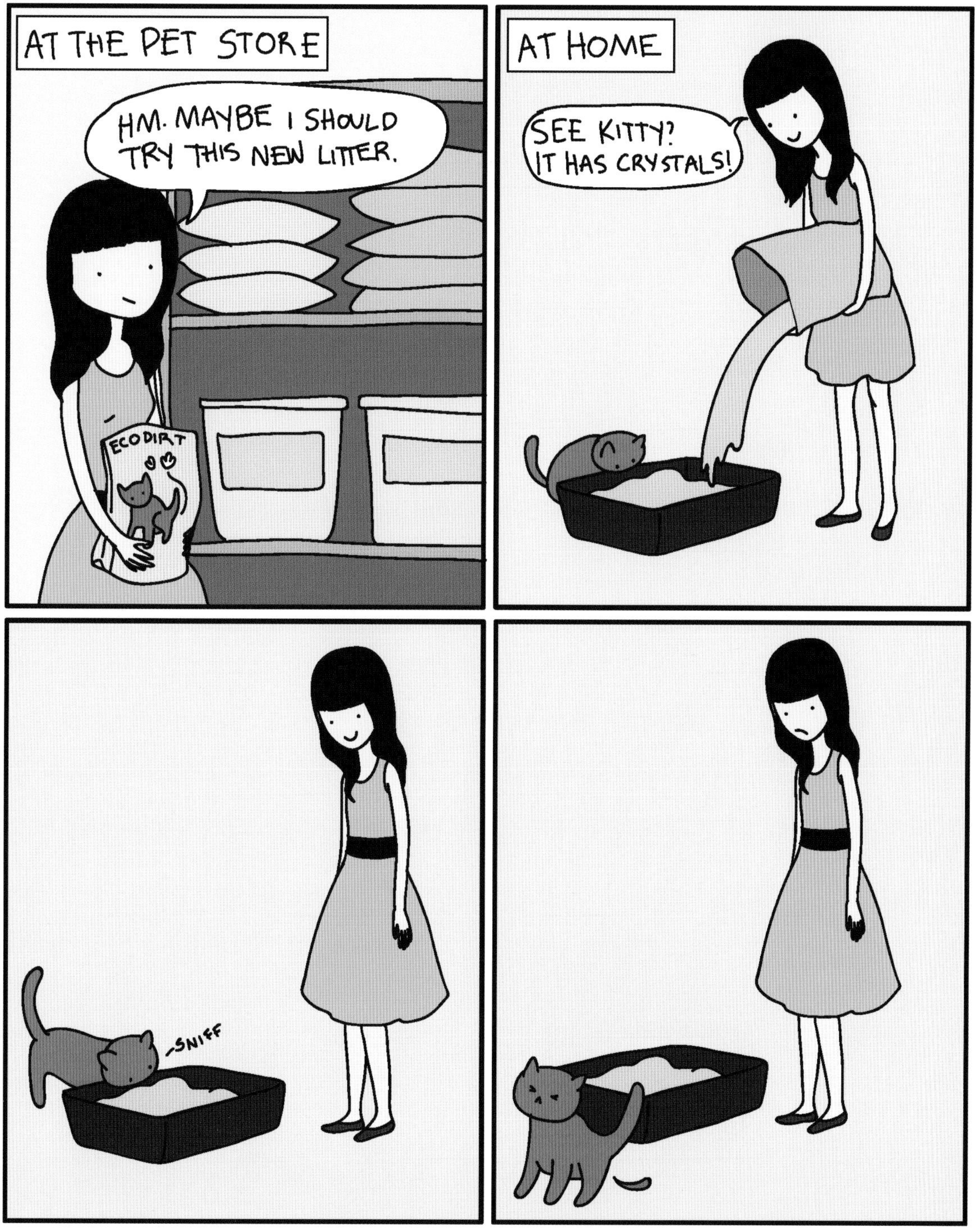
AT THE PET STORE
HM. MAYBE I SHOULD TRY THIS NEW LITTER.
ECODIRT
AT HOME
SEE KITTY? IT HAS CRYSTALS!
~SNIFF

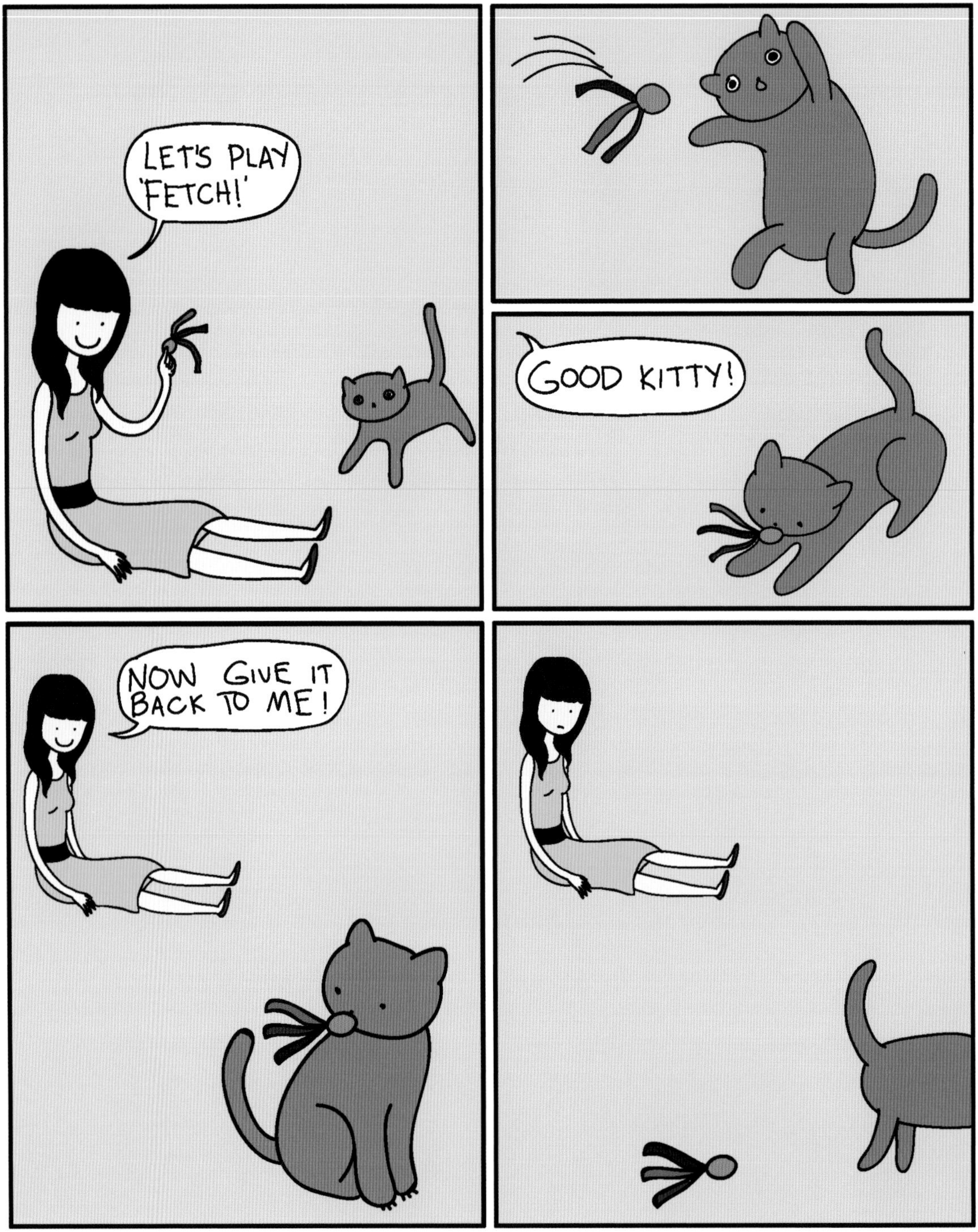
LET'S PLAY 'FETCH!'
GOOD KITTY!
NOW GIVE IT BACK TO ME!

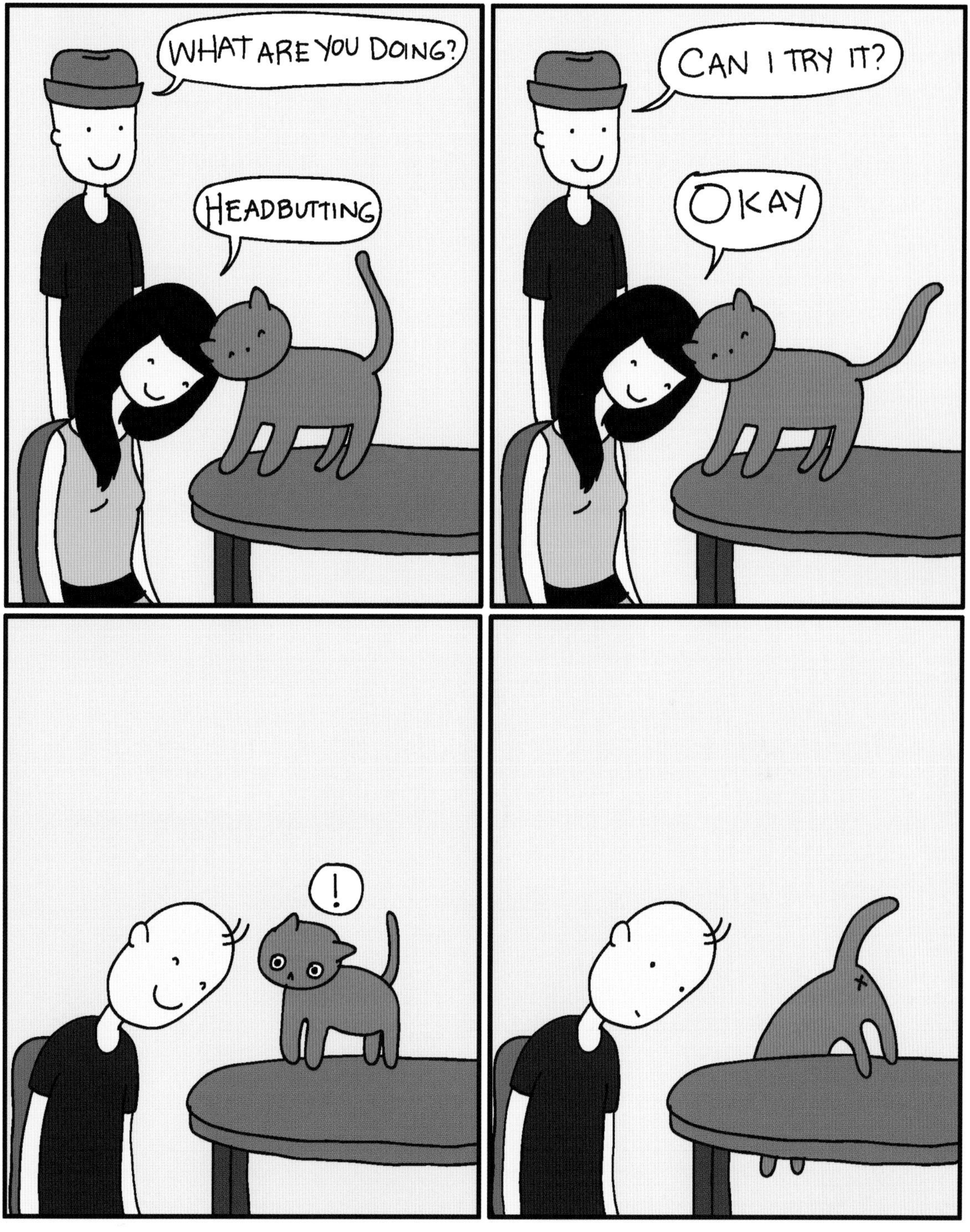
WHAT ARE YOU DOING?
HEADBUTTING
CAN I TRY IT?
OKAY
!

Cat Lady's Soul Mate

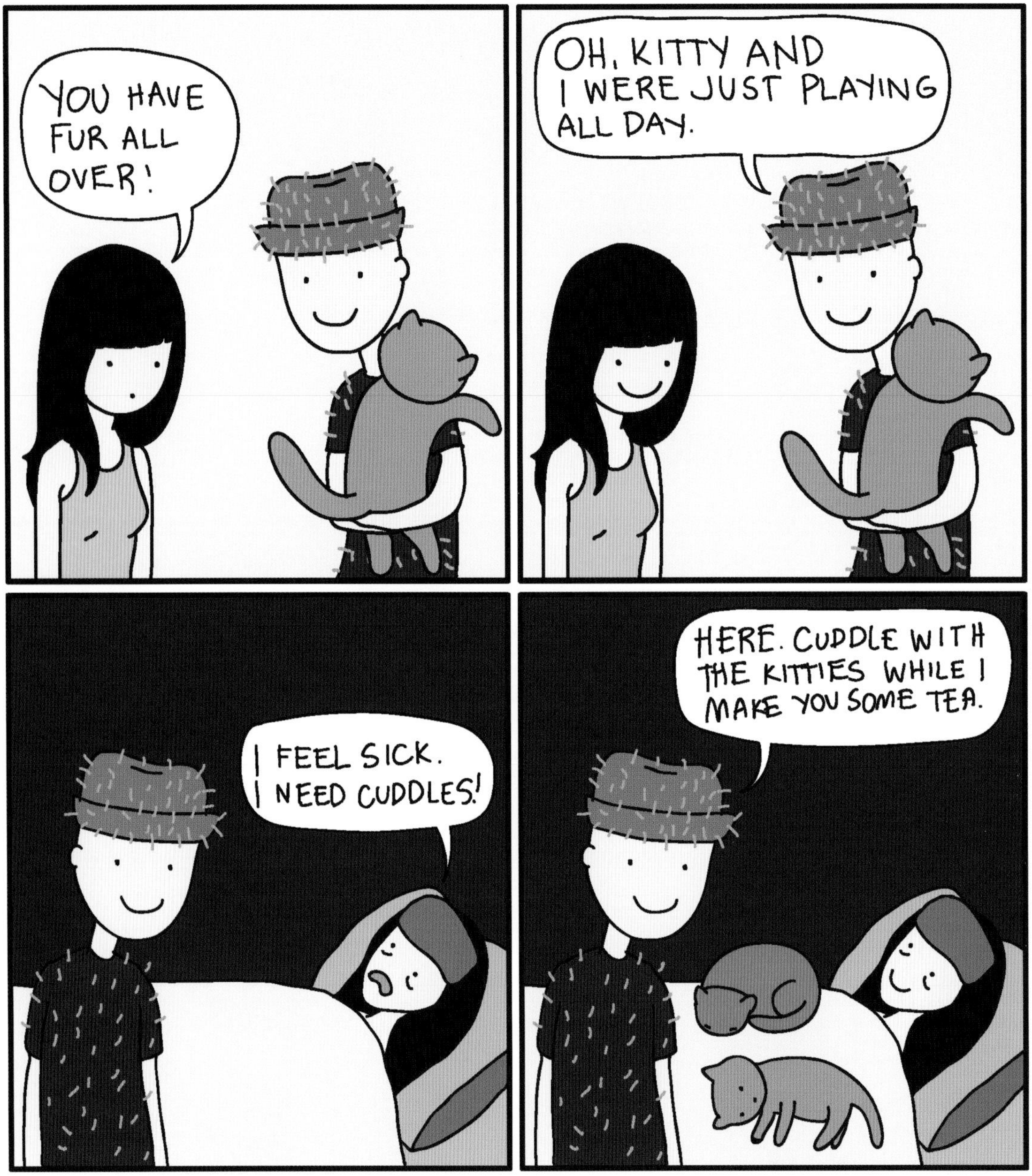
YOU HAVE FUR ALL OVER!
OH, KITTY AND I WERE JUST PLAYING ALL DAY.
I FEEL SICK. I NEED CUDDLES!
HERE. CUDDLE WITH THE KITTIES WHILE I MAKE YOU SOME TEA.

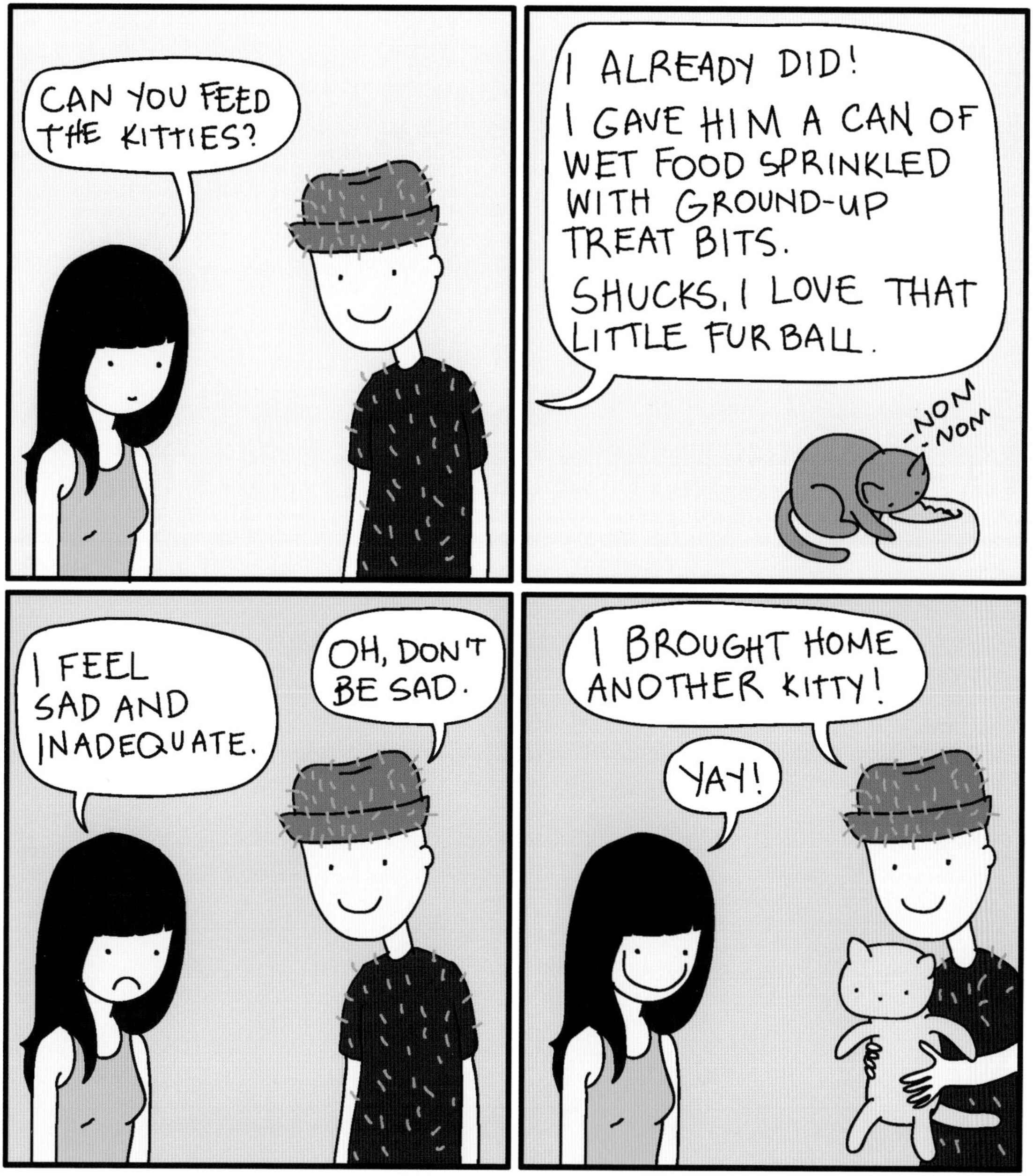
CAN YOU FEED THE KITTIES?
I ALREADY DID!
I GAVE HIM A CAN OF WET FOOD SPRINKLED WITH GROUND-UP TREAT BITS.
SHUCKS, I LOVE THAT LITTLE FUR BALL.
-NOM -NOM
I FEEL SAD AND INADEQUATE.
OH, DON'T BE SAD.
I BROUGHT HOME ANOTHER KITTY!
YAY!

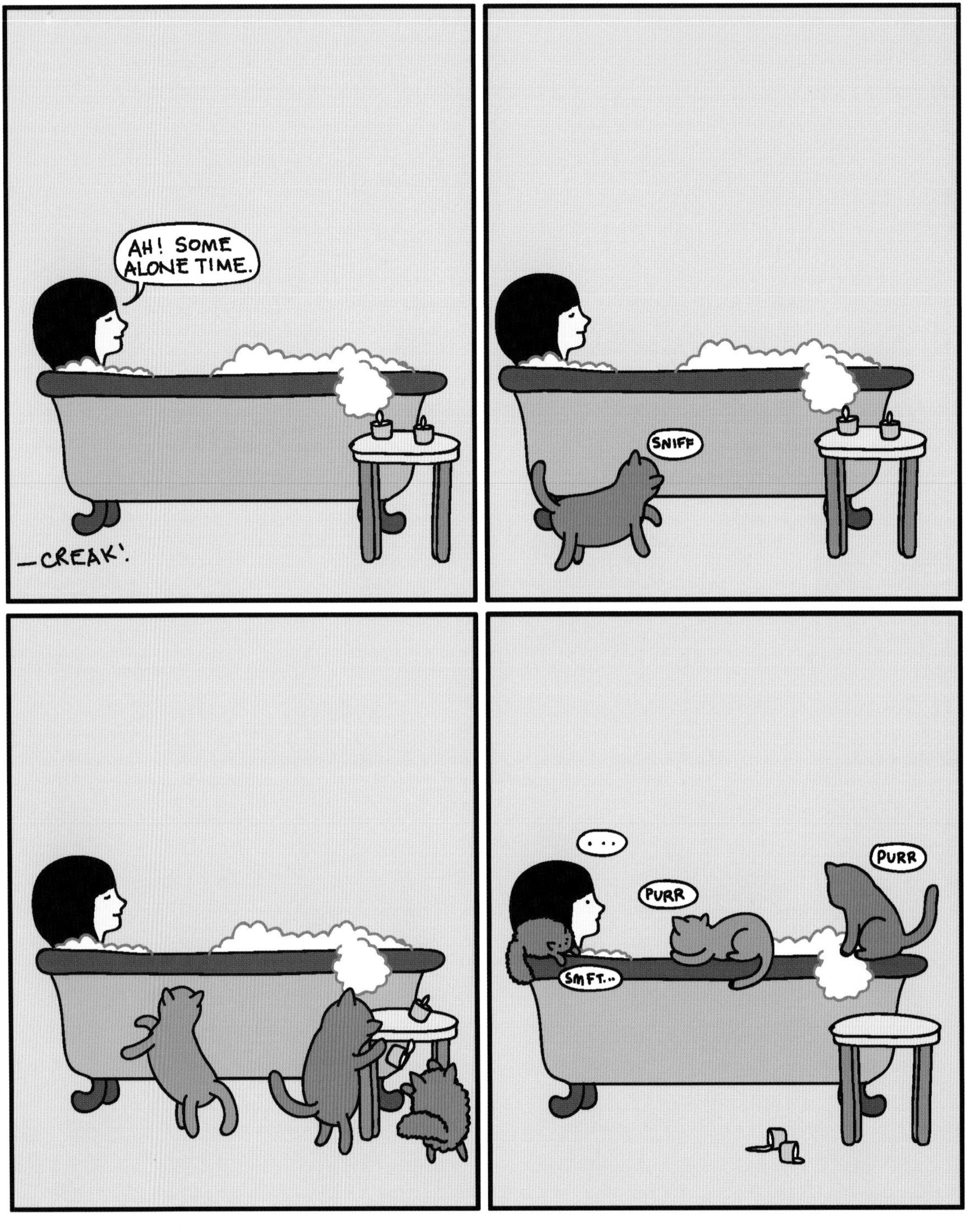
AH! SOME ALONE TIME.
—CREAK!
SNIFF
. . .
PURR
PURR
SMFT...

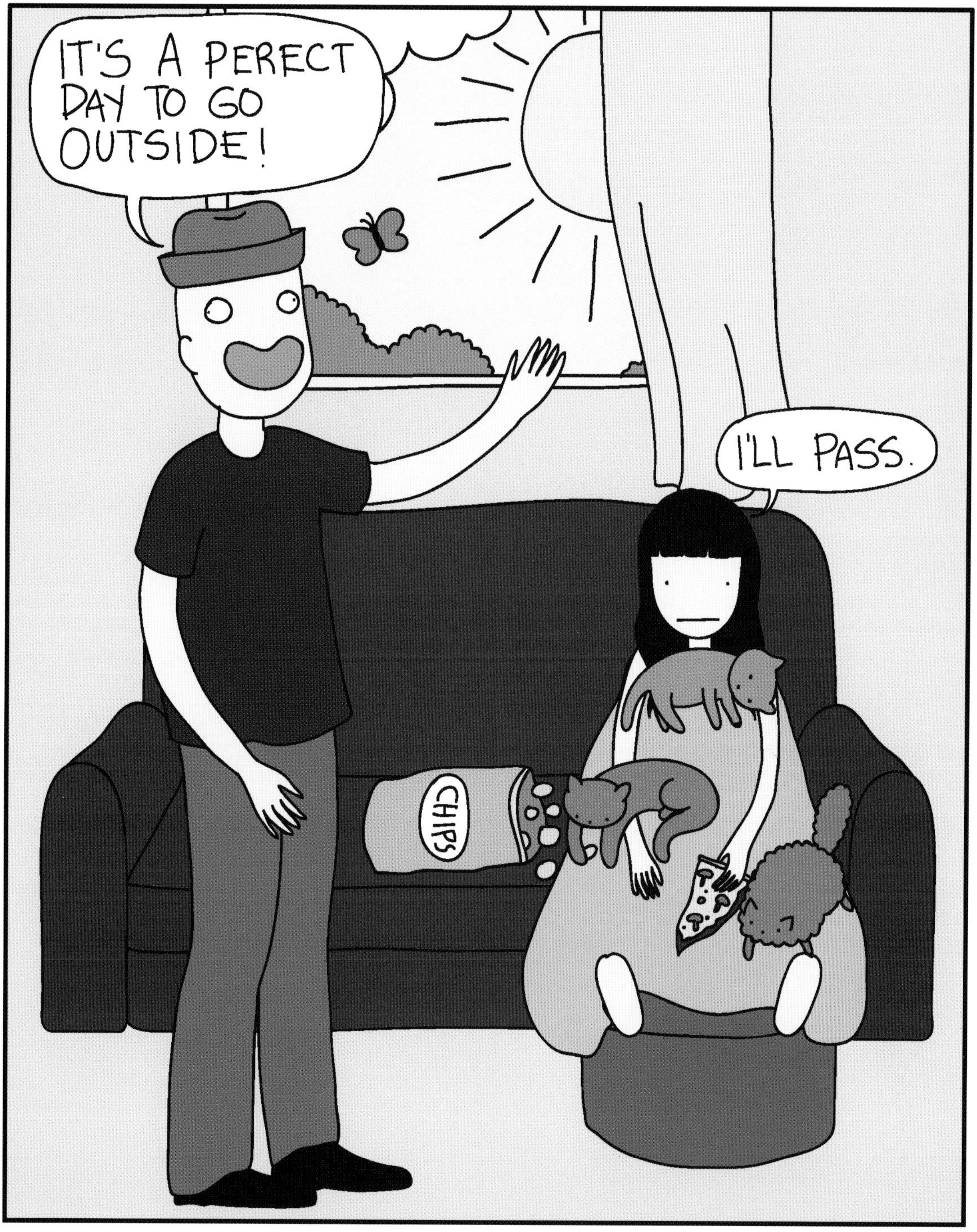
IT'S A PERFECT DAY TO GO OUTSIDE!
I'LL PASS.
CHIPS

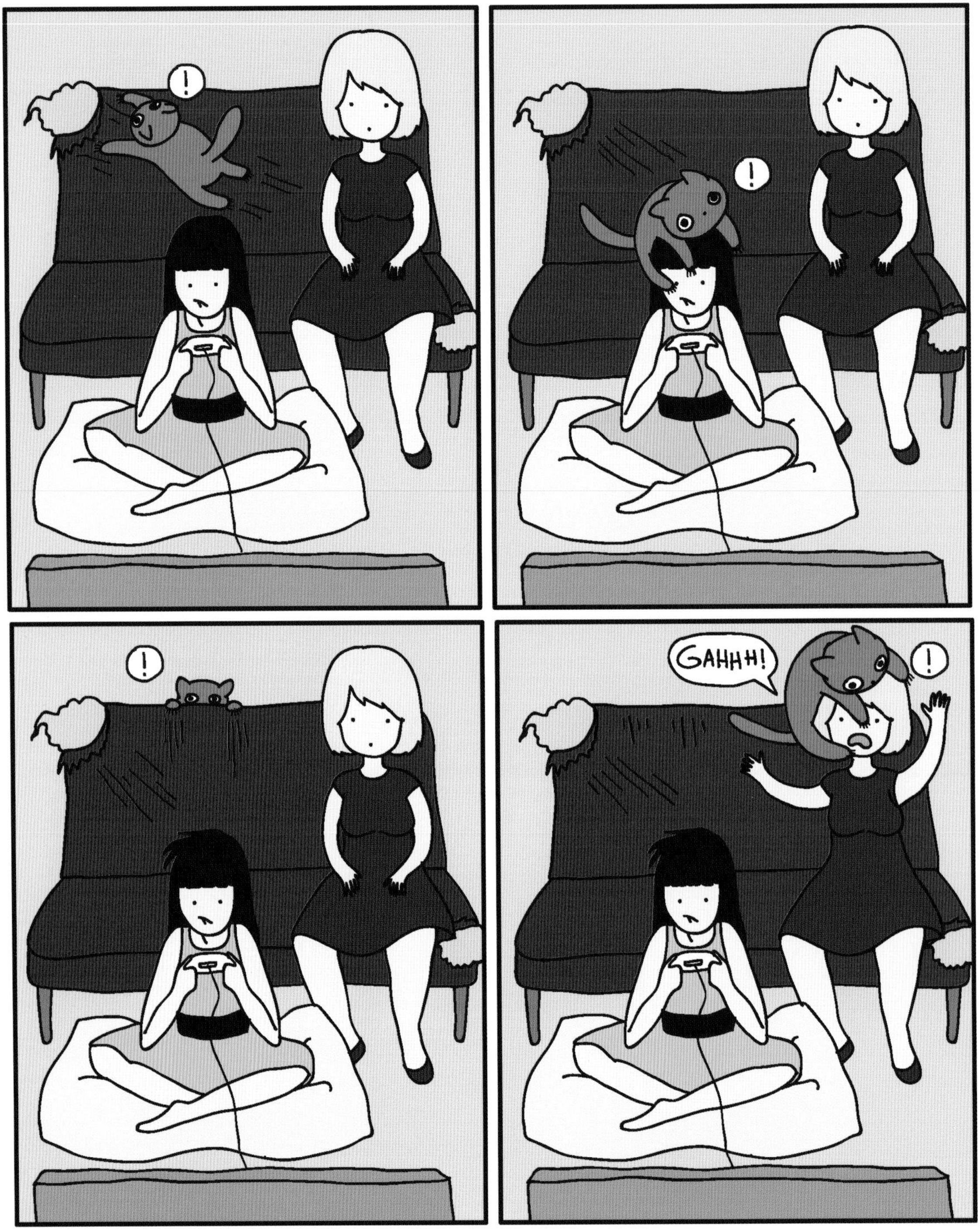
!
!
!
GAHHH!
!

WHAT'S WRONG WITH HER?!!
!
CATNIP.
!

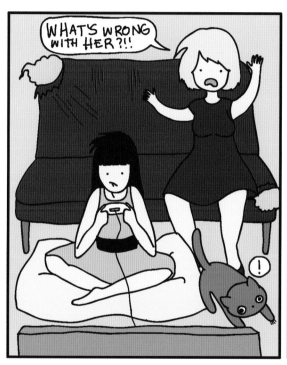

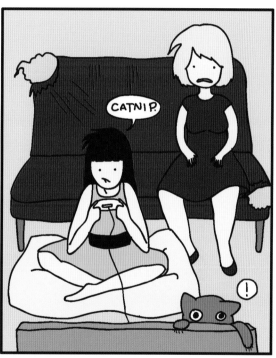

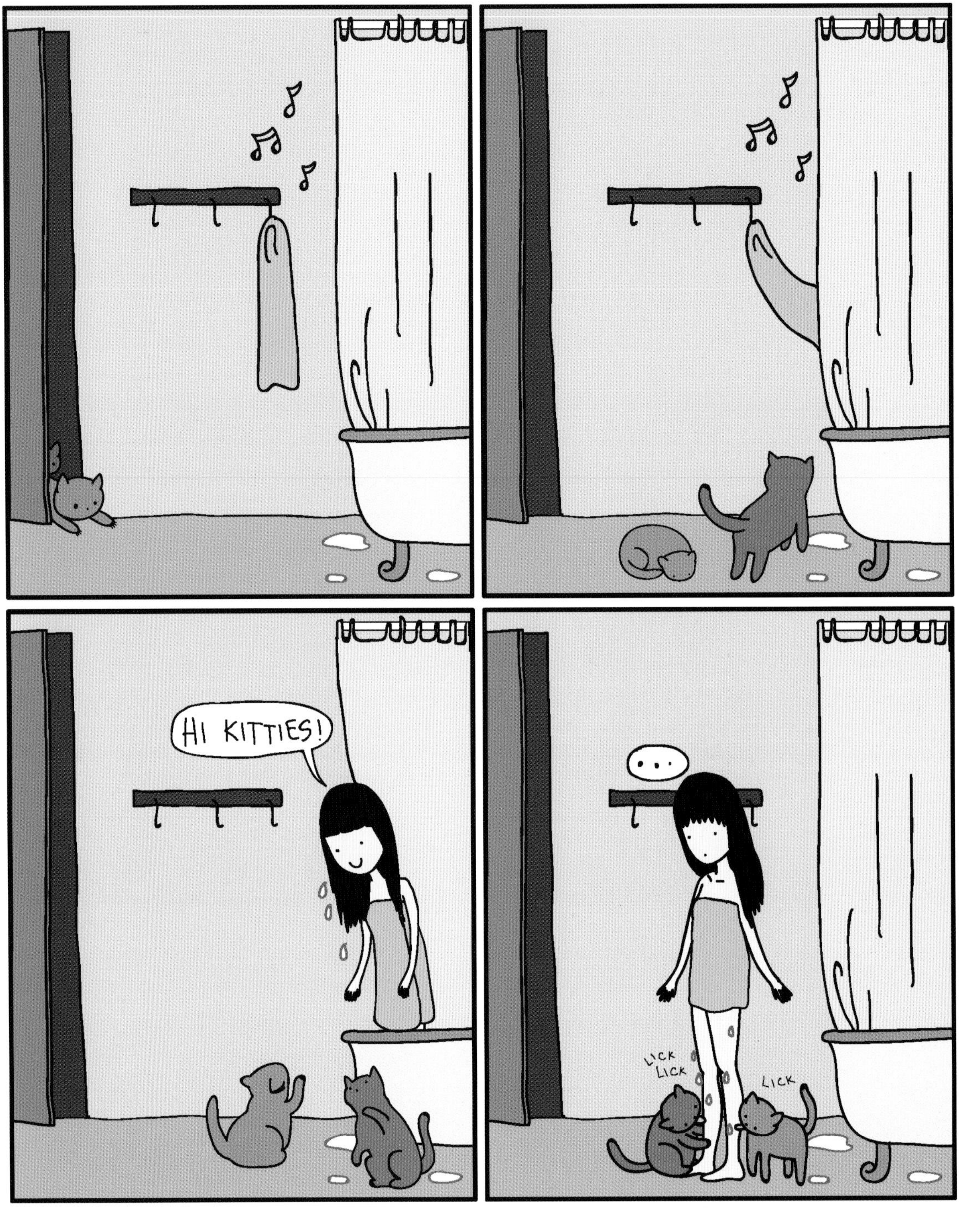
HI KITTIES!
...
LICK
LICK
LICK

KITTY ATTACK MODE

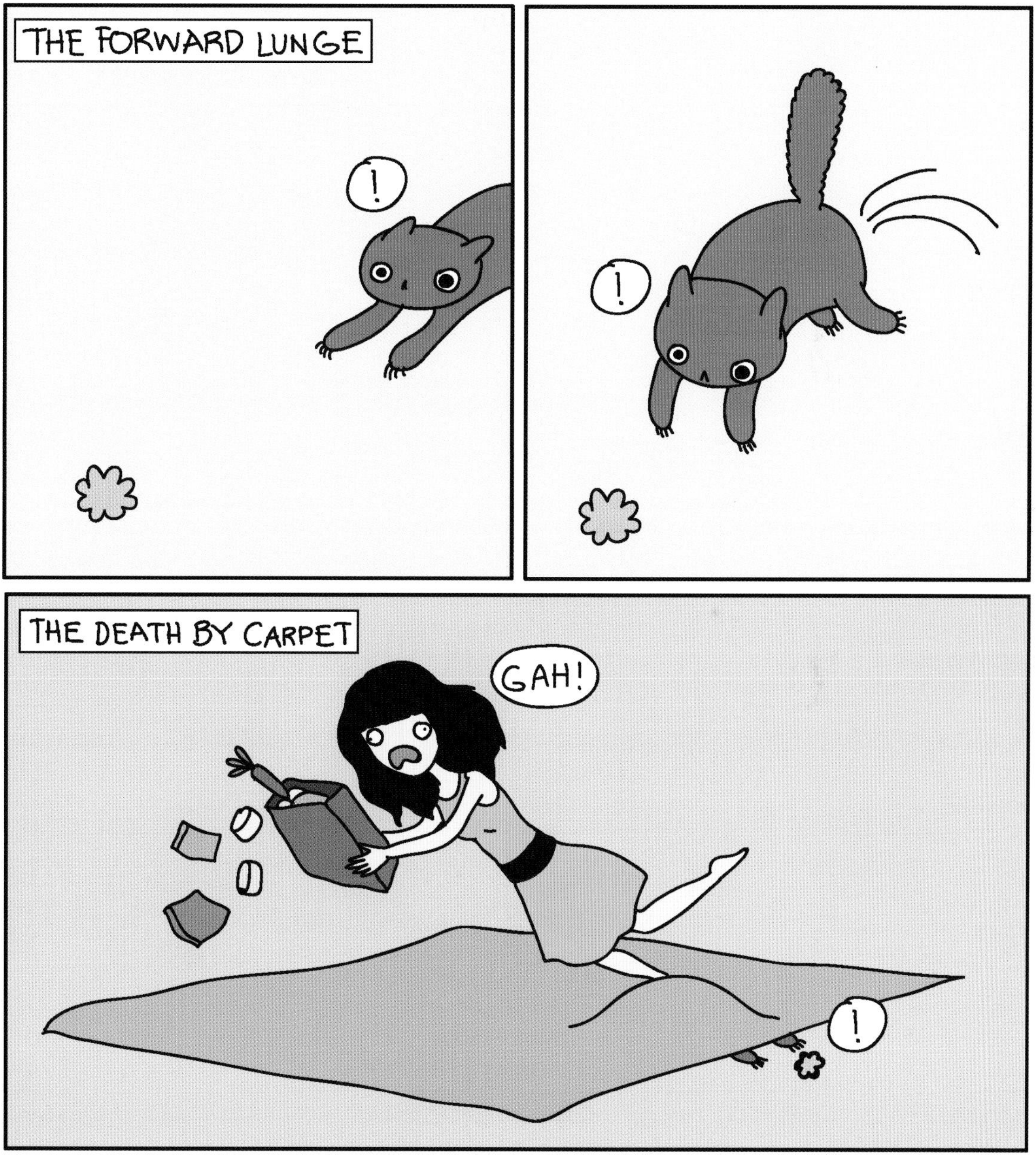
THE FORWARD LUNGE
!
!
THE DEATH BY CARPET
GAH!
!

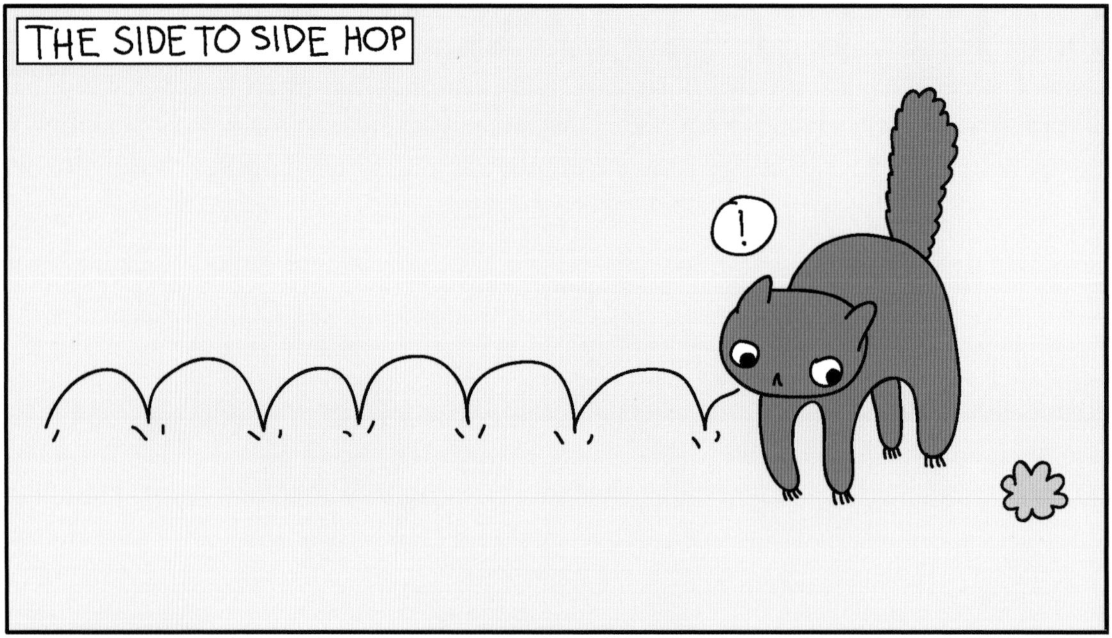
THE SIDE TO SIDE HOP
!

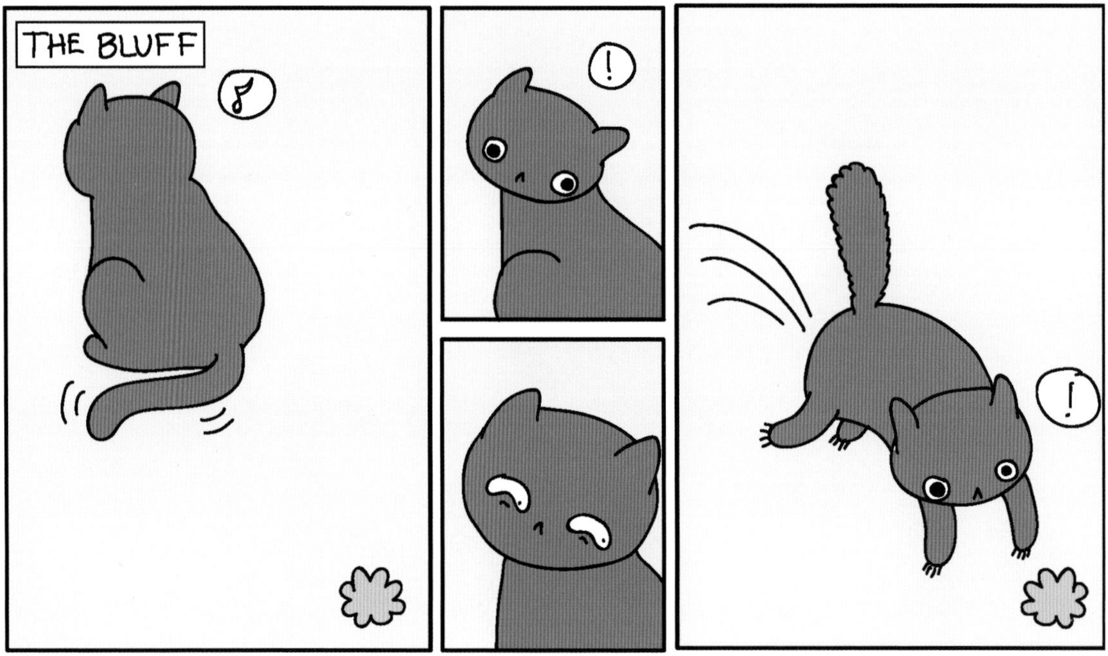
THE BLUFF
!
!

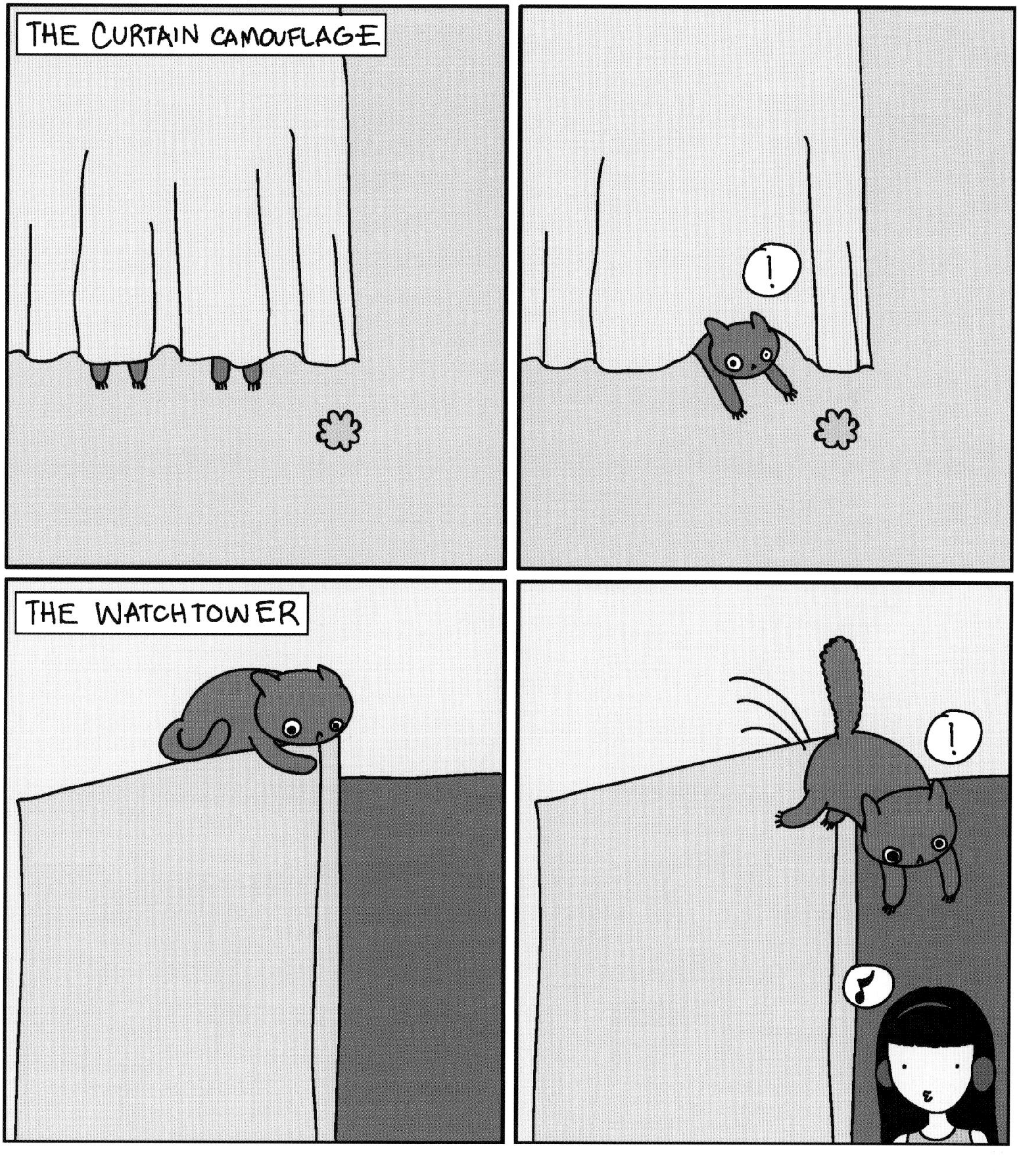
THE CURTAIN CAMOUFLAGE
!
THE WATCHTOWER
!

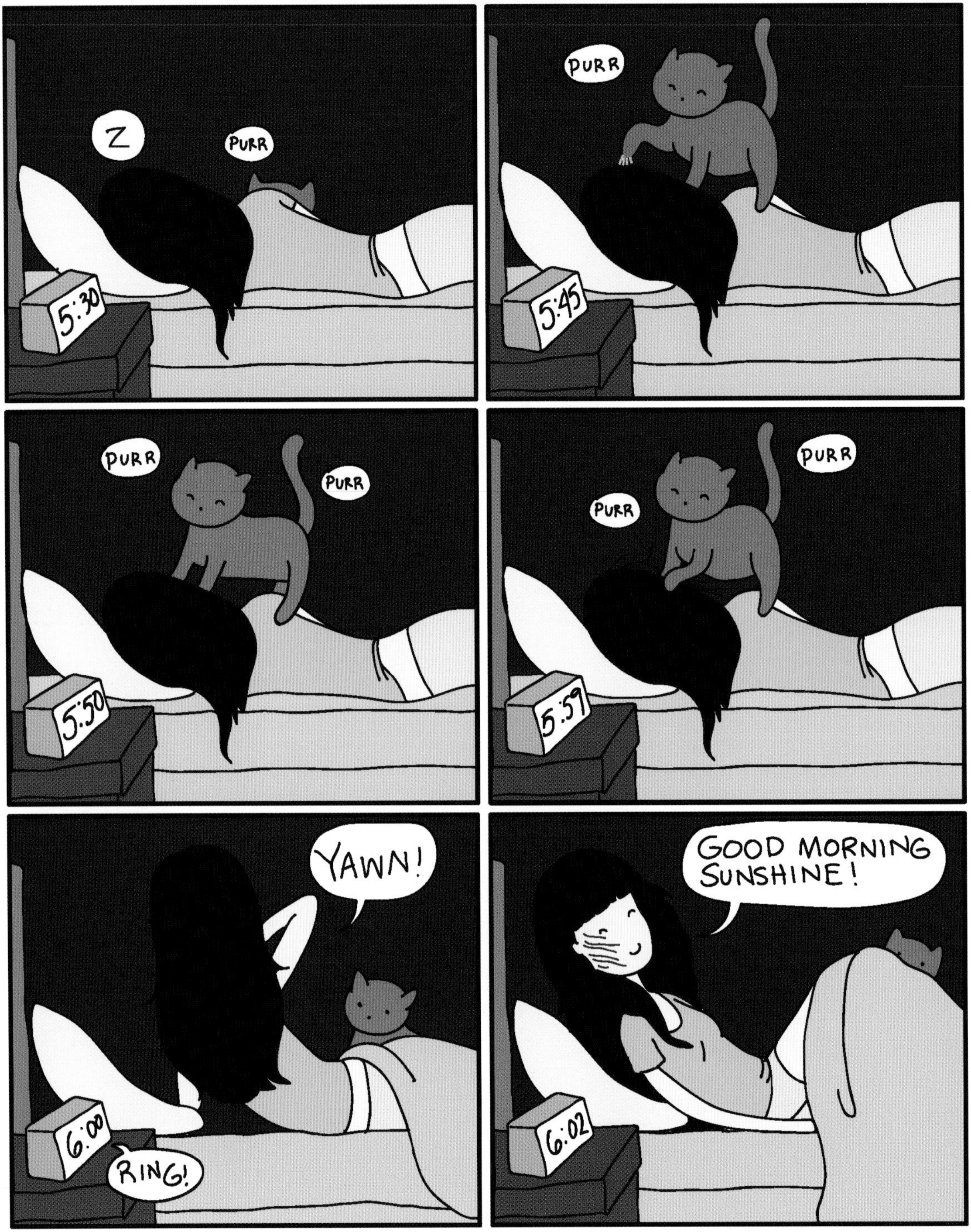
Z
PURR
5:30
PURR
5:45
PURR
PURR
5:50
PURR
PURR
5:59
YAWN!
6:00
RING!
GOOD MORNING SUNSHINE!
6:02

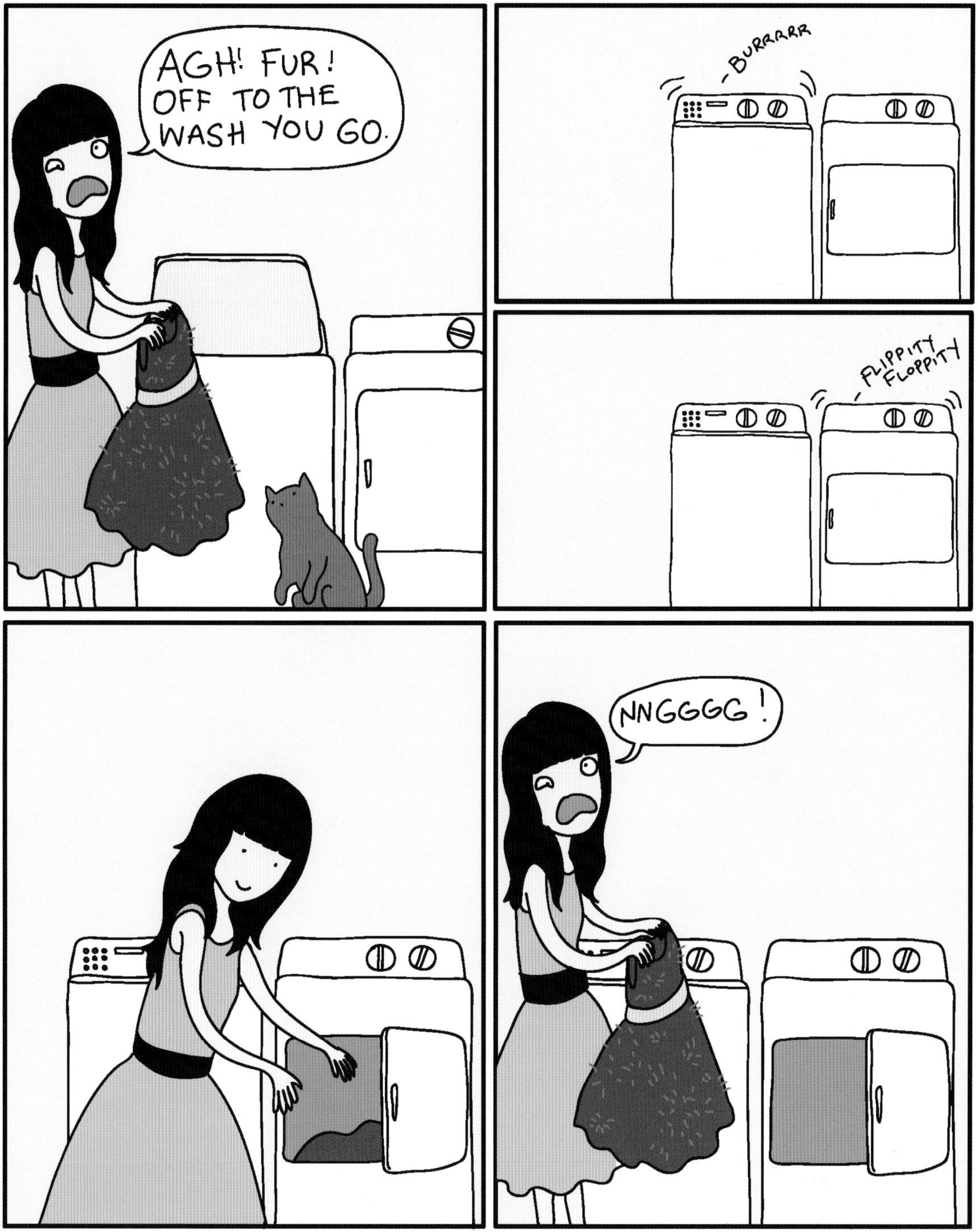
AGH! FUR! OFF TO THE WASH YOU GO.
BURRRRR
FLIPPITY FLOPPITY
NNGGGG!

SLEEPING WITH CATS

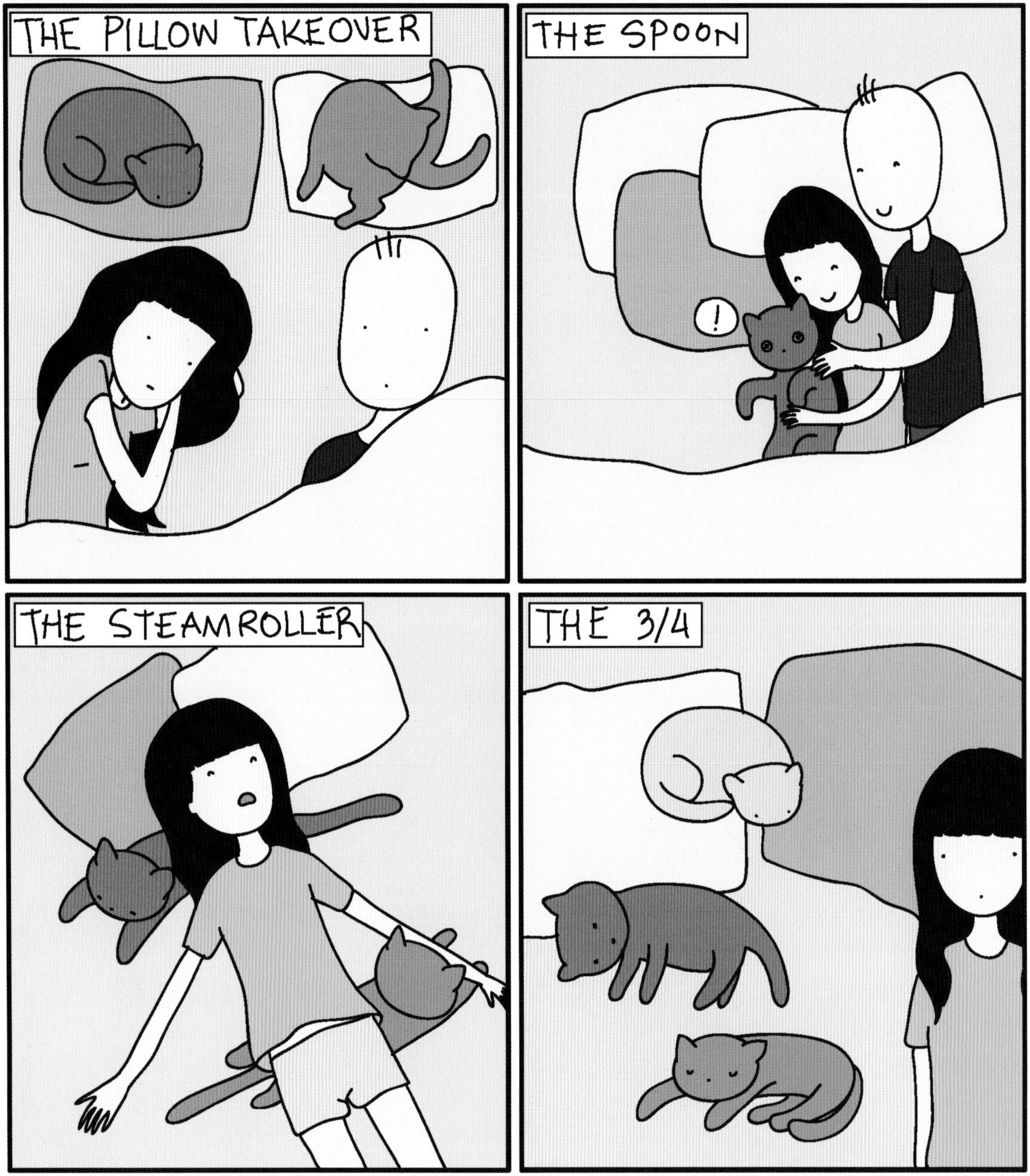
THE PILLOW TAKEOVER
THE SPOON
!
THE STEAMROLLER
THE 3/4

THE IN-BETWEENER

THE BUTT WARMER

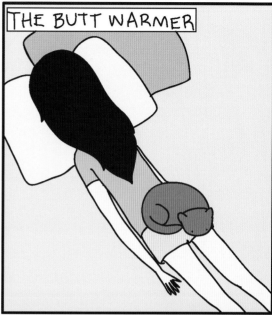

THE SMOTHERERS

THE NIGHTWATCHMAN

CAT LADY AT WORK

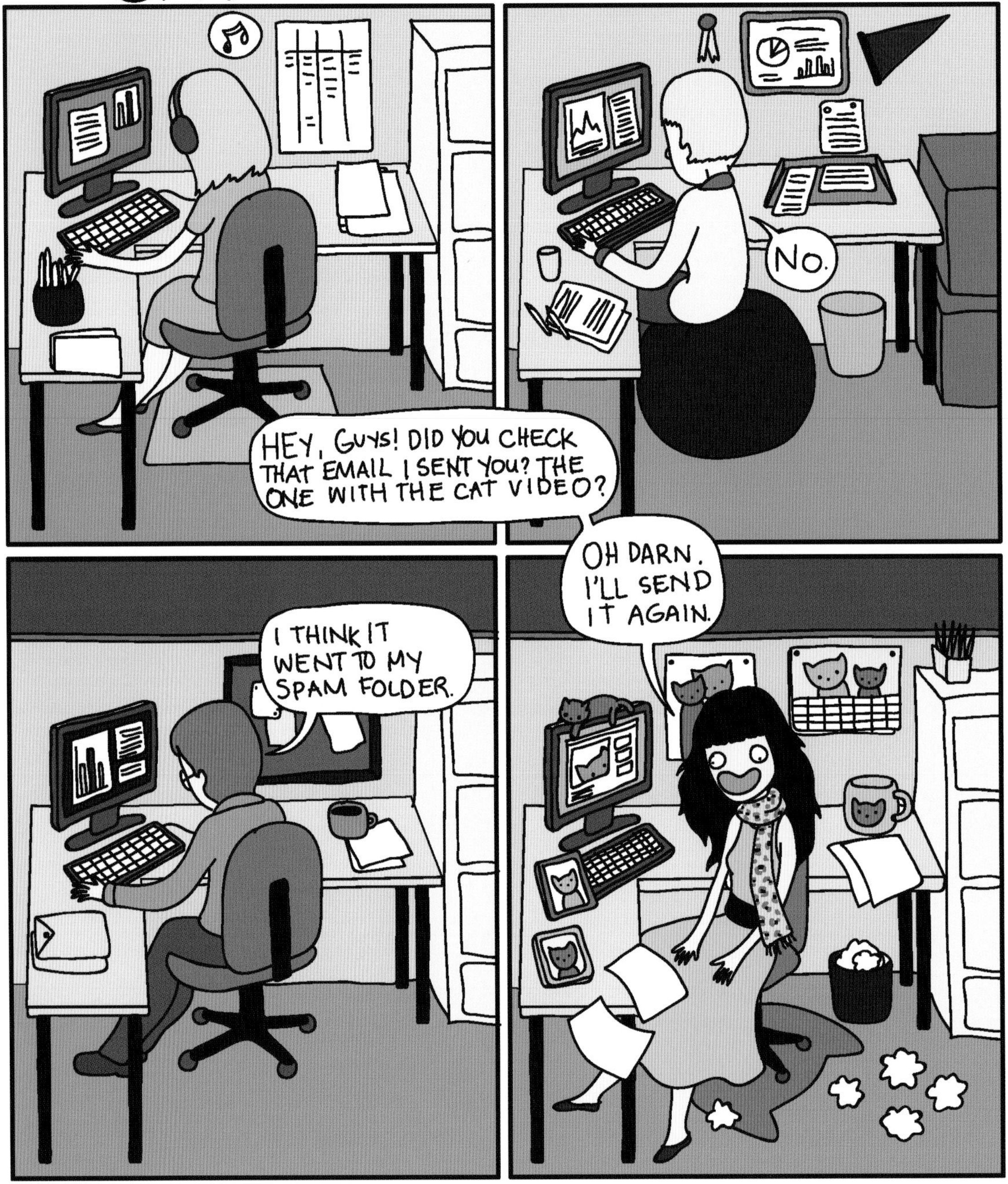
No.
HEY, GUYS! DID YOU CHECK THAT EMAIL I SENT YOU? THE ONE WITH THE CAT VIDEO?
I THINK IT WENT TO MY SPAM FOLDER.
OH DARN. I'LL SEND IT AGAIN.

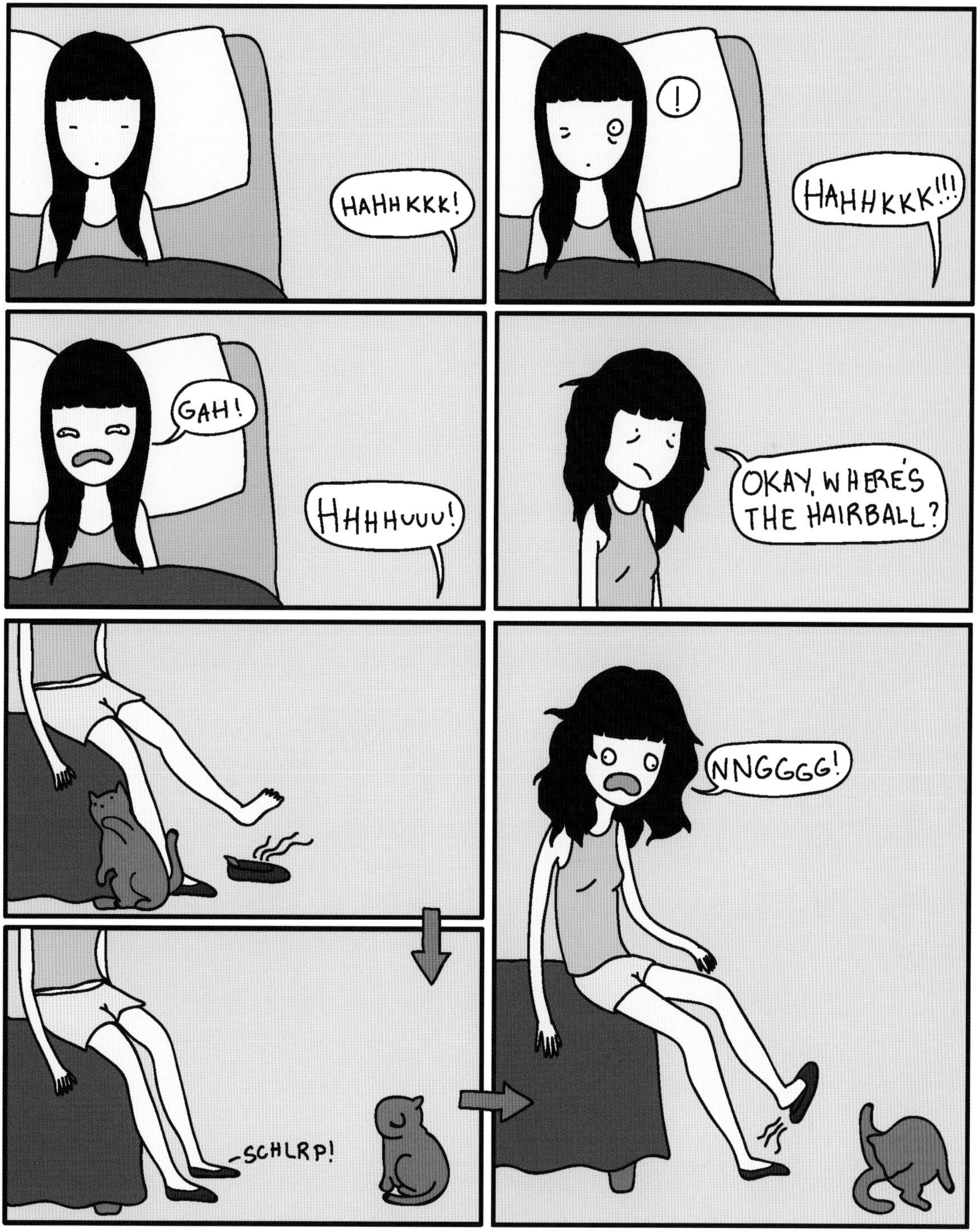
HAHHKKK!
!
HAHHKKK!!!
GAH!
HHHHUUU!
OKAY, WHERE'S THE HAIRBALL?
-SCHLRP!
NNGGGG!

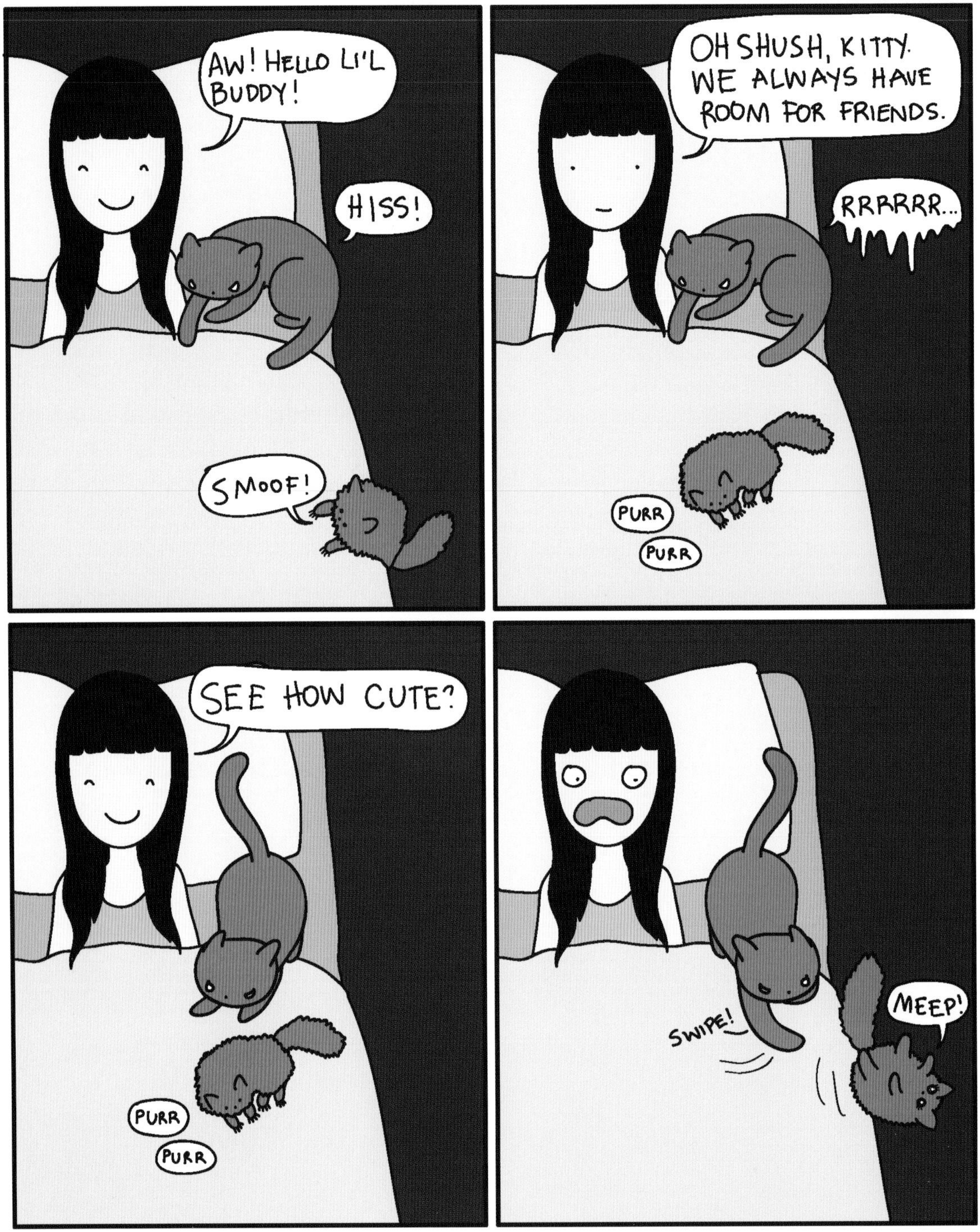
AW! HELLO LI'L BUDDY!
HISS!
SMOOF!
OH SHUSH, KITTY. WE ALWAYS HAVE ROOM FOR FRIENDS.
RRRRRR...
PURR
PURR
SEE HOW CUTE?
PURR
PURR
SWIPE!
MEEP!

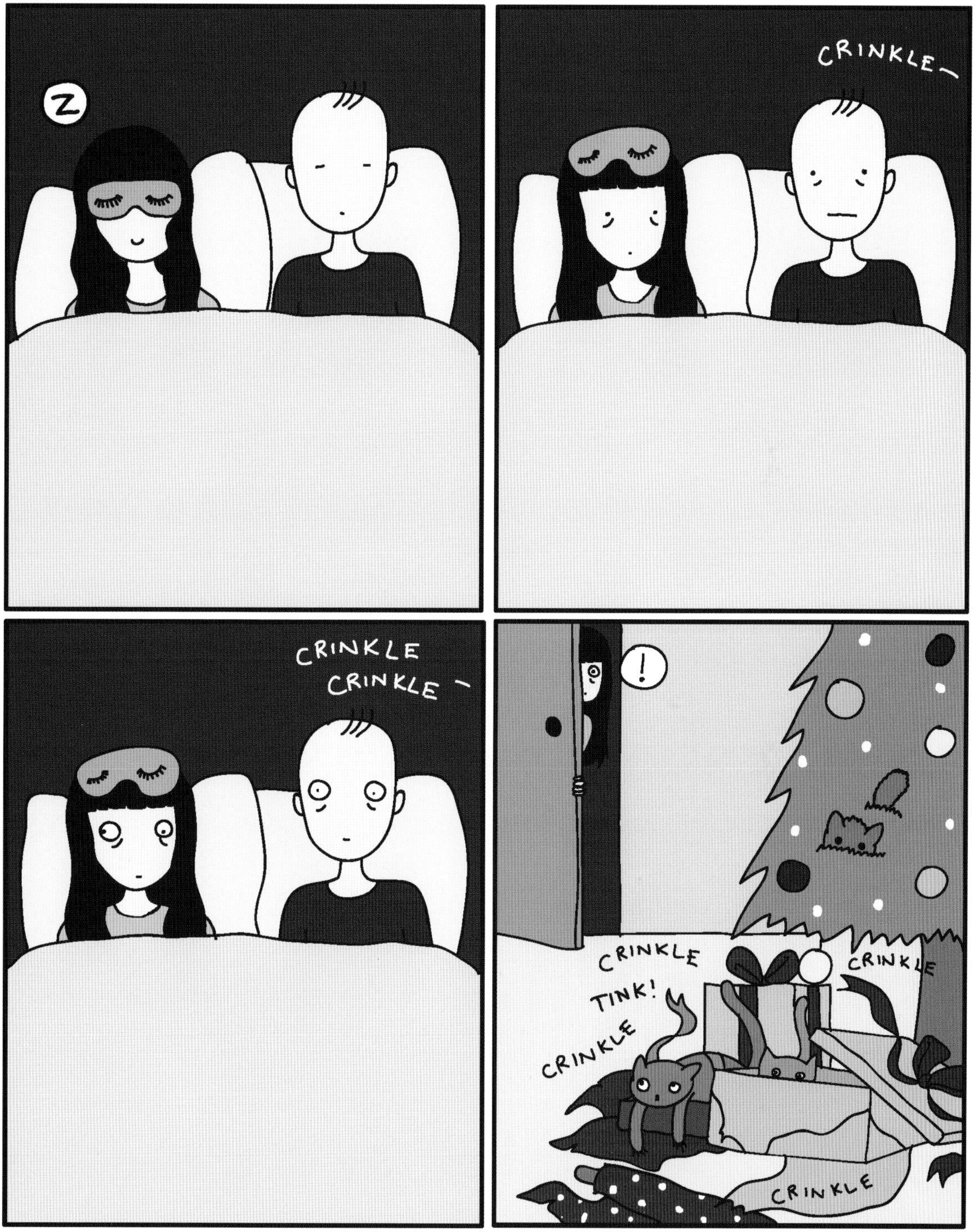
Z
CRINKLE—
CRINKLE
CRINKLE—
!
CRINKLE
CRINKLE
TINK!
CRINKLE
CRINKLE

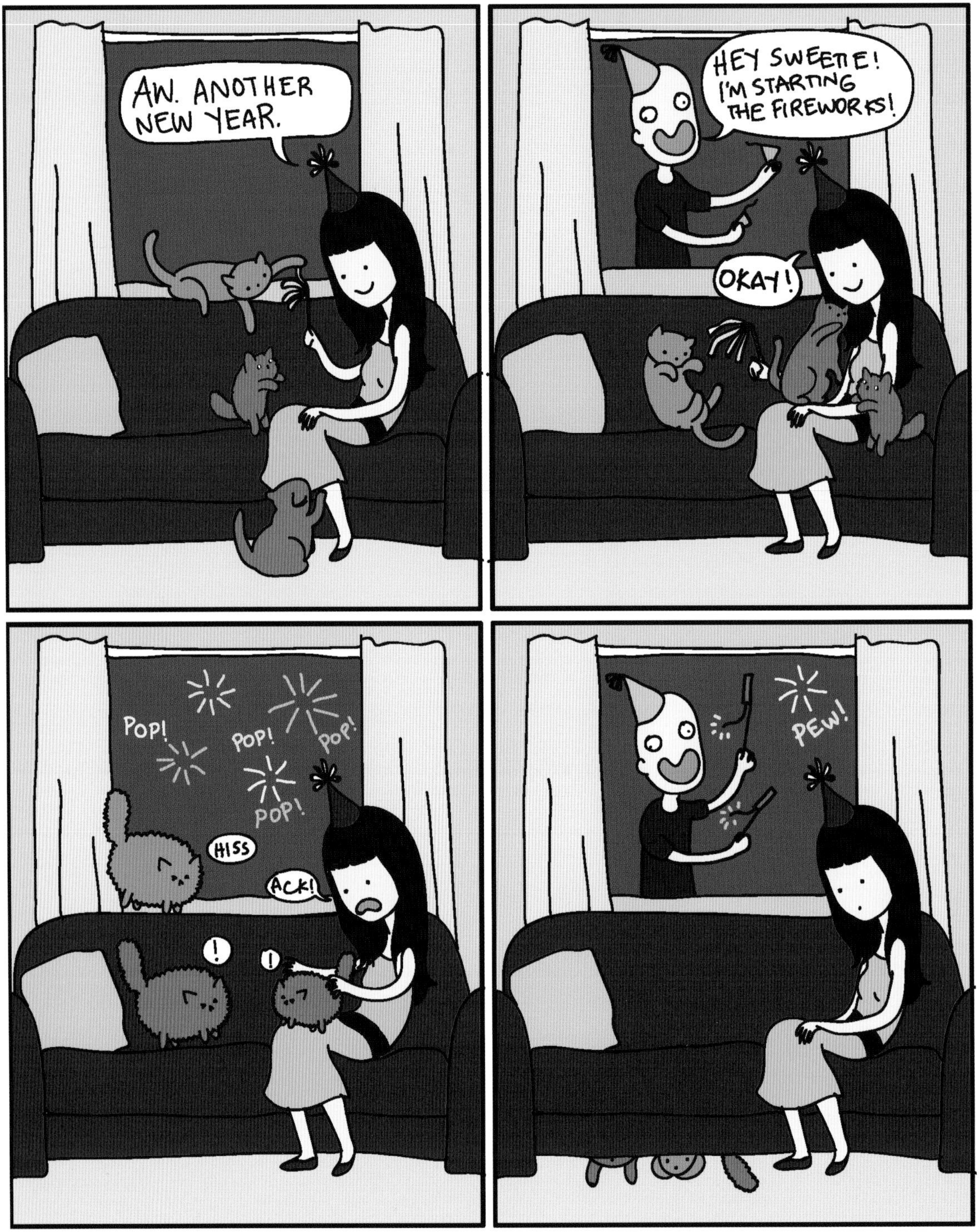
AW. ANOTHER NEW YEAR.
HEY SWEETIE! I'M STARTING THE FIREWORKS!
OKAY!
POP!
POP!
POP!
POP!
HISS
ACK!
!
!
PEW!

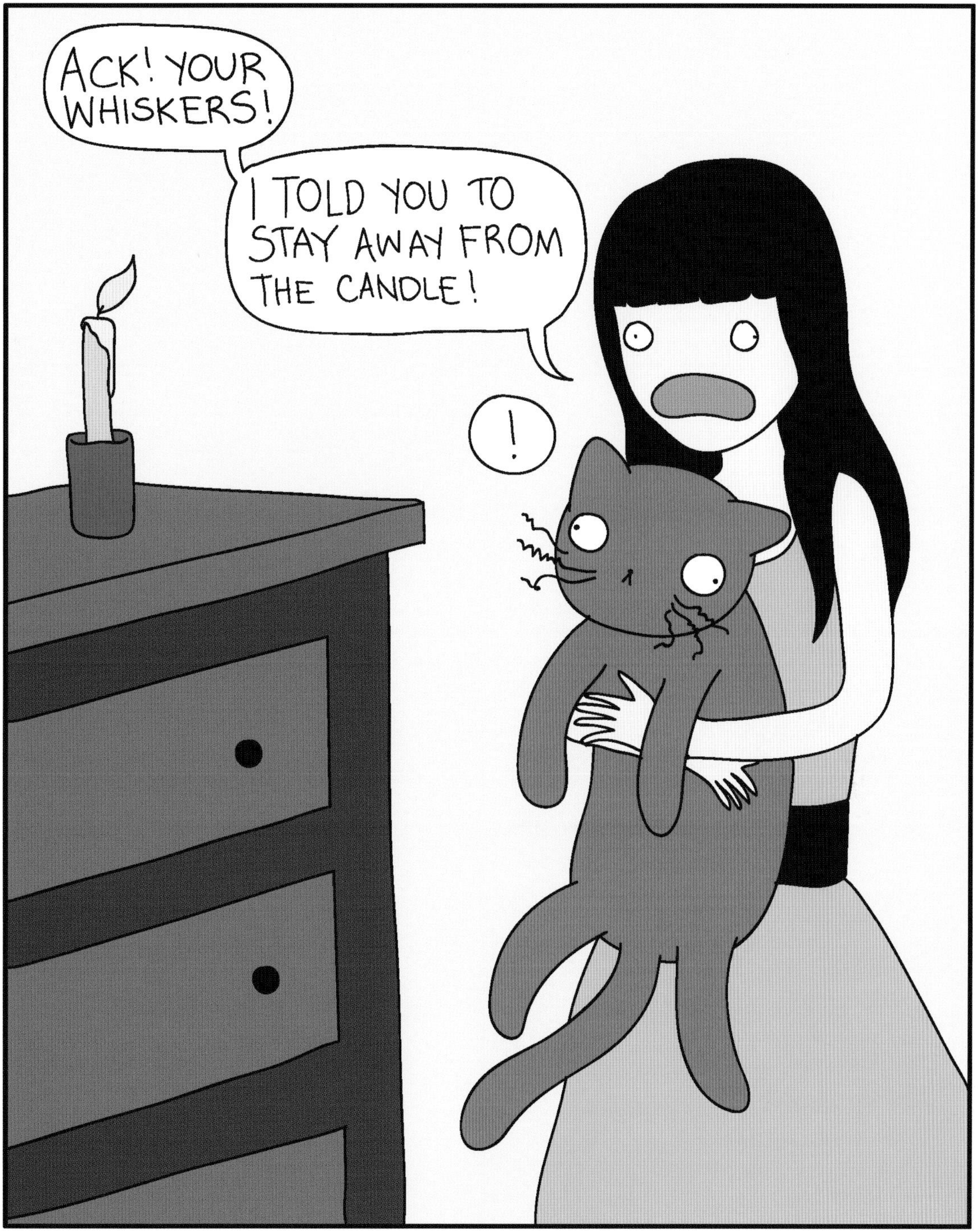
ACK! YOUR WHISKERS!
I TOLD YOU TO STAY AWAY FROM THE CANDLE!
!

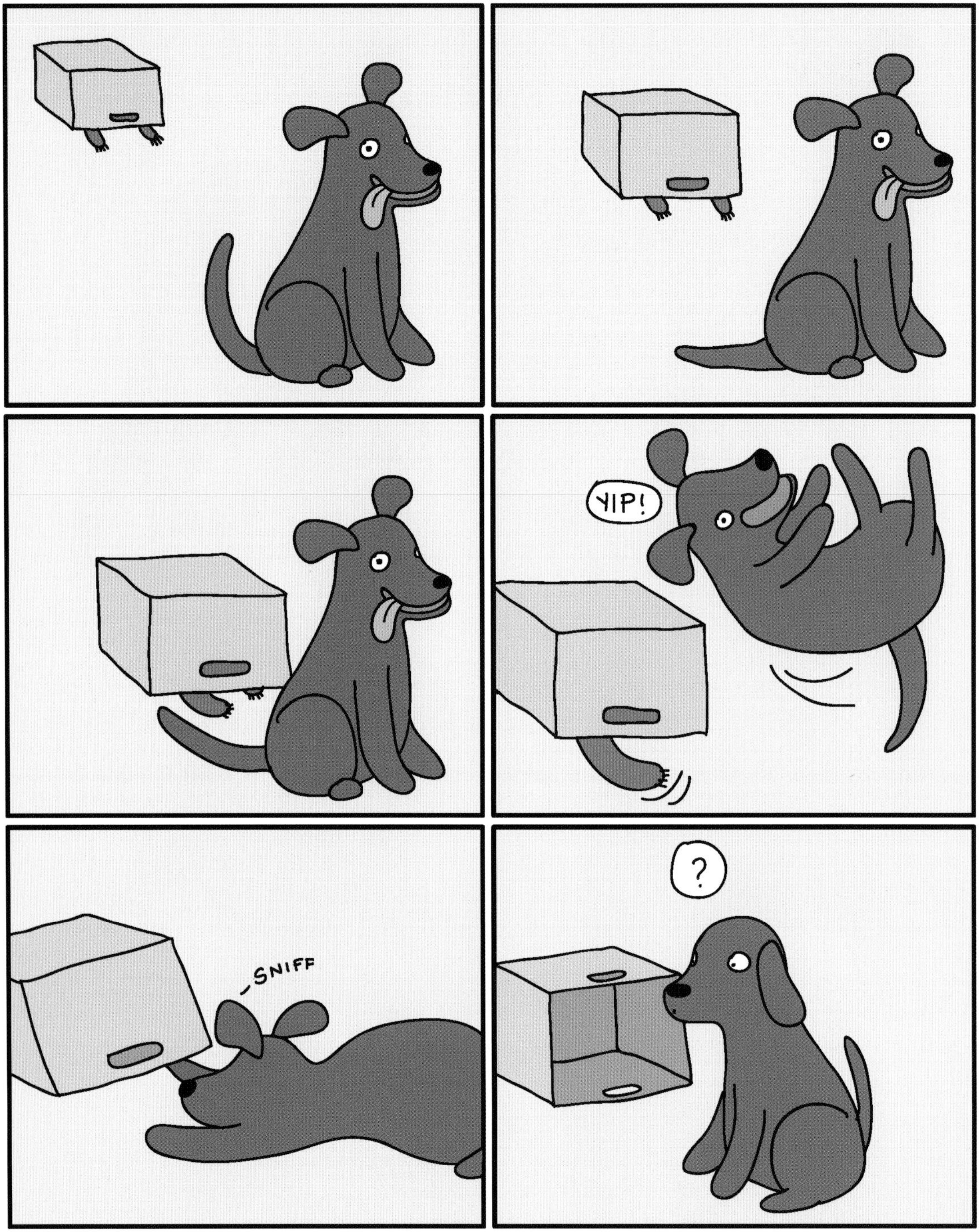
YIP!
SNIFF
?

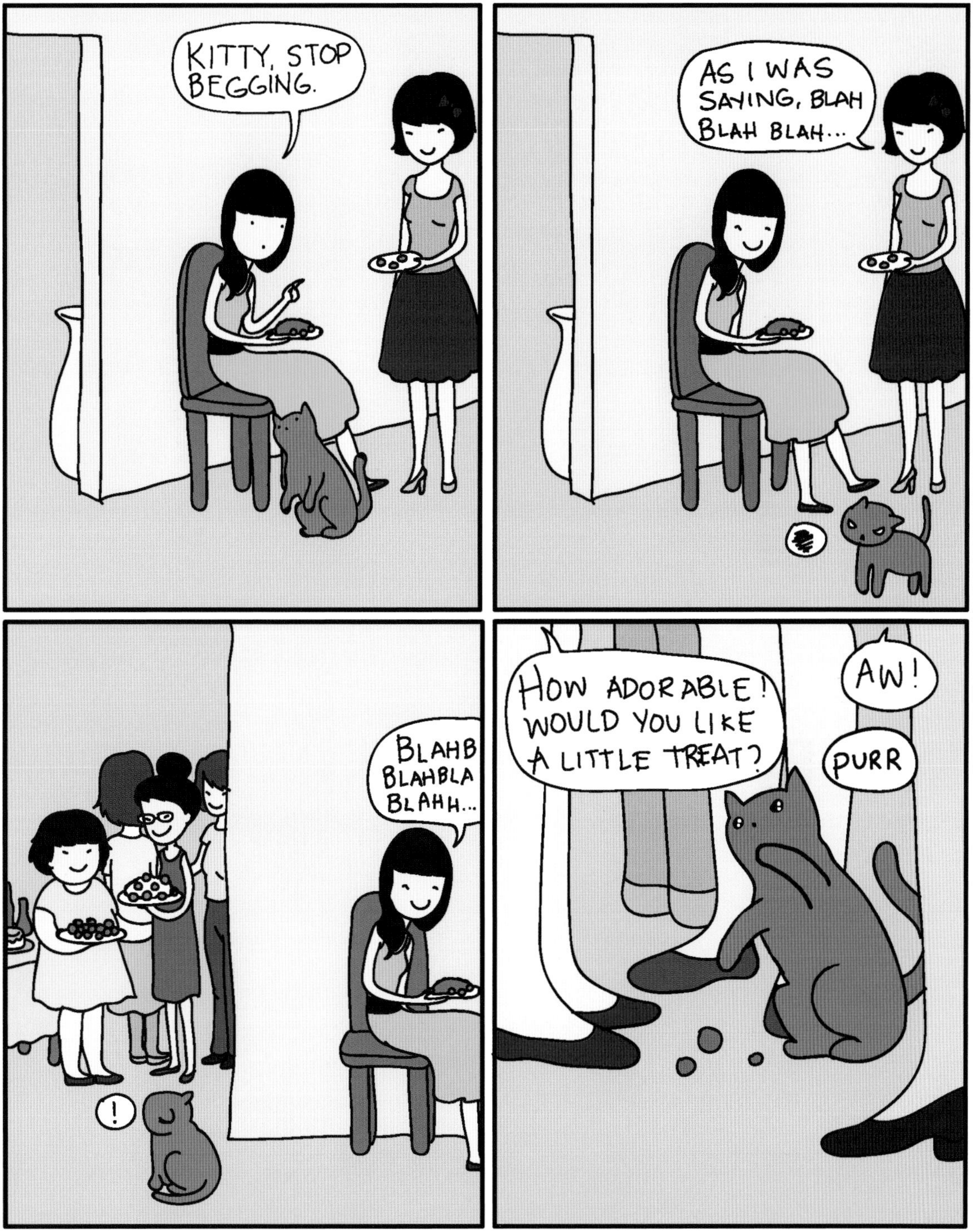
KITTY, STOP BEGGING.
AS I WAS SAYING, BLAH BLAH BLAH...
BLAHB BLAHBLA BLAHH...
!
HOW ADORABLE! WOULD YOU LIKE A LITTLE TREAT?
AW!
PURR

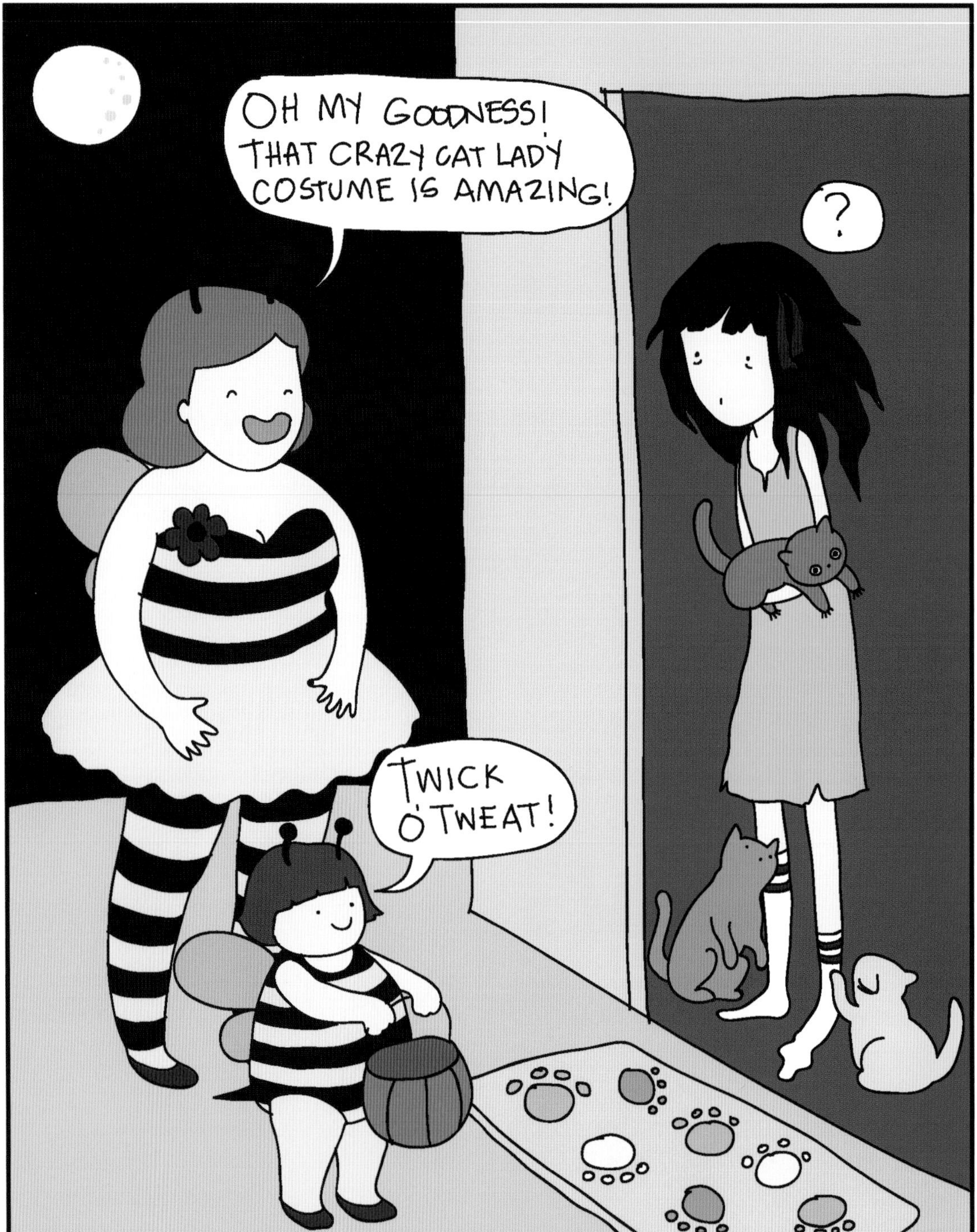
OH MY GOODNESS! THAT CRAZY CAT LADY COSTUME IS AMAZING!
?
TWICK O'TWEAT!

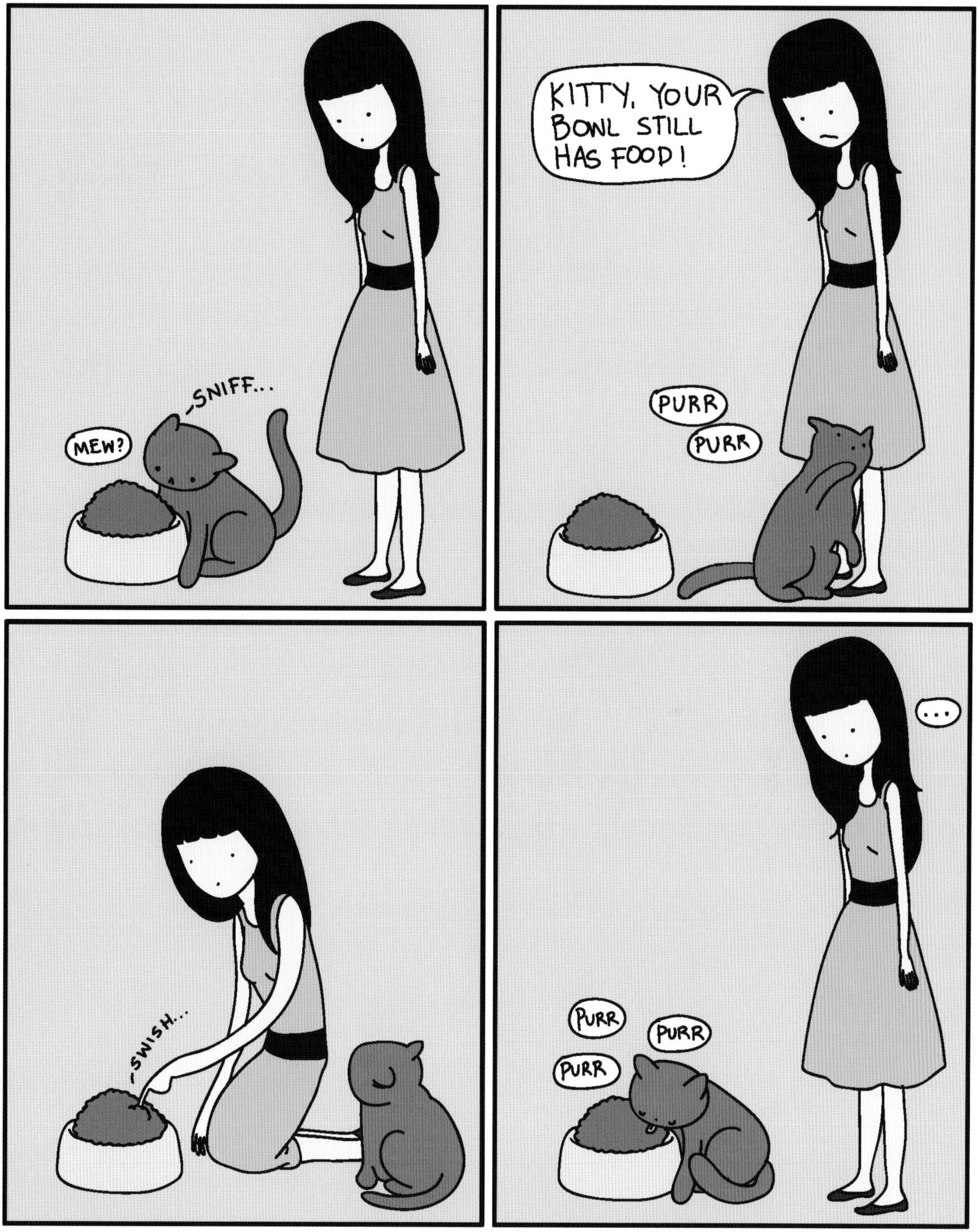
SNIFF...
MEW?
KITTY, YOUR BOWL STILL HAS FOOD!
PURR
PURR
SWISH...
...
PURR
PURR
PURR

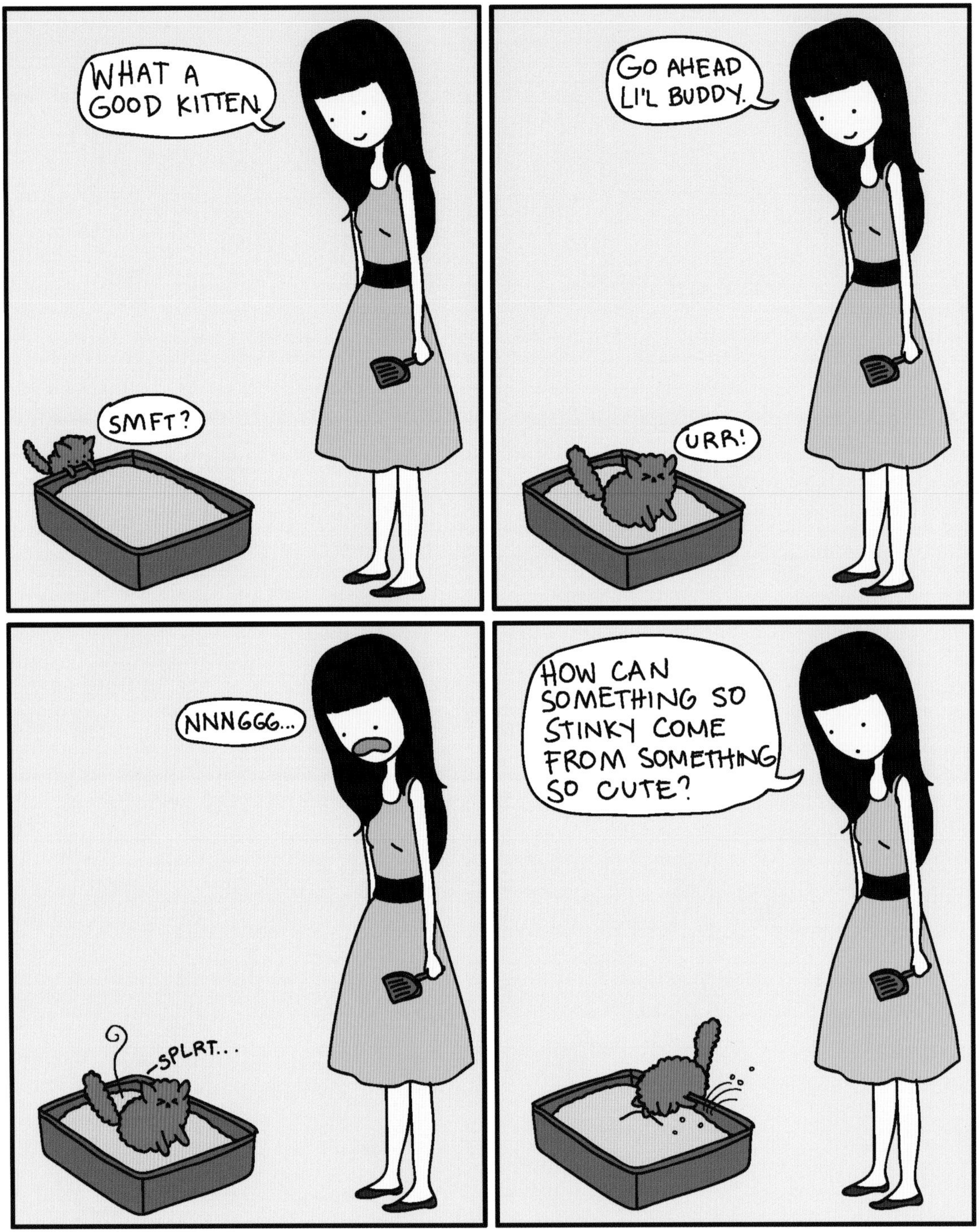
WHAT A GOOD KITTEN
SMFT?
GO AHEAD LI'L BUDDY.
URR!
NNNGGG...
-SPLRT...
HOW CAN SOMETHING SO STINKY COME FROM SOMETHING SO CUTE?

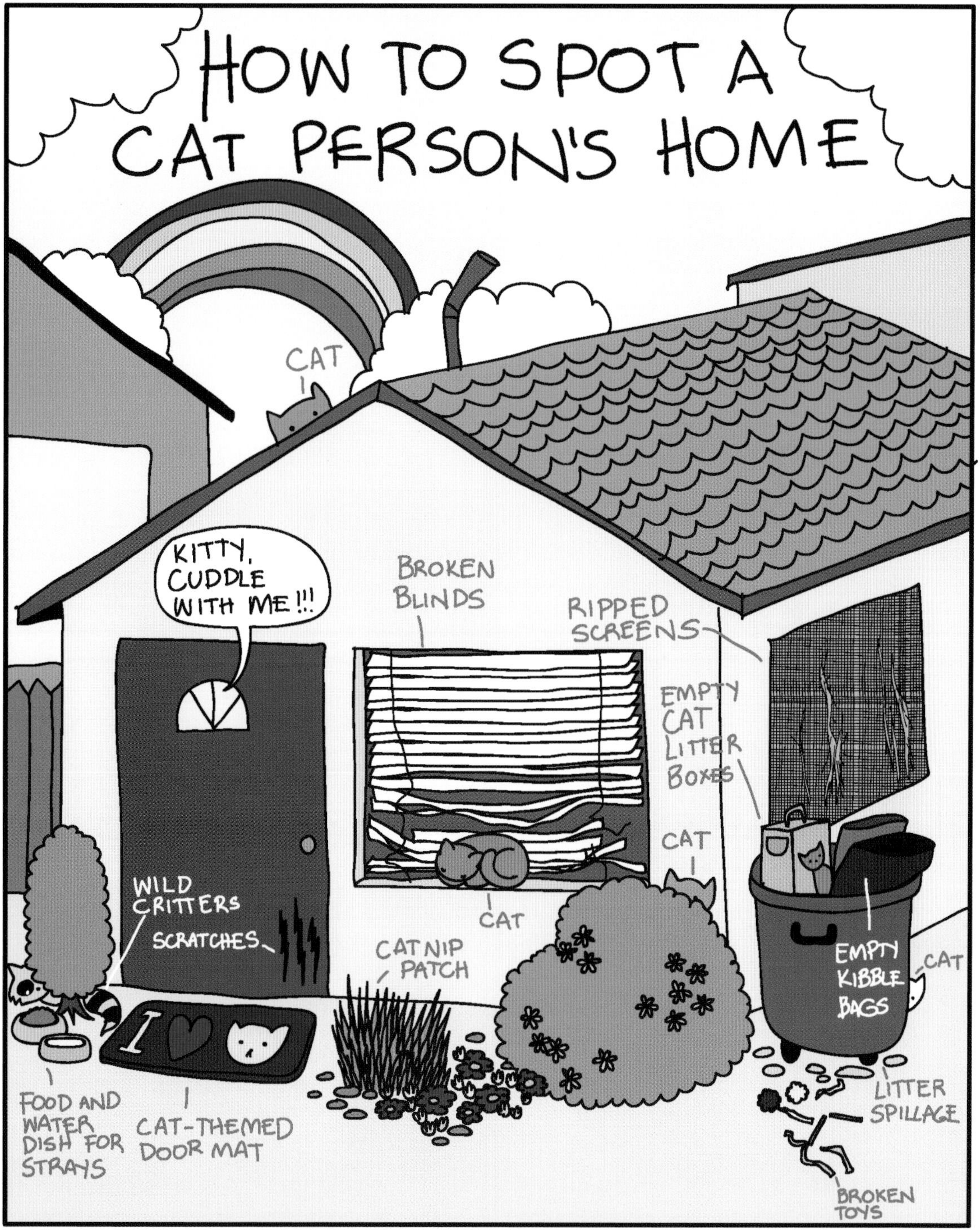
HOW TO SPOT A CAT PERSON'S HOME
CAT
KITTY, CUDDLE WITH ME!!!
BROKEN BLINDS
RIPPED SCREENS
EMPTY CAT LITTER BOXES
CAT
WILD CRITTERS
SCRATCHES
CAT
CATNIP PATCH
EMPTY KIBBLE BAGS
CAT
FOOD AND WATER DISH FOR STRAYS
CAT-THEMED DOOR MAT
LITTER SPILLAGE
BROKEN TOYS

IF CATS COULD TALK

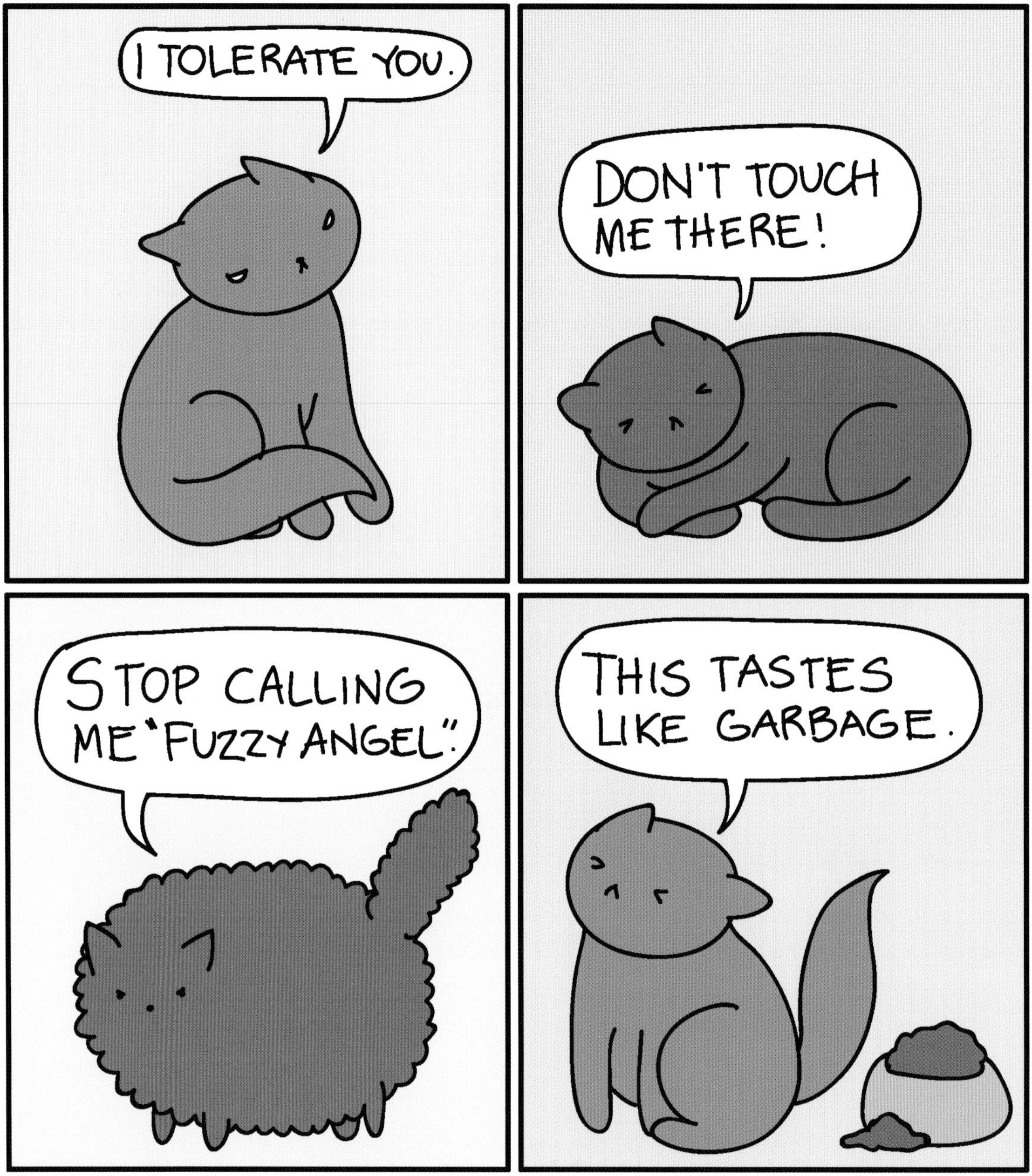
I TOLERATE YOU.
DON'T TOUCH ME THERE!
STOP CALLING ME "FUZZY ANGEL".
THIS TASTES LIKE GARBAGE.

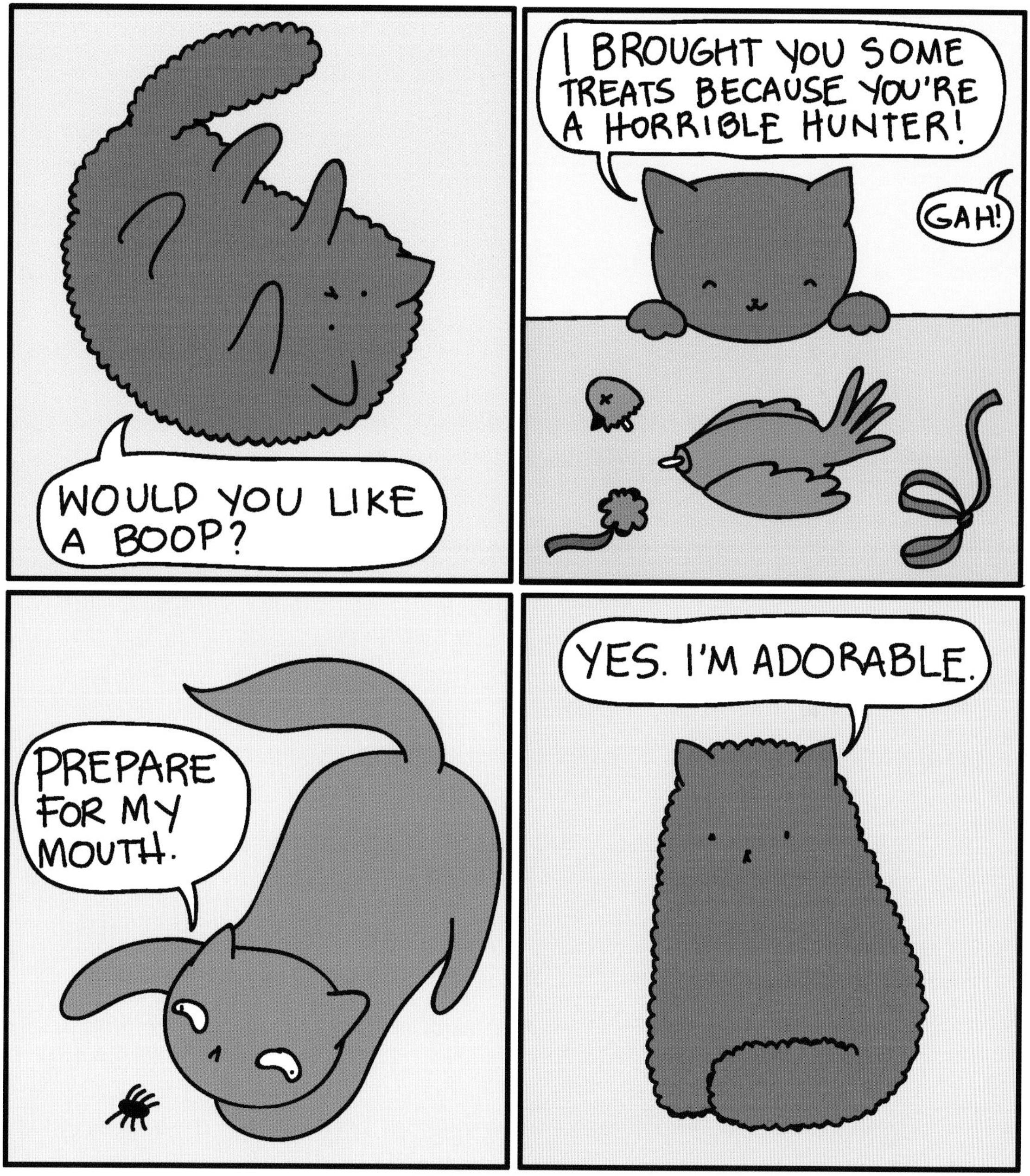
WOULD YOU LIKE A BOOP?
I BROUGHT YOU SOME TREATS BECAUSE YOU'RE A HORRIBLE HUNTER!
GAH!
PREPARE FOR MY MOUTH.
YES. I'M ADORABLE.

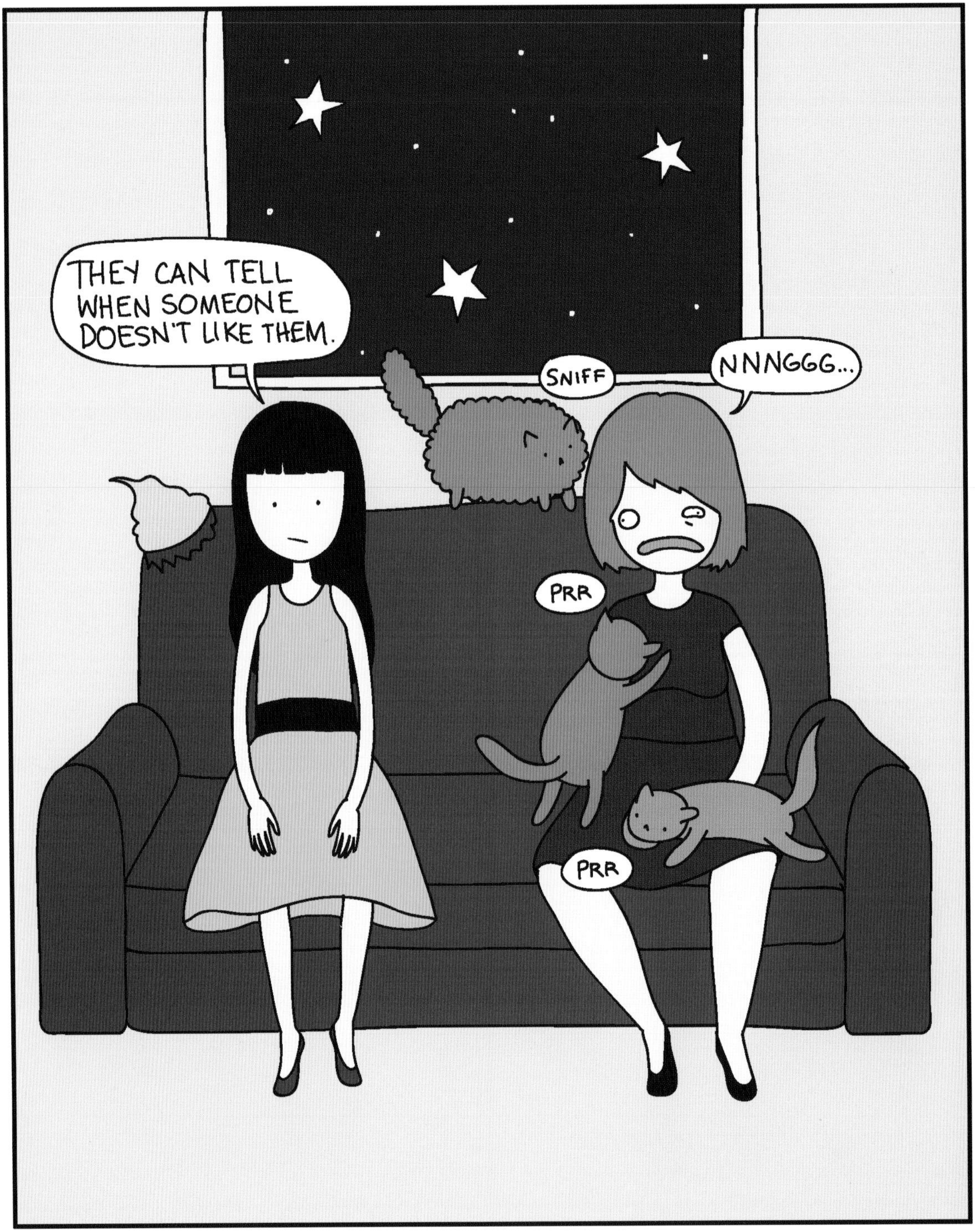
THEY CAN TELL WHEN SOMEONE DOESN'T LIKE THEM.
SNIFF
NNNGGG...
PRR
PRR

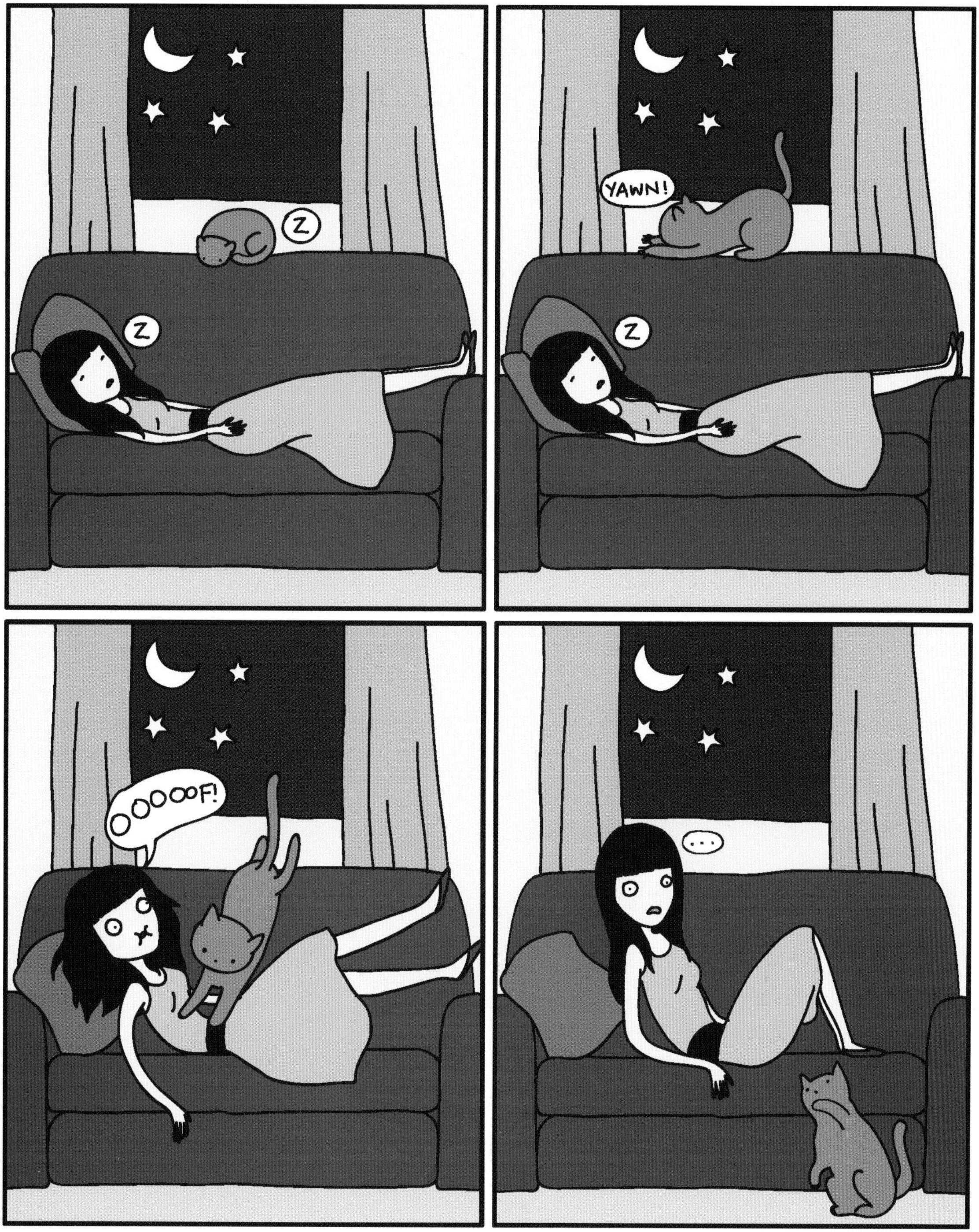
Z
Z
YAWN!
Z
OOOOOF!
...

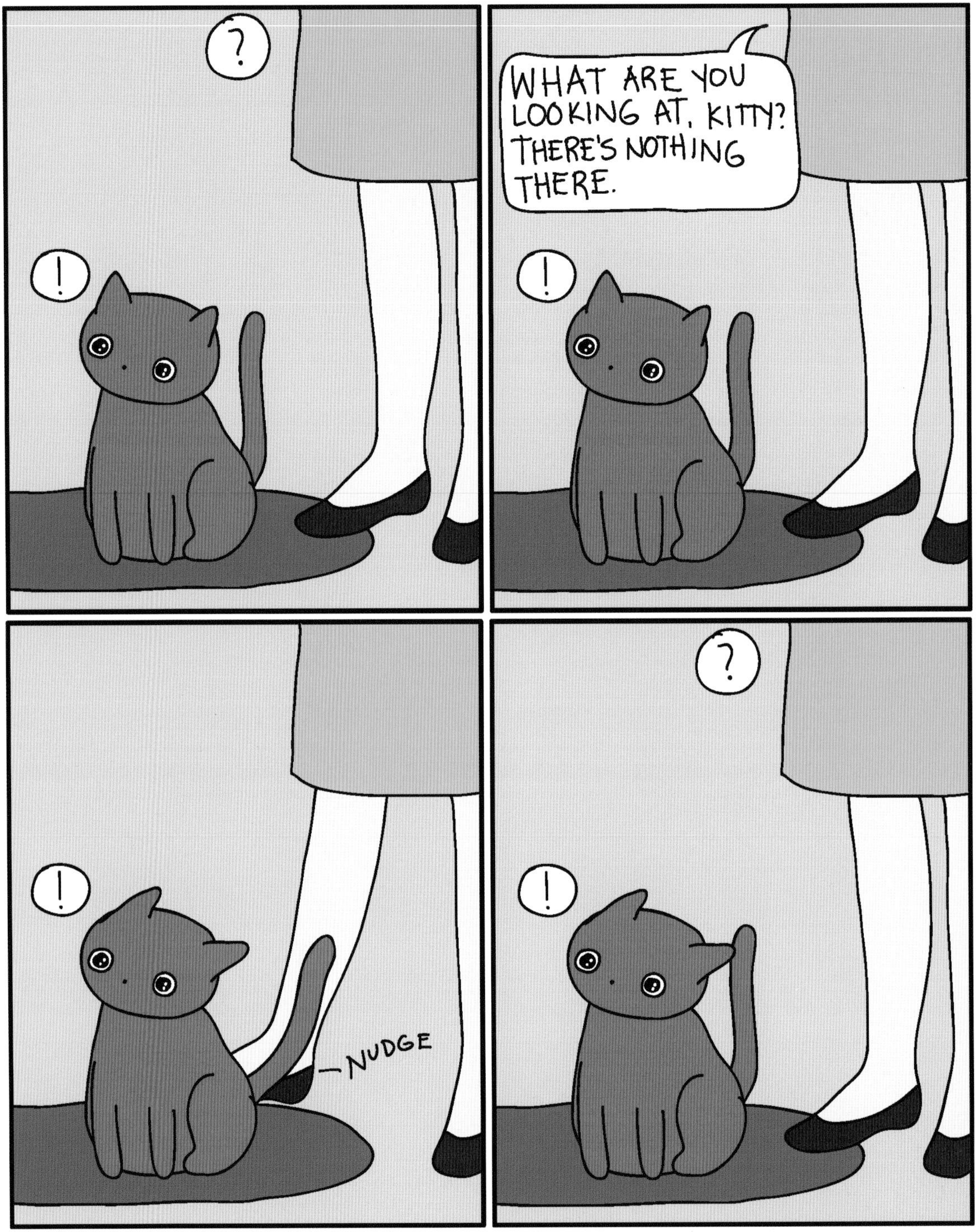
?
!
WHAT ARE YOU LOOKING AT, KITTY? THERE'S NOTHING THERE.
!
!
NUDGE
?
!

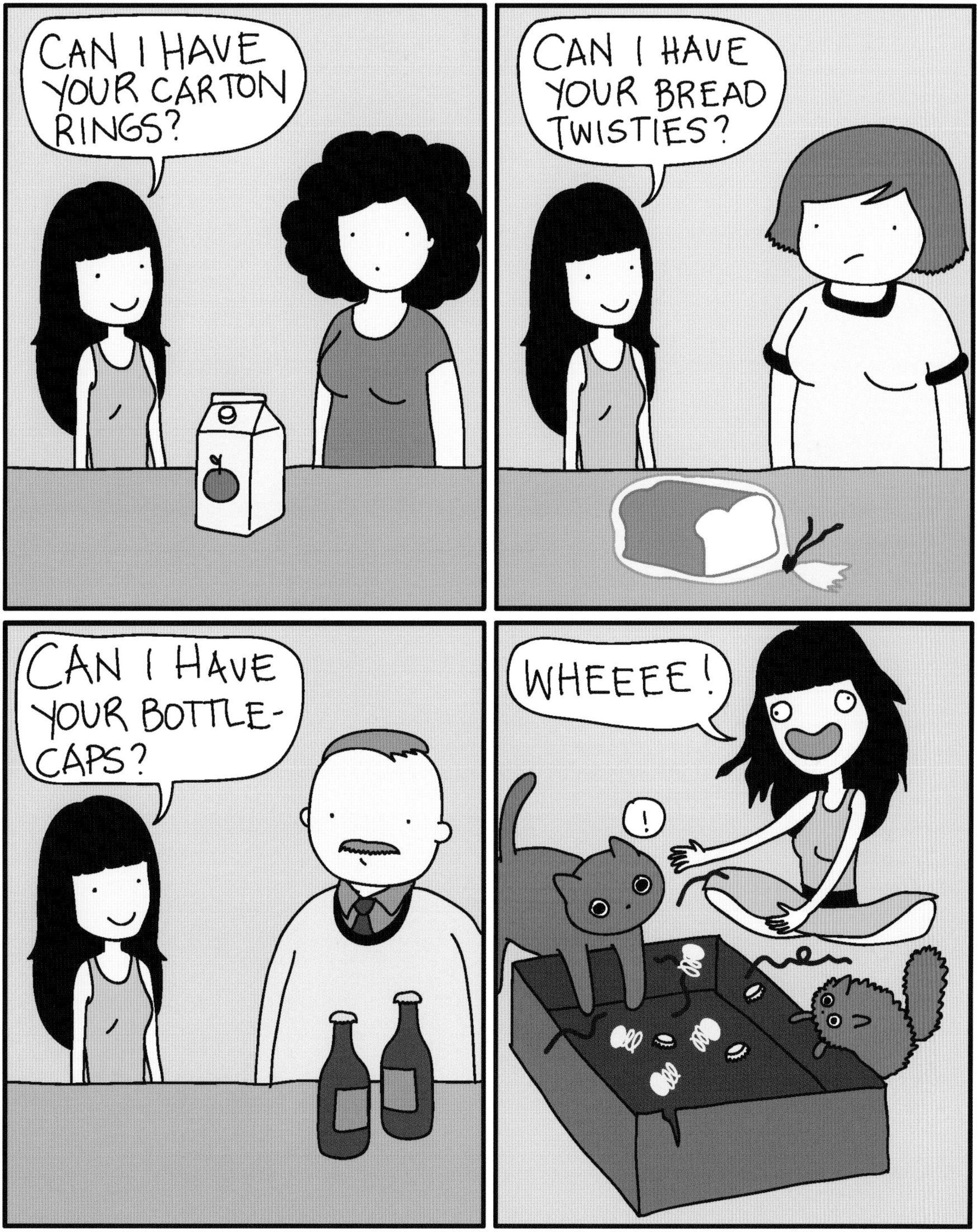
CAN I HAVE YOUR CARTON RINGS?
CAN I HAVE YOUR BREAD TWISTIES?
CAN I HAVE YOUR BOTTLE-CAPS?
WHEEEE!
!

THINGS THAT STRESS ME OUT

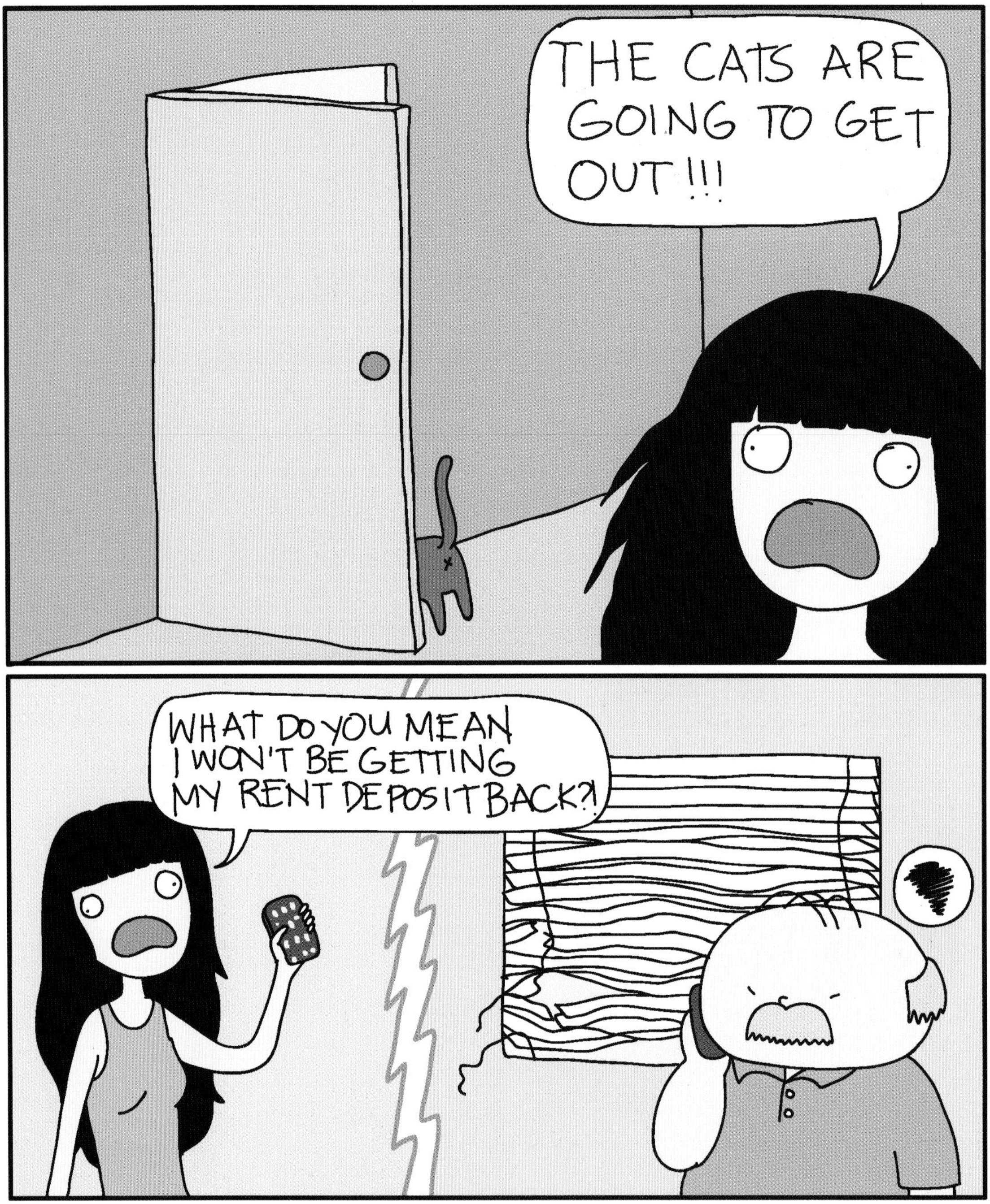
THE CATS ARE GOING TO GET OUT!!!
WHAT DO YOU MEAN I WON'T BE GETTING MY RENT DEPOSIT BACK?!

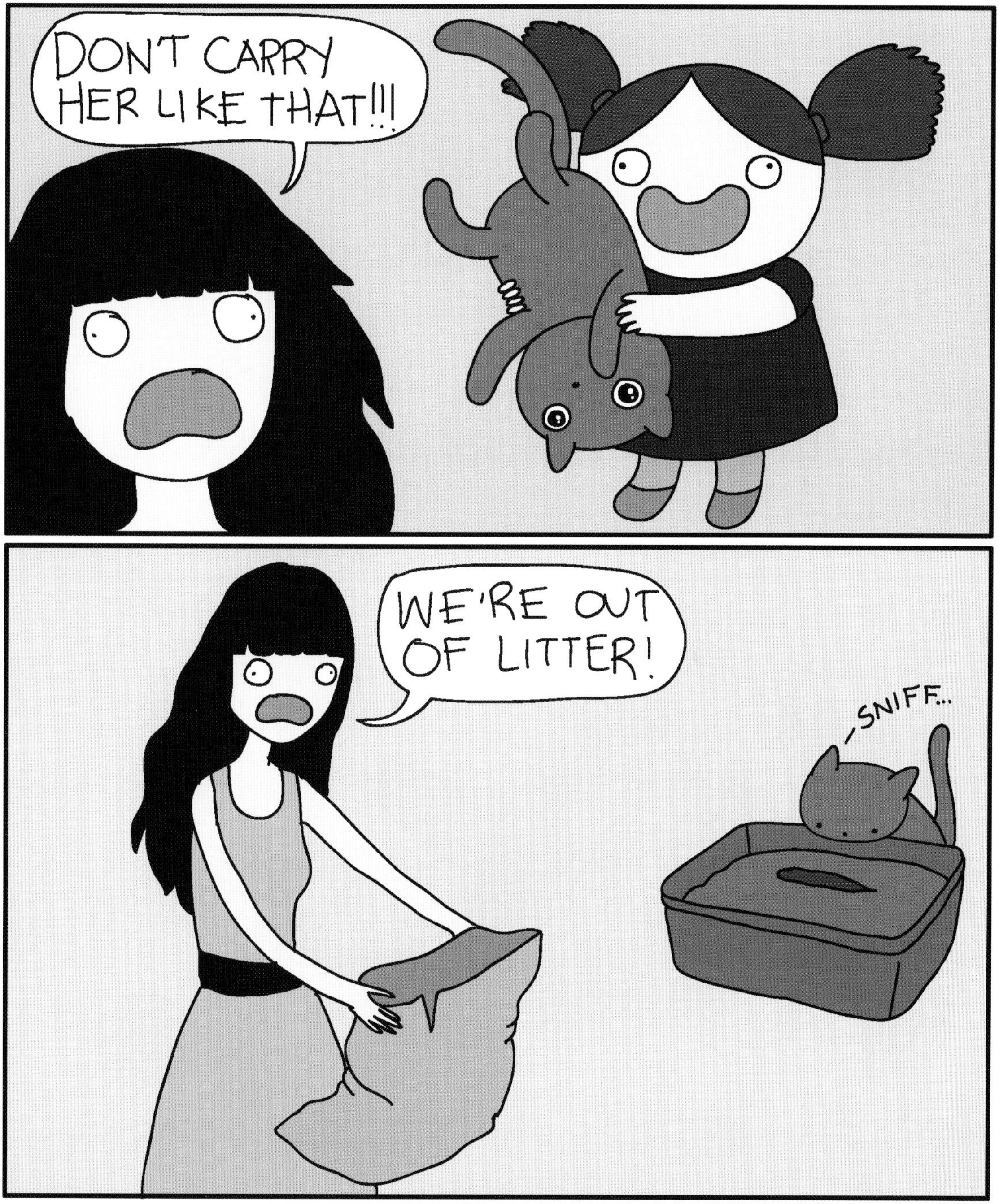
DON'T CARRY HER LIKE THAT!!!
WE'RE OUT OF LITTER!
SNIFF...

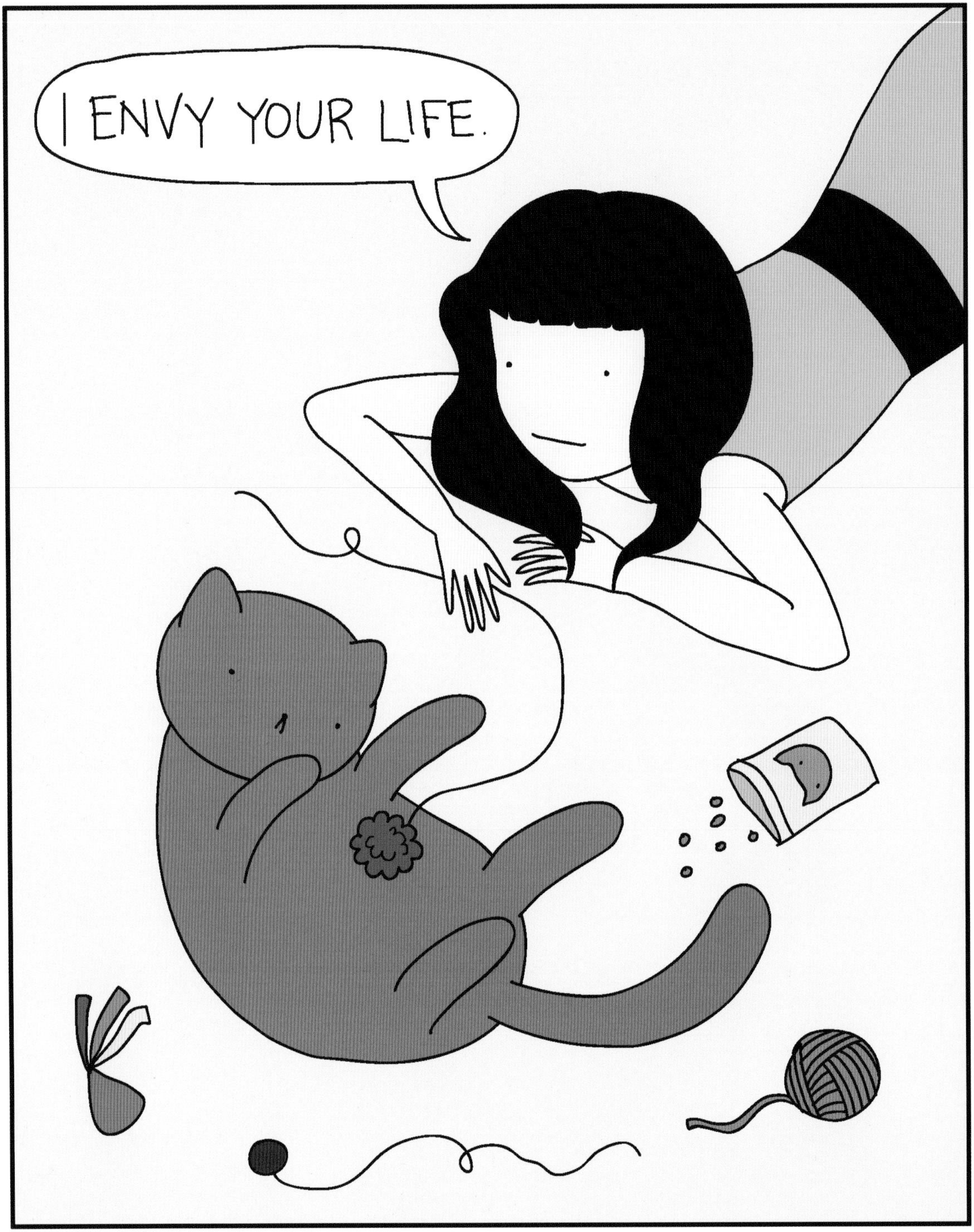
I ENVY YOUR LIFE.

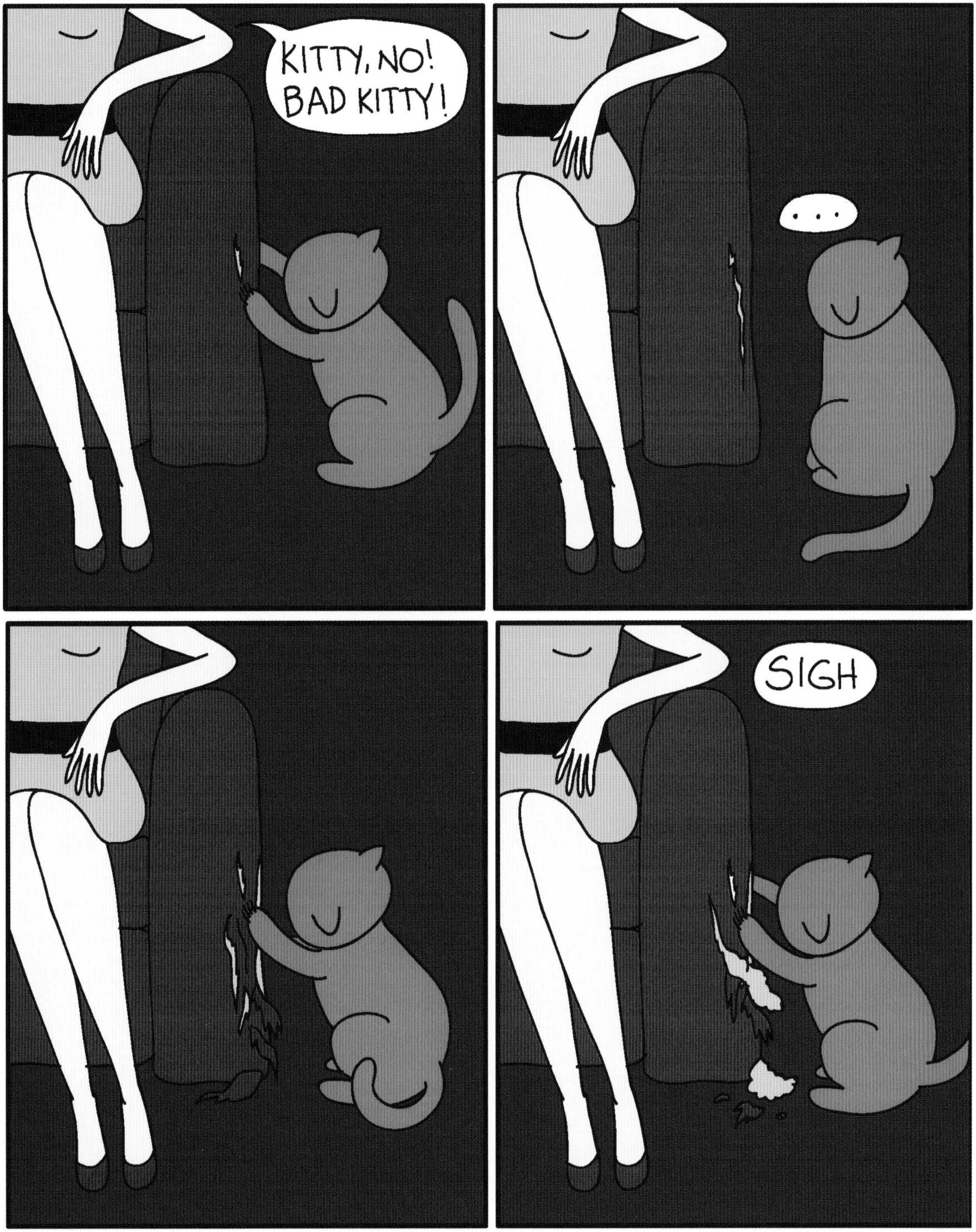
KITTY, NO! BAD KITTY!
...
SIGH

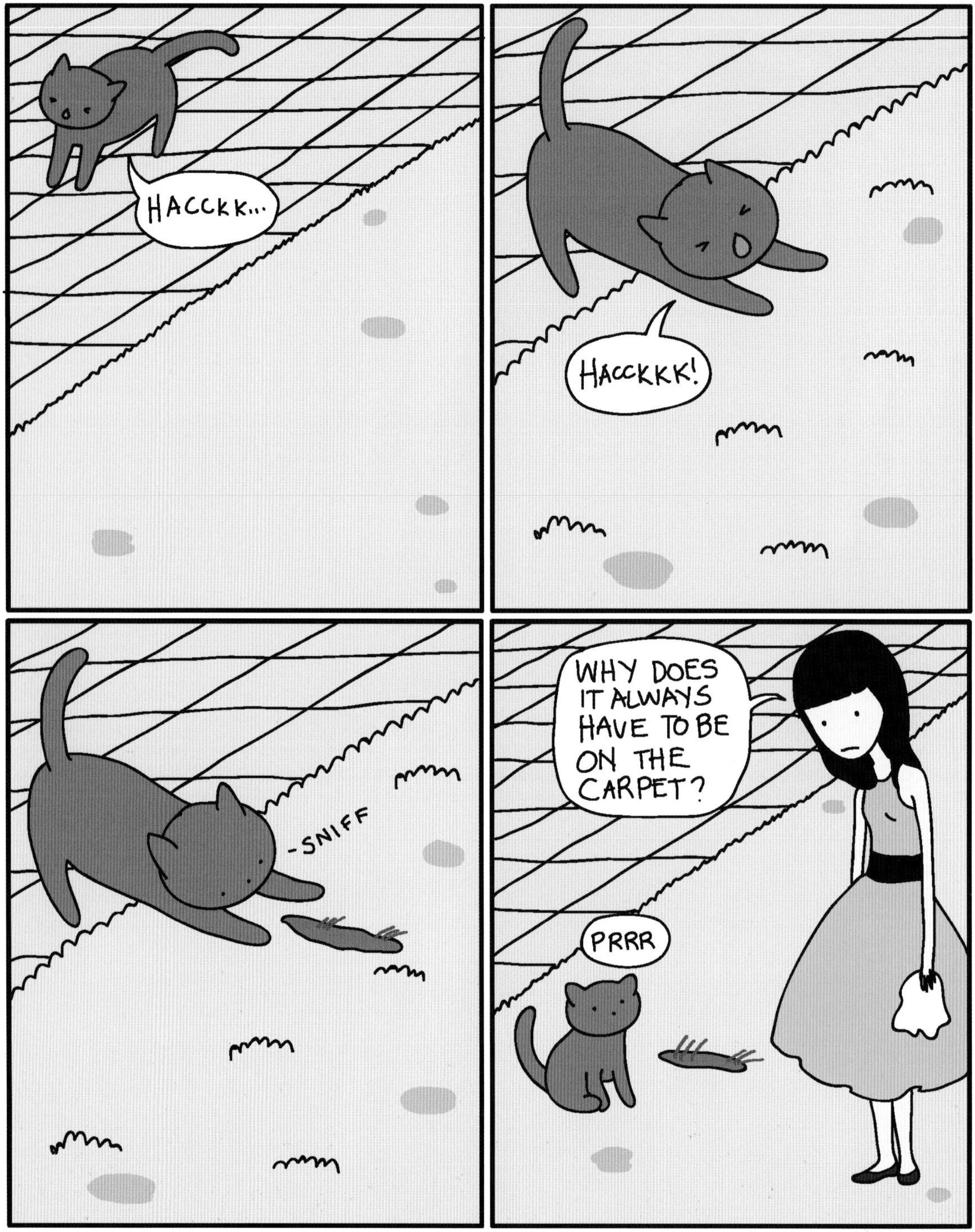
HACCKK...
HACCKKK!
-SNIFF
WHY DOES IT ALWAYS HAVE TO BE ON THE CARPET?
PRRR

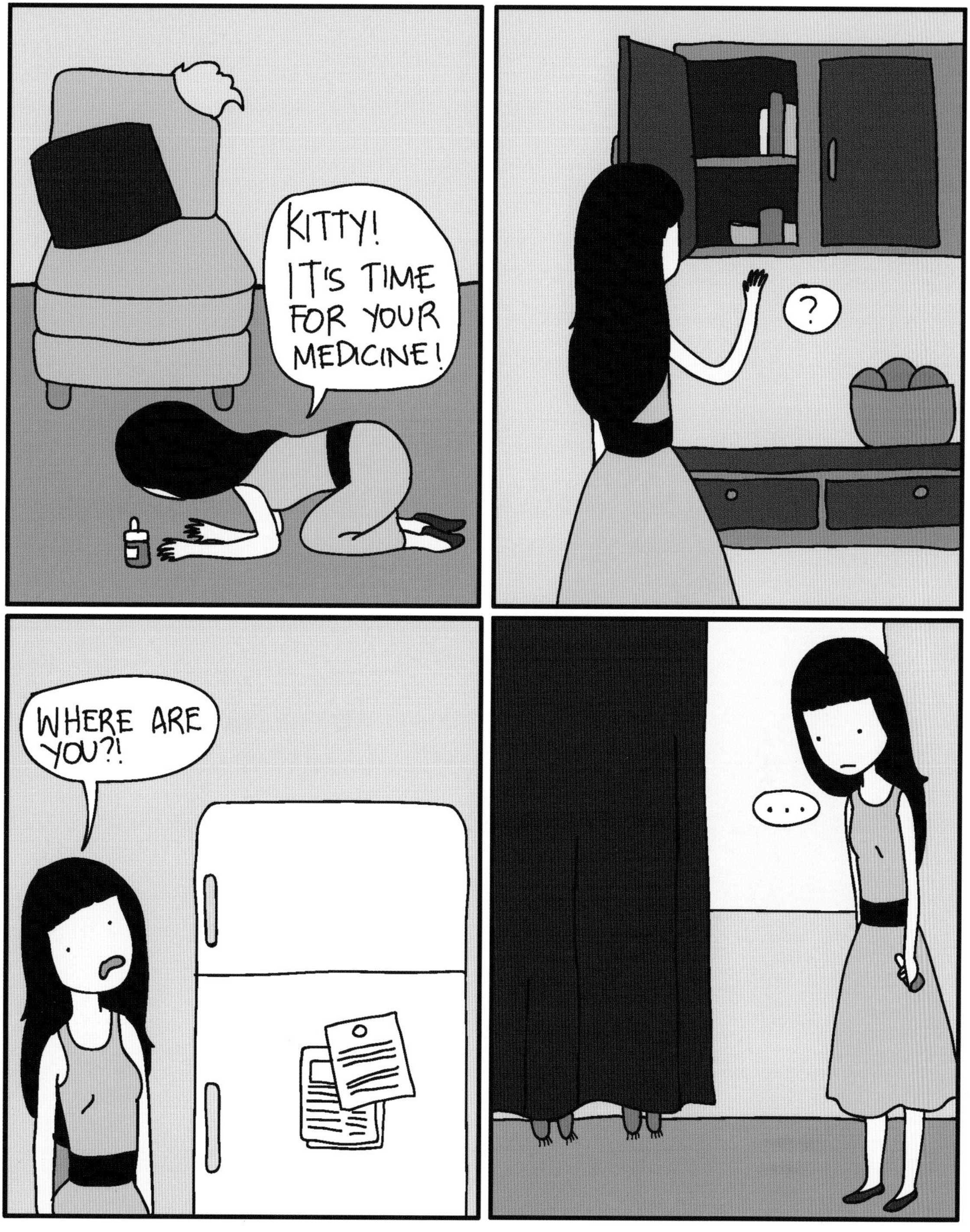
KITTY! IT'S TIME FOR YOUR MEDICINE!
?
WHERE ARE YOU?!
...

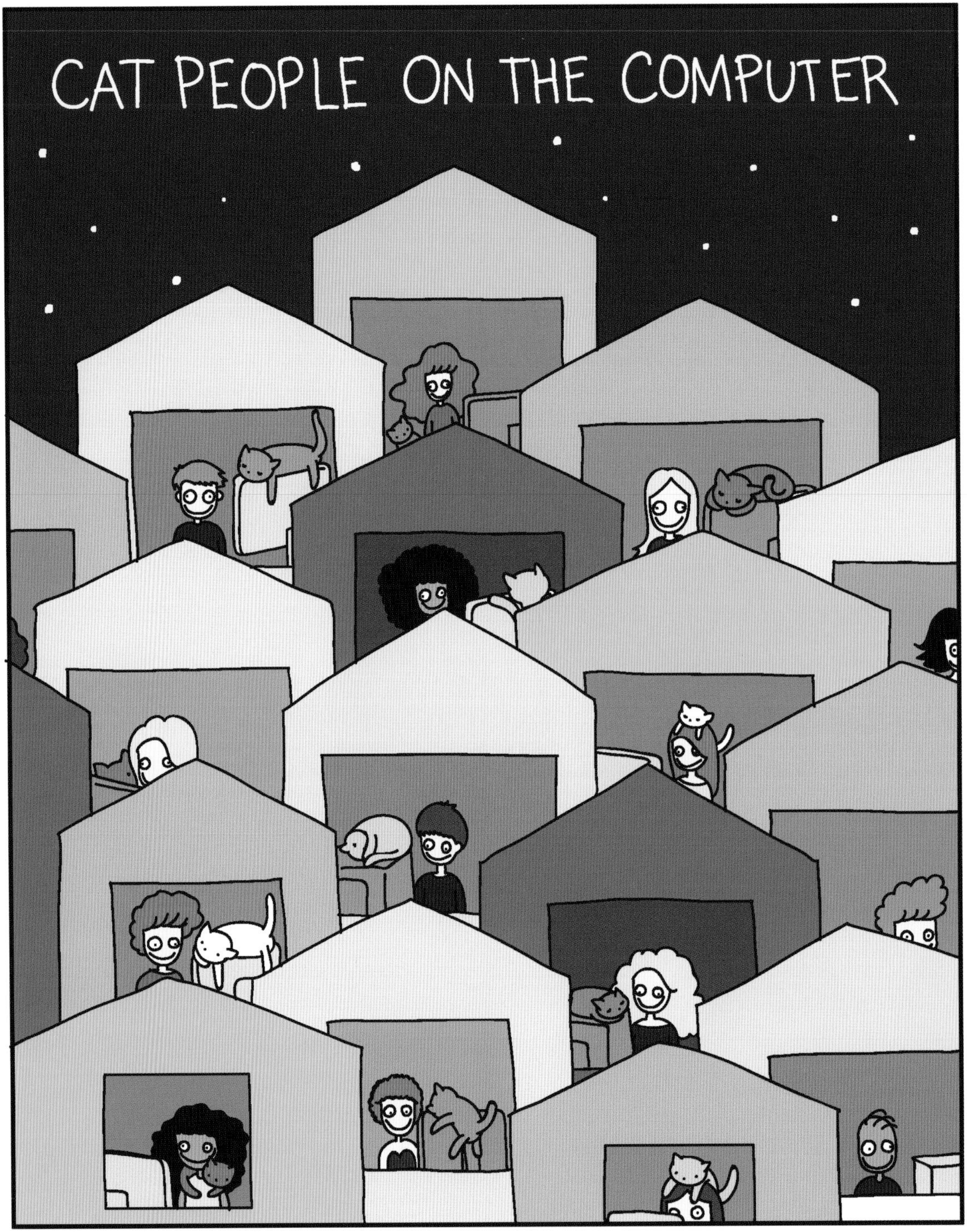
CAT PEOPLE ON THE COMPUTER

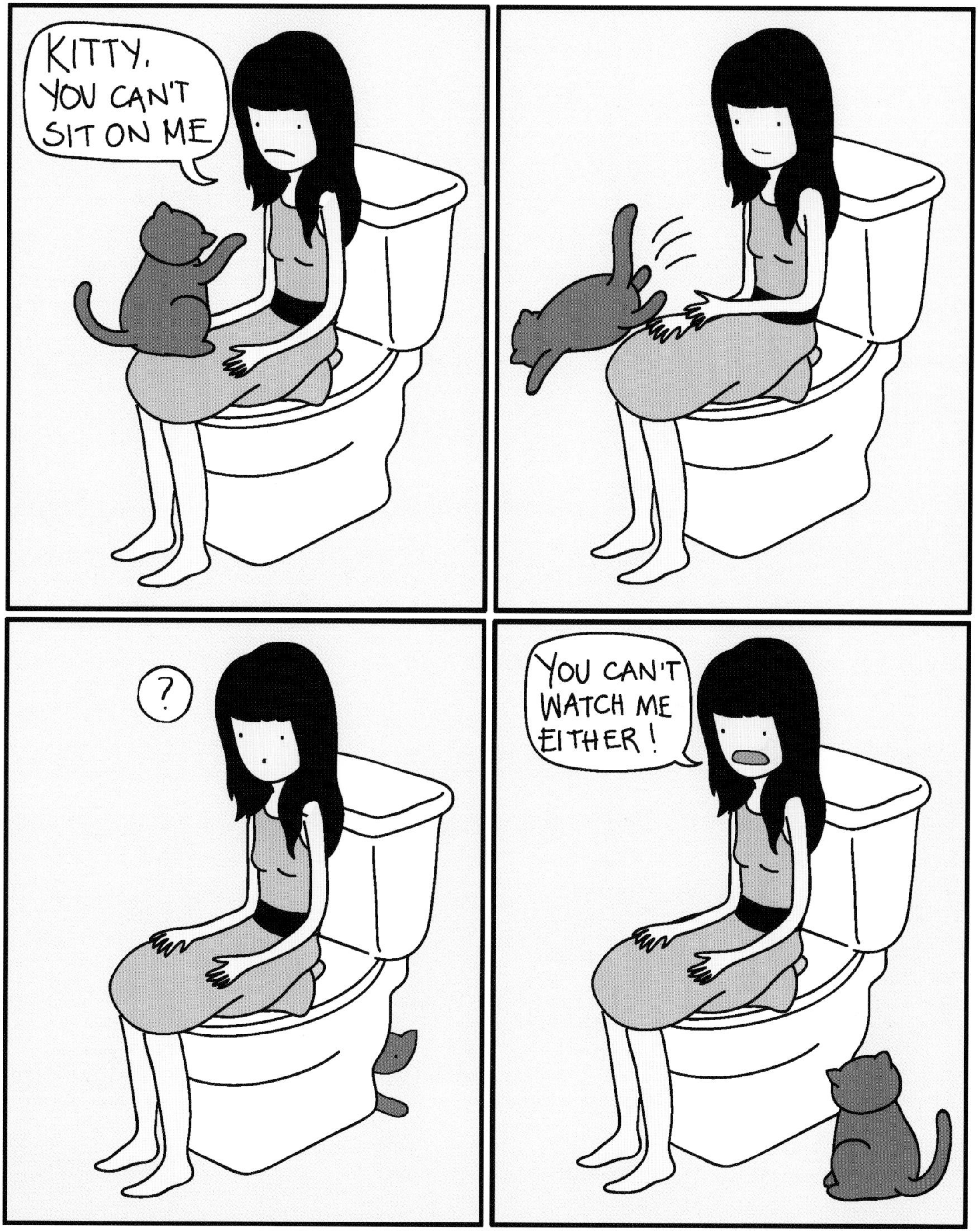
KITTY, YOU CAN'T SIT ON ME
?
YOU CAN'T WATCH ME EITHER!

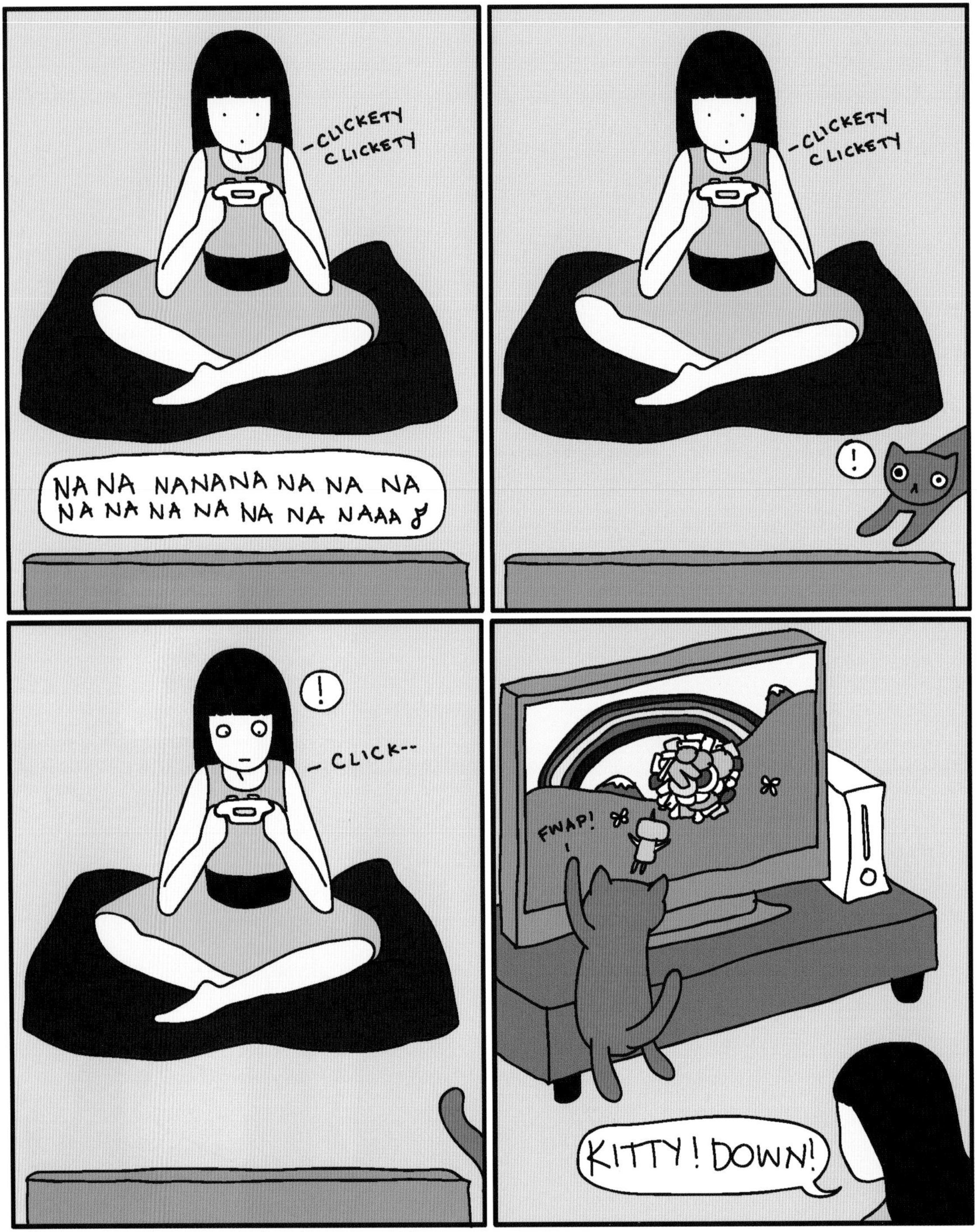
-CLICKETY CLICKETY
NA NA NANANA NA NA NA NA NA NA NA NA NA NAAA
-CLICKETY CLICKETY
!
!
-CLICK--
FWAP!
KITTY! DOWN!

HOW TO TELL WHEN YOUR CAT IS CRAZY

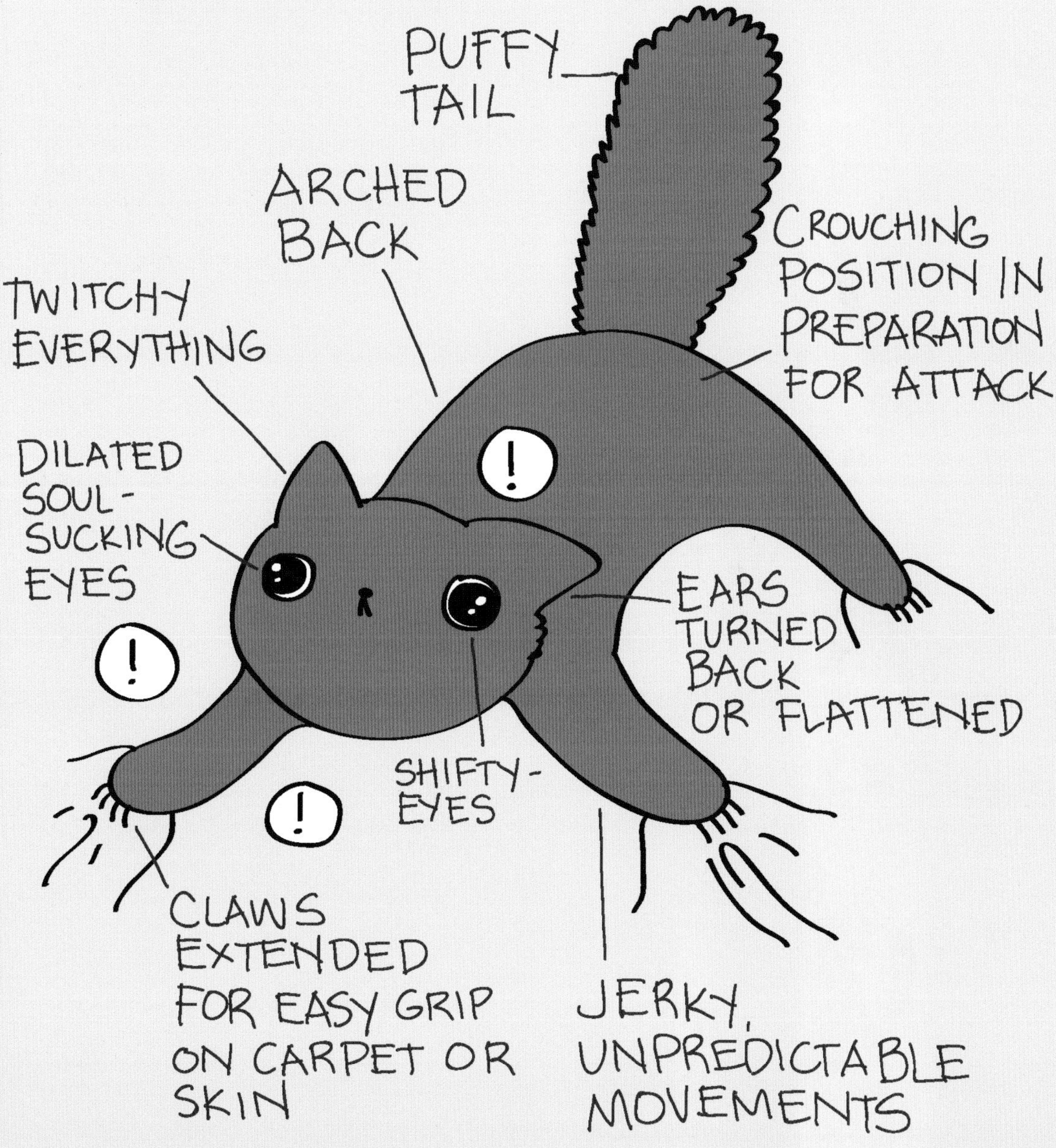
PUFFY TAIL
ARCHED BACK
CROUCHING POSITION IN PREPARATION FOR ATTACK
TWITCHY EVERYTHING
DILATED SOUL-SUCKING EYES
!
!
!
EARS TURNED BACK OR FLATTENED
SHIFTY-EYES
CLAWS EXTENDED FOR EASY GRIP ON CARPET OR SKIN
JERKY, UNPREDICTABLE MOVEMENTS

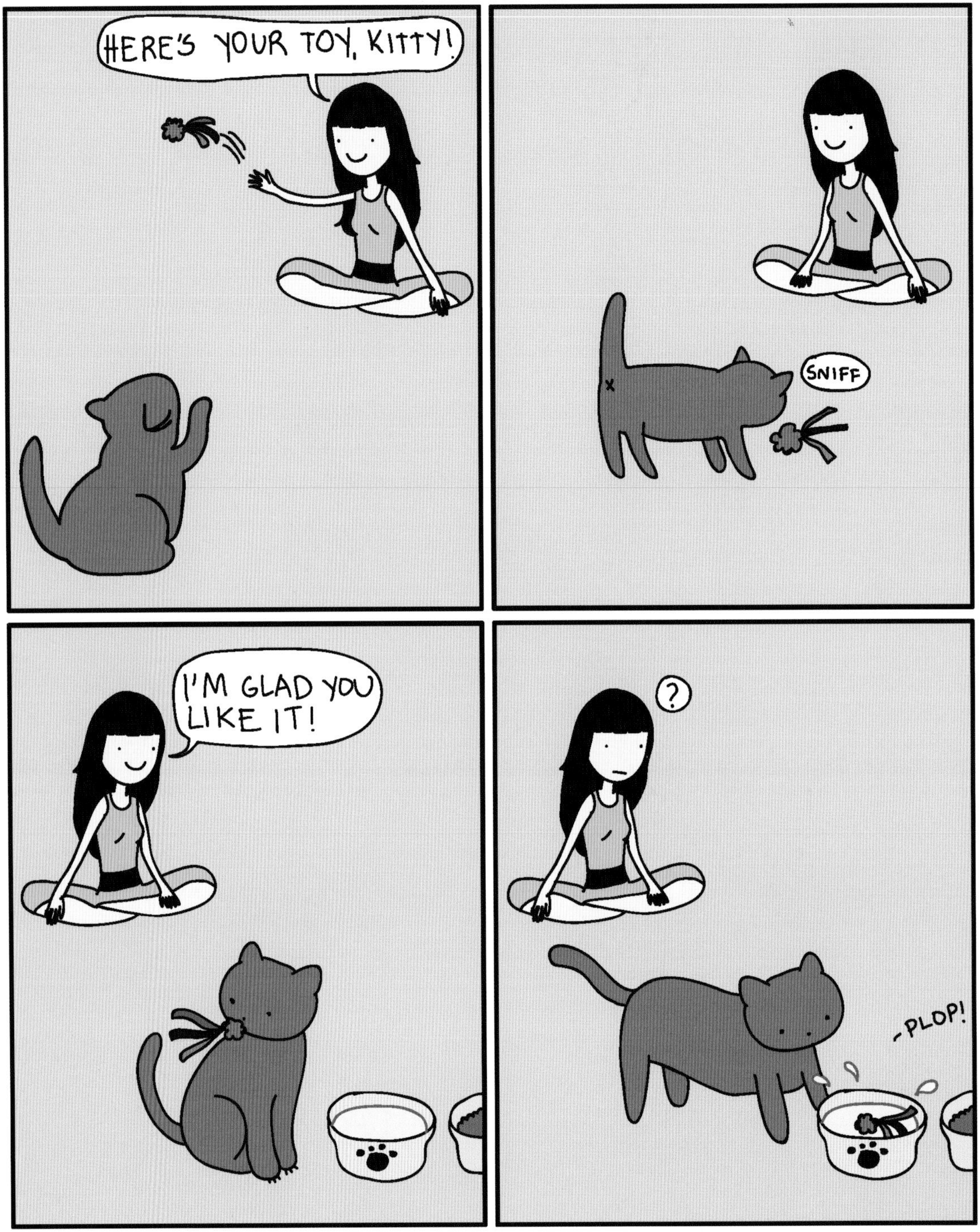
HERE'S YOUR TOY, KITTY!
SNIFF
I'M GLAD YOU LIKE IT!
?
PLOP!

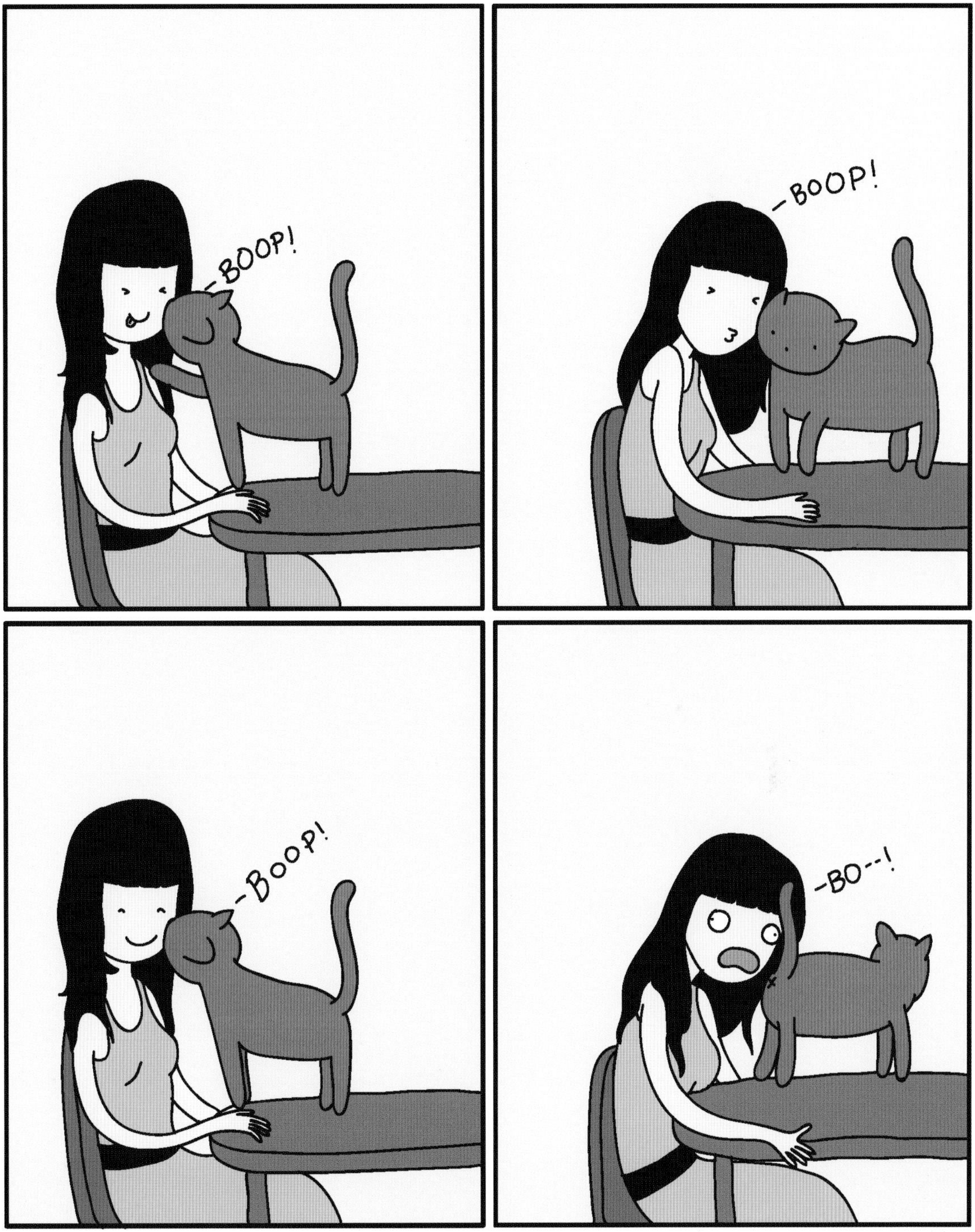
-BOOP!
-BOOP!
-BOOP!
-BO--!

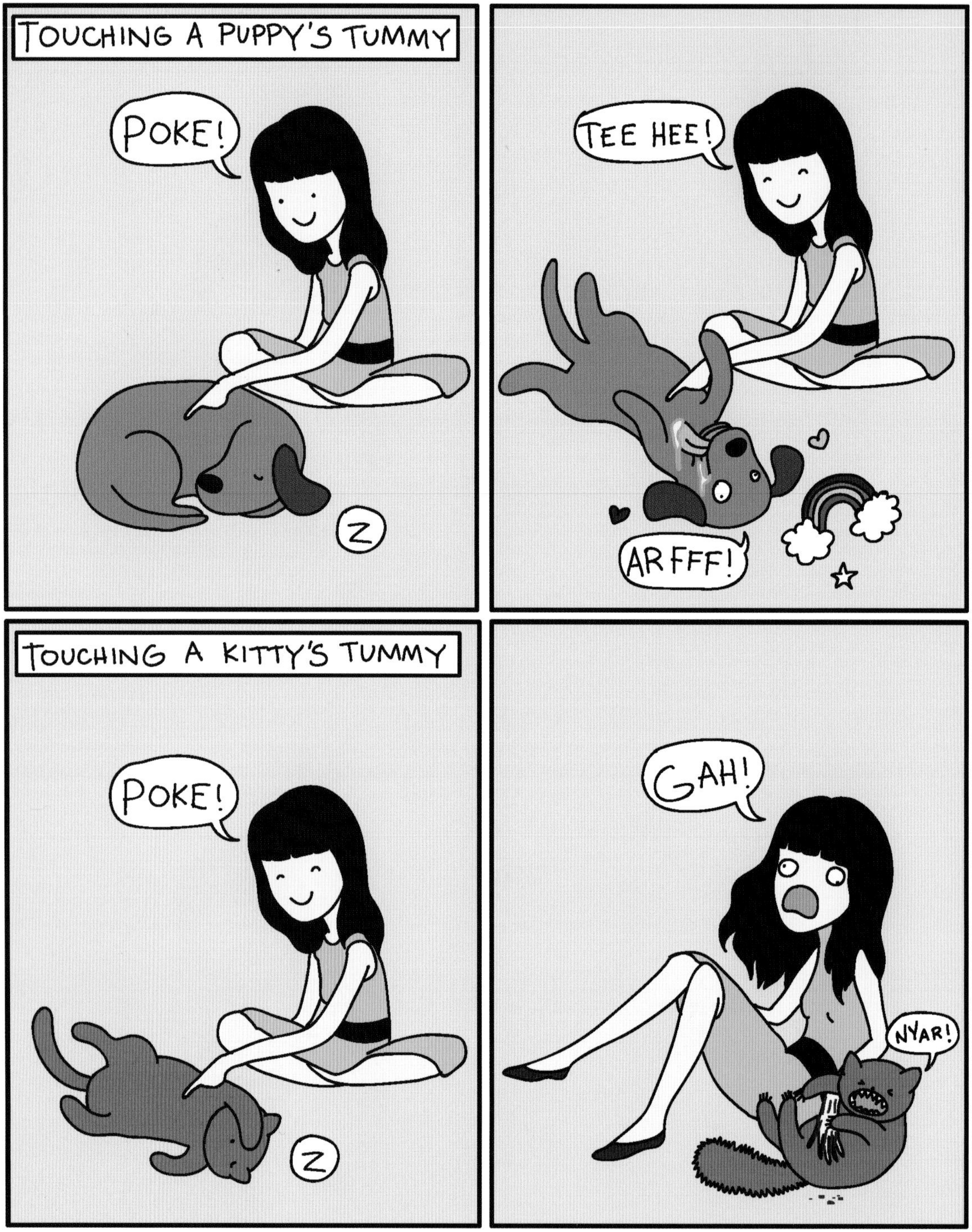
TOUCHING A PUPPY'S TUMMY
POKE!
Z
TEE HEE!
ARFFF!
TOUCHING A KITTY'S TUMMY
POKE!
Z
GAH!
NYAR!

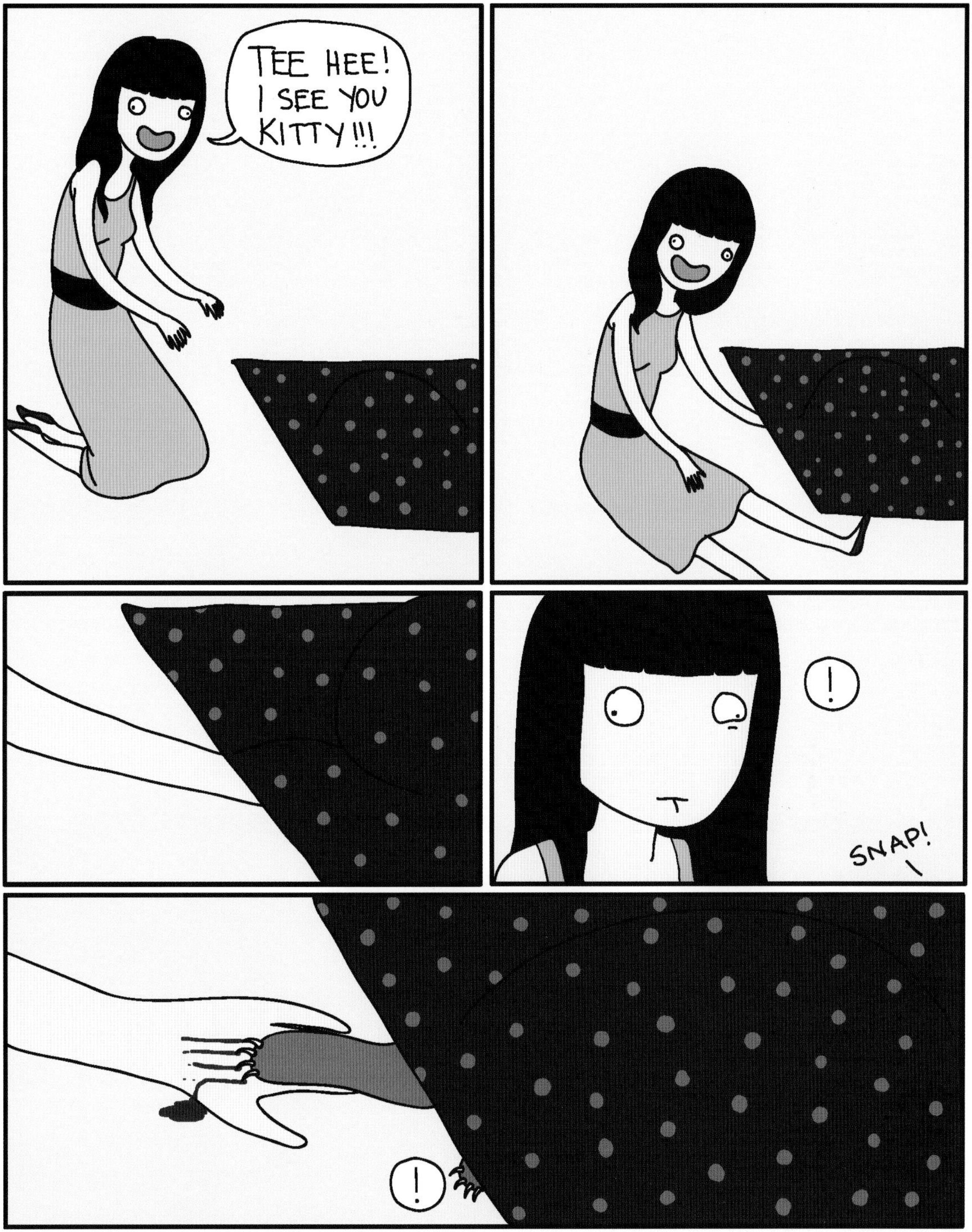
TEE HEE! I SEE YOU KITTY!!!
!
SNAP!
!

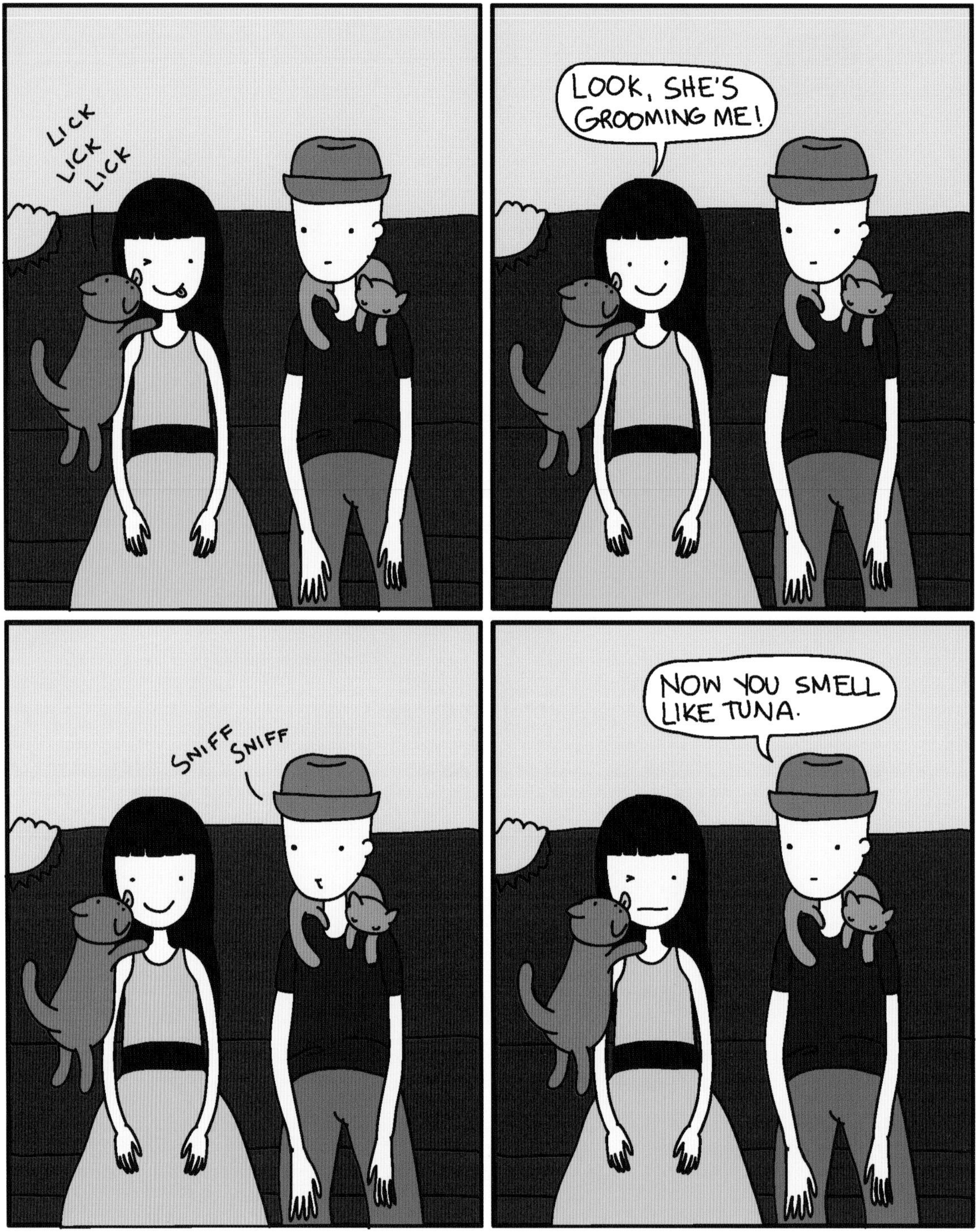
LICK LICK LICK
LOOK, SHE'S GROOMING ME!
SNIFF SNIFF
NOW YOU SMELL LIKE TUNA.

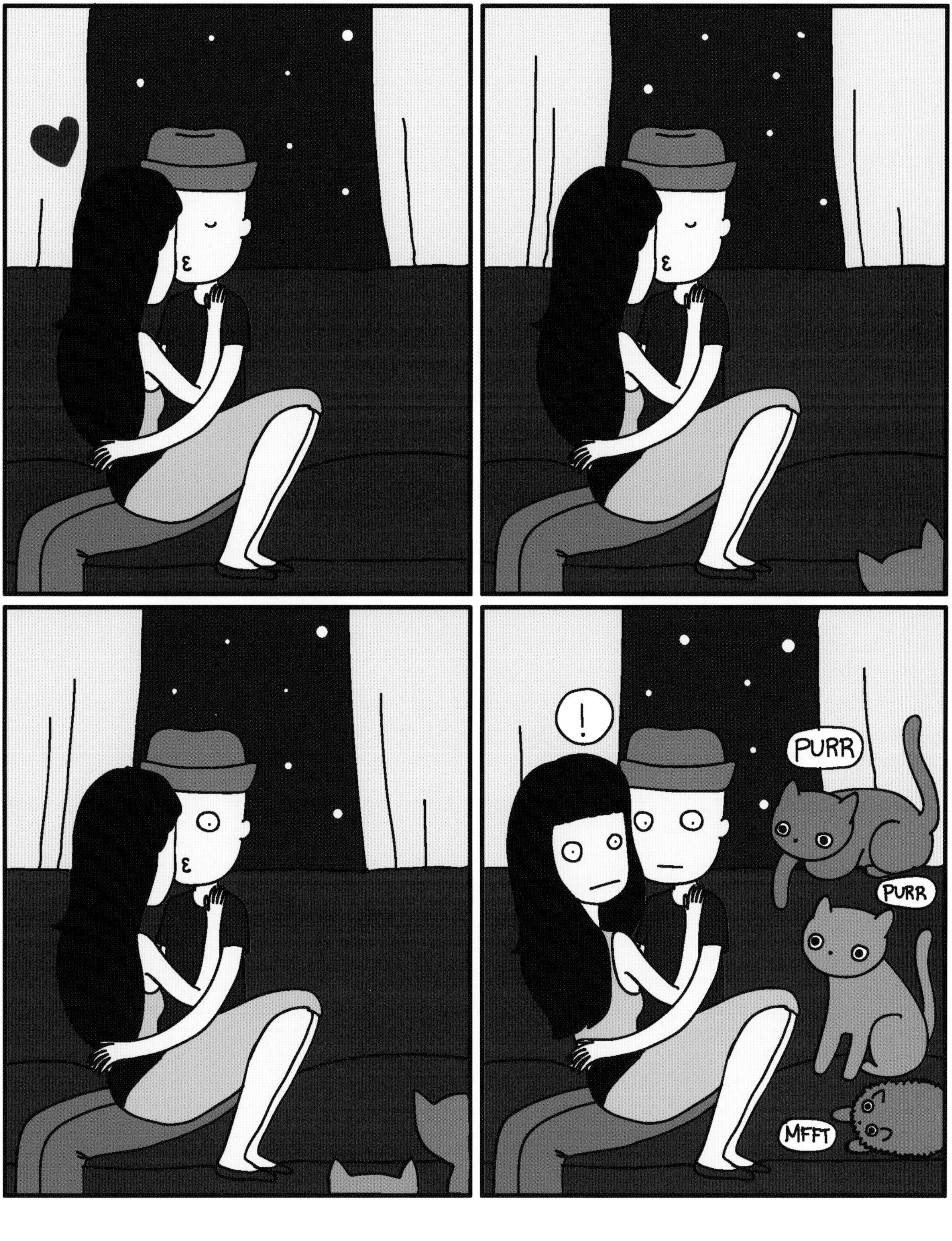
!
PURR
PURR
MFFT

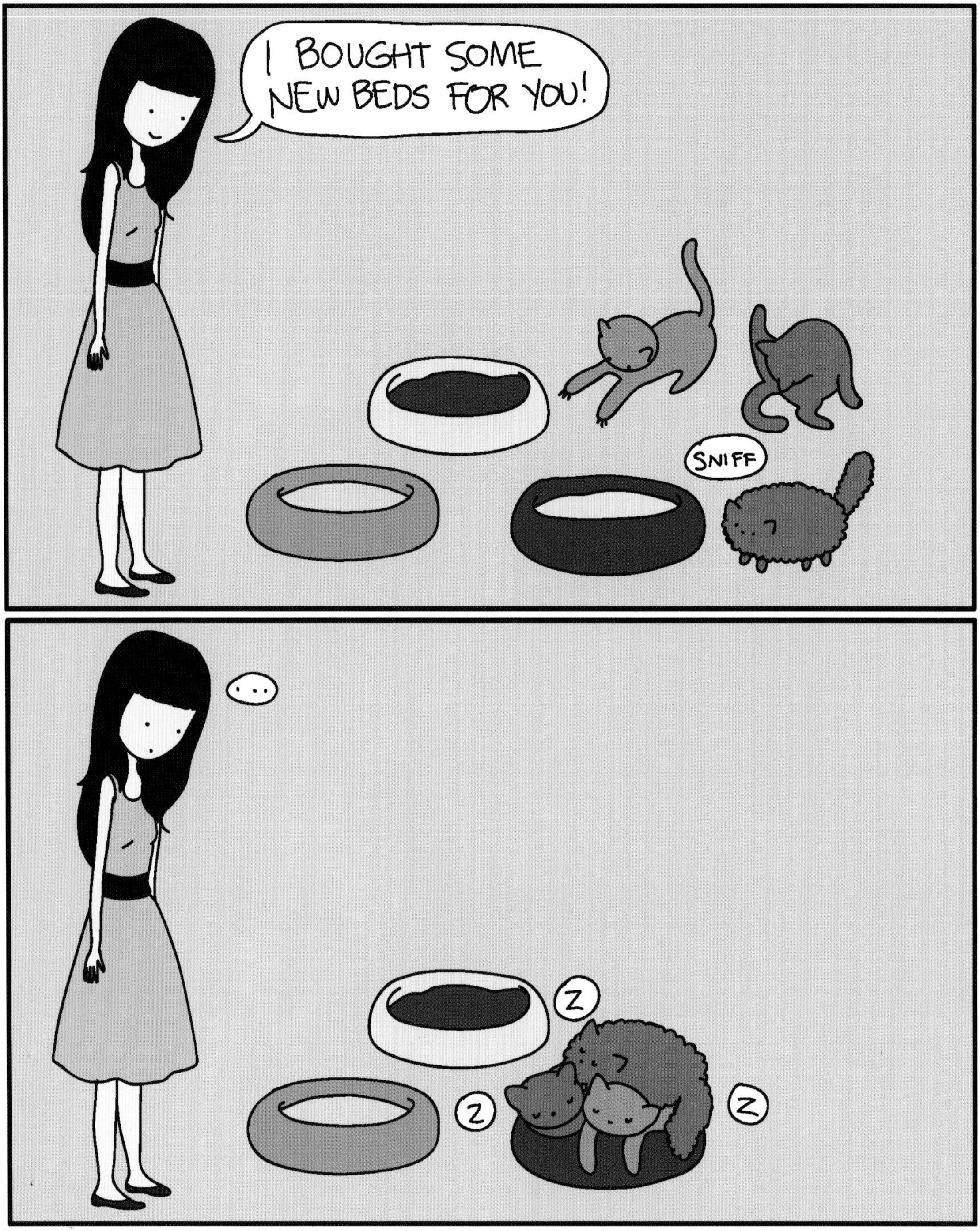
I BOUGHT SOME NEW BEDS FOR YOU!
SNIFF
...
Z
Z
Z

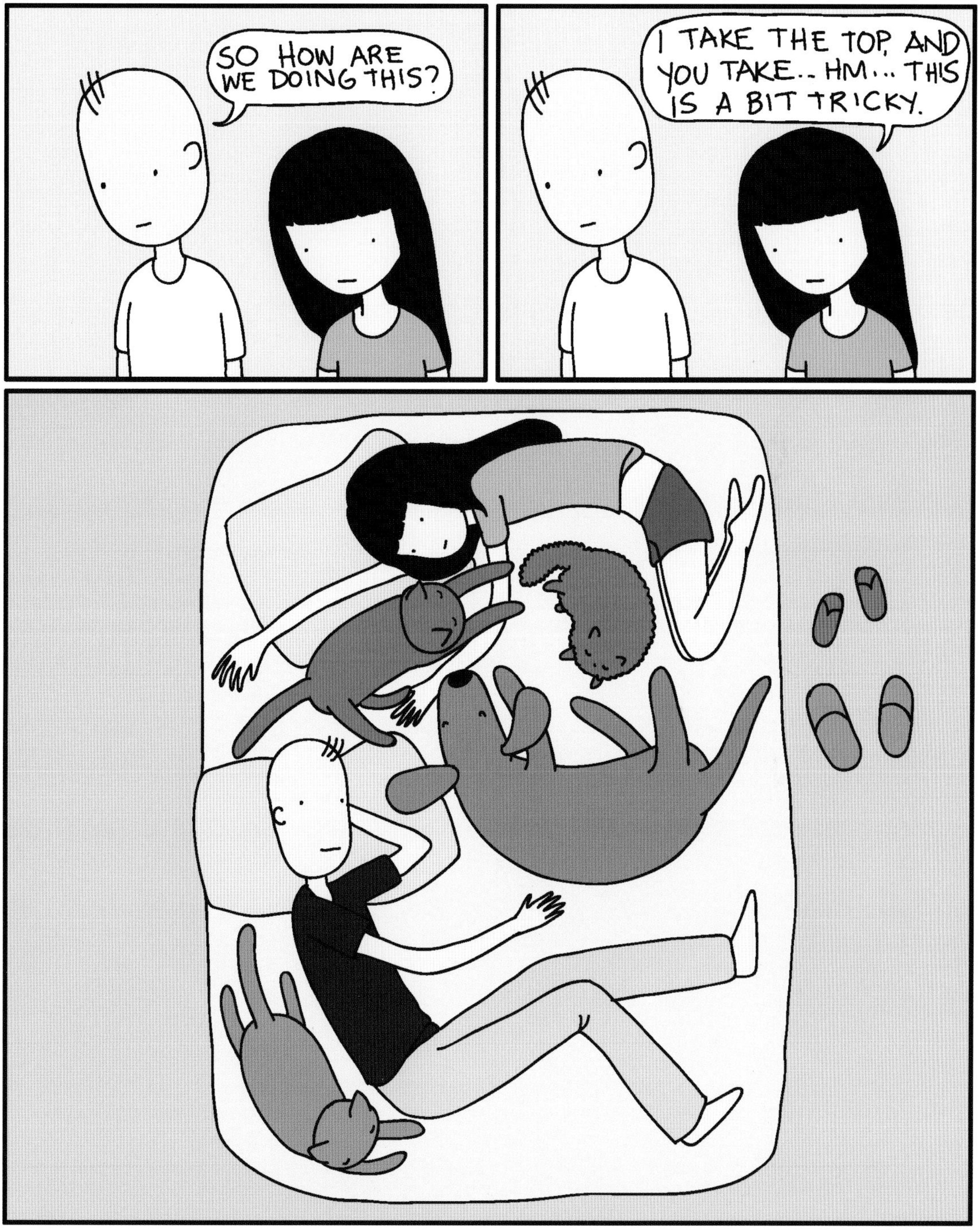
SO HOW ARE WE DOING THIS?
I TAKE THE TOP, AND YOU TAKE.. HM... THIS IS A BIT TRICKY.

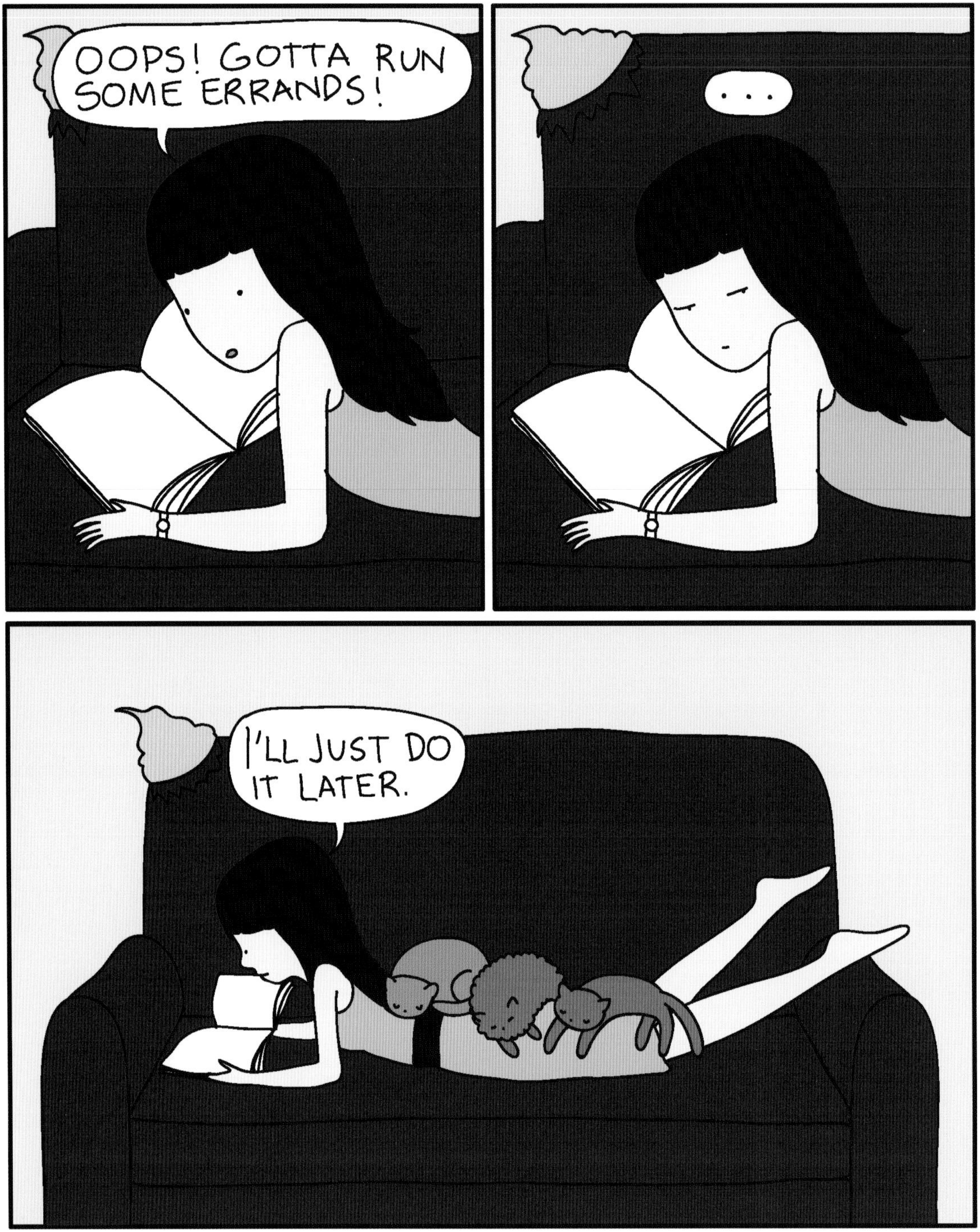
OOPS! GOTTA RUN SOME ERRANDS!
...
I'LL JUST DO IT LATER.

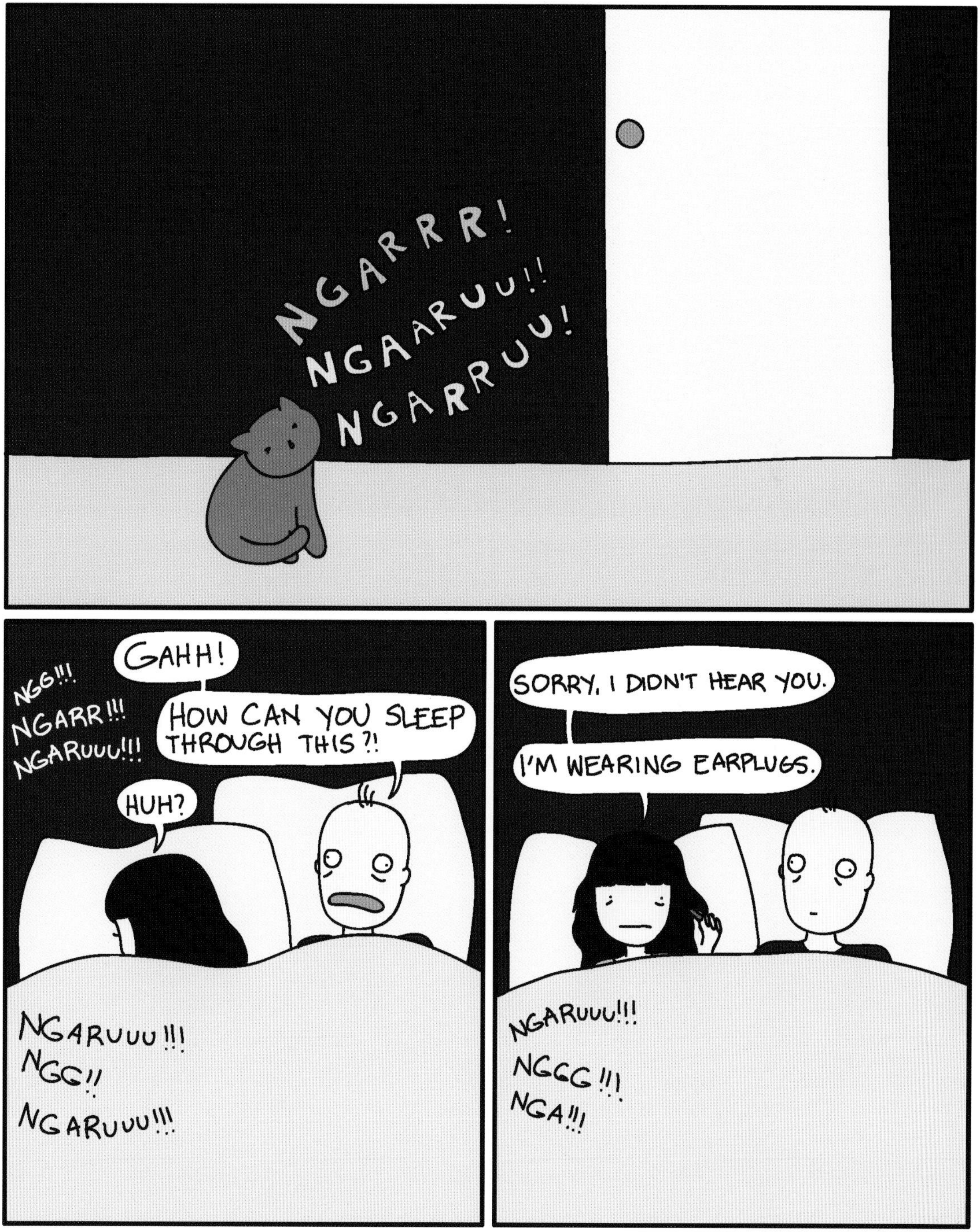

NGARRR!
NGAARUU!!
NGARRUU!
NGG!!!
NGARR!!!
NGARUUU!!!
GAHH!
HOW CAN YOU SLEEP THROUGH THIS?!
HUH?
NGARUUU!!!
NGG!!
NGARUUU!!!
SORRY, I DIDN'T HEAR YOU.
I'M WEARING EARPLUGS.
NGARUUU!!!
NGGG!!!
NGA!!!

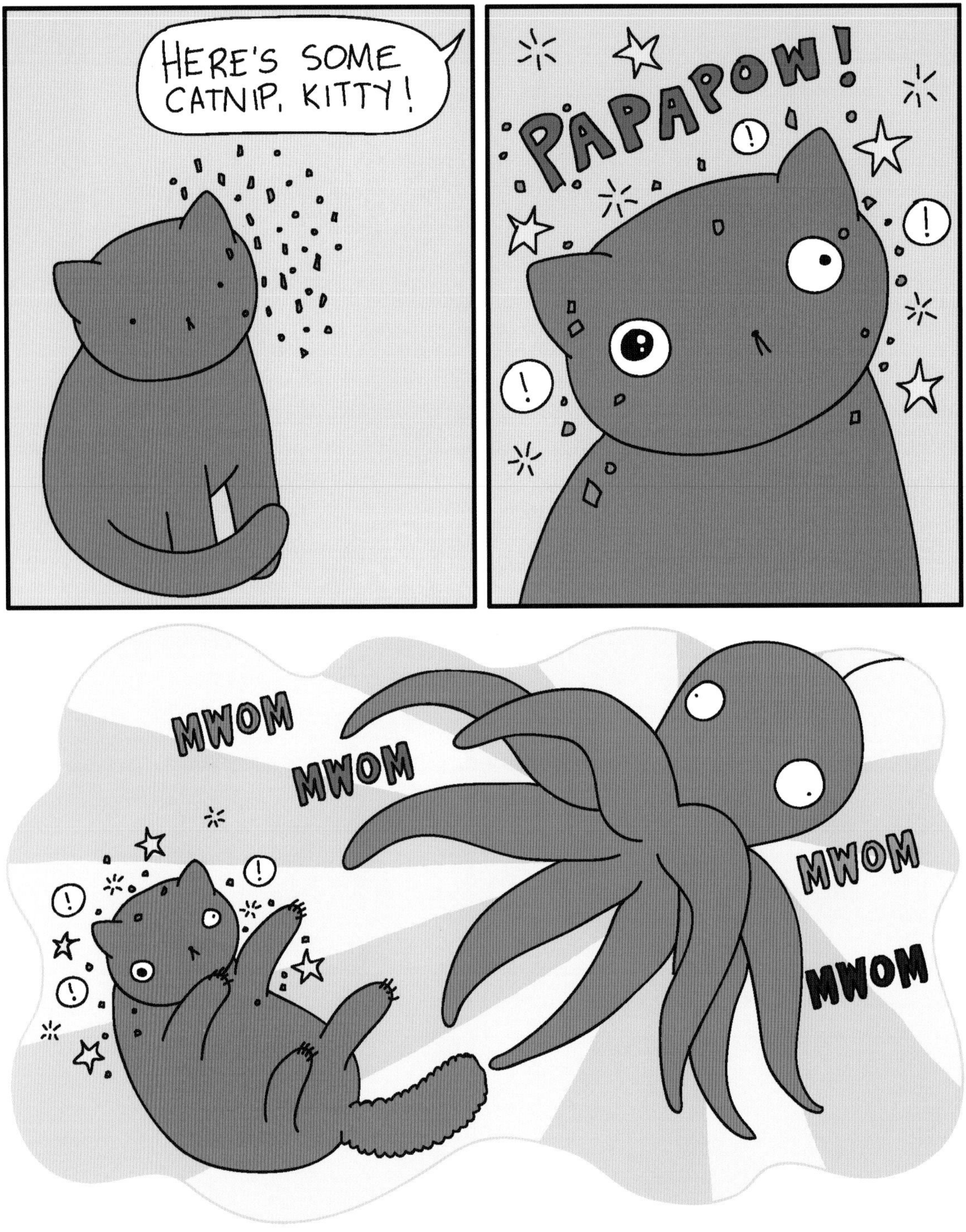
HERE'S SOME CATNIP, KITTY!
PAPAPOW!
!
!
!
!
!
!
MWOM
MWOM
MWOM
MWOM

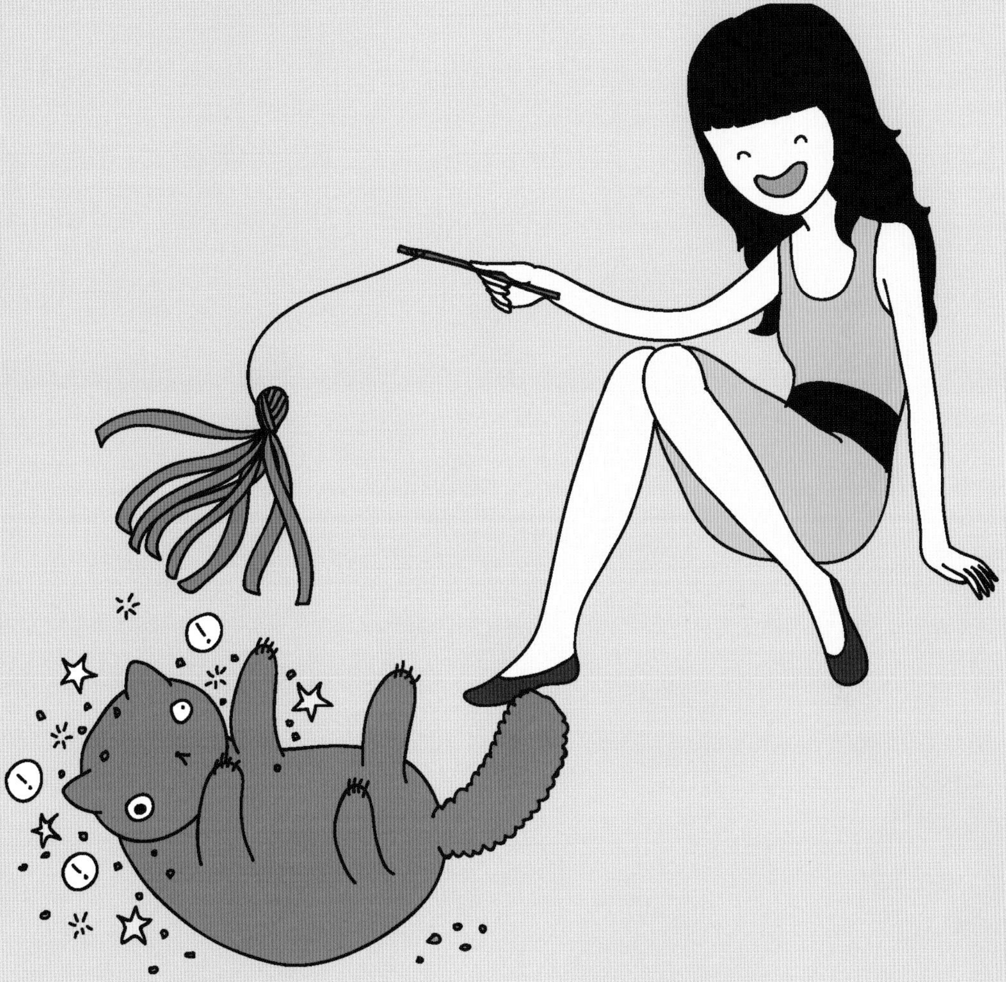

Cat Lady's Soul Mate

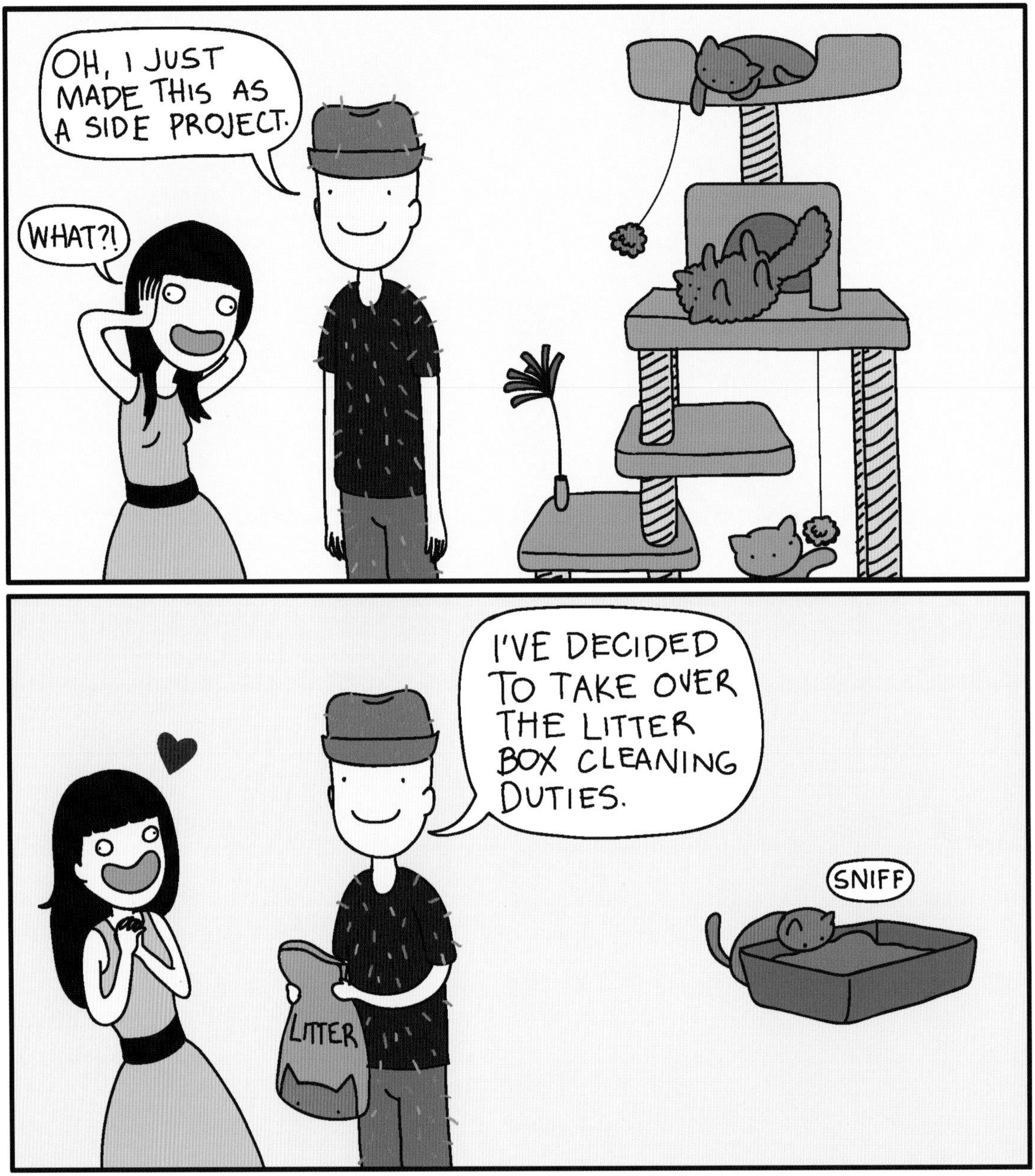

OH, I JUST MADE THIS AS A SIDE PROJECT.
WHAT?!
I'VE DECIDED TO TAKE OVER THE LITTER BOX CLEANING DUTIES.
LITTER
SNIFF

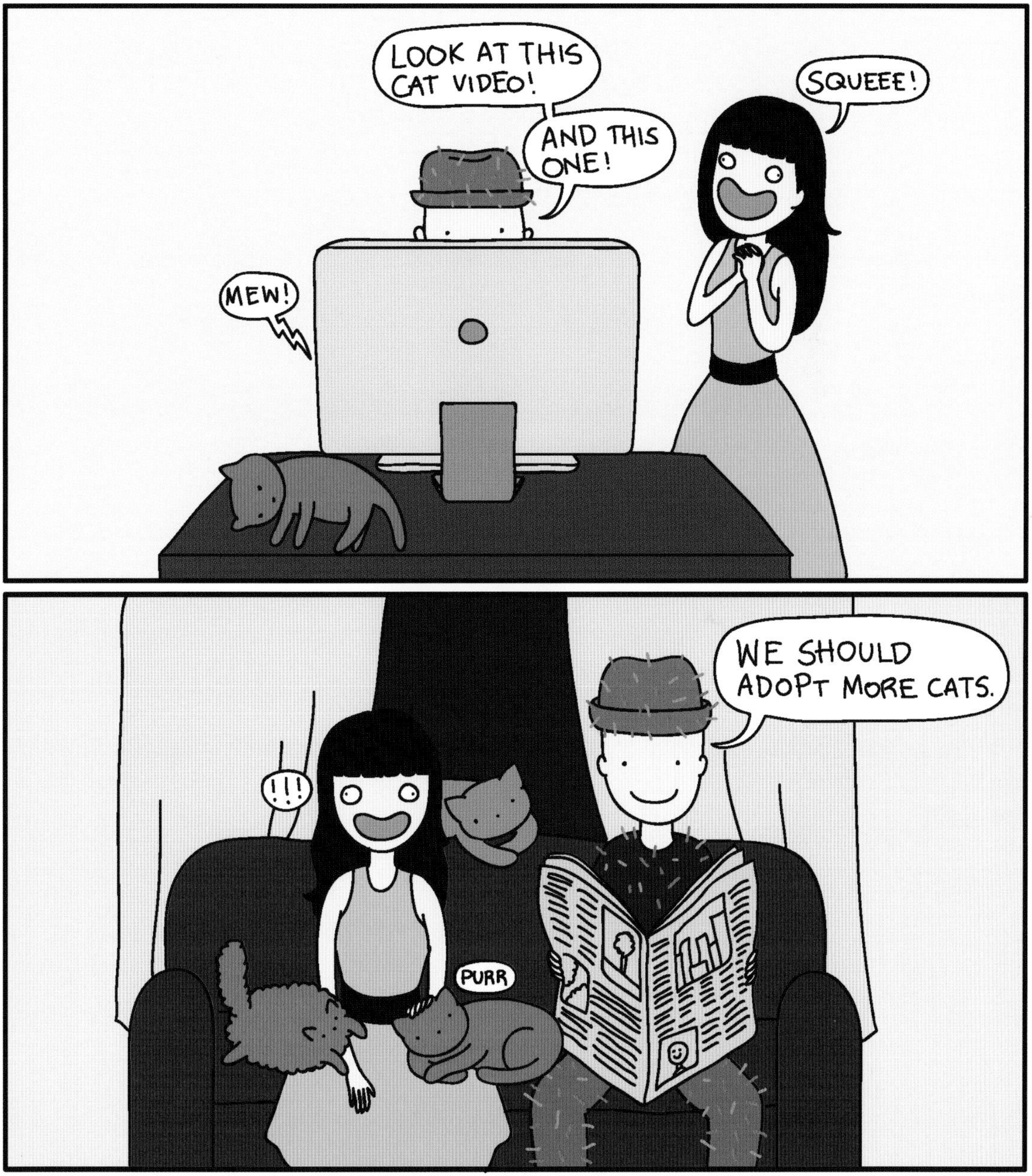
LOOK AT THIS CAT VIDEO!
AND THIS ONE!
SQUEEE!
MEW!
WE SHOULD ADOPT MORE CATS.
!!!
PURR

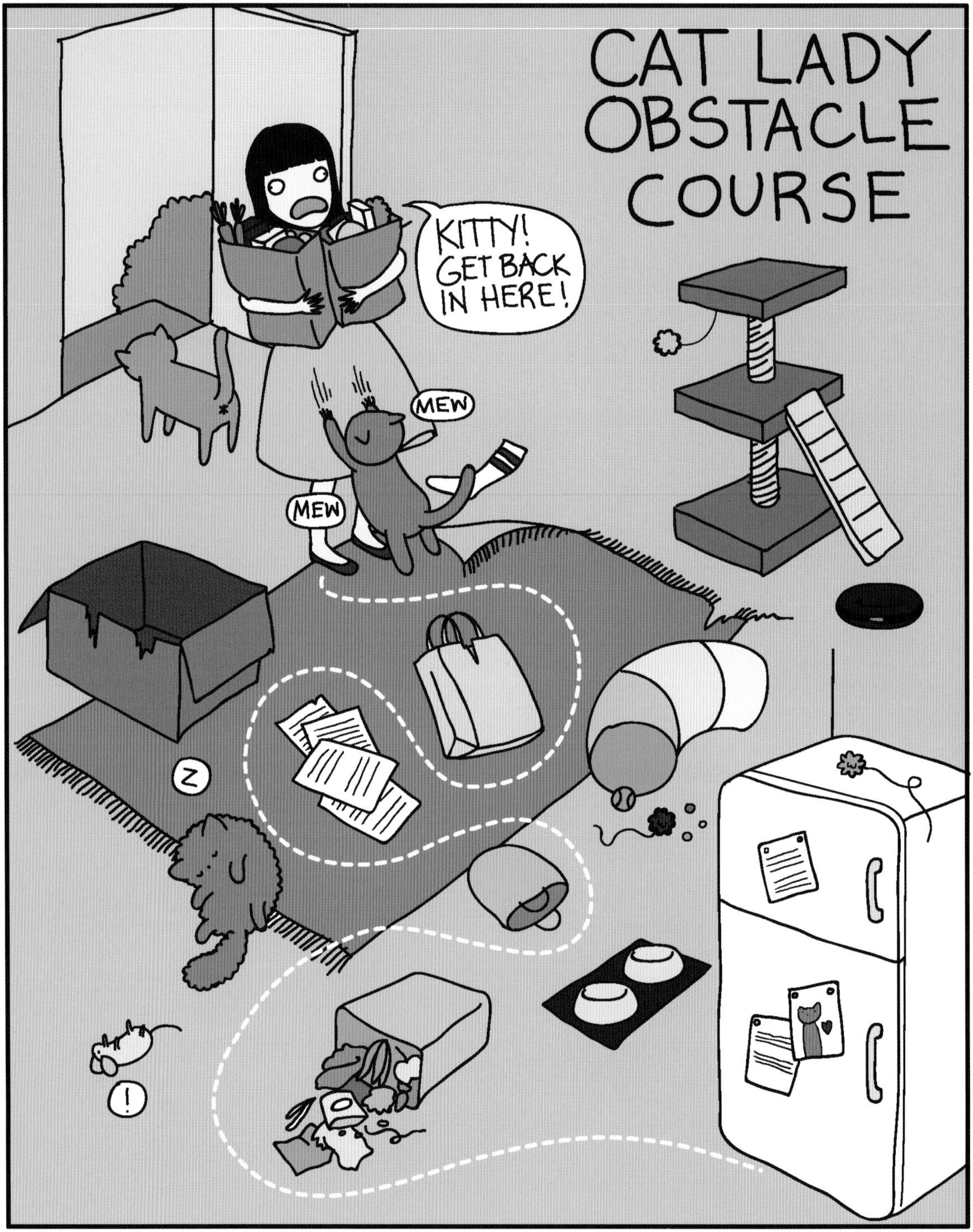
CAT LADY OBSTACLE COURSE
KITTY! GET BACK IN HERE!
MEW
MEW
Z
!

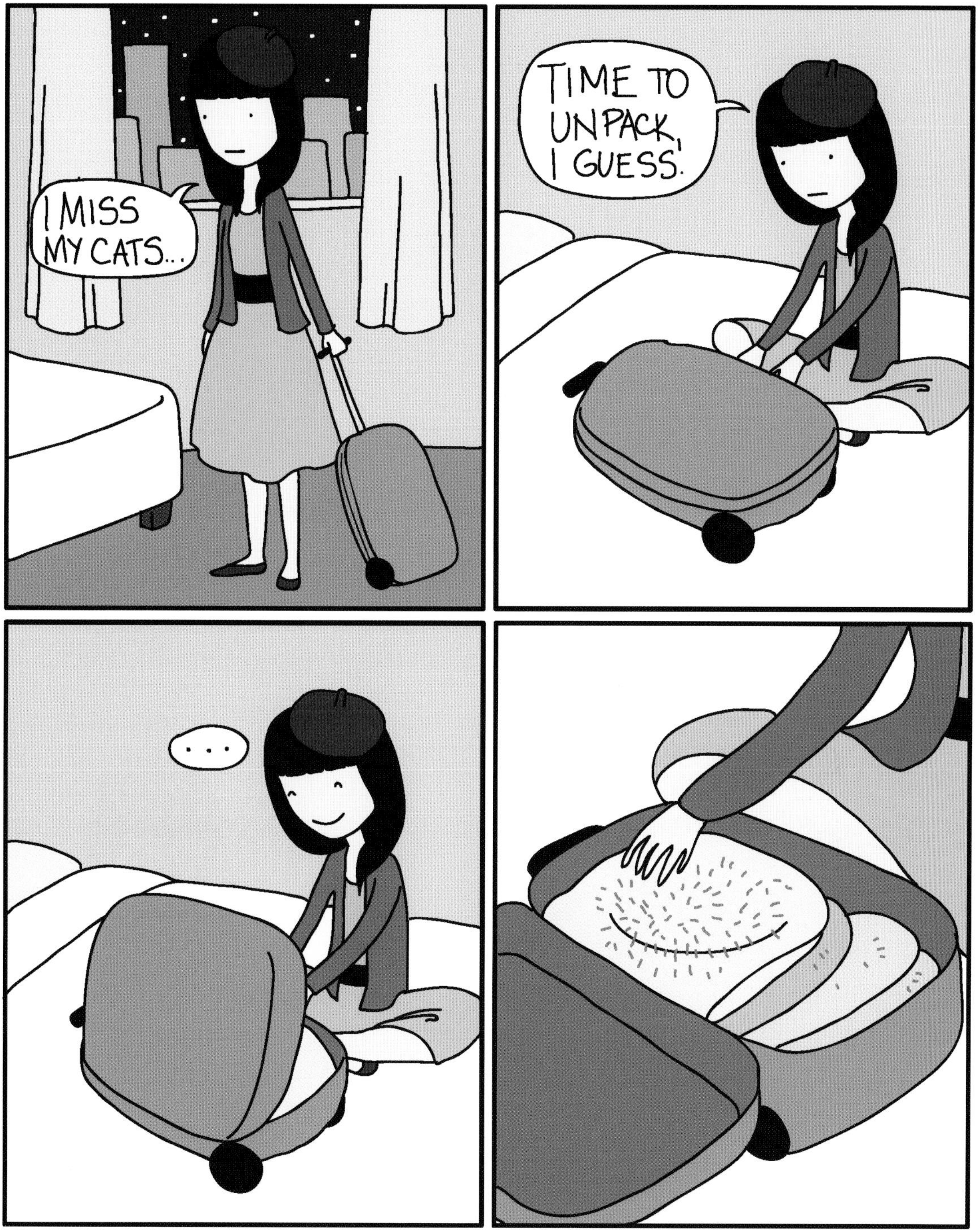
I MISS MY CATS...
TIME TO UNPACK, I GUESS.
...

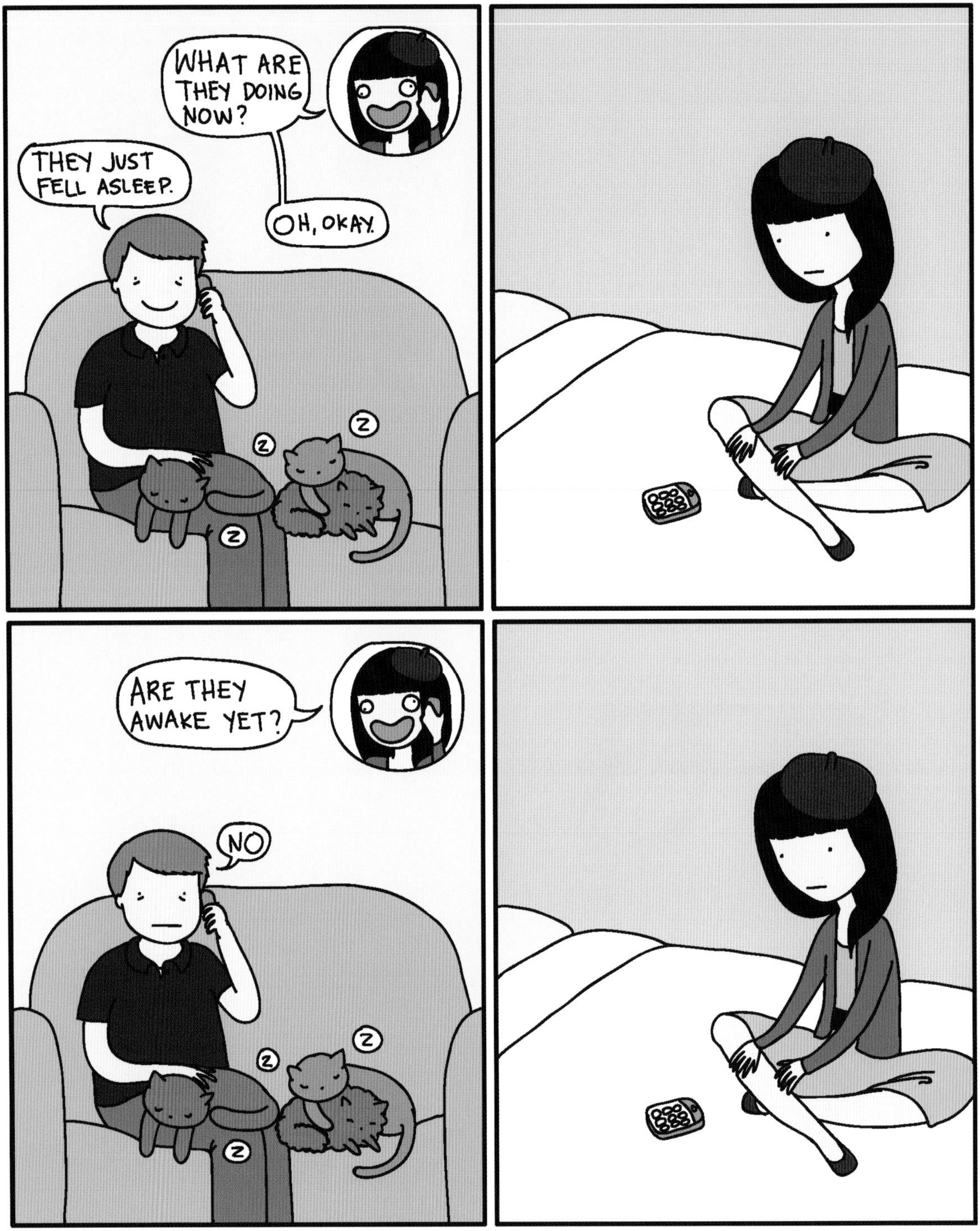
THEY JUST FELL ASLEEP.
WHAT ARE THEY DOING NOW?
OH, OKAY.
ARE THEY AWAKE YET?
NO

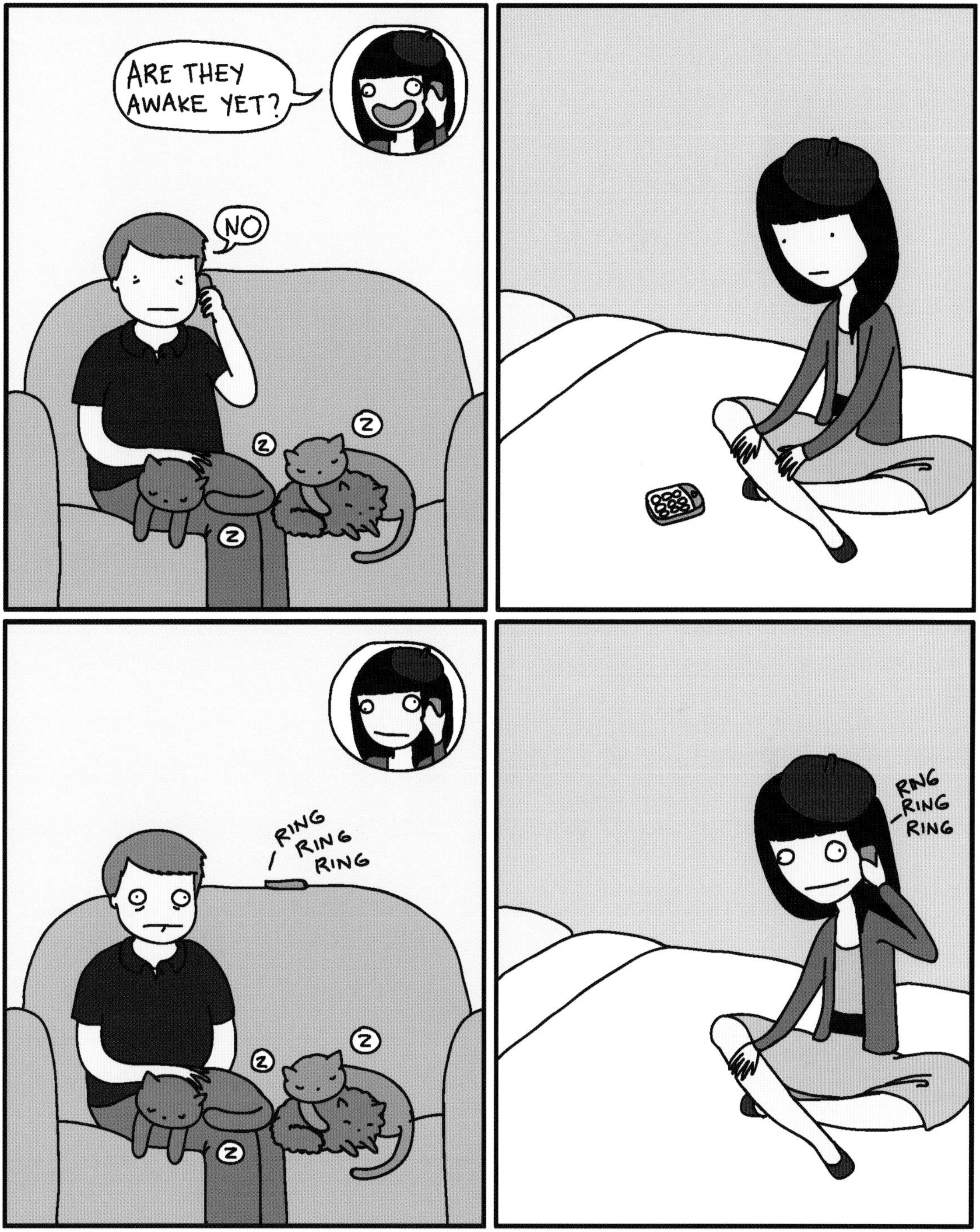
ARE THEY AWAKE YET?
NO
Z
Z
Z
RING RING RING
RING RING RING

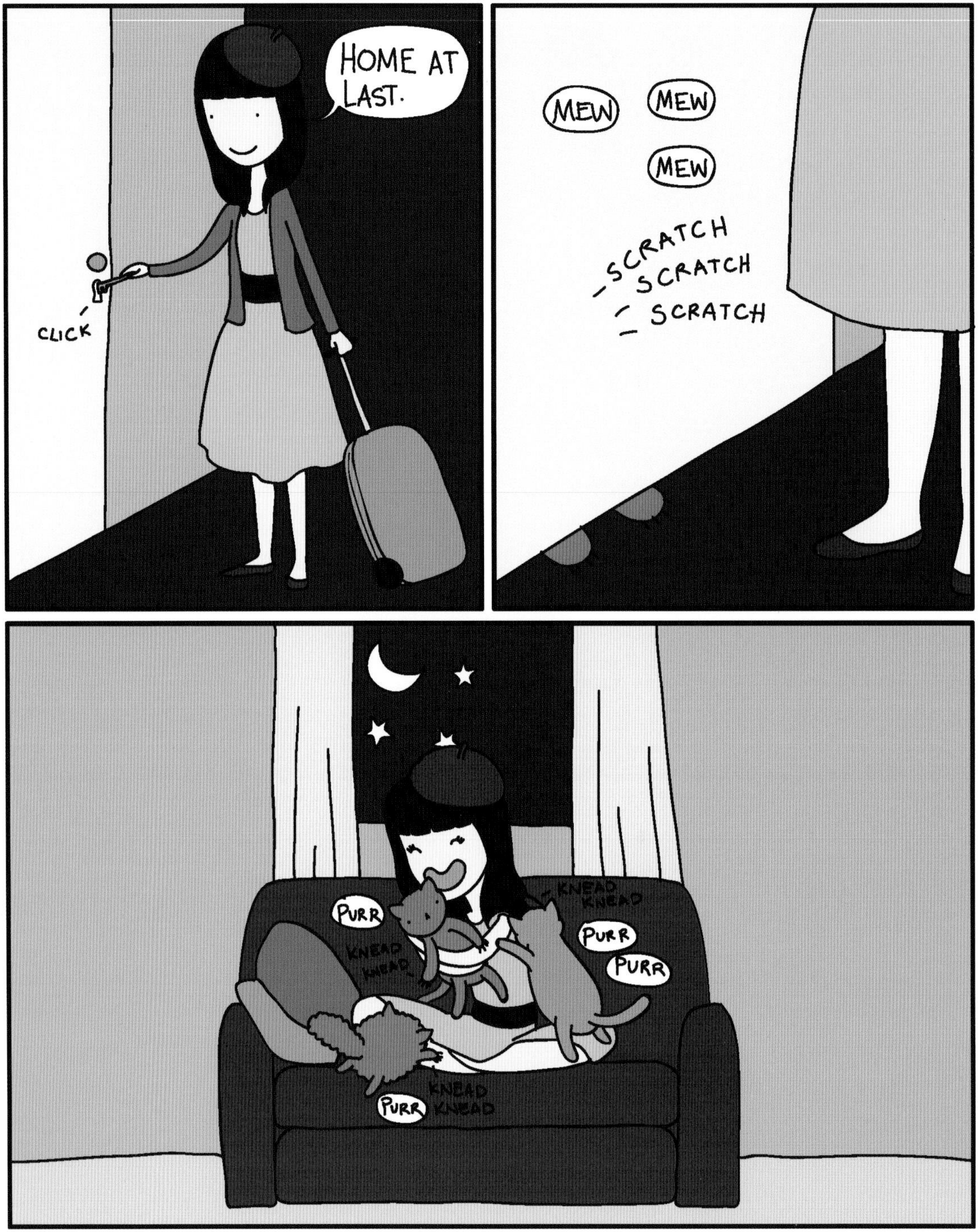

HOME AT LAST.
CLICK
MEW
MEW
MEW
SCRATCH
SCRATCH
SCRATCH
PURR
KNEAD KNEAD
KNEAD KNEAD
PURR
PURR
PURR
KNEAD KNEAD

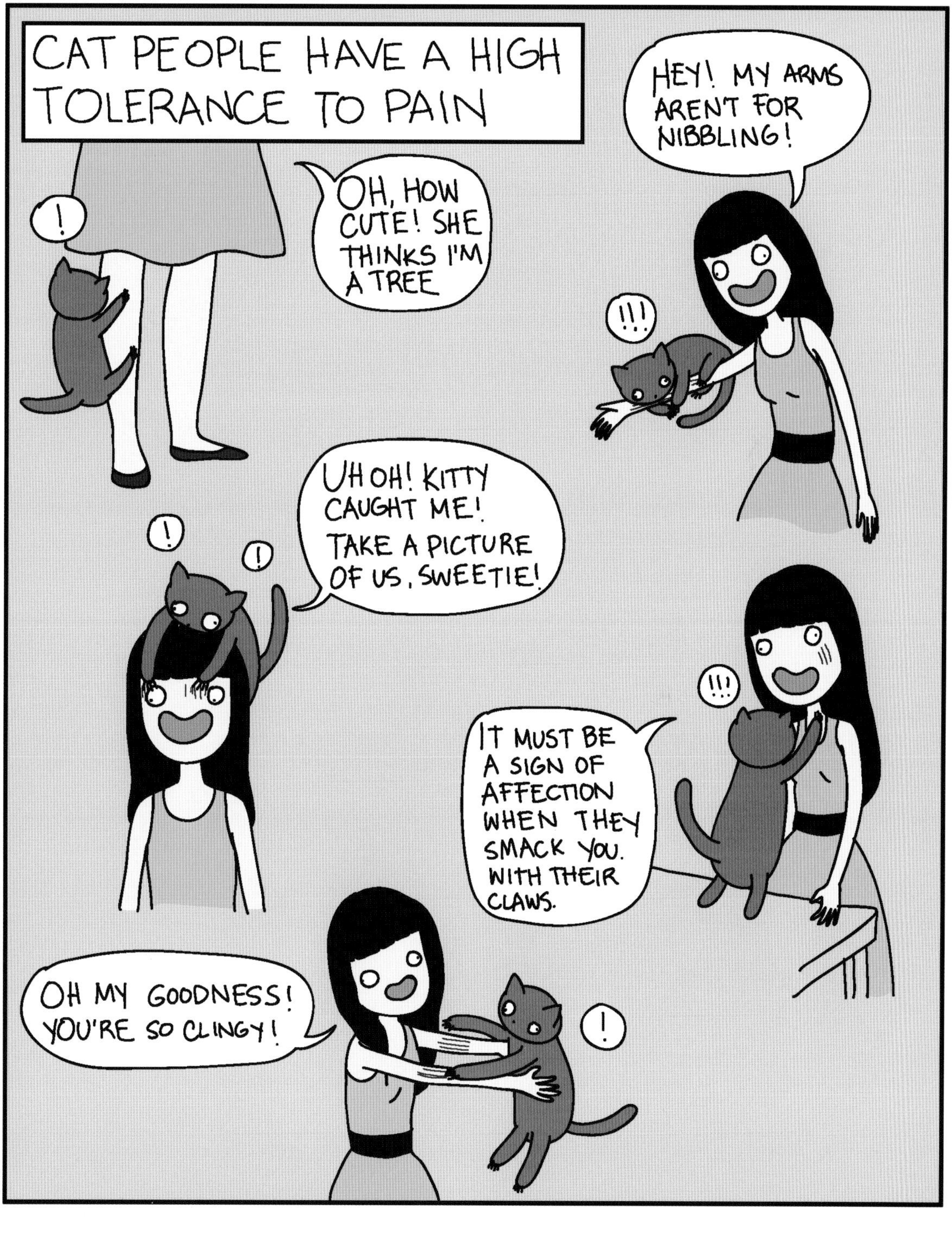
CAT PEOPLE HAVE A HIGH TOLERANCE TO PAIN
!
OH, HOW CUTE! SHE THINKS I'M A TREE
HEY! MY ARMS AREN'T FOR NIBBLING!
!!!
UH OH! KITTY CAUGHT ME! TAKE A PICTURE OF US, SWEETIE!
!
!
IT MUST BE A SIGN OF AFFECTION WHEN THEY SMACK YOU. WITH THEIR CLAWS.
!!!
OH MY GOODNESS! YOU'RE SO CLINGY!
!

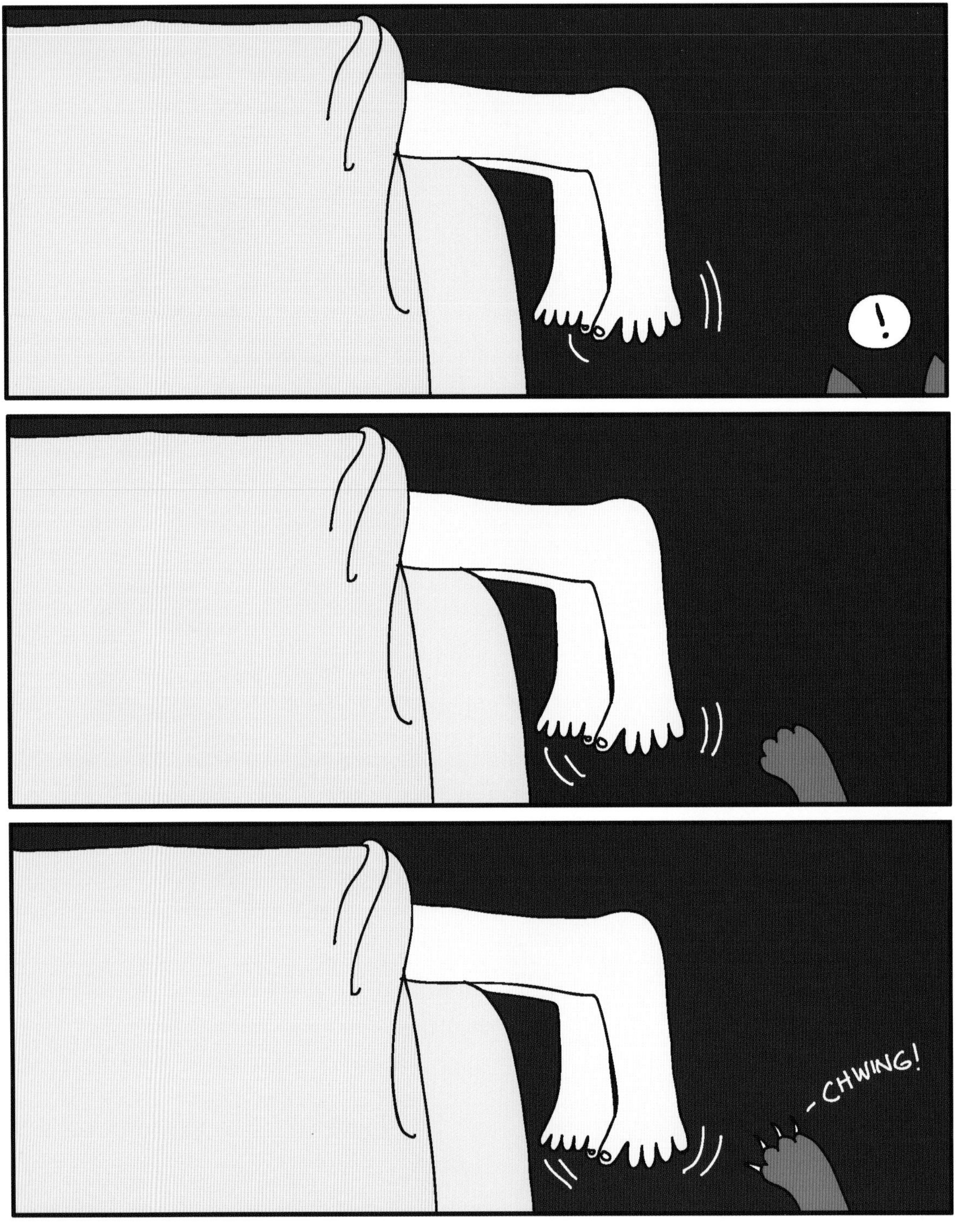
!
-CHWING!

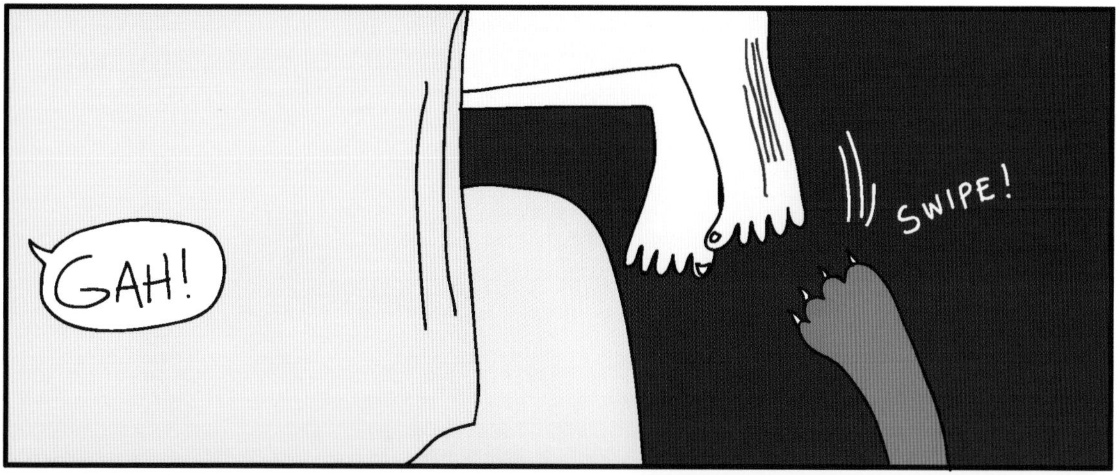
GAH!
SWIPE!

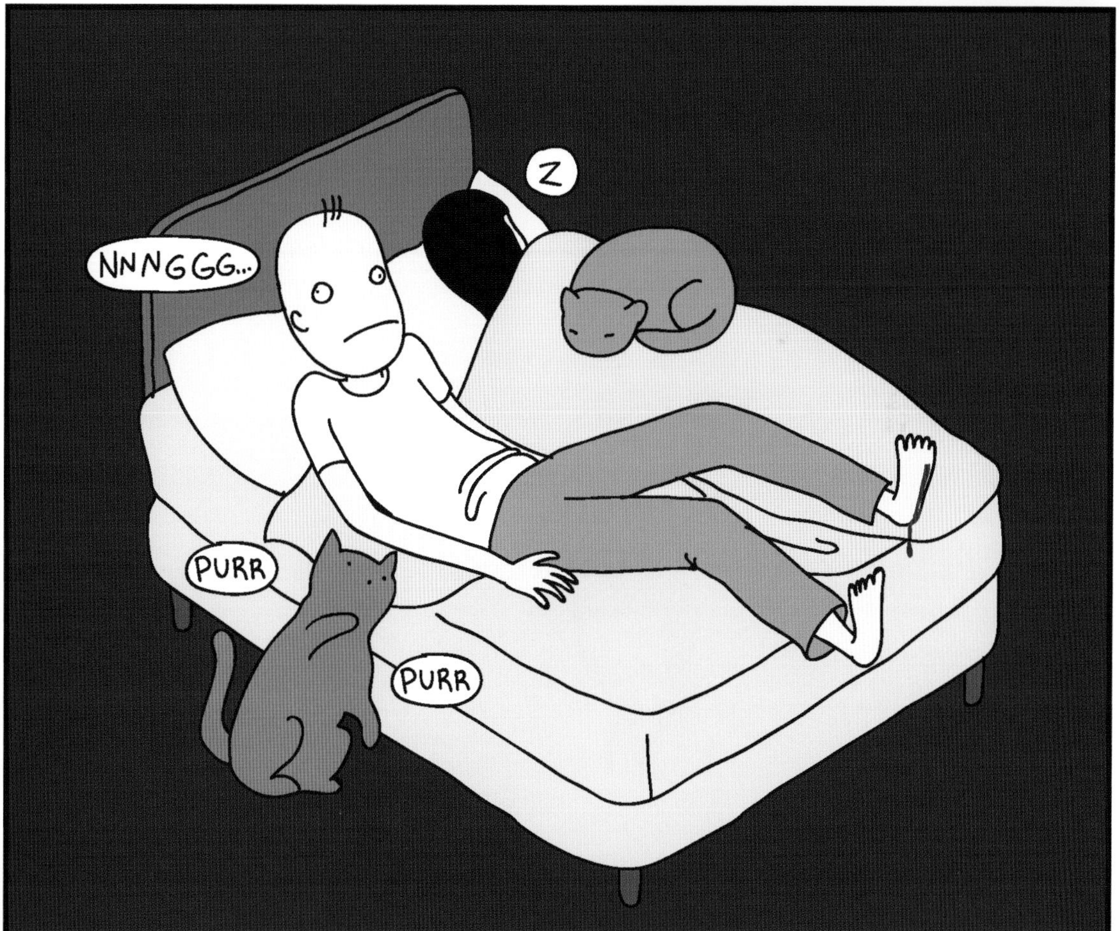
Z
NNNGGG...
PURR
PURR

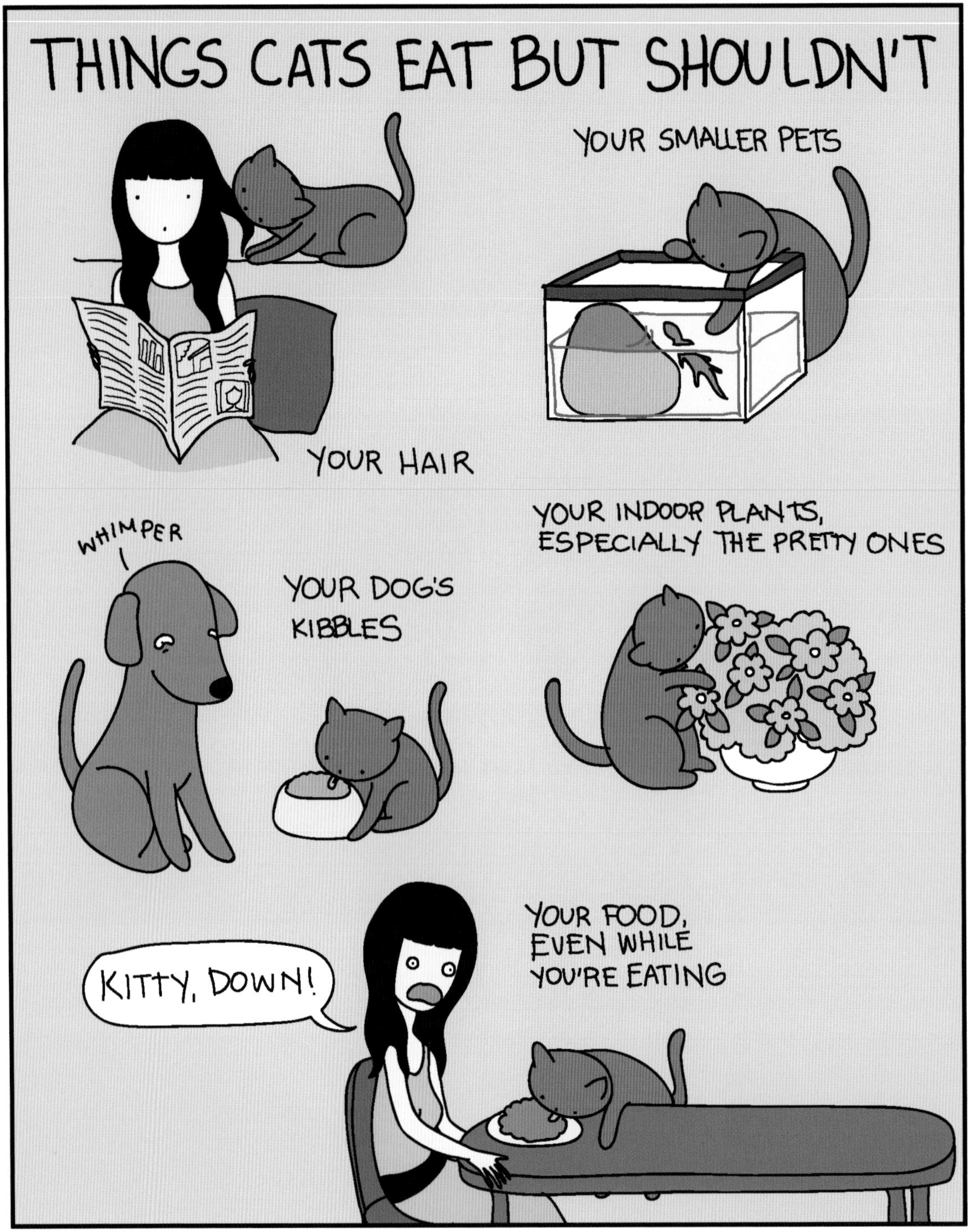
THINGS CATS EAT BUT SHOULDN'T
YOUR HAIR
YOUR SMALLER PETS
WHIMPER
YOUR DOG'S KIBBLES
YOUR INDOOR PLANTS, ESPECIALLY THE PRETTY ONES
KITTY, DOWN!
YOUR FOOD, EVEN WHILE YOU'RE EATING

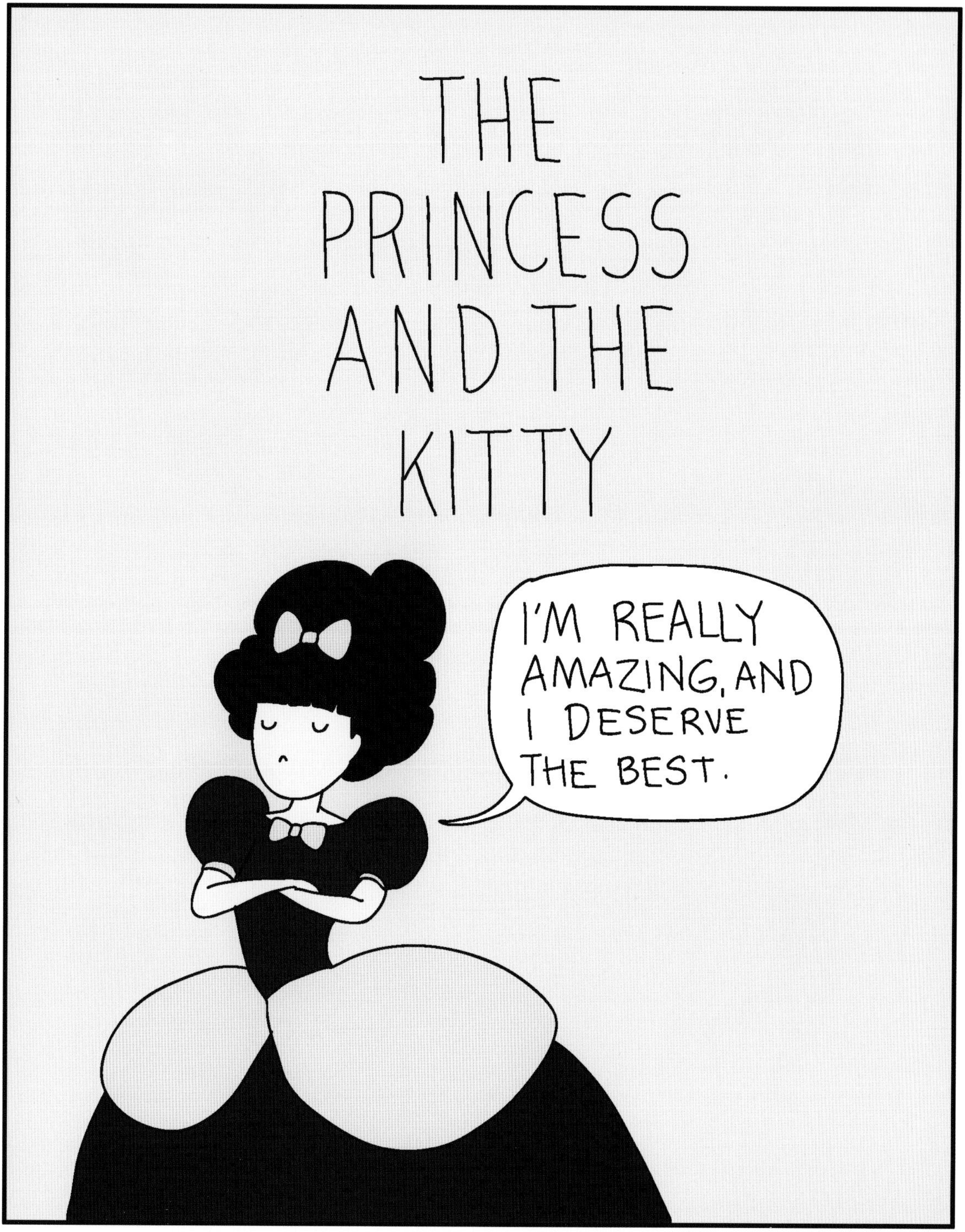
THE PRINCESS AND THE KITTY
I'M REALLY AMAZING, AND I DESERVE THE BEST.

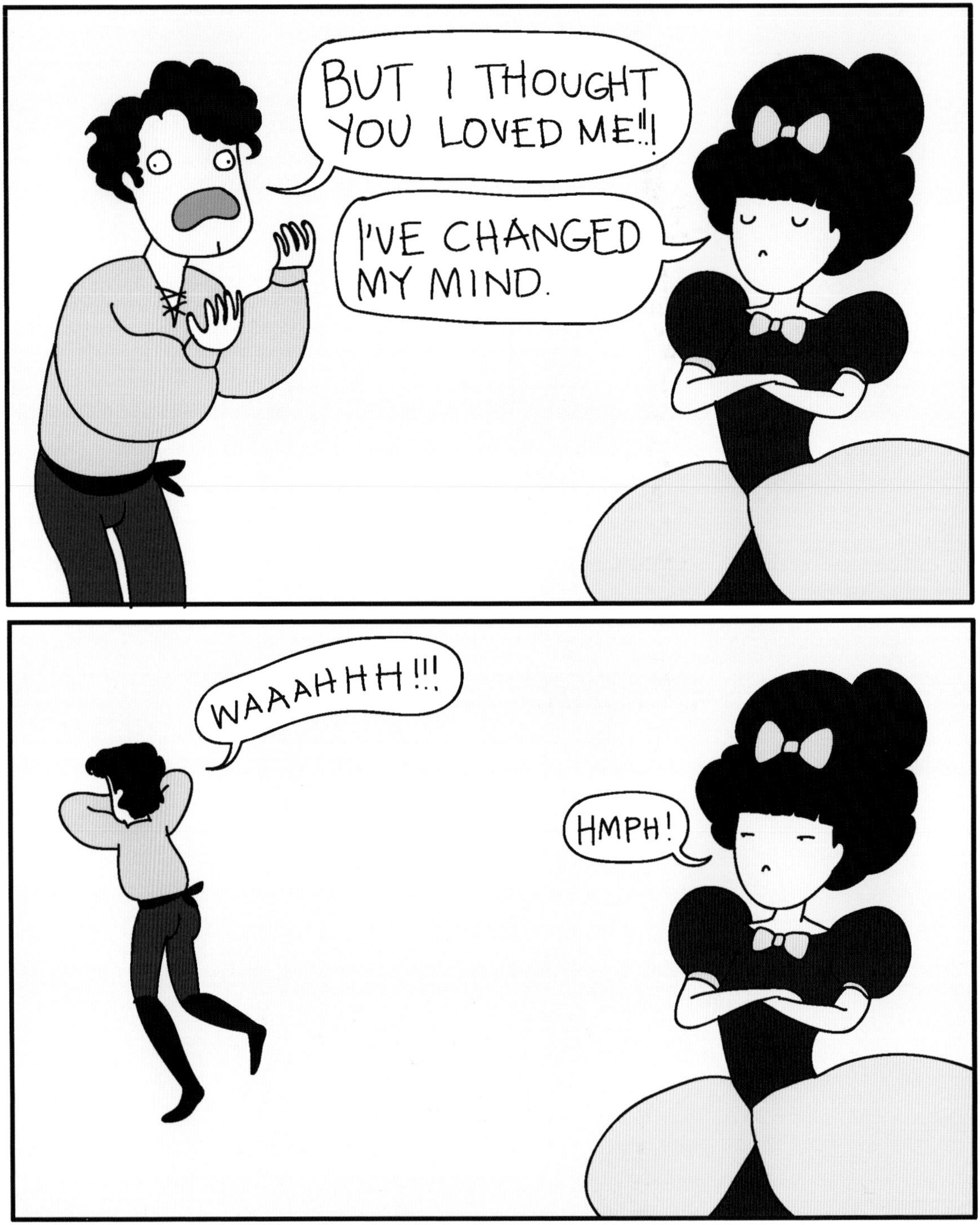
BUT I THOUGHT YOU LOVED ME!!!
I'VE CHANGED MY MIND.
WAAAHHH!!!
HMPH!

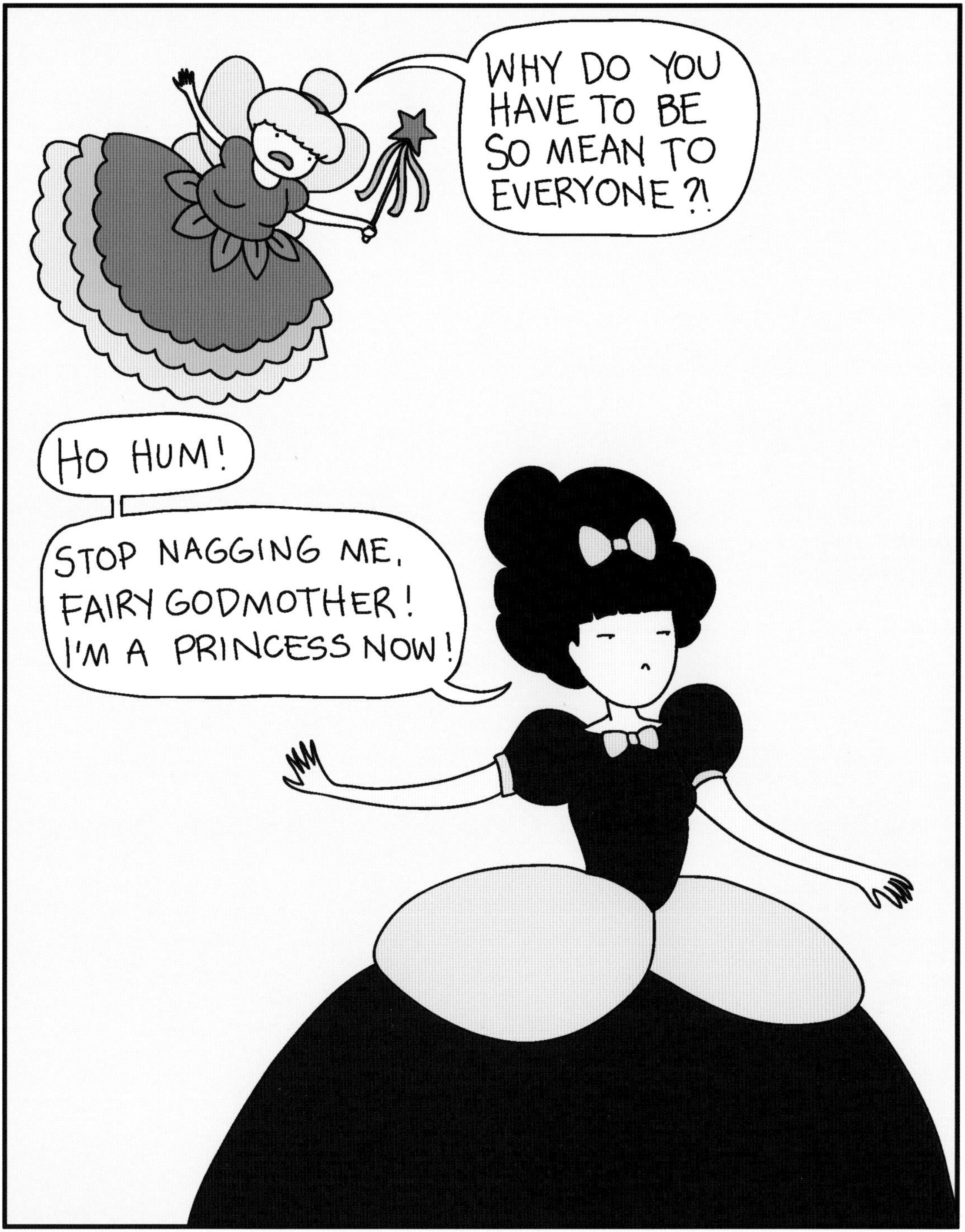
WHY DO YOU HAVE TO BE SO MEAN TO EVERYONE?!
HO HUM!
STOP NAGGING ME, FAIRY GODMOTHER! I'M A PRINCESS NOW!

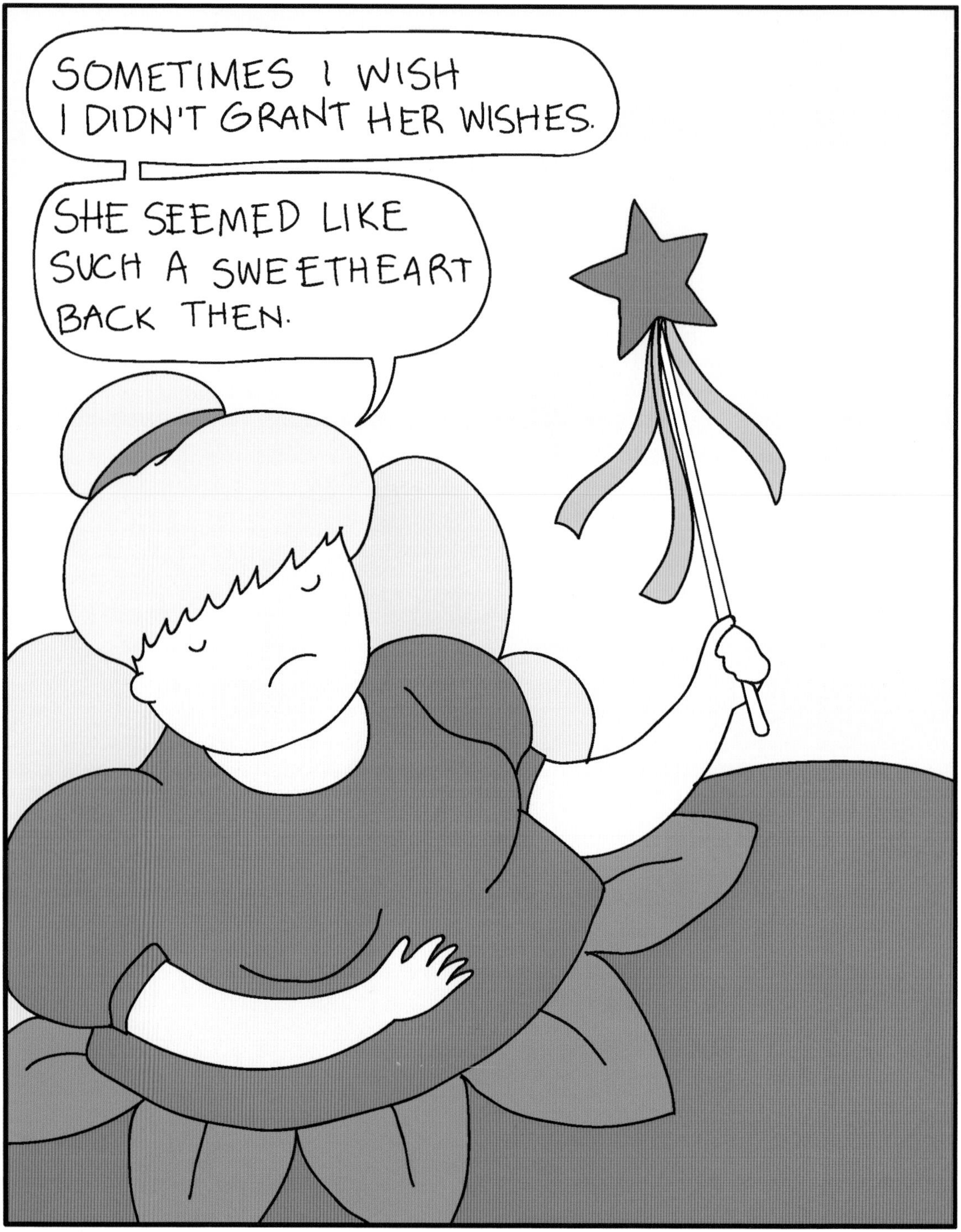
SOMETIMES I WISH I DIDN'T GRANT HER WISHES.
SHE SEEMED LIKE SUCH A SWEETHEART BACK THEN.

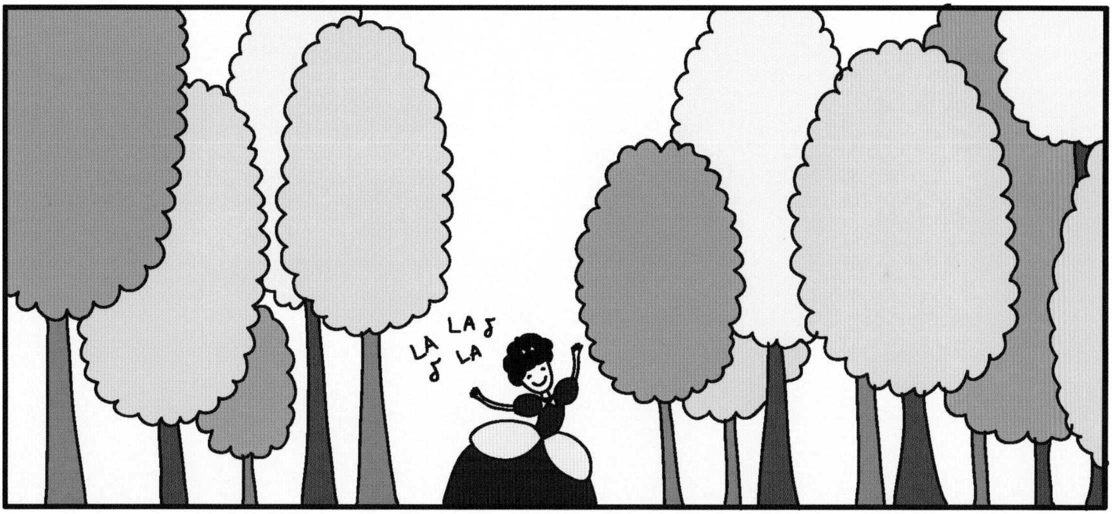
LA LA
LA LA

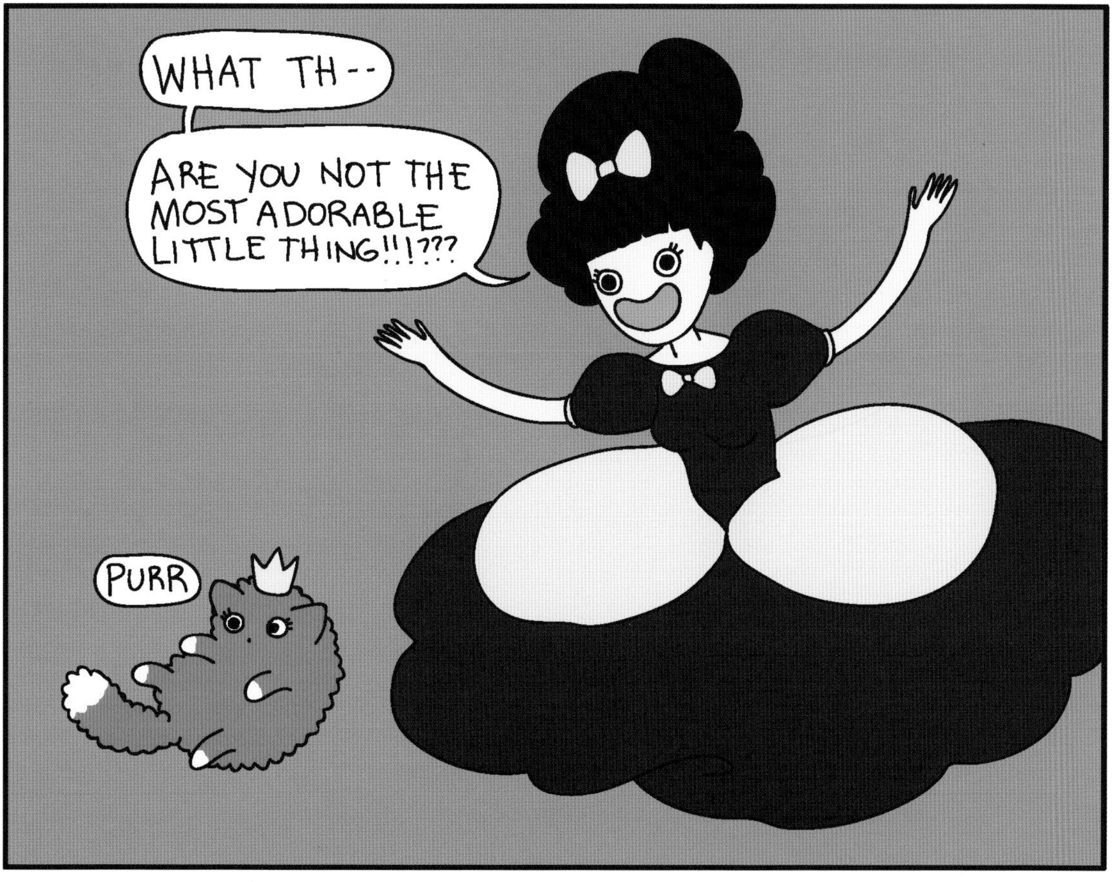
WHAT TH--
ARE YOU NOT THE MOST ADORABLE LITTLE THING!!!???
PURR

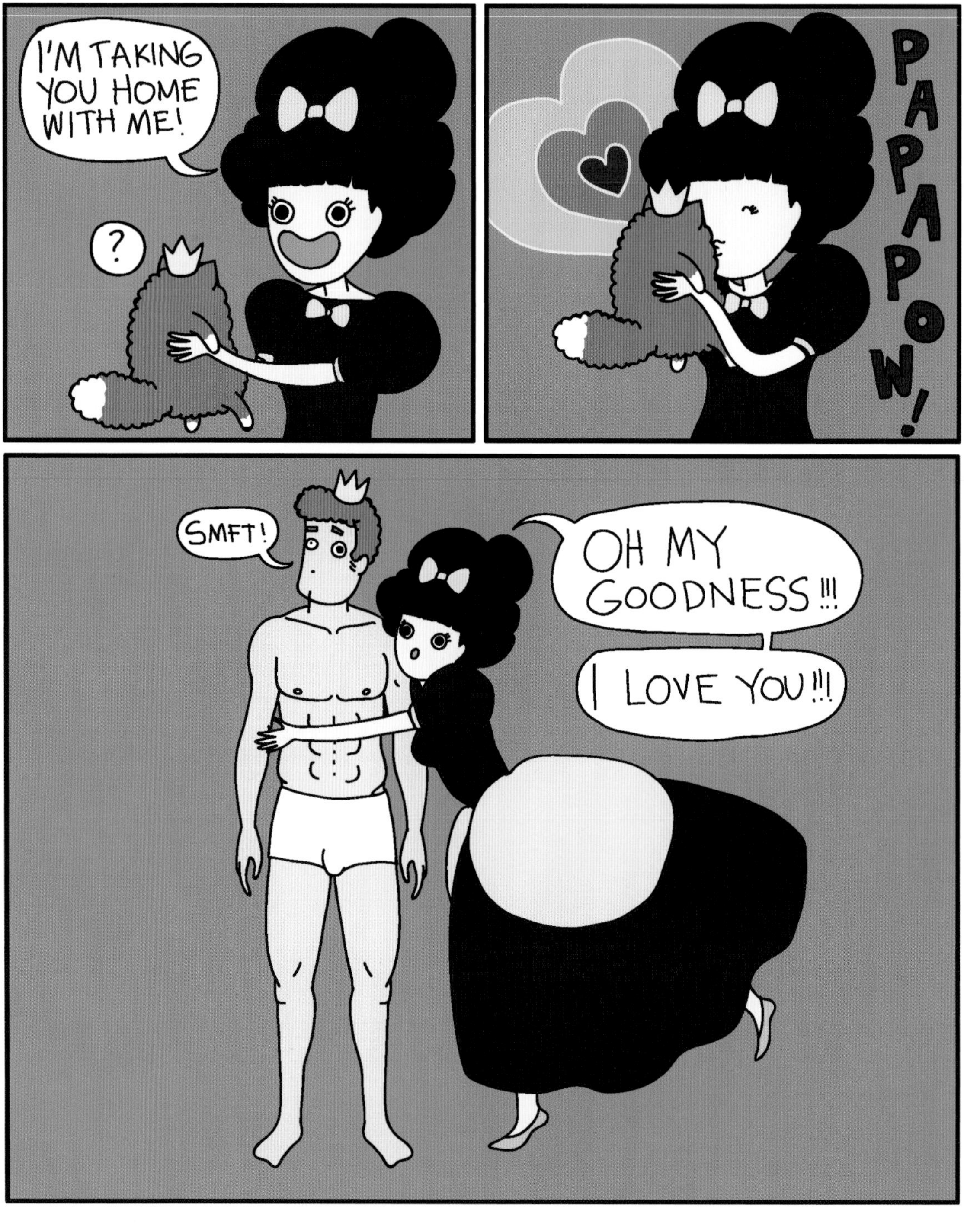
I'M TAKING YOU HOME WITH ME!
?
PAPAPAPOW!
SMFT!
OH MY GOODNESS!!!
I LOVE YOU!!!

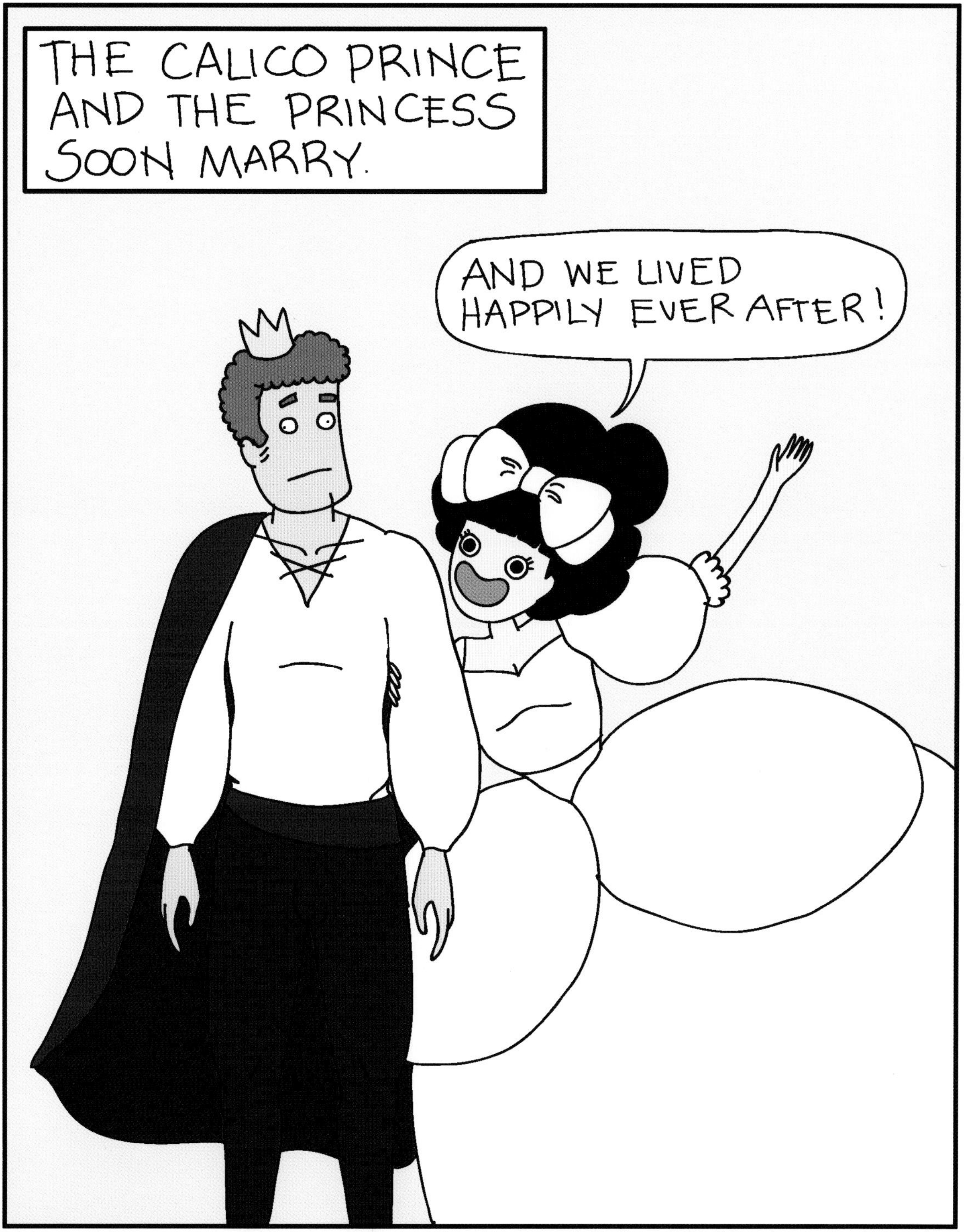
THE CALICO PRINCE AND THE PRINCESS SOON MARRY.
AND WE LIVED HAPPILY EVER AFTER!

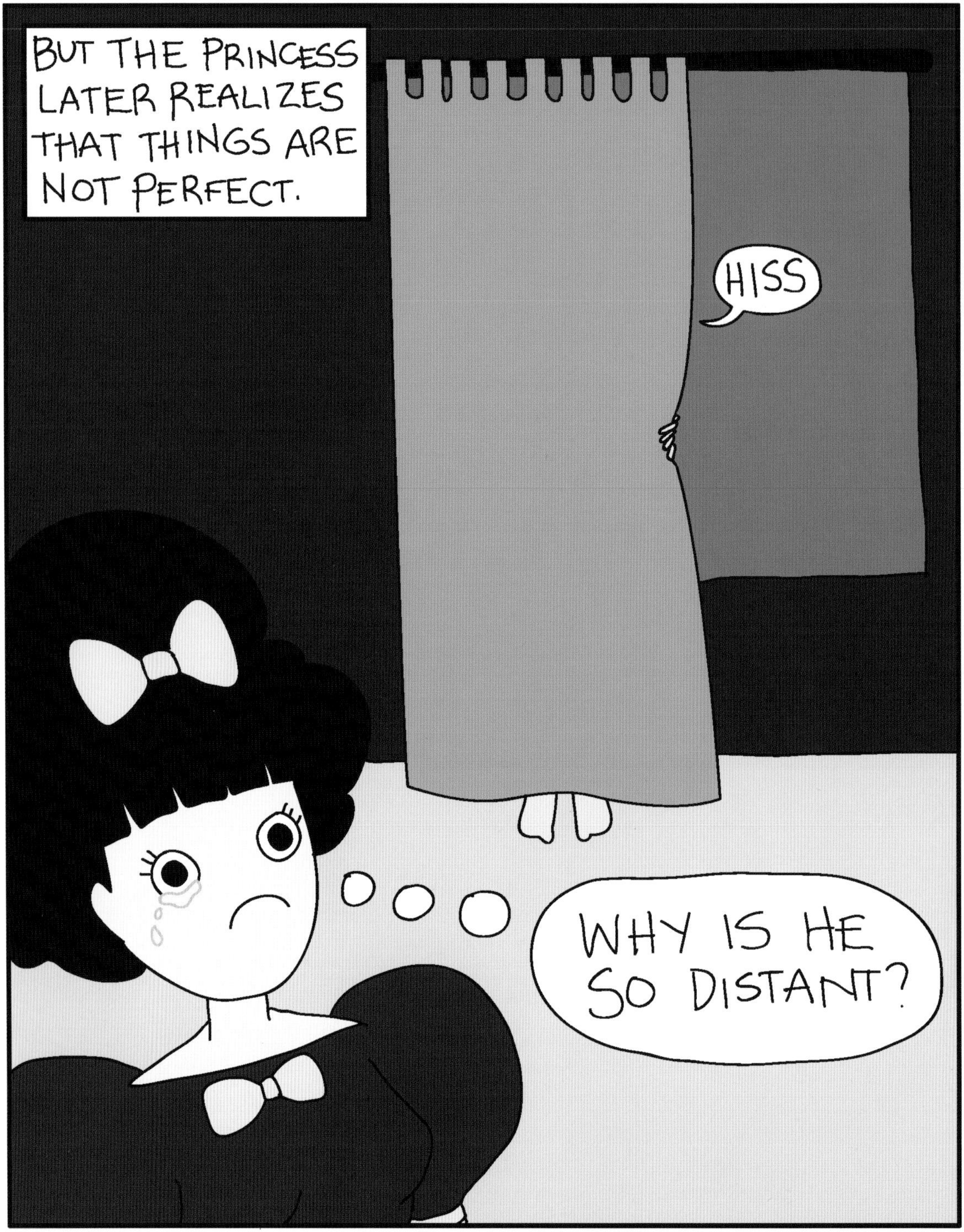
BUT THE PRINCESS LATER REALIZES THAT THINGS ARE NOT PERFECT.
HISS
WHY IS HE SO DISTANT?

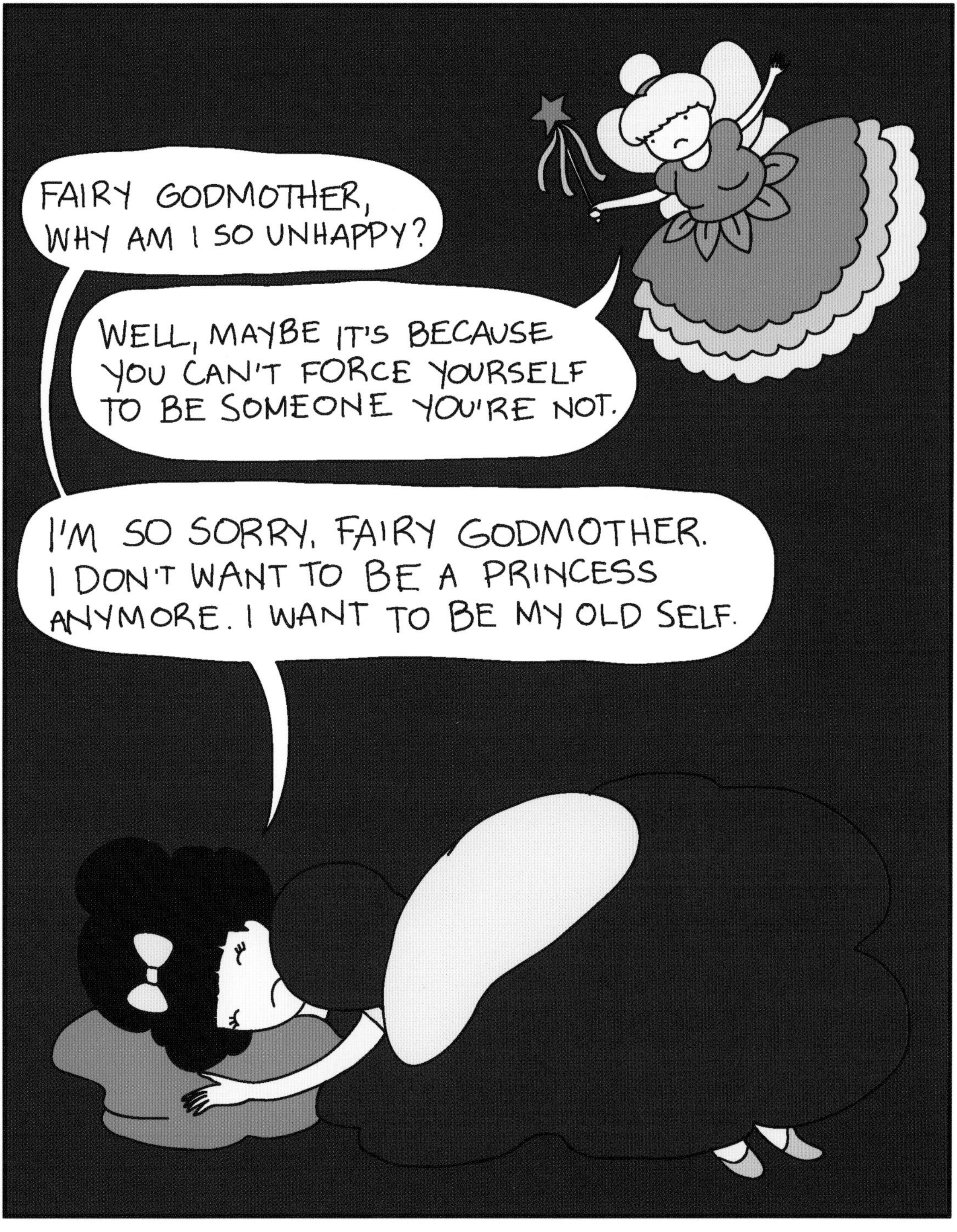
FAIRY GODMOTHER, WHY AM I SO UNHAPPY?
WELL, MAYBE IT'S BECAUSE YOU CAN'T FORCE YOURSELF TO BE SOMEONE YOU'RE NOT.
I'M SO SORRY, FAIRY GODMOTHER. I DON'T WANT TO BE A PRINCESS ANYMORE. I WANT TO BE MY OLD SELF.

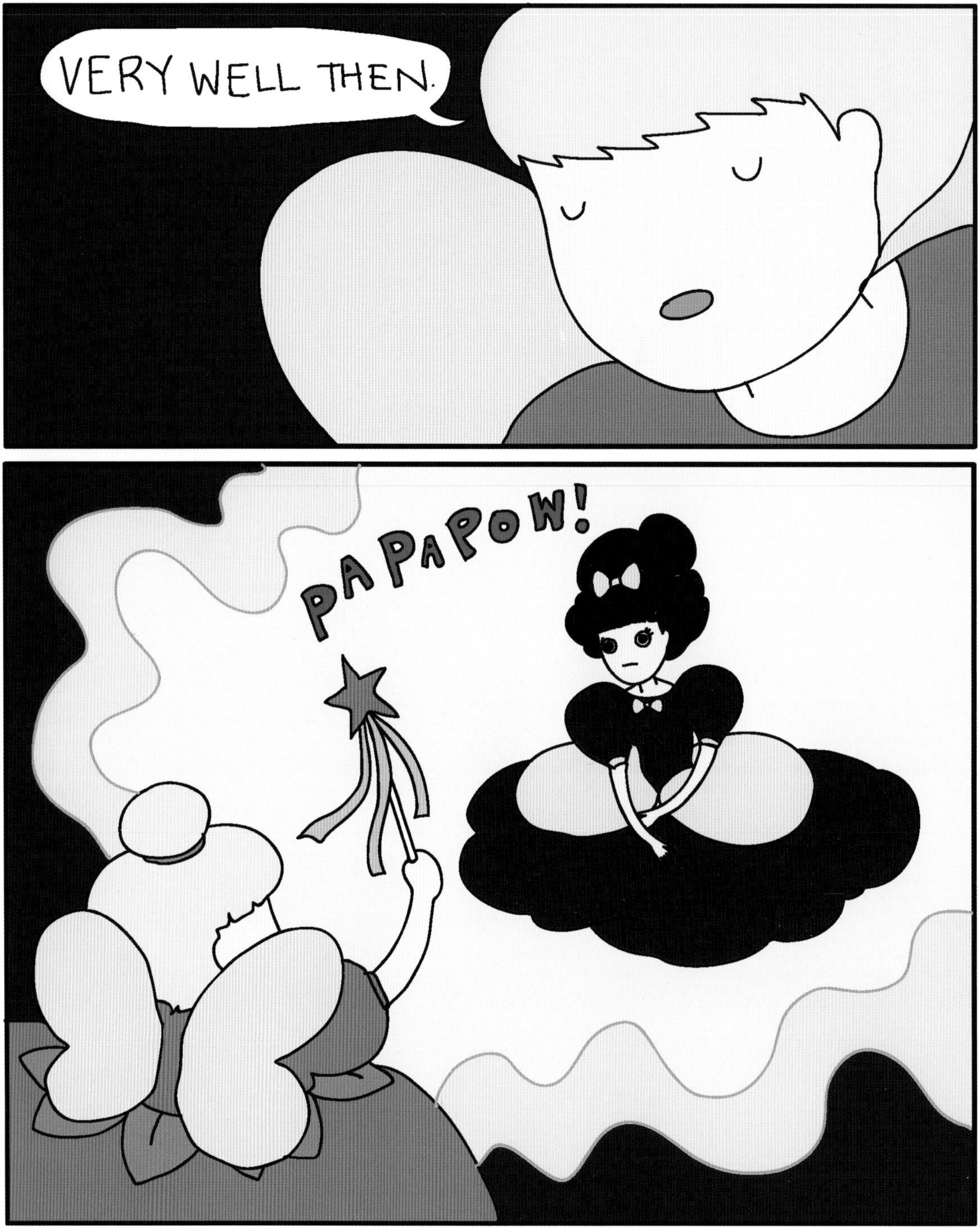
VERY WELL THEN.
PAPAPOW!

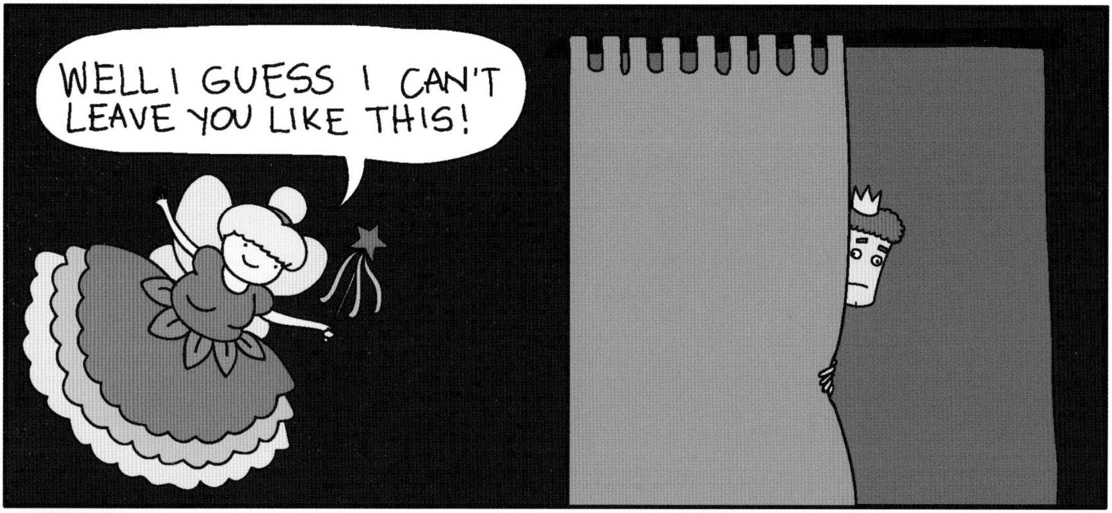
WELL I GUESS I CAN'T LEAVE YOU LIKE THIS!

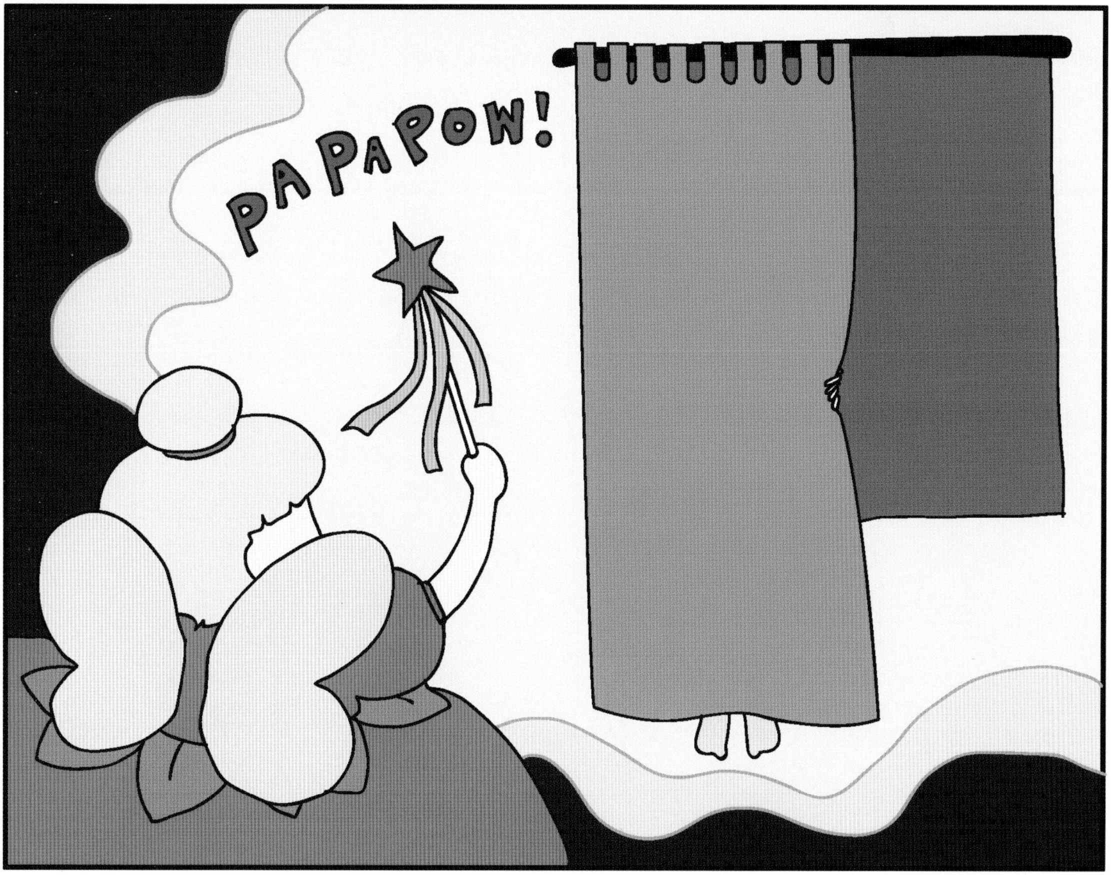
PAPAPOW!

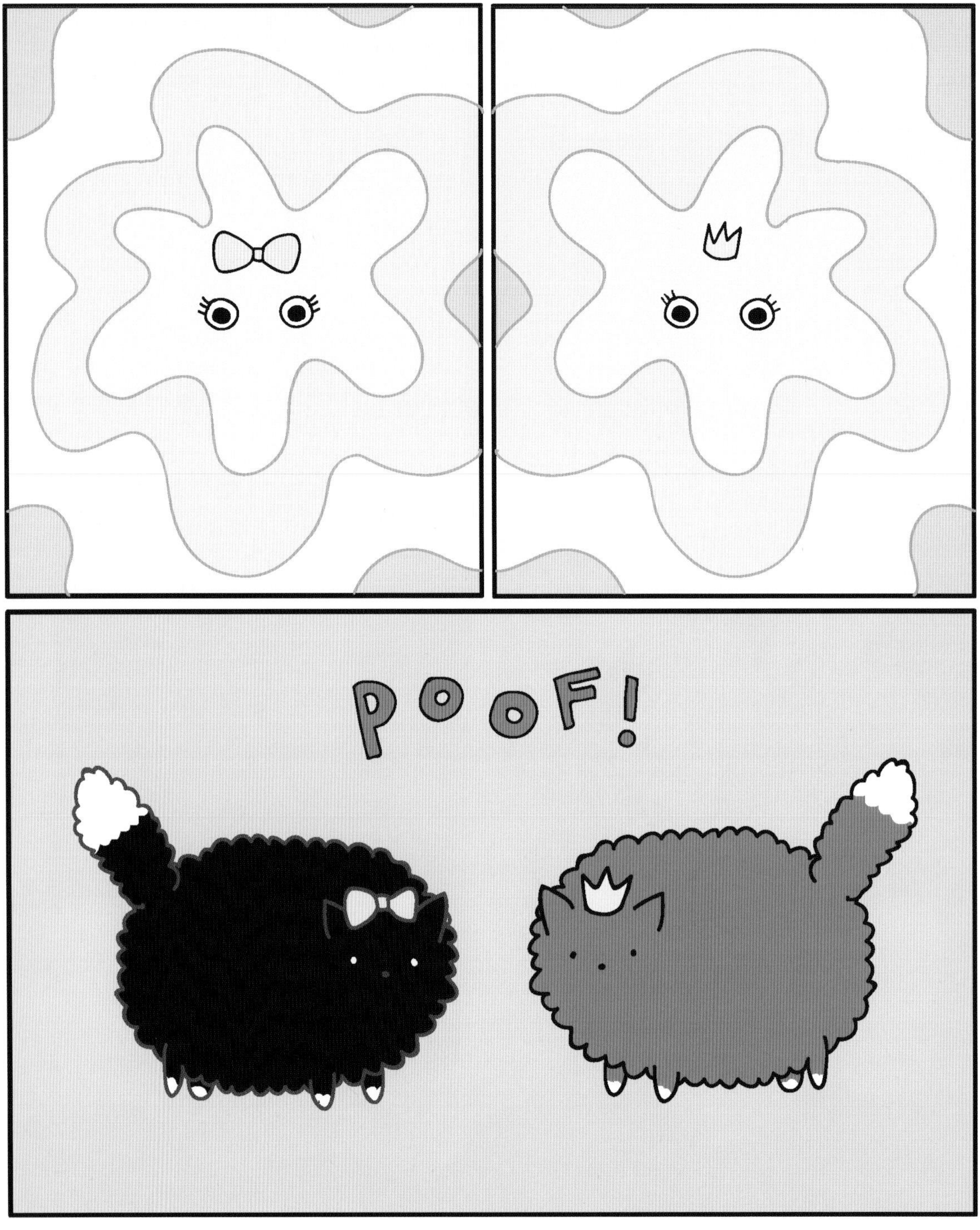
POOF!

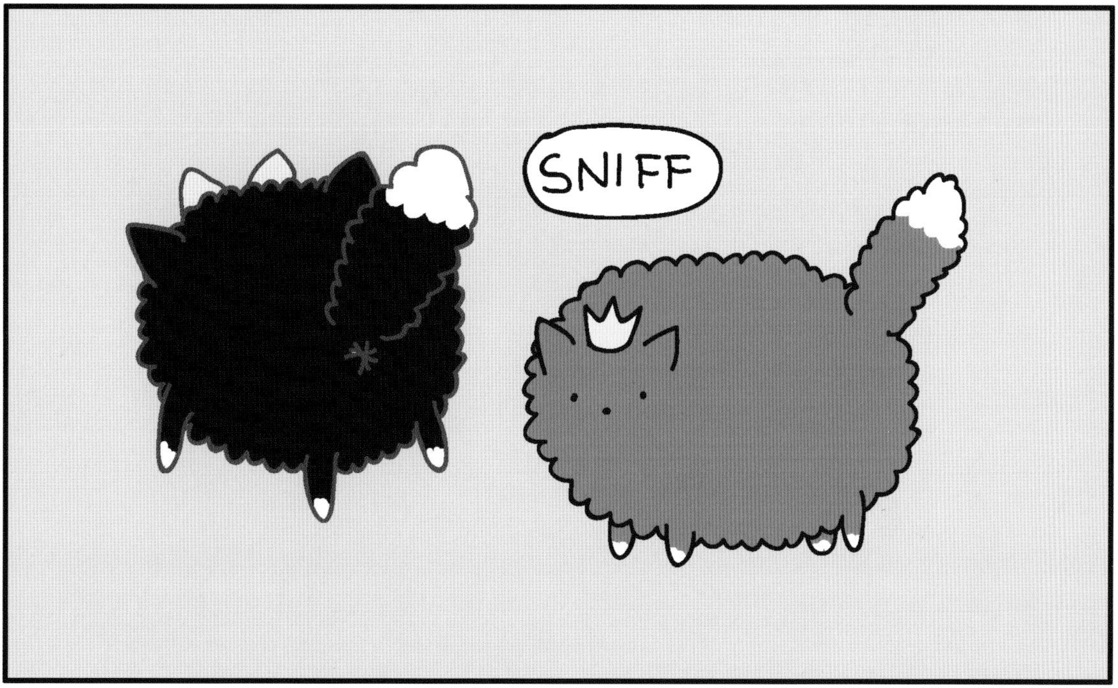
SNIFF

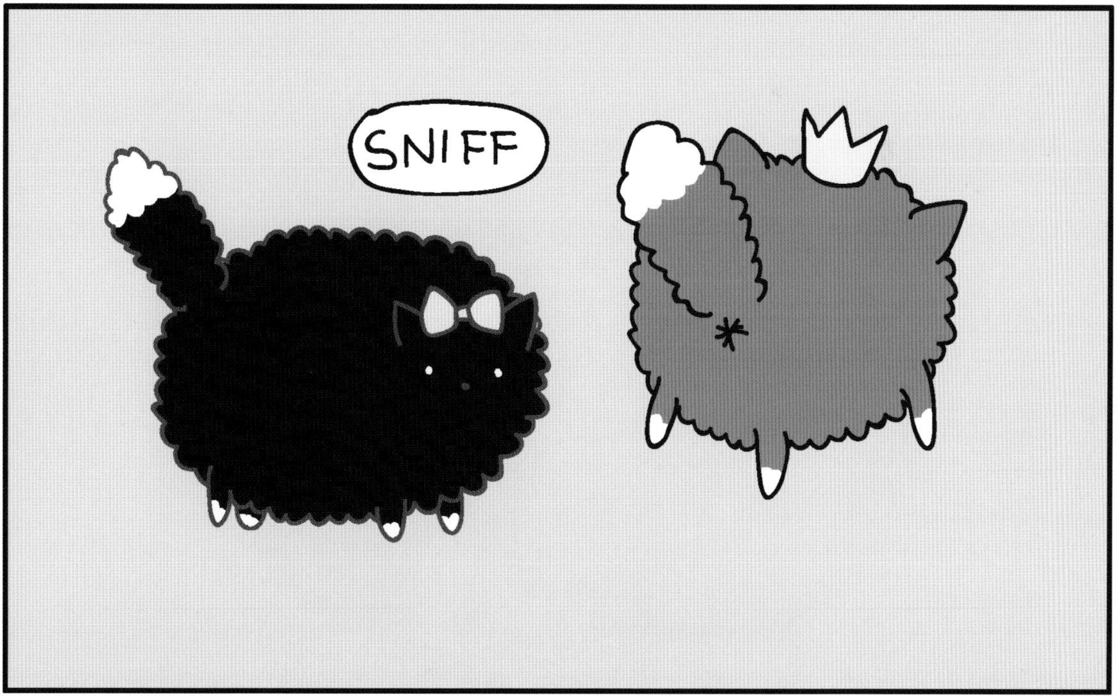
SNIFF

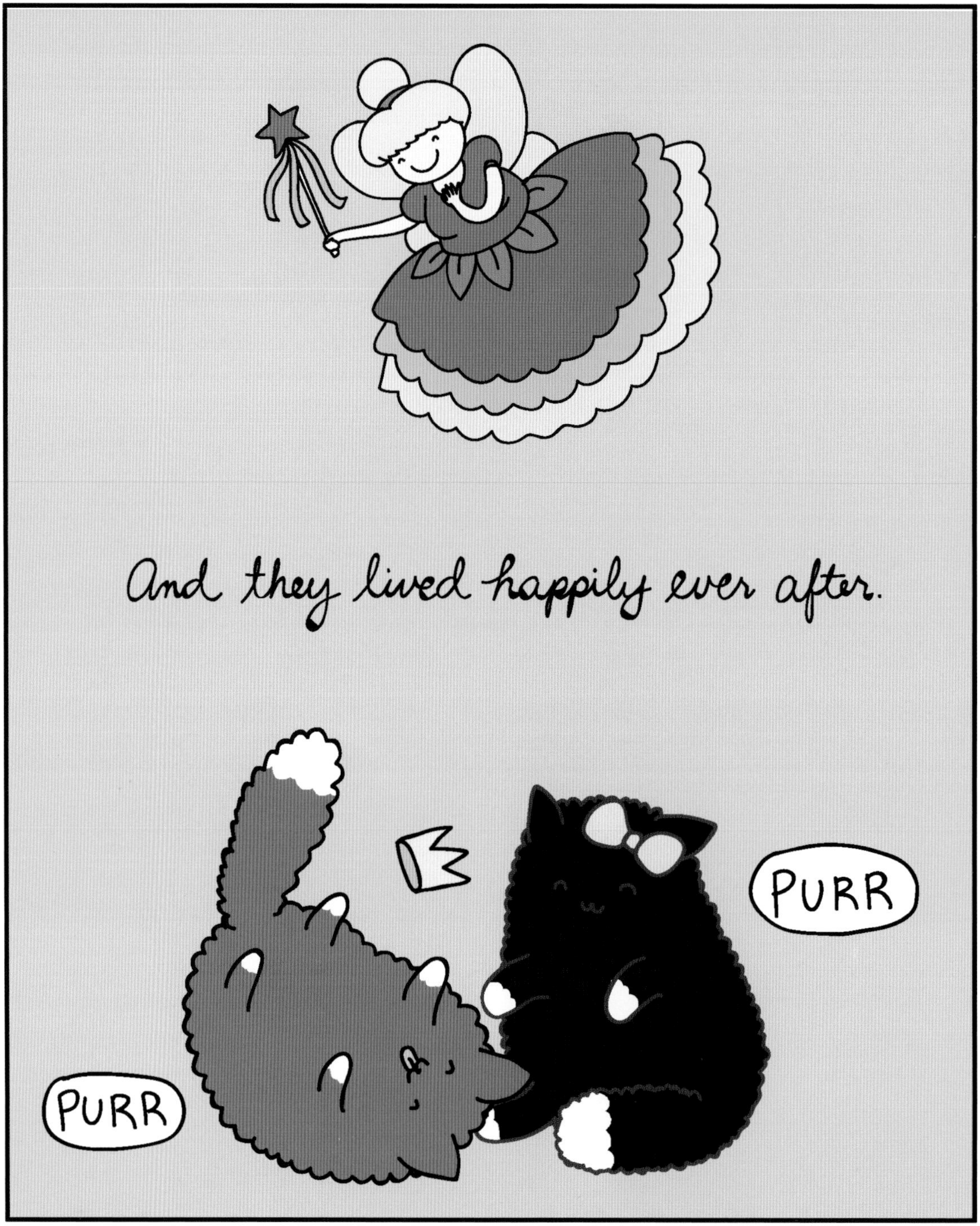
And they lived happily ever after.
PURR
PURR

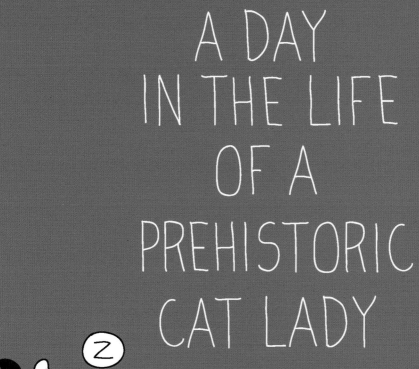

A DAY
IN THE LIFE
OF A
PREHISTORIC
CAT LADY

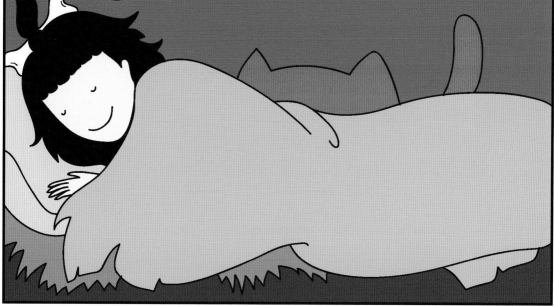

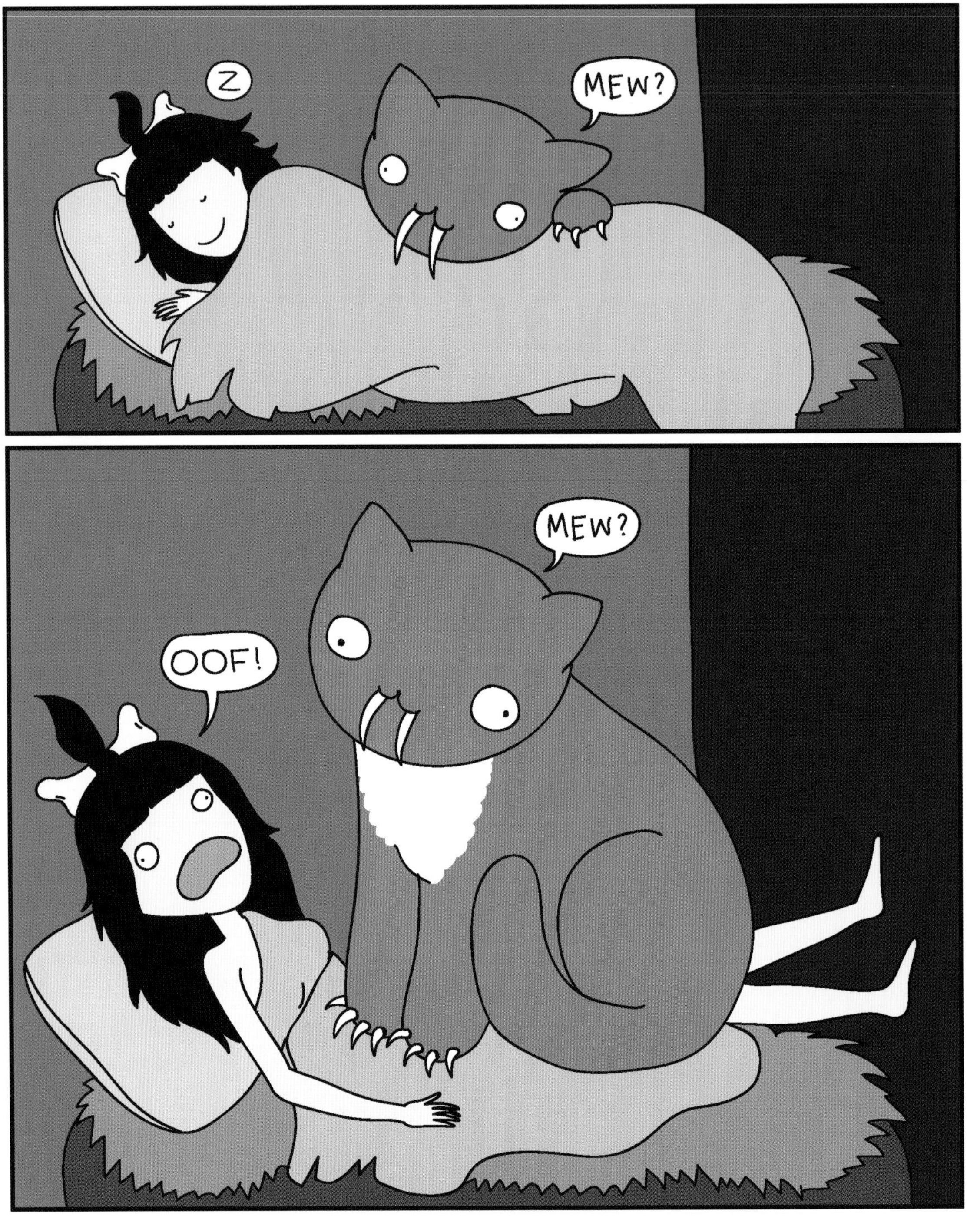
Z
MEW?
MEW?
OOF!

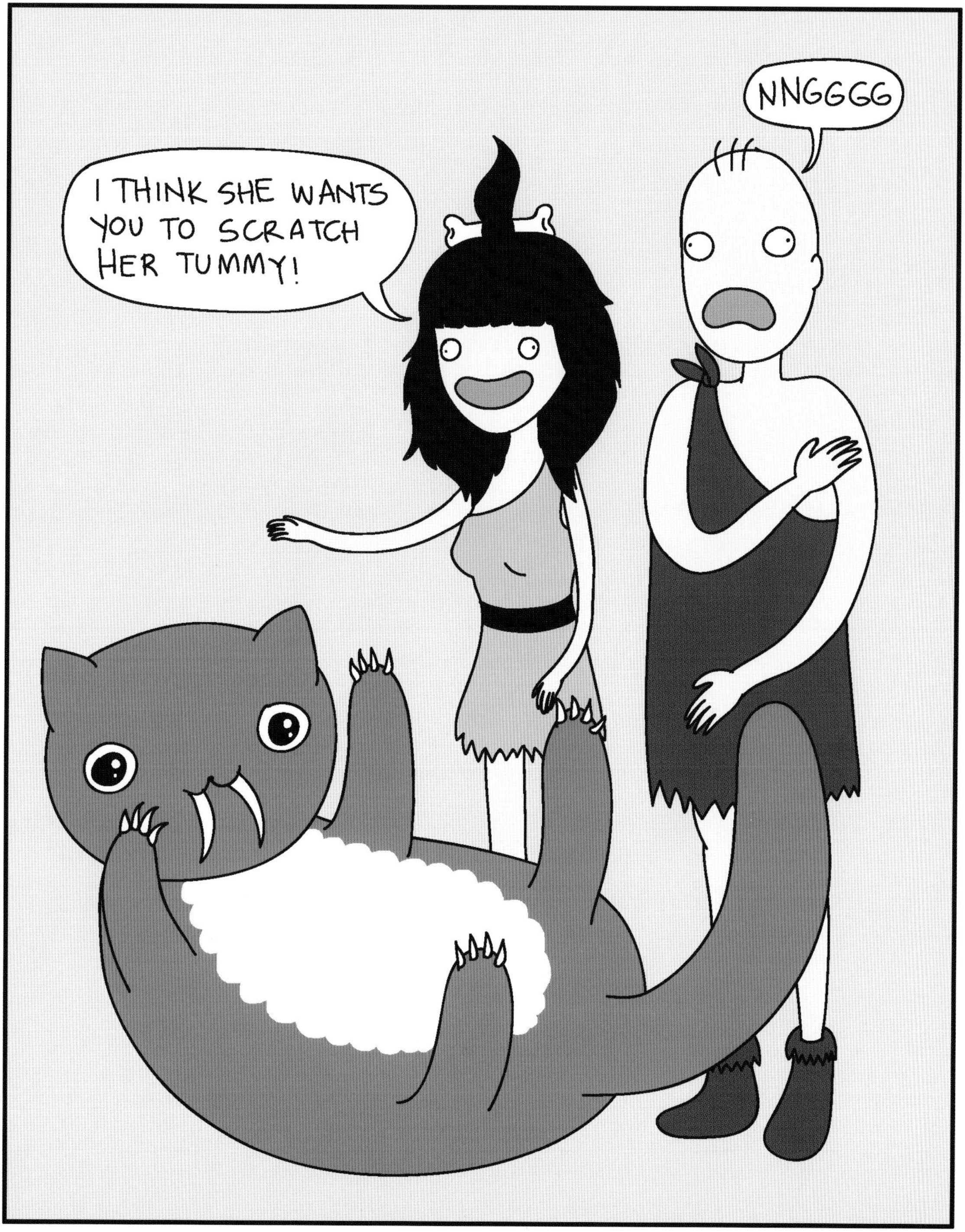
I THINK SHE WANTS YOU TO SCRATCH HER TUMMY!
NNGGGG

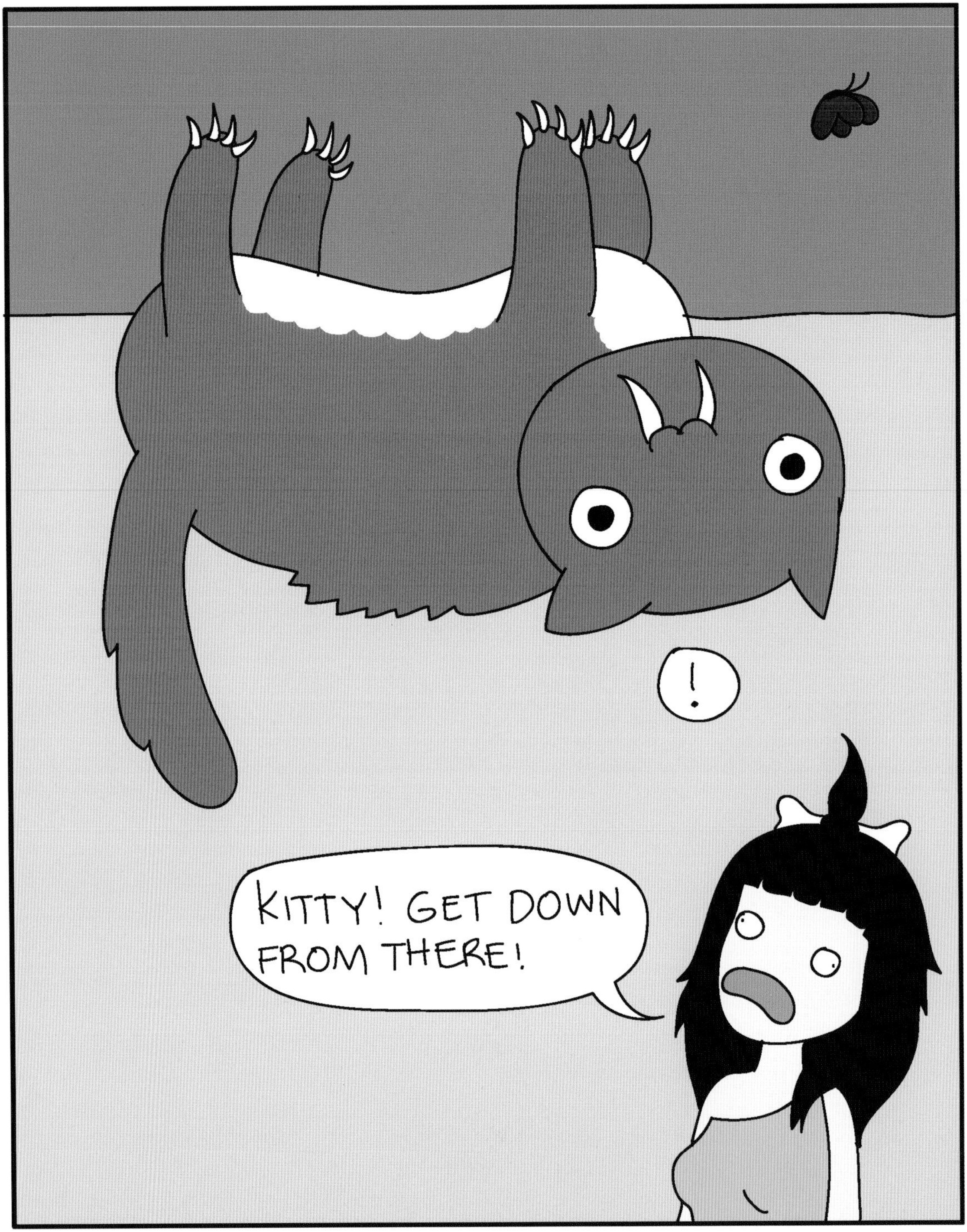
!
KITTY! GET DOWN FROM THERE!

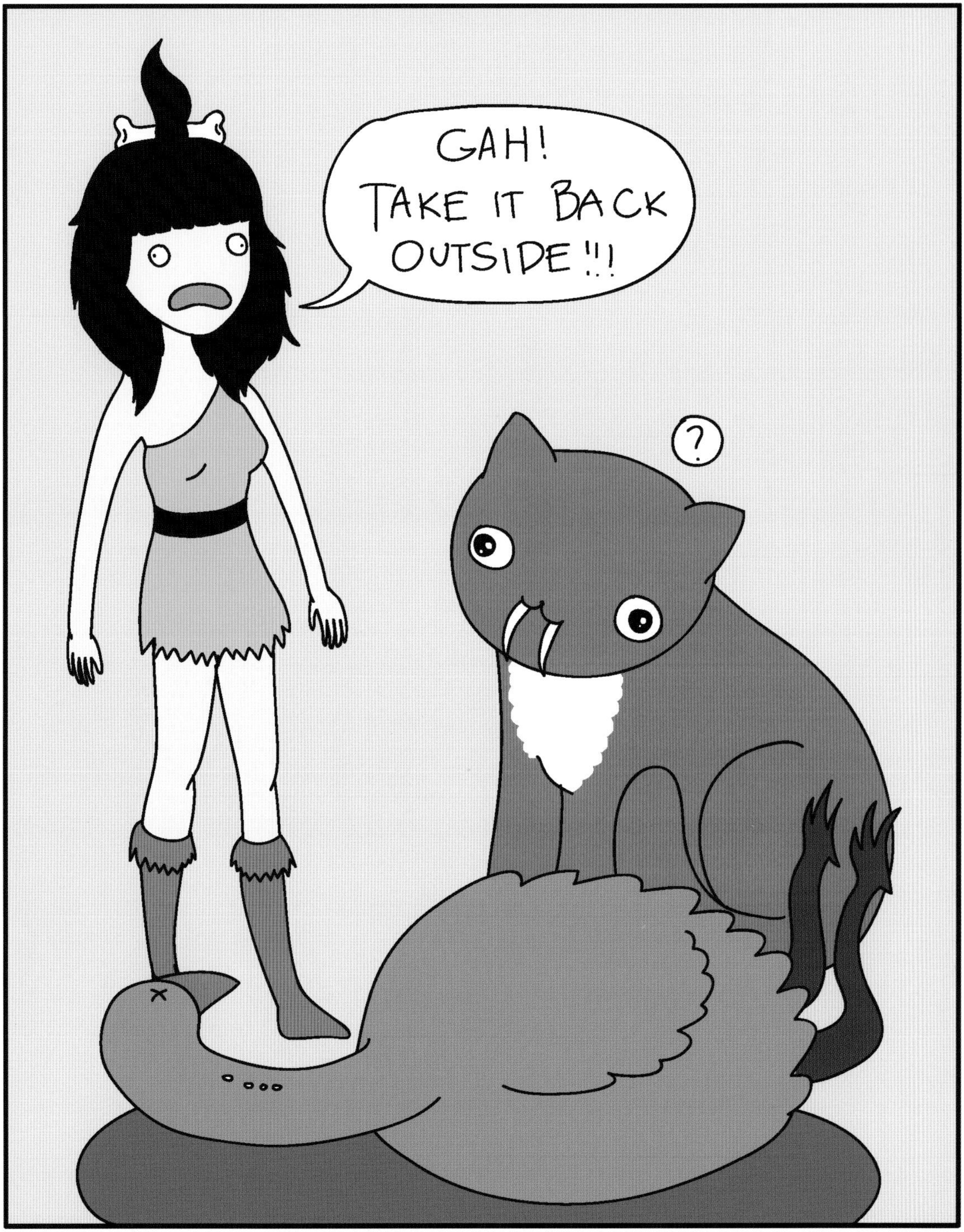
GAH! TAKE IT BACK OUTSIDE!!!
?

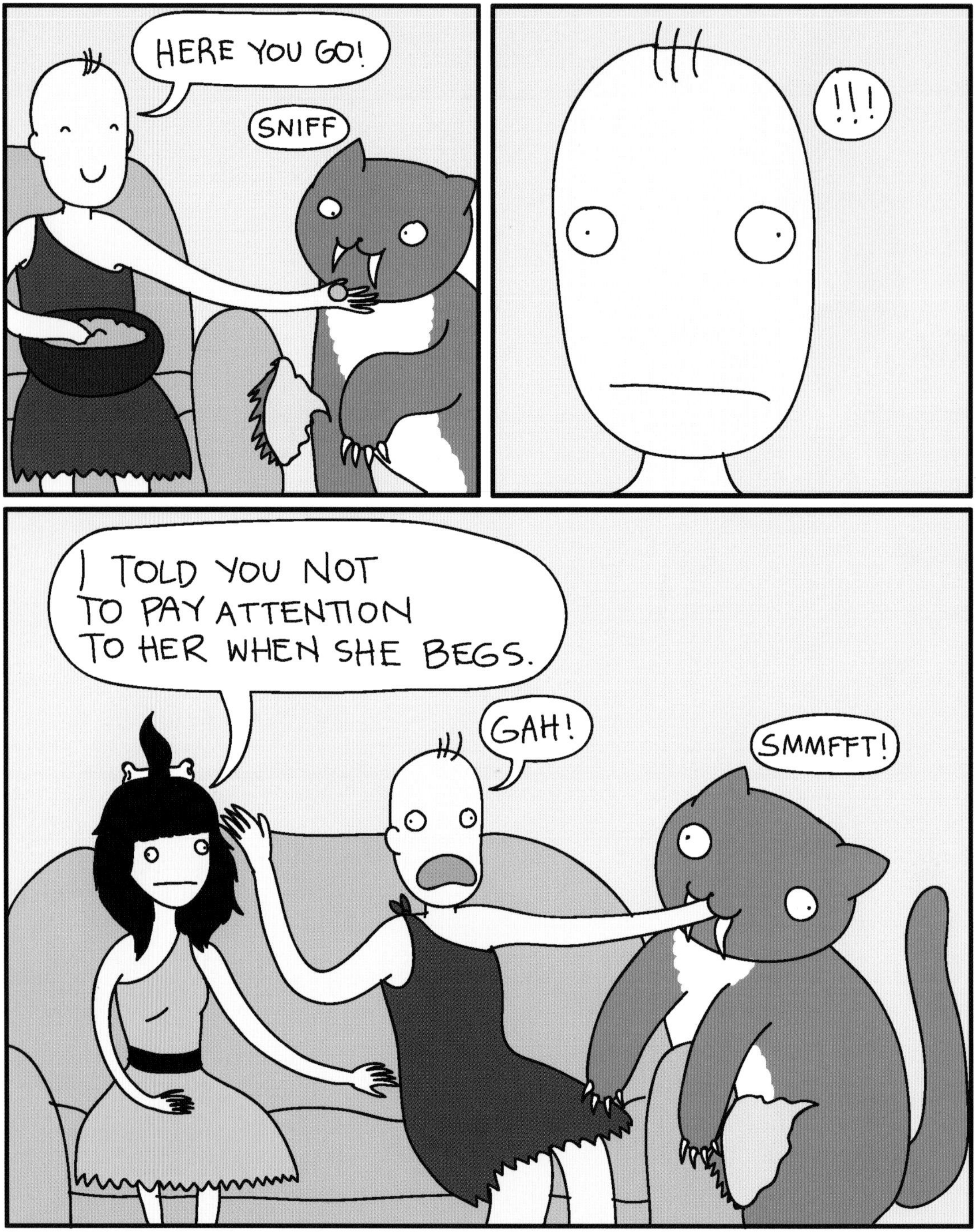
HERE YOU GO!
SNIFF
!!!
I TOLD YOU NOT TO PAY ATTENTION TO HER WHEN SHE BEGS.
GAH!
SMMFFT!

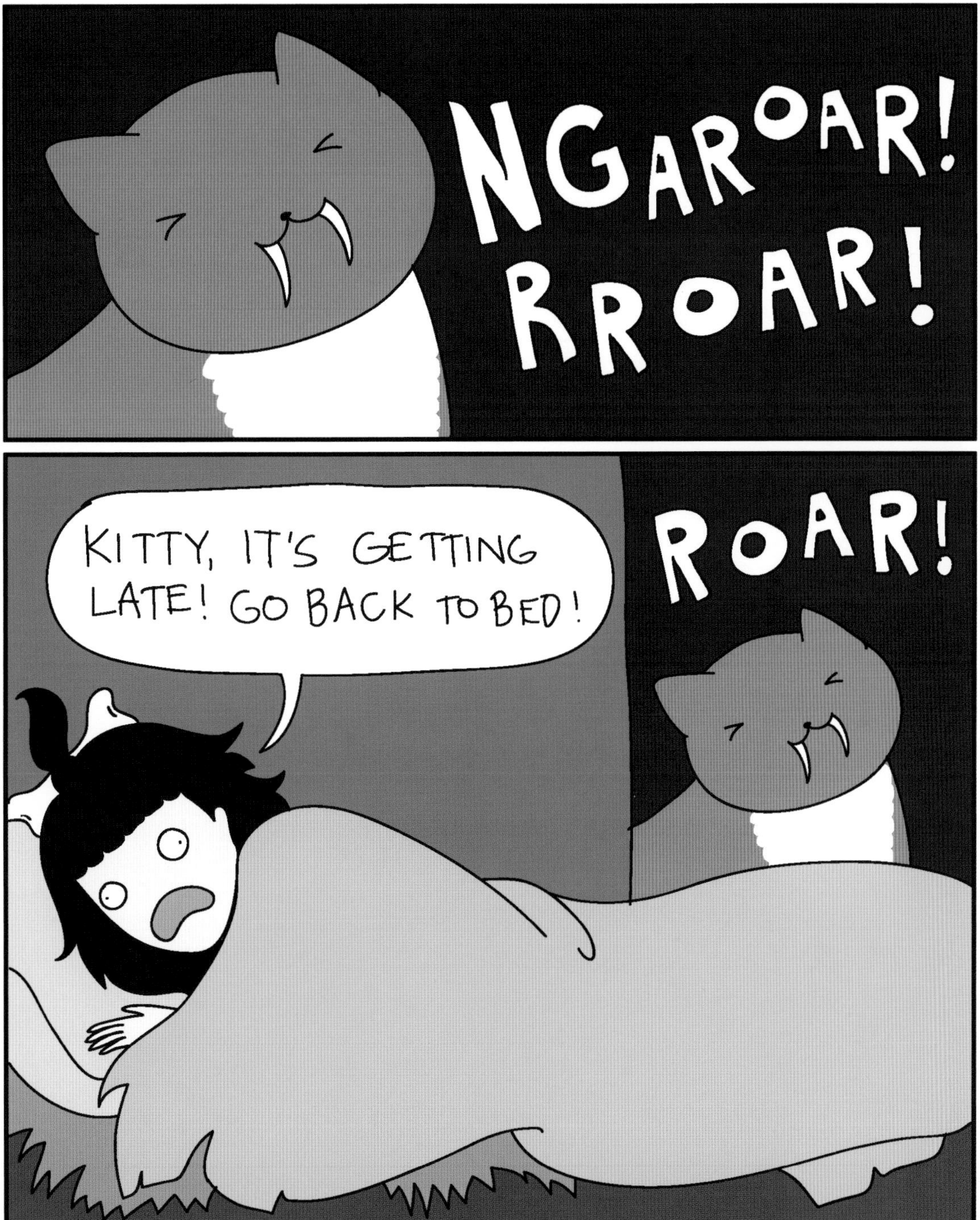
NGAROAR!
RROAR!
KITTY, IT'S GETTING LATE! GO BACK TO BED!
ROAR!

CAT LADIES THROUGHOUT HISTORY

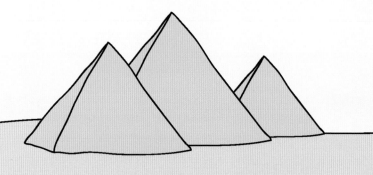

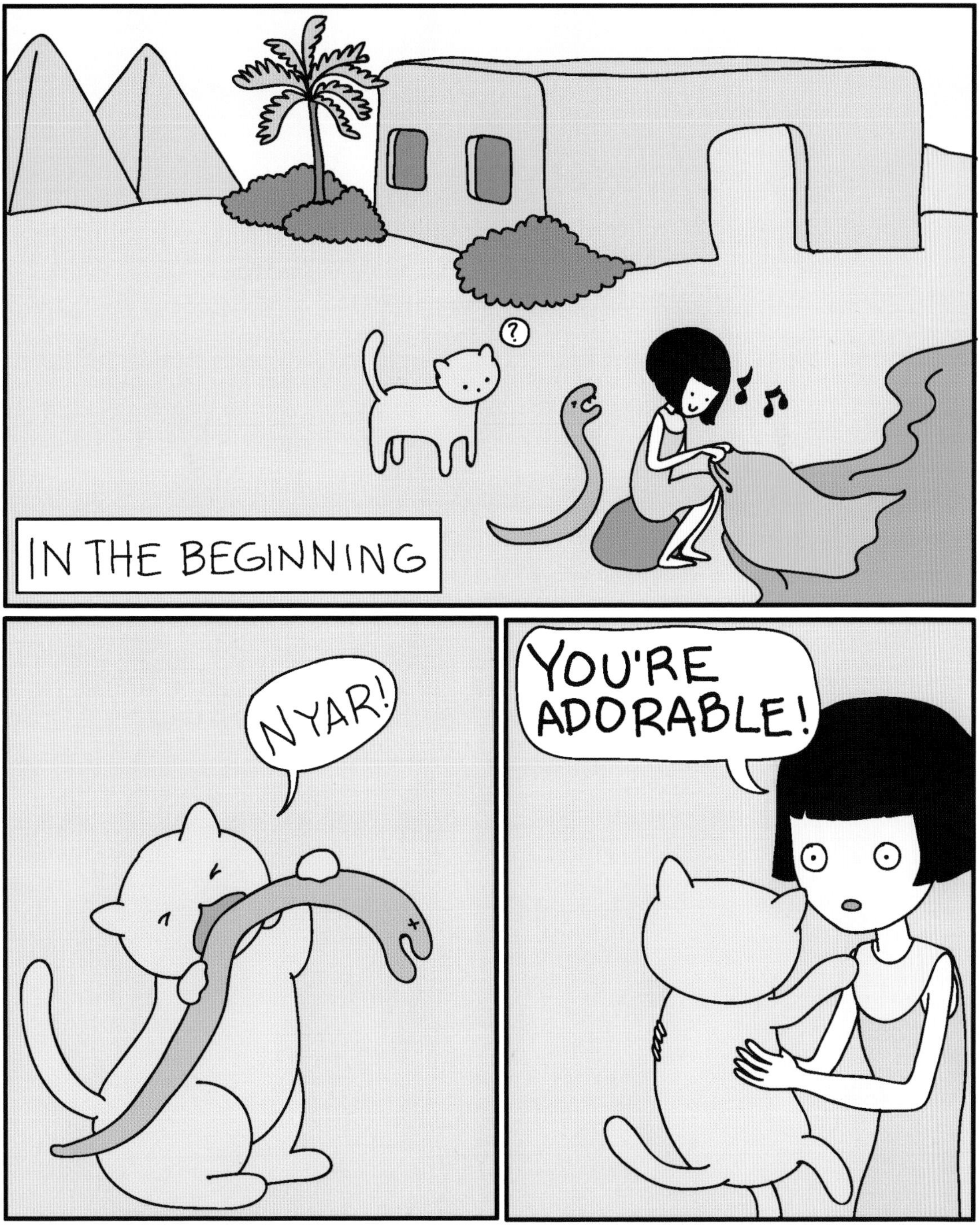
IN THE BEGINNING
?
NYAR!
YOU'RE ADORABLE!

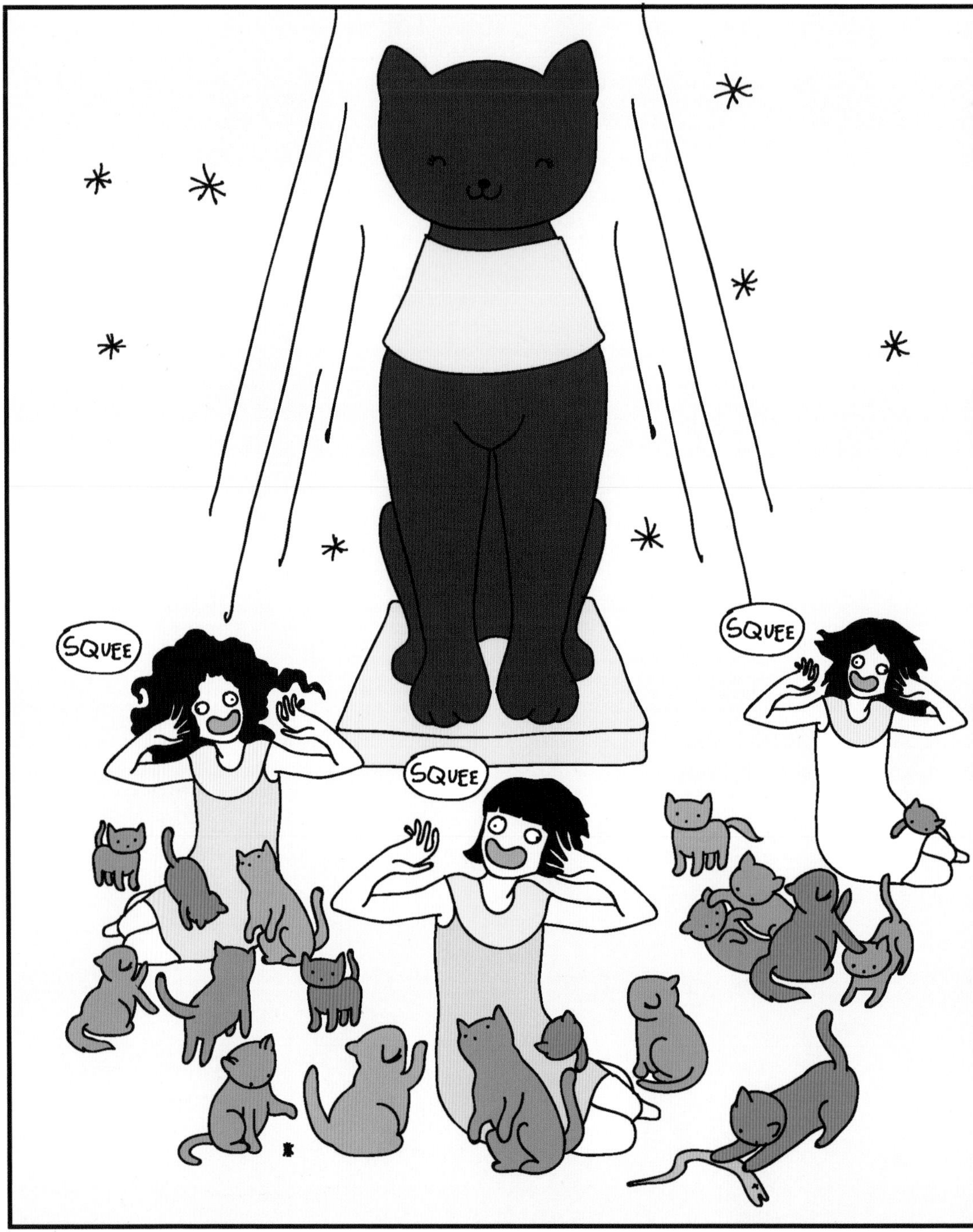
SQUEE
SQUEE
SQUEE

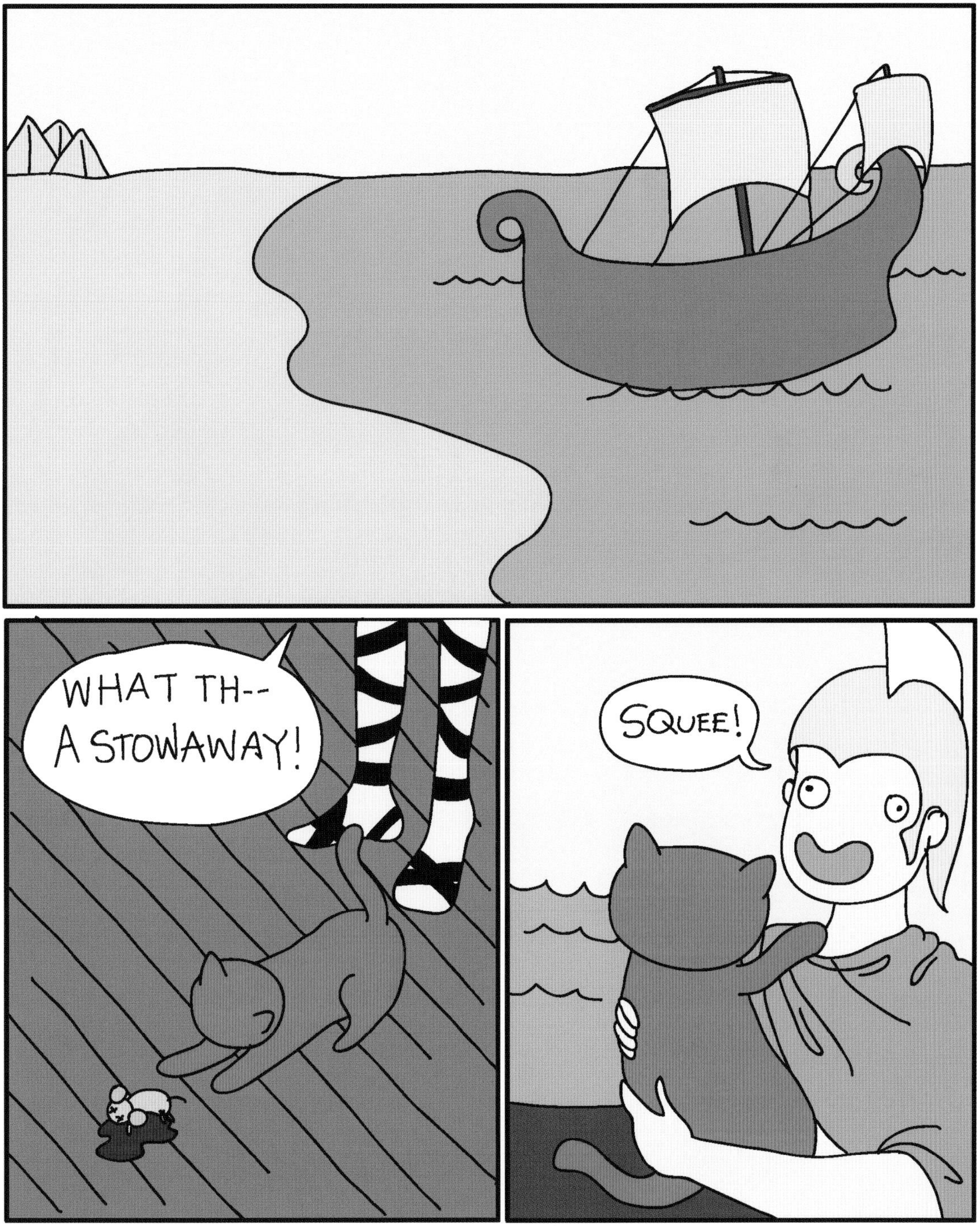
WHAT TH--
A STOWAWAY!
SQUEE!

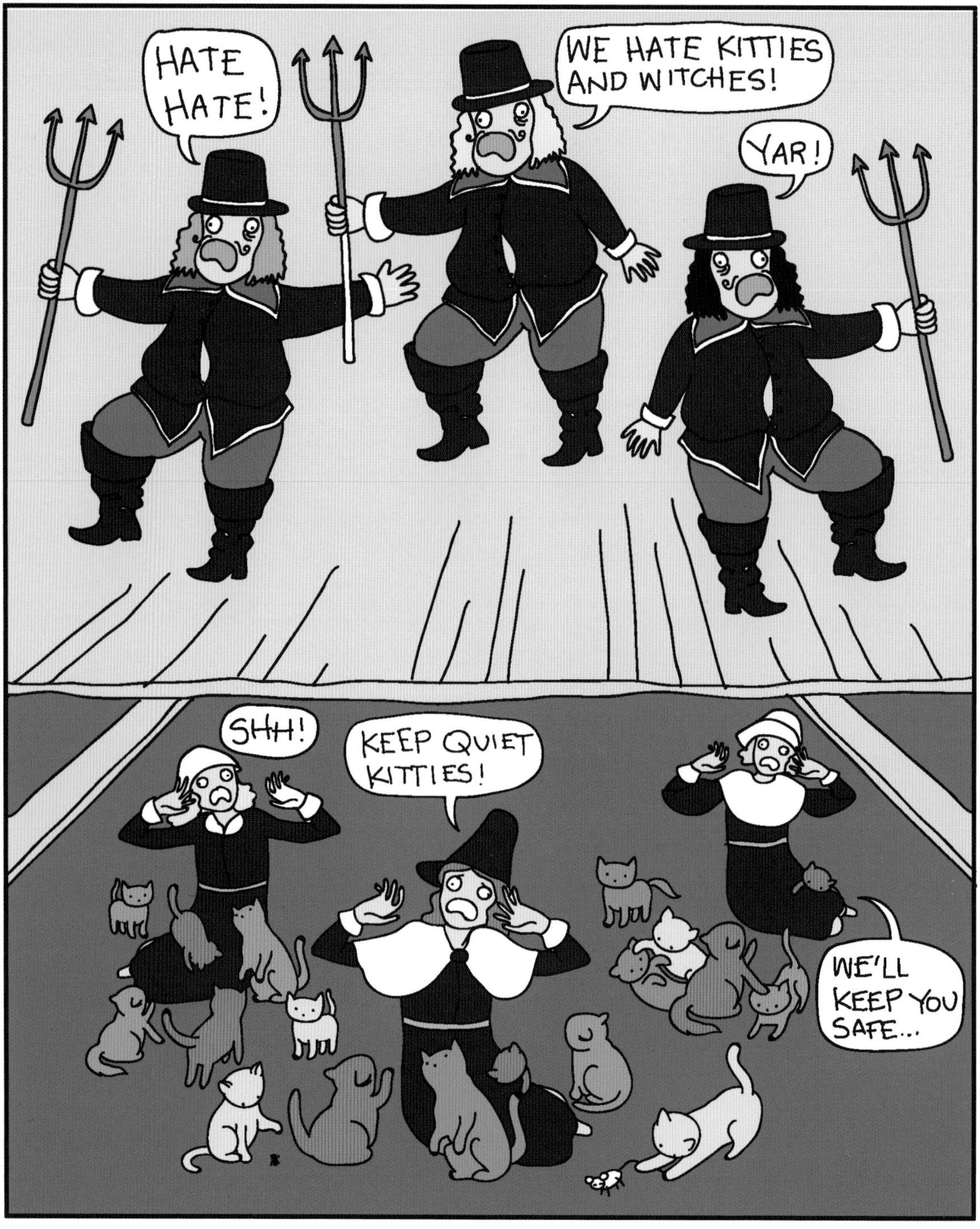
HATE HATE!
WE HATE KITTIES AND WITCHES!
YAR!
SHH!
KEEP QUIET KITTIES!
WE'LL KEEP YOU SAFE...

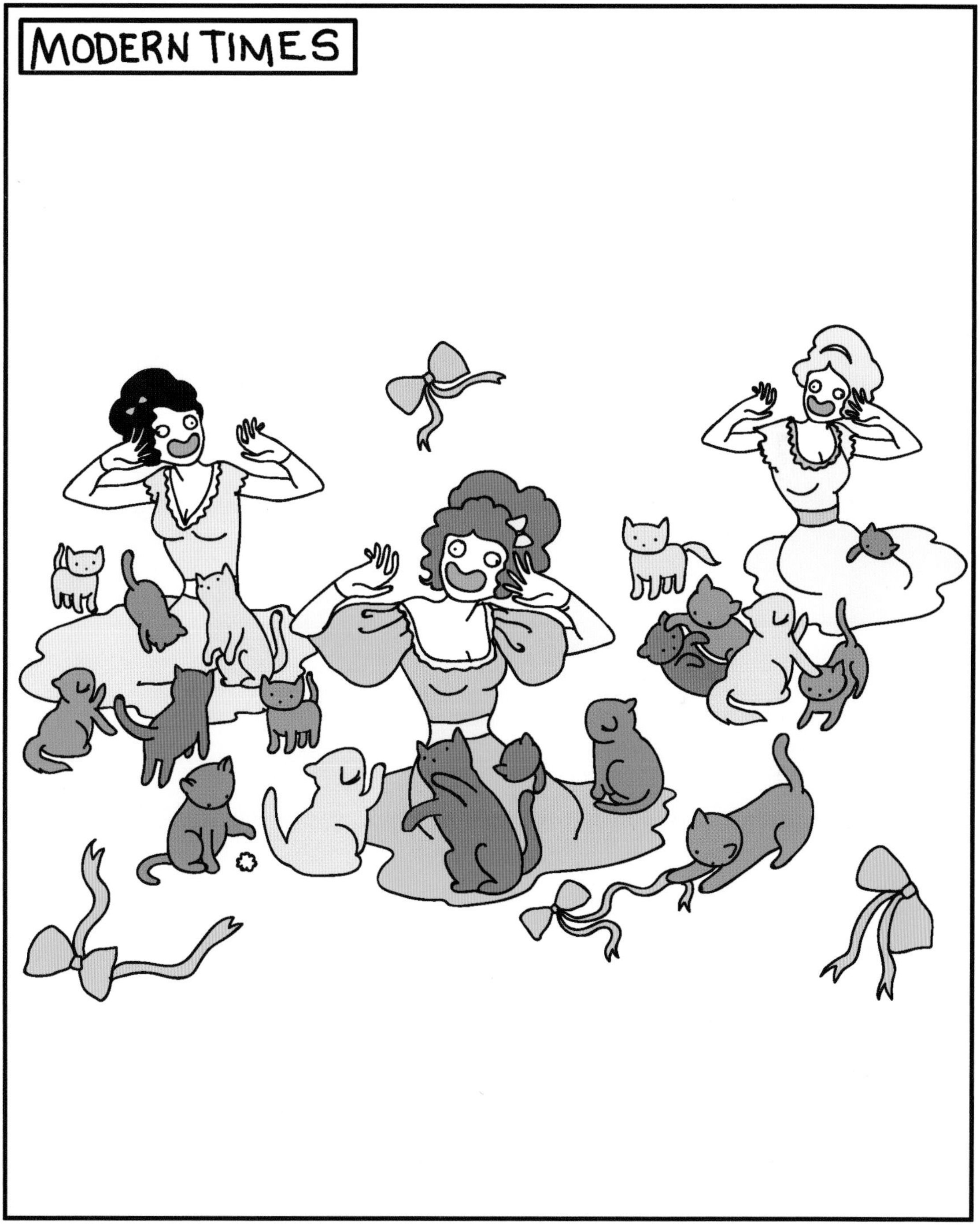
MODERN TIMES

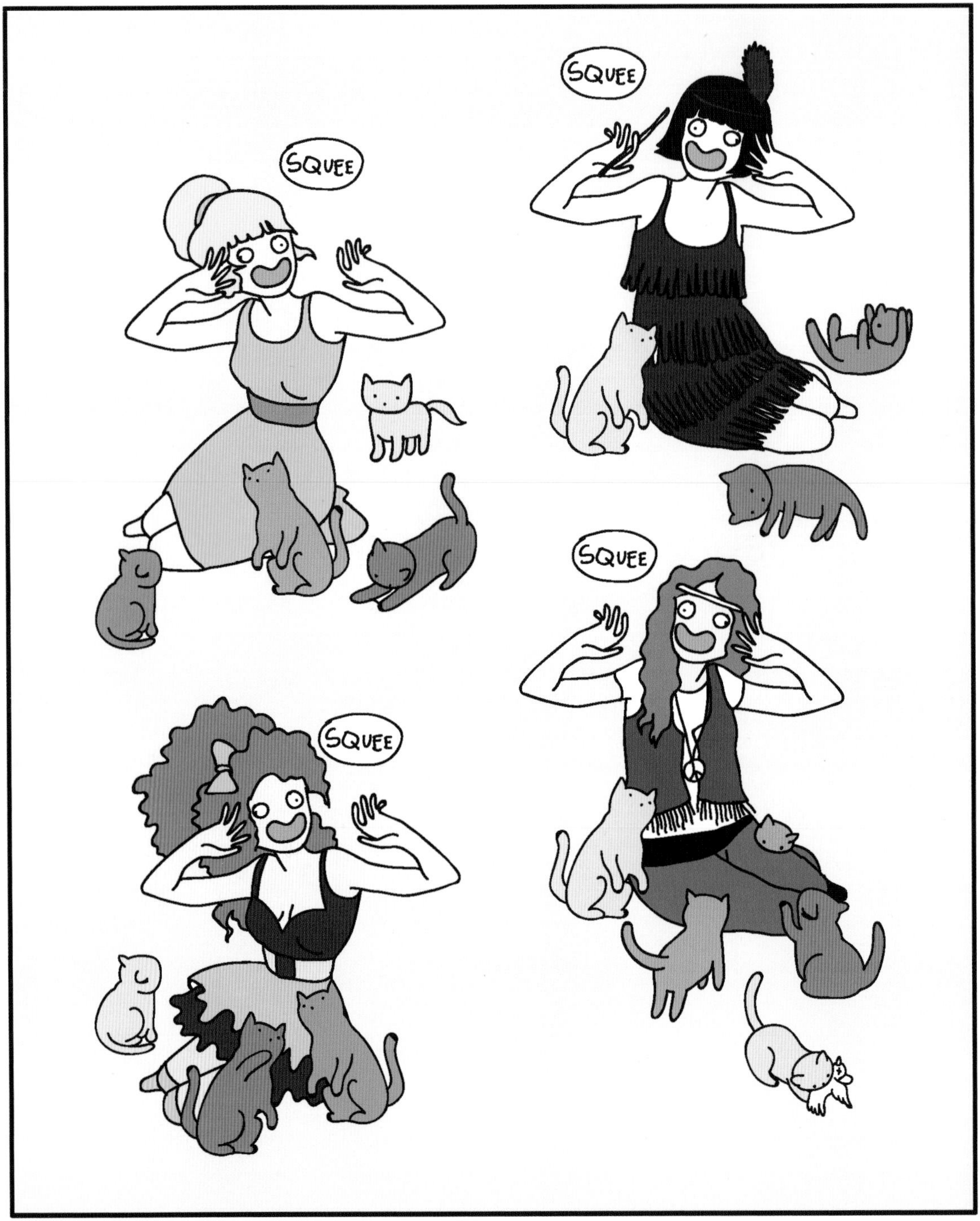
SQUEE
SQUEE
SQUEE
SQUEE

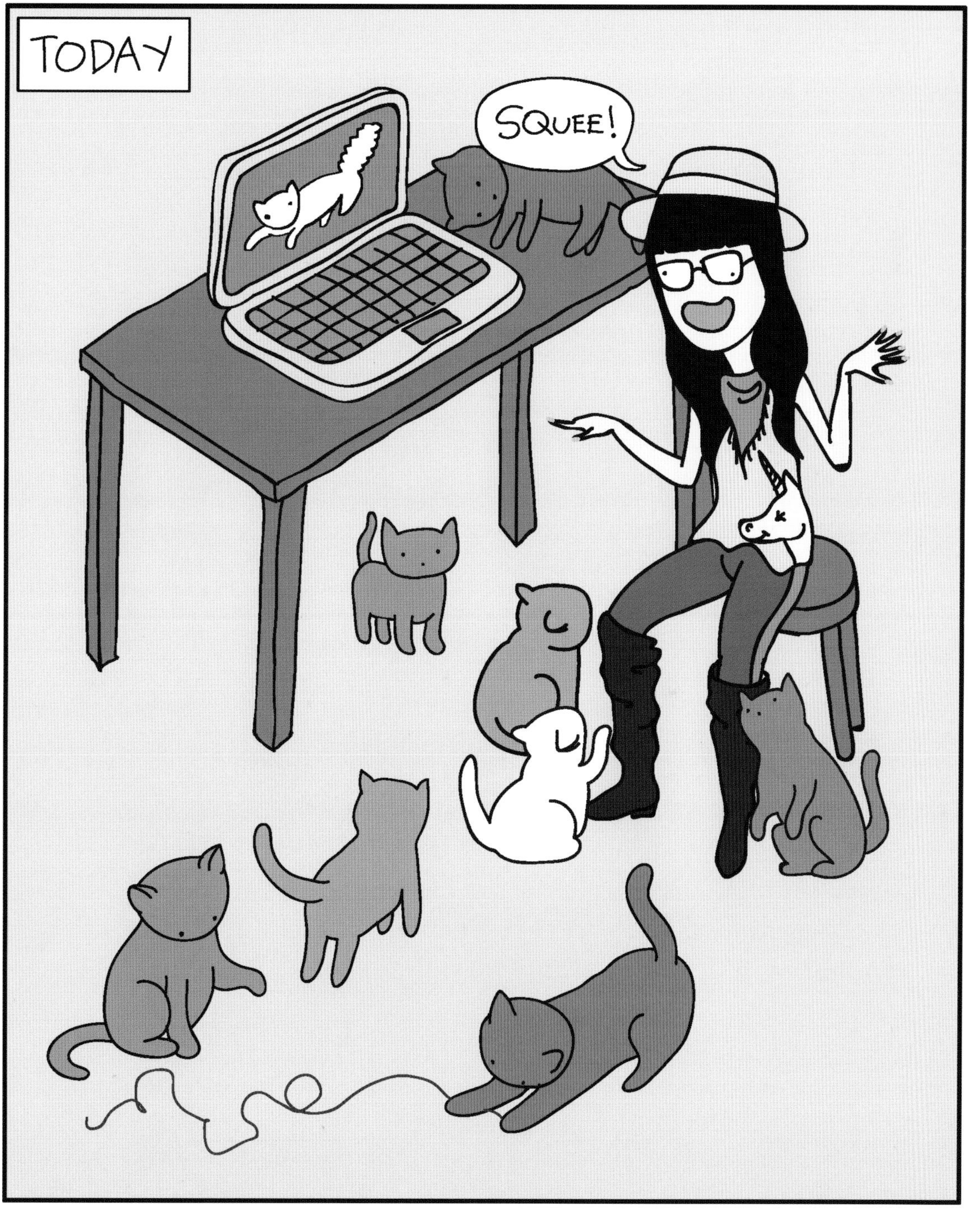
TODAY
SQUEE!

HUNGRY HUNGRY KITTEN

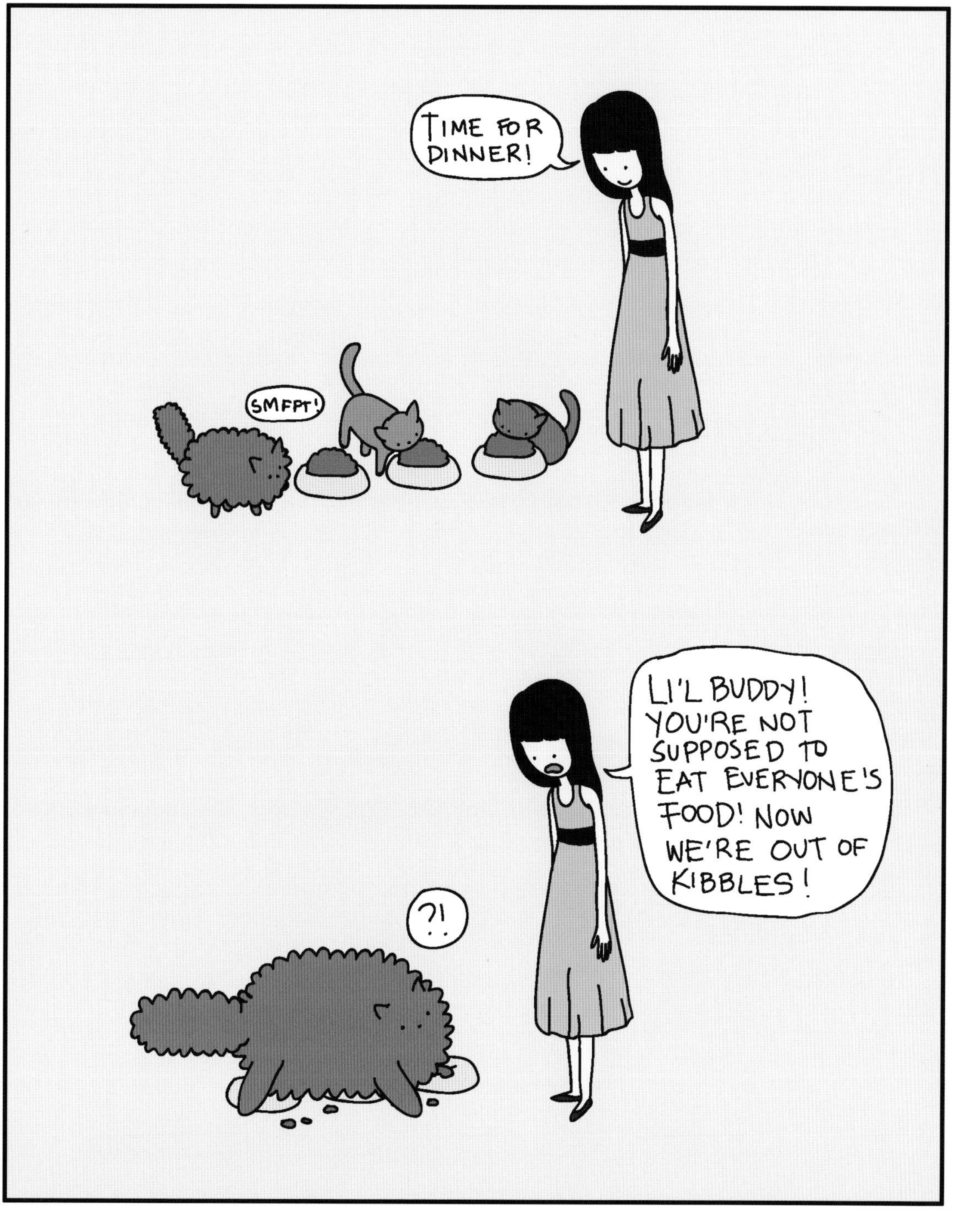
TIME FOR DINNER!
SMFPT!
LI'L BUDDY! YOU'RE NOT SUPPOSED TO EAT EVERYONE'S FOOD! NOW WE'RE OUT OF KIBBLES!
?!

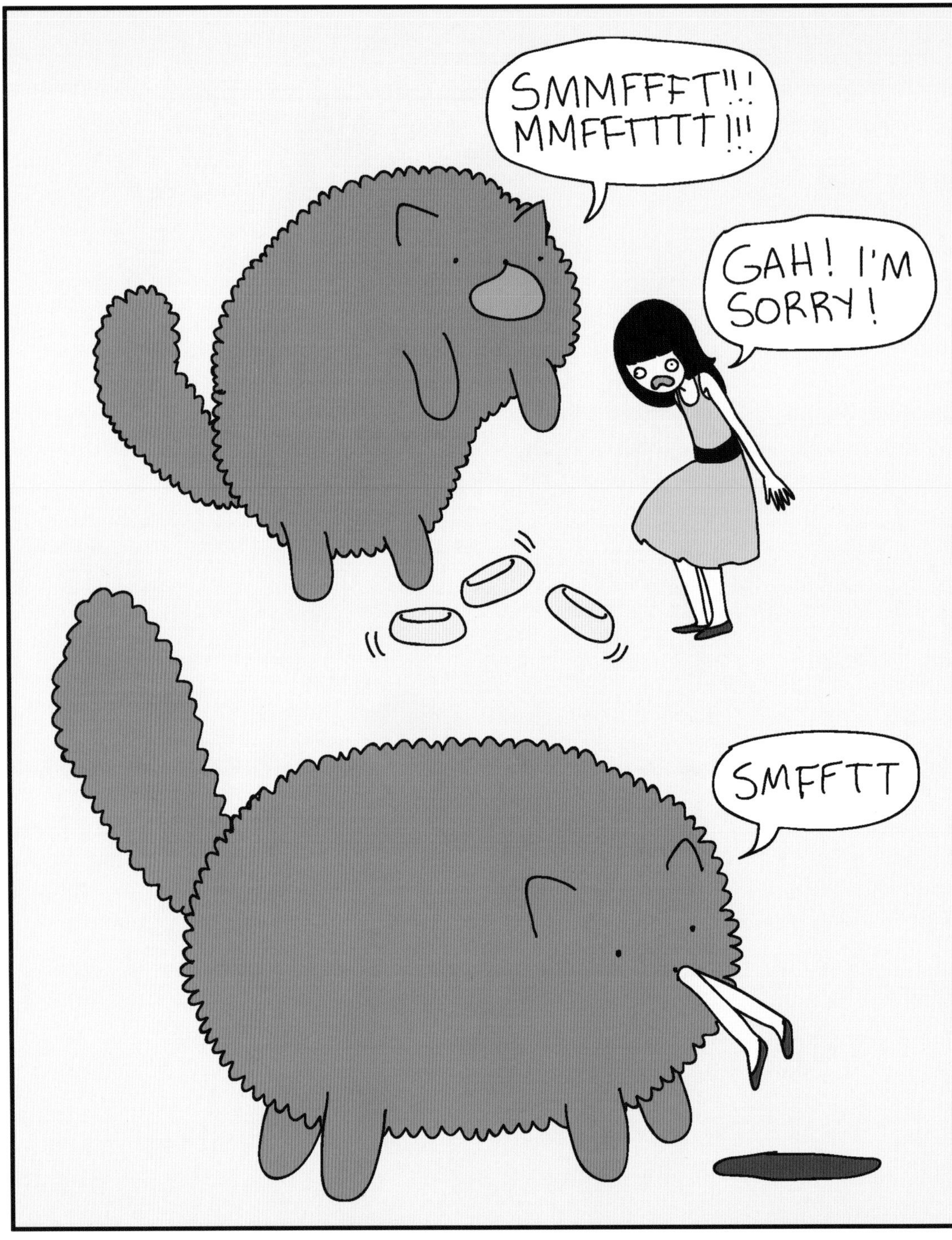
SMMFFFT!!! MMFFTTTTT!!!
GAH! I'M SORRY!
SMFFTT

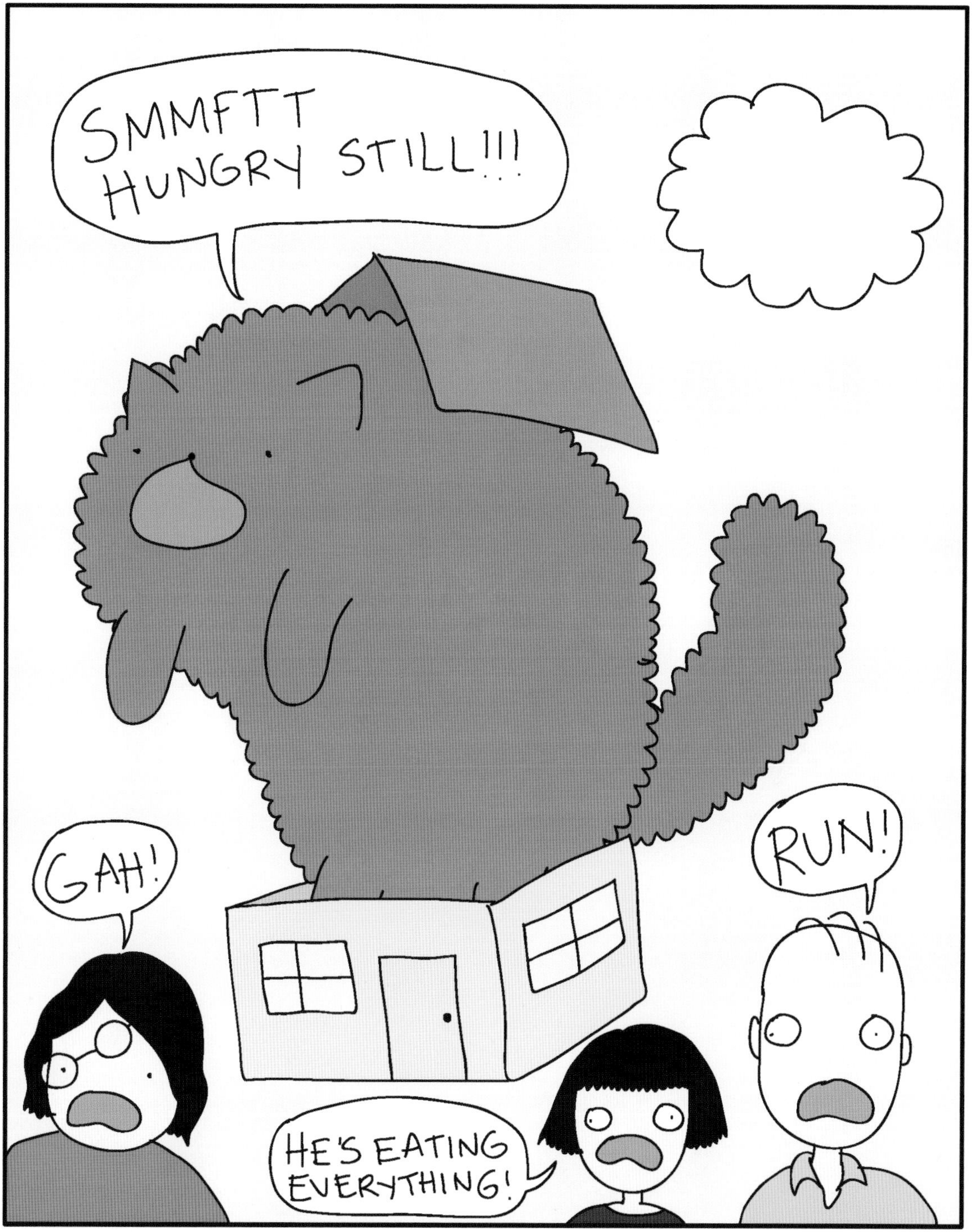
SMMFTT HUNGRY STILL!!!
GAH!
RUN!
HE'S EATING EVERYTHING!

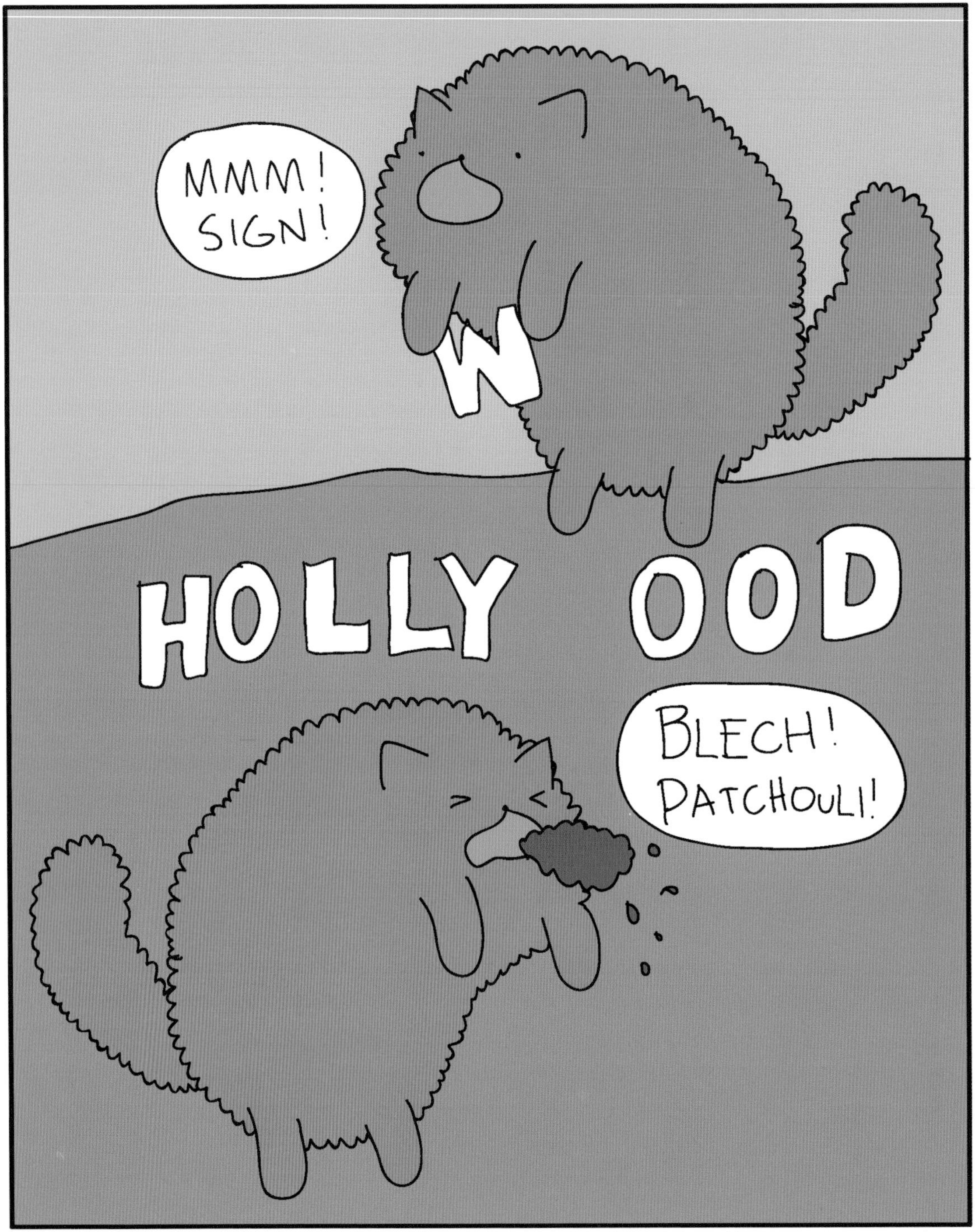
MMM! SIGN!
W
HOLLY OOD
BLECH! PATCHOULI!

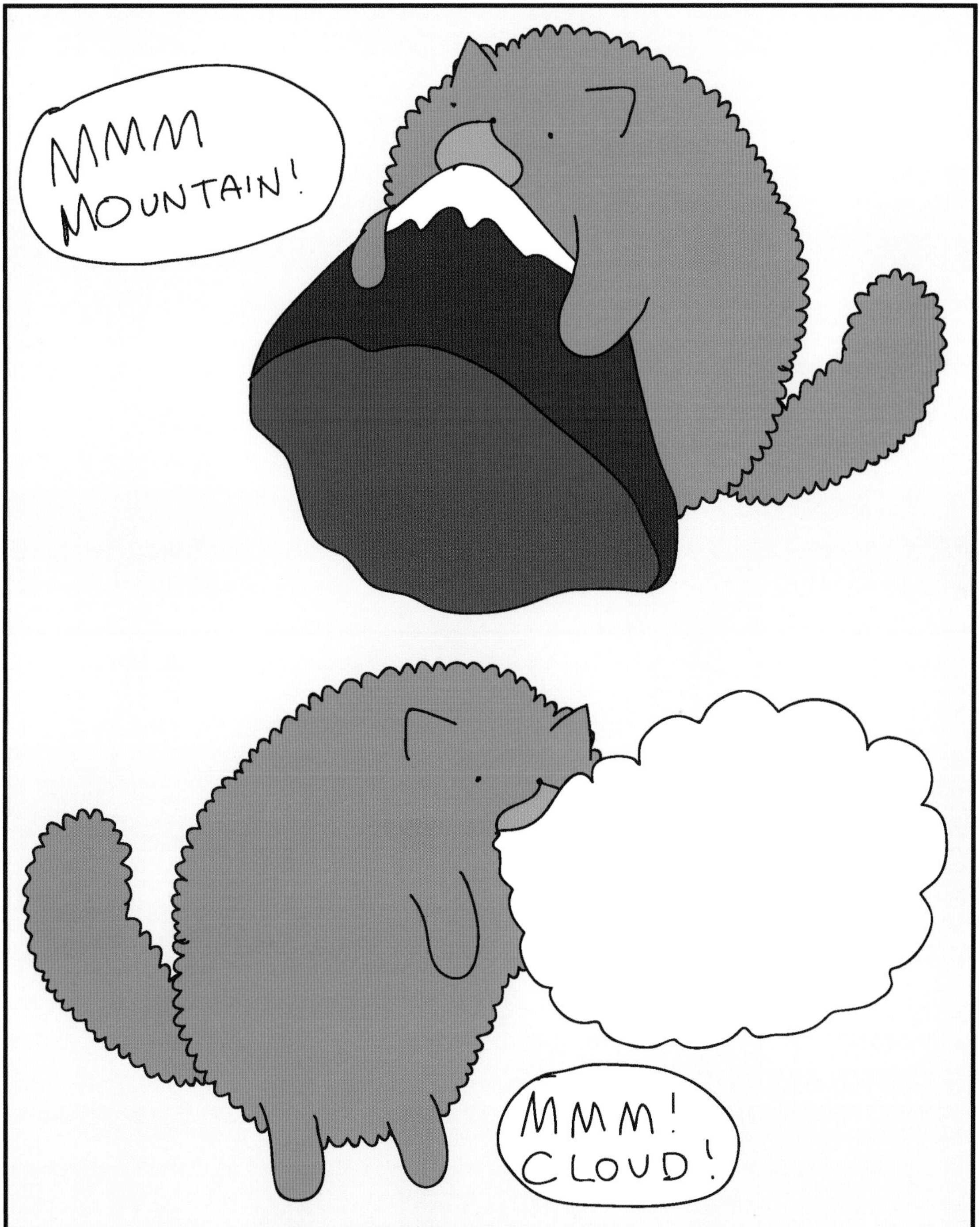
MMM MOUNTAIN!
MMM! CLOUD!

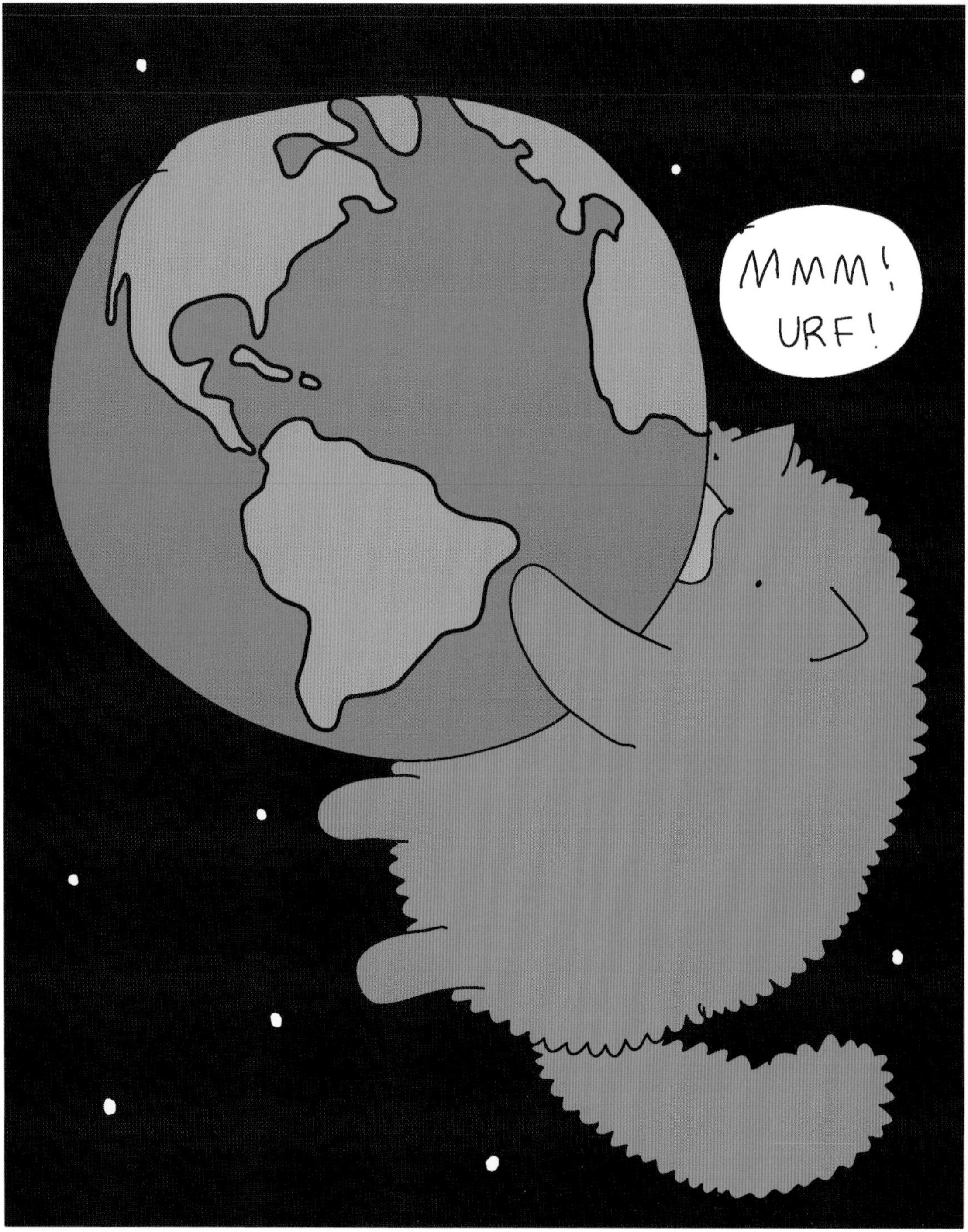
MMM! URF!

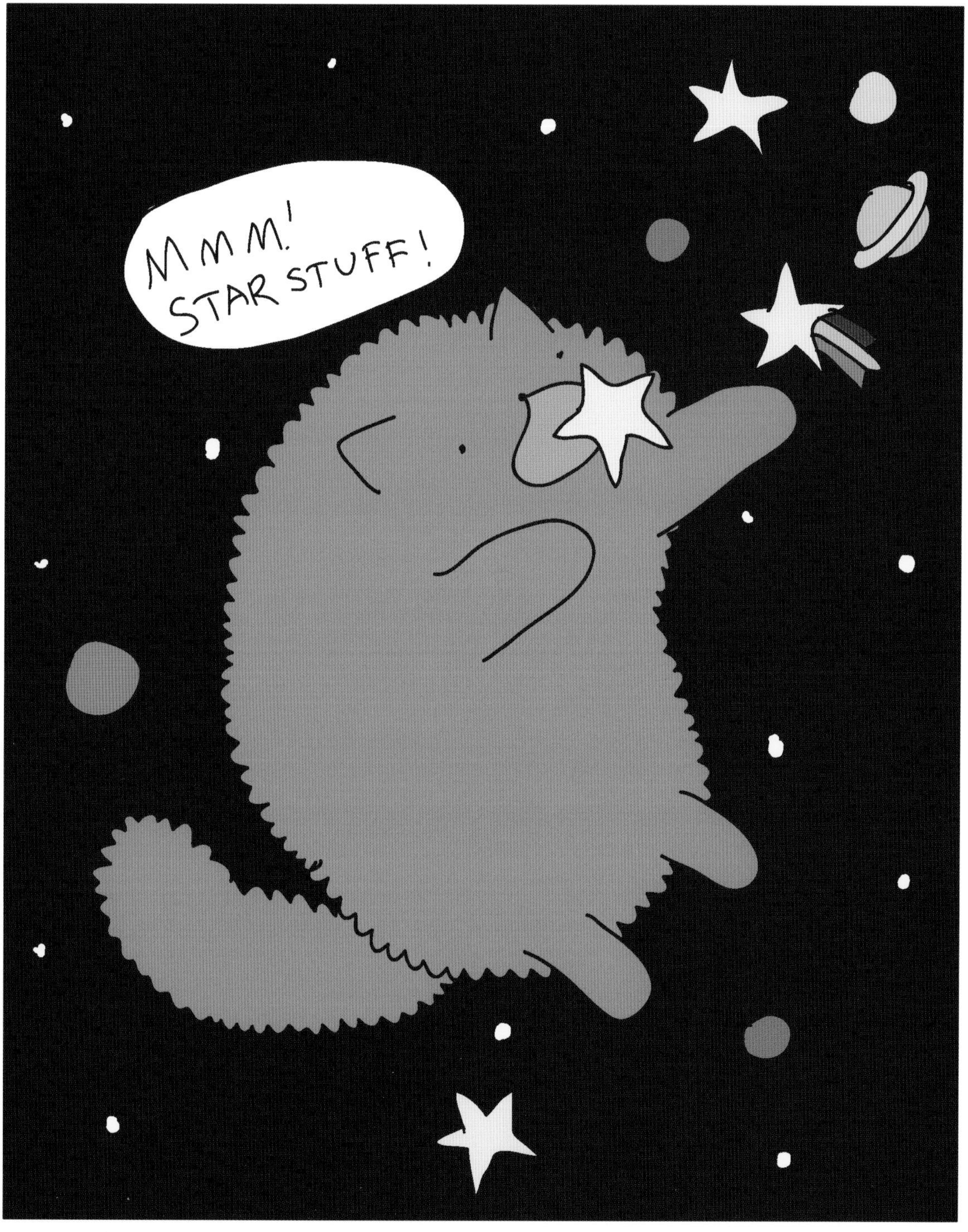
MMM! STAR STUFF!

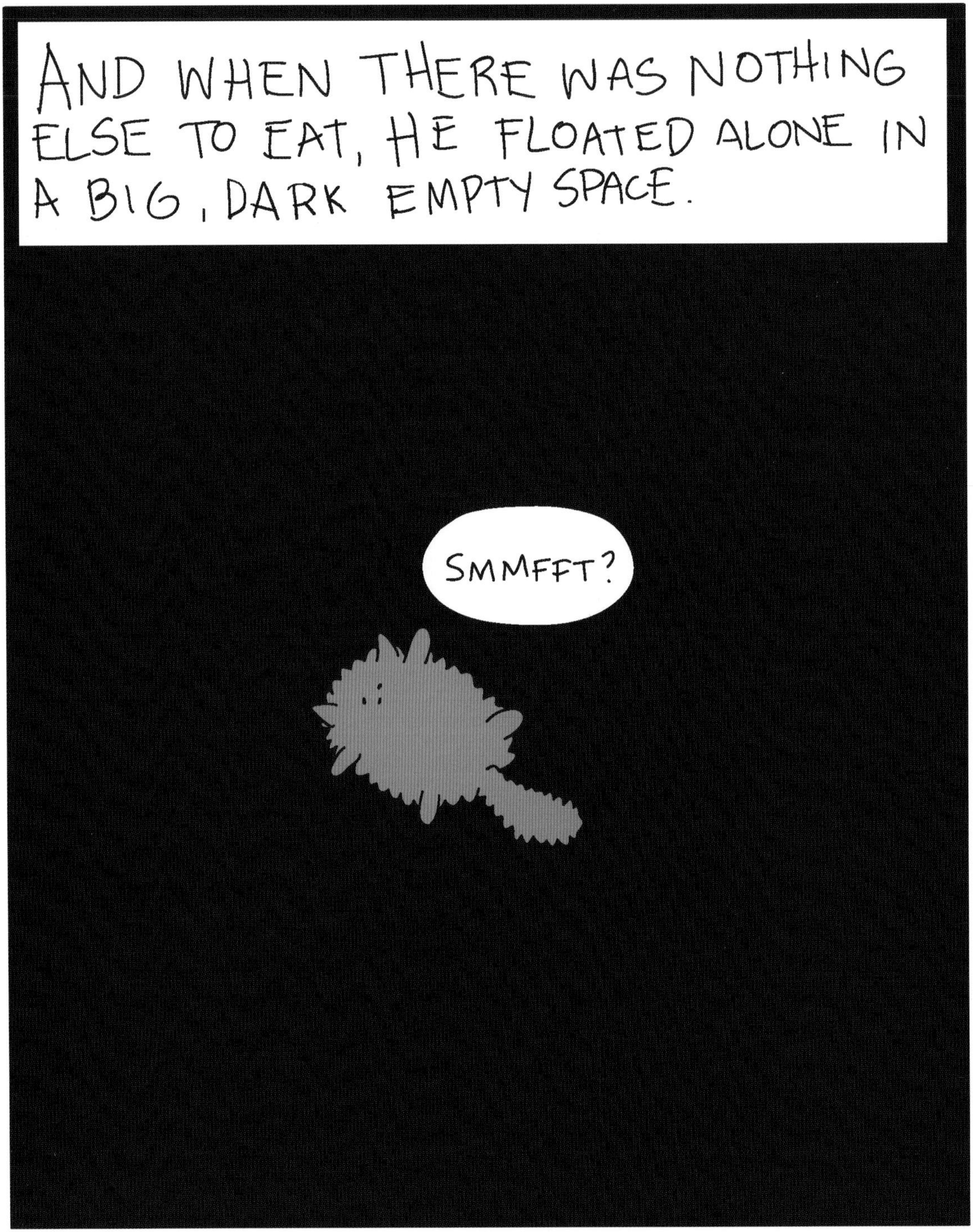
AND WHEN THERE WAS NOTHING ELSE TO EAT, HE FLOATED ALONE IN A BIG, DARK EMPTY SPACE.
SMMFFT?

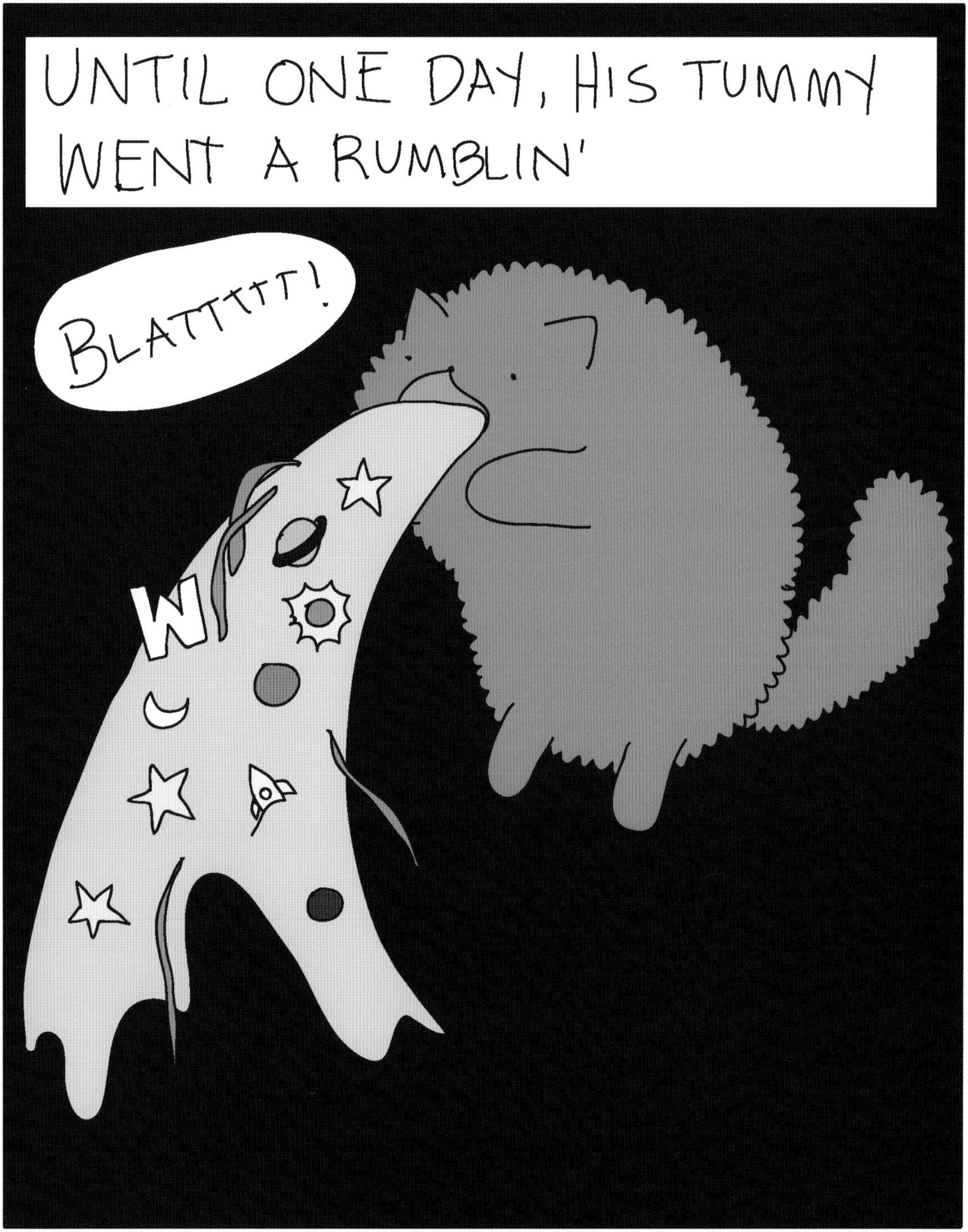
UNTIL ONE DAY, HIS TUMMY WENT A RUMBLIN'
BLATTTTTT!
W

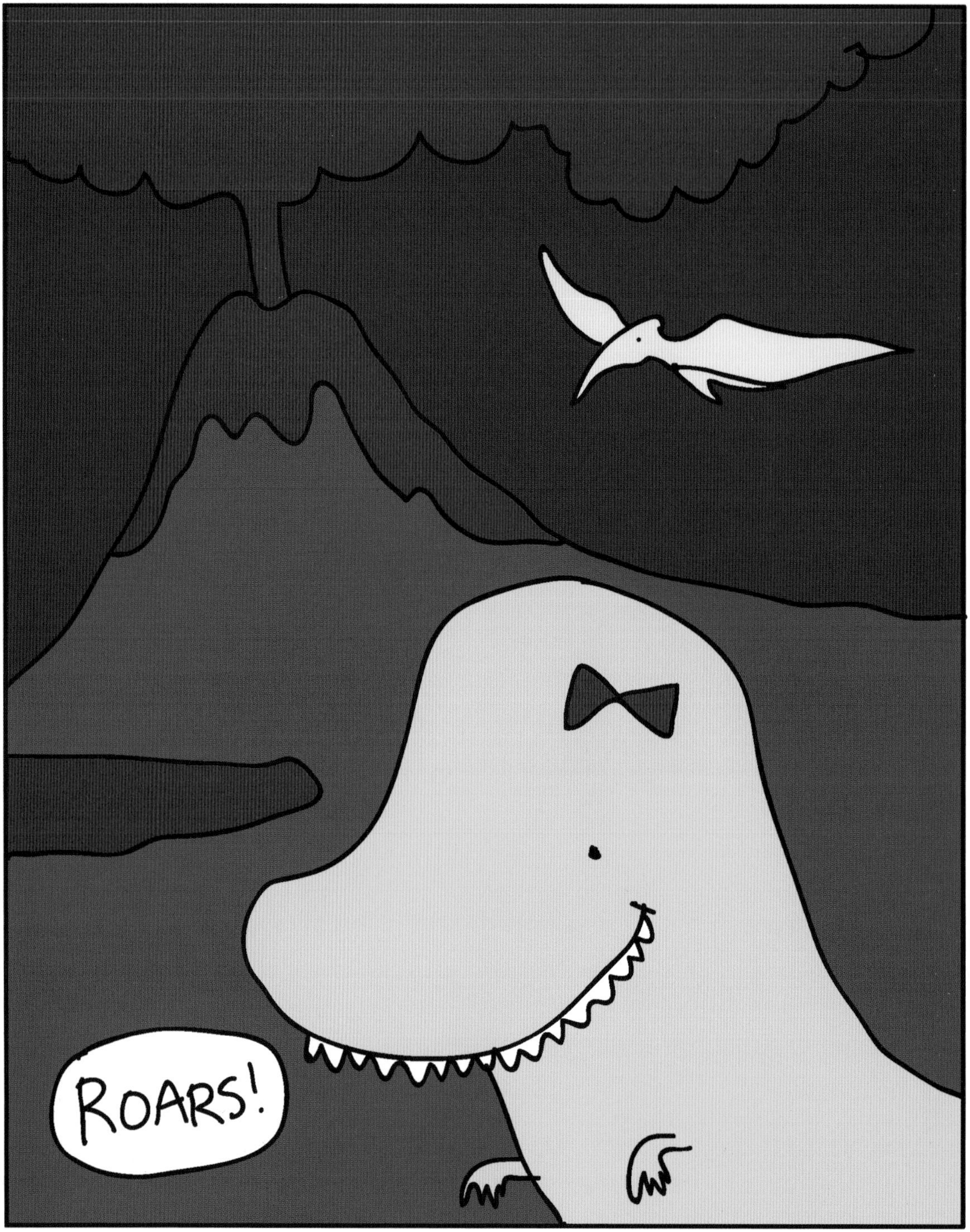
ROARS!

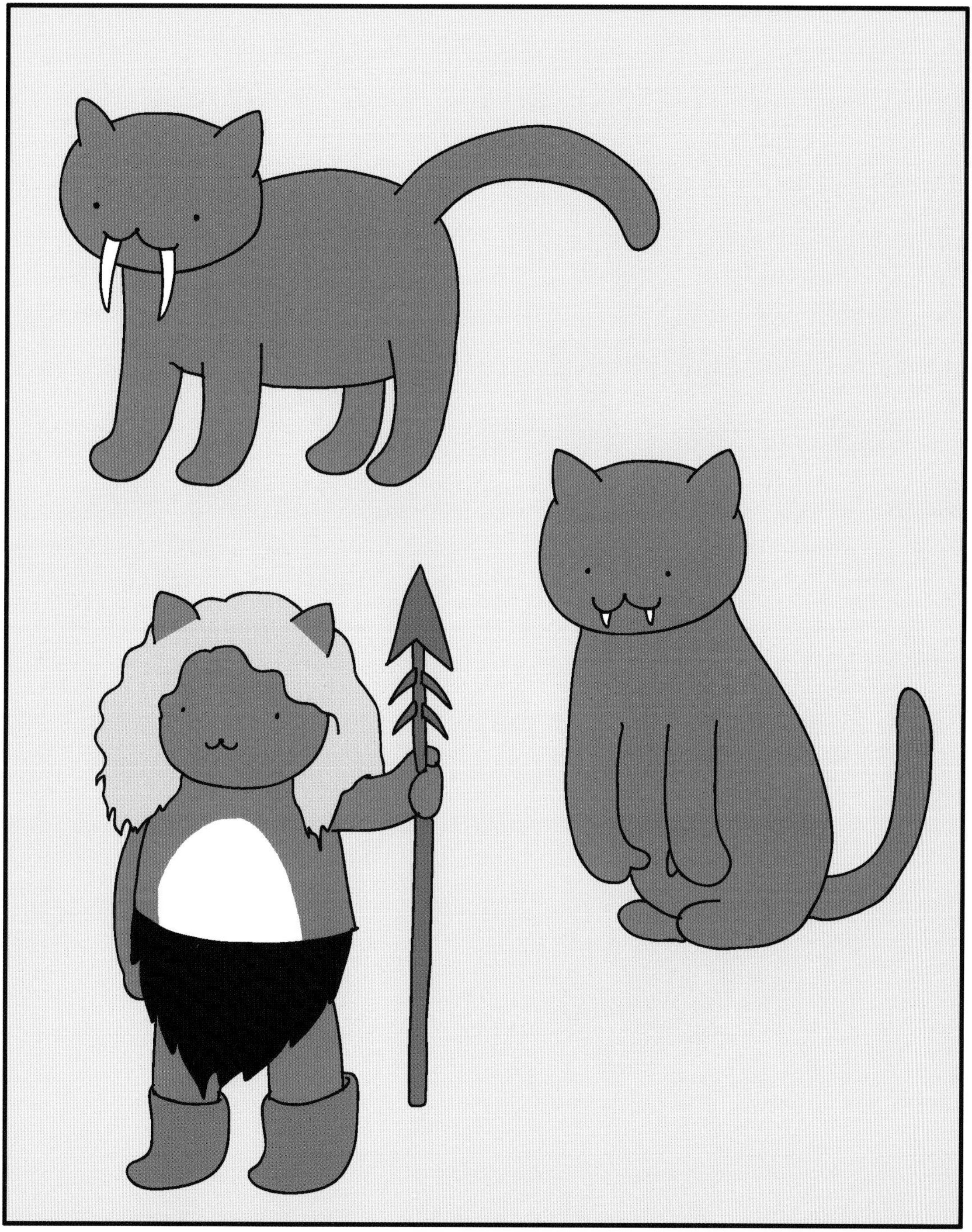

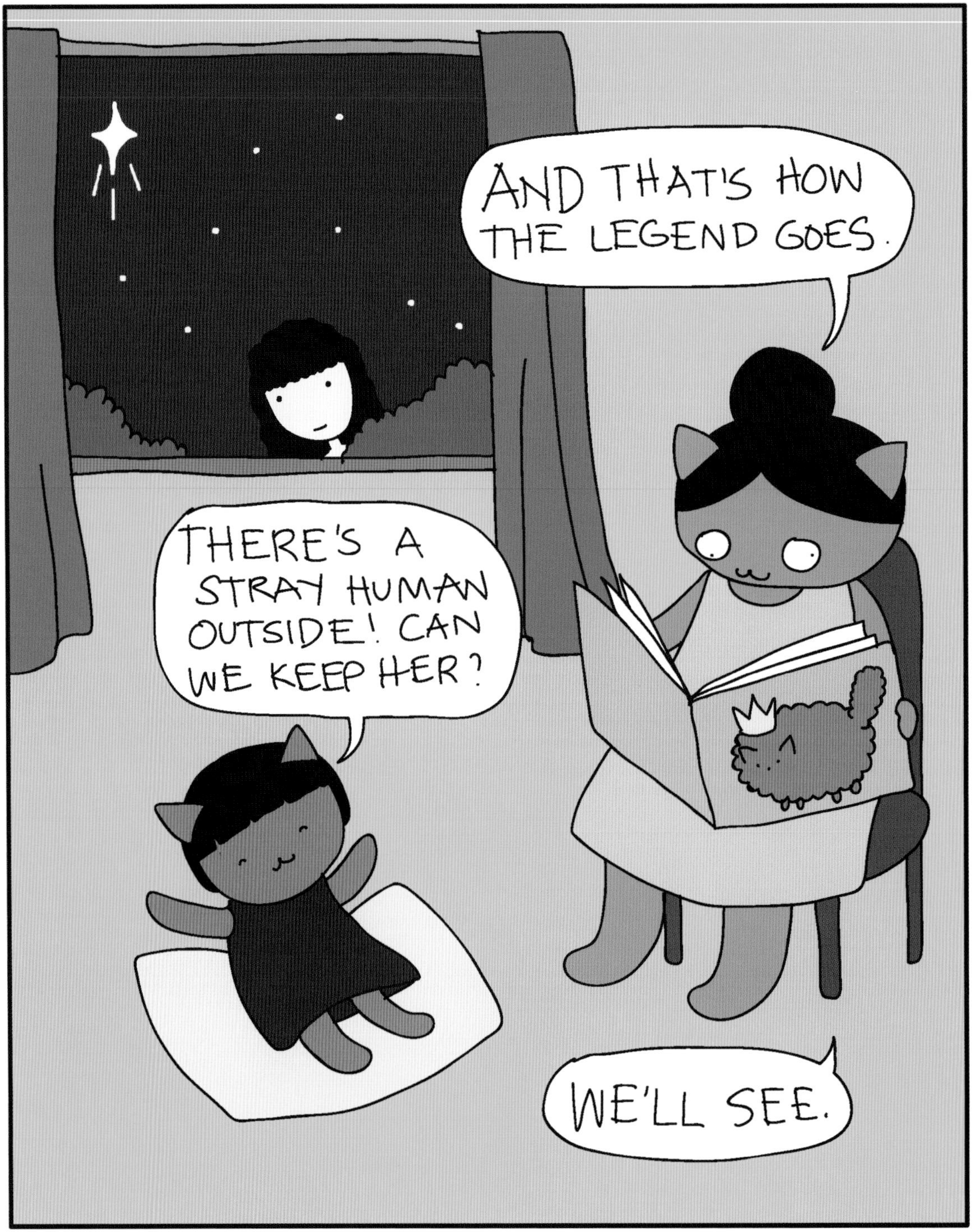
AND THAT'S HOW THE LEGEND GOES.
THERE'S A STRAY HUMAN OUTSIDE! CAN WE KEEP HER?
WE'LL SEE.

PIE CHART OF MY LIFE

WHEN I AM OLD AND GRAY, I SHALL LOOK
BACK AT MY LIFE AND SEE THIS:

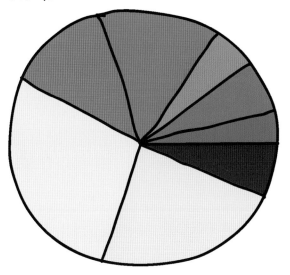

- CATS
- MADE A FEW FRIENDS (I THINK)
- SOMETHING THAT ESCAPES ME AT THE MOMENT

- FOUND SOMEONE AWESOME (NOT A CAT) WHO LOVES ME
- CATS
- WATCHED CAT VIDEOS ON THE INTERNET AND LOOKED AT CAT PICTURES ON THE INTERNET
- CATS
- WORK

ALSO BY YASMINE SUROVEC:

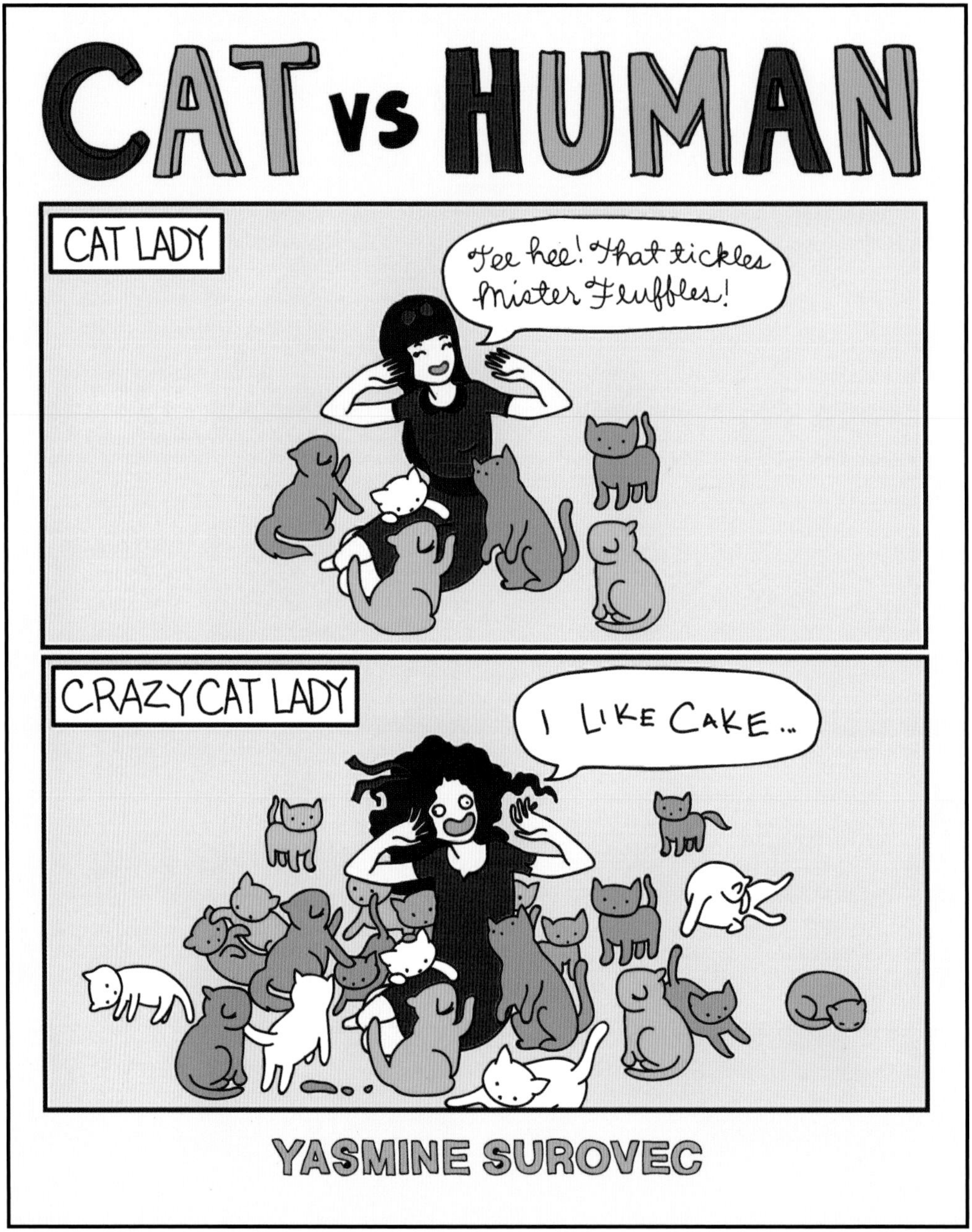
CAT VS HUMAN
CAT LADY
Tee hee! That tickles Mister Fluffles!
CRAZY CAT LADY
I LIKE CAKE...
YASMINE SUROVEC

THIS IS THE INSPIRATION BEHIND THE RED COUCH
SEEN IN MUCH OF THE CAT VS HUMAN COMICS.
IT HAS SINCE BEEN REPLACED BY ANOTHER
COUCH, WHICH WILL MOST LIKELY SEE THE SAME FATE.

YASMINE SUROVEC IS
AN ILLUSTRATOR AND
CARTOONIST WHO DIVIDES
HER TIME BETWEEN
CALIFORNIA AND ARIZONA
WITH HER HUSBAND, THREE
KITTIES AND PUPPY.

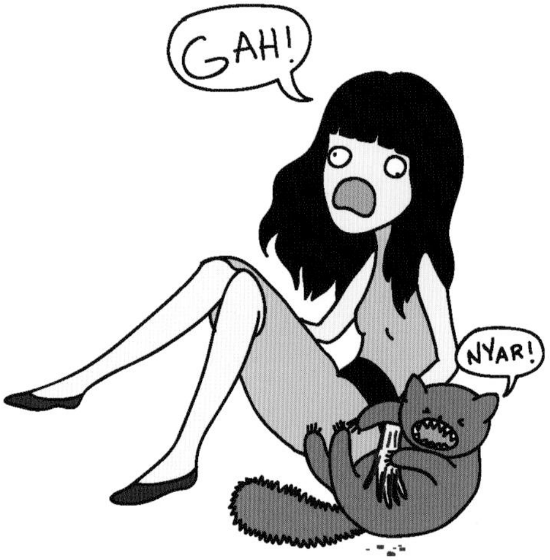
GAH!
NYAR!